Praise for *Scaling Graph Learning for the Enterprise*

Scaling Graph Learning for the Enterprise is a comprehensive, hands-on guide to building scalable and enterprise-ready graph learning pipelines. From dynamic graph representation to real-time inference with federated graph learning, it equips you with all the tools and knowledge to bring cutting-edge graph capabilities into your enterprise environments.

—*Lipi Patnaik, senior software developer, Zeta*

In an era of boundless connectivity, this book walks you through the phases of building scalable graph representation learning to unlock the structure and meaning concealed within complex networks.

—*Dr Emir Muñoz, senior manager AI/ML,*
Genesys Cloud Services

I am incredibly impressed by the sheer volume of topics this book covers, taking you all the way from foundational concepts to advanced, enterprise-scale strategies. What truly makes it exceptional is how every complex idea is grounded in a clear, practical example. It's that rare resource that serves as both a comprehensive reference and an easy-to-follow, hands-on guide.

—*Mahmoud Fahmy Mohammed, lead AI engineer*

I thoroughly enjoyed this book. It provided a clear and well-structured path to understanding graph learning and its value in the corporate world. It's presented in such an intuitive way that I'd recommend it to anyone being introduced to the subject for the first time.

—*Mohamed Elemam, senior cloud developer, HPE*

Scaling Graph Learning
for the Enterprise
Production-Ready Graph Learning and Inference

Ahmed Menshawy, Sameh Mohamed,
and Maraim Rizk Masoud

O'REILLY®

Scaling Graph Learning for the Enterprise

by Ahmed Menshawy, Sameh Mohamed, and Maraim Rizk Masoud

Published by O'Reilly Media, Inc., 141 Stony Circle, Suite 195, Santa Rosa, CA 95401.

O'Reilly books may be purchased for educational, business, or sales promotional use. Online editions are also available for most titles (*http://oreilly.com*). For more information, contact our corporate/institutional sales department: 800-998-9938 or *corporate@oreilly.com*.

Acquisitions Editor: Nicole Butterfield

Development Editor: Michele Cronin

Production Editor: Elizabeth Faerm

Copyeditor: Charles Roumeliotis

Proofreader: Helena Stirling

Indexer: WordCo Indexing Services, Inc.

Cover Designer: Karen Montgomery

Cover Illustrator: Karen Montgomery

Interior Designer: David Futato

Interior Illustrator: Kate Dullea

August 2025: First Edition

Revision History for the First Edition

2025-08-06: First Release

See *http://oreilly.com/catalog/errata.csp?isbn=9781098146061* for release details.

978-1-098-14606-1

[LSI]

Table of Contents

Preface

Welcome to *Scaling Graph Learning for the Enterprise*. We wrote this book with a single aim: to give professionals a clear, direct path from a first idea to a working system. In many technical books, the gap between theory and practice can feel like a canyon; in ours, it is meant to be a footbridge. We've tried to balance every page with just enough background information to make sense of the subject, along with concrete guidance that you can apply in the same afternoon.

What Is Graph Learning for the Enterprise?

During the last few years, developments in the field of graph technology and machine learning have been astonishing. With the growing recognition of the interconnectedness of data, graph methods have moved from academic niches to a critical tool for understanding complex systems. From detecting sophisticated fraud rings to optimizing supply chains and personalizing recommendations, graph learning is becoming vital across every industry.

Despite this surge in interest, many practitioners find themselves navigating a landscape with powerful tools but limited guidance on how to systematically apply graph learning in real-world enterprise settings. While model architectures and theoretical concepts have received significant attention, the practical aspects of building, deploying, and maintaining robust graph-based systems often receive less focus.

This book aims to bridge that gap. We believe that applying graph learning effectively in an enterprise context requires more than just understanding algorithms; it demands a structured approach to problem-solving, data integration, model deployment, and ongoing maintenance. We will show you how to build a robust graph learning system that delivers actionable insights and is designed for the challenges of production environments.

Why Does Graph Learning Matter for the Enterprise?

In the rush for the most performant machine learning solutions, we've observed a few things that have received less attention, particularly in the realm of graph data. Data scientists and machine learning engineers often lack good sources of information for concepts and tools to accelerate, reuse, manage, and deploy graph-based developments. What's needed is a practical framework for applying graph learning.

From our personal experience, most data science projects aiming to deploy models into production don't have the luxury of a large team, especially when dealing with the unique complexities of graph data. This can make it incredibly difficult to build an entire graph learning pipeline in-house from scratch. Without a structured approach, graph projects often turn into one-off efforts where scaling becomes a significant challenge, performance degrades over time, or the model isn't widely used across the enterprise. An automated, reproducible, and scalable pipeline for graph learning is therefore crucial, as it dramatically reduces the effort required to scale the deployment and maintenance of these powerful models.

Our intention with this book is to contribute to the standardization of graph learning projects by walking readers through an entire graph learning pipeline, end to end. Clear writing alone isn't enough if the reader is left guessing about context. For that reason, each technique is anchored to a story drawn from the banking, retail, cybersecurity, or healthcare domains, areas where a mistake is costly and timelines are tight. Just as important, you'll read where early versions failed and what was changed to keep the project alive. These small detours are included so you can identify similar issues in your own work and hopefully avoid them later. We also know that most enterprise teams work under strict rules concerning data privacy, fairness, and uptime. Whenever those rules collide with a modeling choice, we call it out and show how to innovate within those boundaries to achieve your goals compliantly. The same applies to hardware limits and budget caps. The goal is to save you from discovering a deal-breaking constraint after weeks of effort.

Open source tools now make it possible to build and run large graph models with a few commands, and the surge of interest in large language models lets us combine free-text knowledge with graph structure in ways that were impossible just a year ago. The book reflects that momentum but keeps the focus on what you can ship today. We describe emerging ideas, yet always bring the discussion back to code that will run on a modest cluster without an army of researchers behind it.

Who Is This Book For?

The primary audience for this book includes data scientists and machine learning engineers who want to go beyond training a one-off graph model and successfully productize their data science projects. You should be comfortable with basic machine learning concepts and familiar with at least one machine learning framework (e.g., PyTorch, TensorFlow, Keras).

A secondary audience for this book includes managers of data science projects, software developers, and DevOps engineers who want to enable their organization to accelerate their data science projects with graph technologies. If you are interested in better understanding automated graph learning life cycles and how they can benefit your organization, this book will introduce a toolchain to achieve exactly that.

Overview of the Chapters

In each chapter, we will introduce specific steps for building effective graph learning systems and demonstrate how these work with practical examples.

Chapter 1, "Introduction to Graphs", provides an overview of graph structures, their applications, and why they are powerful for enterprise problems.

Chapter 2, "The Graph Machine Learning Pipeline", outlines the end-to-end process for building, deploying, and maintaining graph-based machine learning systems.

Chapter 3, "Traditional Machine Learning for Graphs", explores how classical machine learning techniques can be adapted and applied to graph data.

Chapter 4, "PyGraf: End-to-End Graph Learning and Serving", introduces PyGraf, a practical framework for building and serving graph learning models in a production environment.

Chapter 5, "Graph Neural Networks", dives into the foundational concepts and architectures of graph neural networks (GNNs).

Chapter 6, "Advanced Techniques in Graph Learning", covers more sophisticated graph learning methods and their applications.

Chapter 7, "Scalable Graph Neural Networks", addresses the challenges of scaling GNNs to large, enterprise-sized datasets and discusses solutions.

Chapter 8, "Enterprise Applications of Graphs", showcases real-world use cases of graph learning across various industries, drawing from our experience.

Chapter 9, "Privacy-Preserving Graph Learning", explores techniques for building graph models while adhering to strict data privacy regulations.

Chapter 10, "Graph Inference and Deployment Strategies", focuses on deploying graph learning models efficiently for real-time and batch inference.

Chapter 11, "Monitoring and Feedback Loops", discusses how to monitor the performance of deployed graph models and establish feedback mechanisms for continuous improvement.

Chapter 12, "Future Trends: Graph Learning and LLMs", provides an outlook on emerging technologies, particularly the intersection of graph learning and large language models (LLMs), and their potential impact.

As you turn the pages, try to look at each new dataset through a simple lens: how do the records affect one another, and what can those links tell us that single rows cannot? That habit is often the spark that changes a minor improvement into a breakthrough.

Thank you for giving this book a place on your desk. May it guide you to cleaner designs, stronger models, faster deployment, and more accurate insights. Open your favorite editor, start a notebook, and let's map some relationships. Happy reading, and happy graphing!

Conventions Used in This Book

The following typographical conventions are used in this book:

Italic
> Indicates new terms, URLs, email addresses, filenames, and file extensions.

`Constant width`
> Used for program listings, as well as within paragraphs to refer to program elements such as variable or function names, databases, data types, environment variables, statements, and keywords.

`Constant width bold`
> Shows commands or other text that should be typed literally by the user.

`Constant width italic`
> Shows text that should be replaced with user-supplied values or by values determined by context.

> This element signifies a general note.

Using Code Examples

Supplemental material (code examples, exercises, etc.) is available for download at *https://github.com/gl4ebook/py-graf*.

If you have a technical question or a problem using the code examples, please send email to *support@oreilly.com*.

This book is here to help you get your job done. In general, if example code is offered with this book, you may use it in your programs and documentation. You do not need to contact us for permission unless you're reproducing a significant portion of the code. For example, writing a program that uses several chunks of code from this book does not require permission. Selling or distributing examples from O'Reilly books does require permission. Answering a question by citing this book and quoting example code does not require permission. Incorporating a significant amount of example code from this book into your product's documentation does require permission.

We appreciate, but generally do not require, attribution. An attribution usually includes the title, author, publisher, and ISBN. For example: "*Scaling Graph Learning for the Enterprise* by Ahmed Menshawy, Sameh Mohamed, and Maraim Rizk Masoud (O'Reilly). Copyright 2025 Ahmed Menshawy, Sameh Mohamed, and Maraim Masoud, 978-1-098-14606-1."

If you feel your use of code examples falls outside fair use or the permission given above, feel free to contact us at *permissions@oreilly.com*.

O'Reilly Online Learning

O'REILLY® For more than 40 years, *O'Reilly Media* has provided technology and business training, knowledge, and insight to help companies succeed.

Our unique network of experts and innovators share their knowledge and expertise through books, articles, and our online learning platform. O'Reilly's online learning platform gives you on-demand access to live training courses, in-depth learning paths, interactive coding environments, and a vast collection of text and video from O'Reilly and 200+ other publishers. For more information, visit *https://oreilly.com*.

How to Contact Us

Please address comments and questions concerning this book to the publisher:

O'Reilly Media, Inc.
141 Stony Circle, Suite 195
Santa Rosa, CA 95401
800-889-8969 (in the United States or Canada)
707-827-7019 (international or local)
707-829-0104 (fax)
support@oreilly.com
https://oreilly.com/about/contact.html

We have a web page for this book, where we list errata, examples, and any additional information. You can access this page at *https://oreil.ly/scaling-graph-learning-for-the-enterprise*.

For news and information about our books and courses, visit *https://oreilly.com*.

Find us on LinkedIn: *https://linkedin.com/company/oreilly-media*.

Watch us on YouTube: *https://youtube.com/oreillymedia*.

Acknowledgements

A project like this stands on many shoulders, and we are profoundly grateful to everyone who contributed to its creation.

We extend our sincere thanks to the team at O'Reilly for their guidance and support throughout this process: Nicole Butterfield, Michele Cronin, Elizabeth Faerm, and Charles Roumeliotis.

Our technical reviewers provided invaluable feedback that sharpened our examples and clarified our explanations. We are especially grateful to Emir Muñoz, Mahmoud Fahmy, and Lipi Deepaakshi Patnaik for their diligent review and insightful suggestions.

## CHAPTER 1

Introduction to Graphs

The Power of Enterprise Graph Learning and Inference at Scale

Graphs serve as a fundamental tool for representing various natural phenomena, evident in ecological and hydrological networks. In ecological networks, such as the food webs (*https://oreil.ly/SyFGn*) illustrated in Figure 1-1, nodes symbolize distinct species, and edges represent predator–prey interactions or trophic relationships. Similarly, hydrological networks exemplify this natural graph phenomena, with the nodes representing bodies of water (such as lakes, streams, and rivers), and edges depicting the water flow between them. The graph structures encapsulate how the energy flows within natural ecosystems in the initial ecological example.

Conversely, in the second scenario, the graph representation aids researchers in comprehending the complexities of water distribution patterns. In natural systems, like biology and neuroscience, the internal organization resembles a graph. In biology, graphs simulate molecular interactions, such as protein–protein interaction networks, metabolic pathways, and gene regulatory networks. Similarly, in neuroscience, graphs illustrate neuronal connections in the brain, shedding light on brain structure and function. By representing these systems with graphs, it is possible to visualize and analyze these systems, leading to advancements in medicine, neuroscience, and biotechnology.

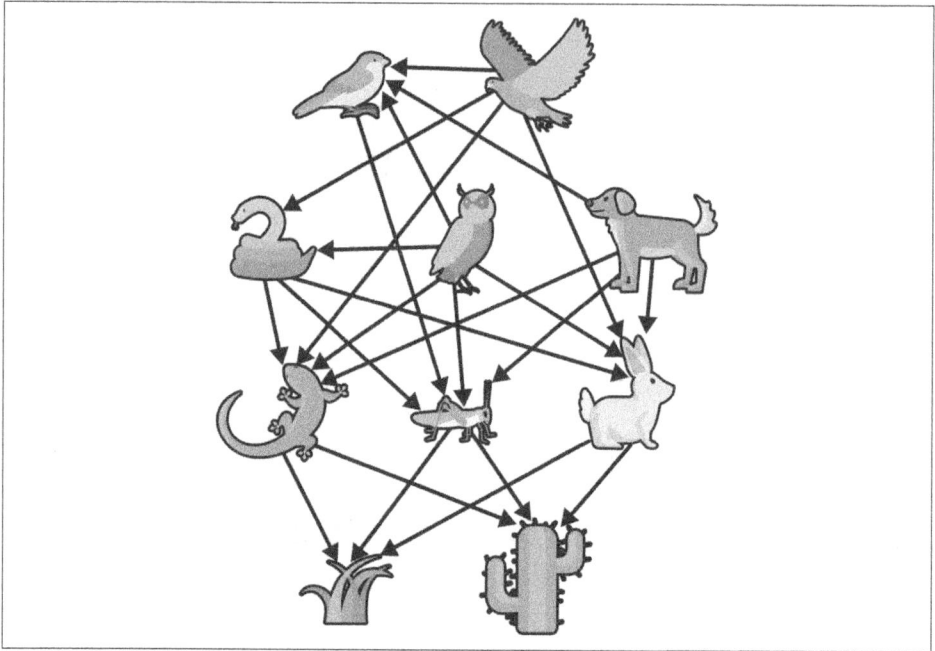

Figure 1-1. A sample desert ecosystem food web

Additionally, the power of graphs is evident in designed technologies and systems, such as social networks, as illustrated in Figure 1-2, and in transportation networks. Both systems can be represented by graphs. In social networks, individuals are represented as nodes, and their friendship relationships are indicated by edges, creating a vast graph that represents millions of people around the world. Graph algorithms can be applied to this network to suggest new friendships (creating edges) between individuals, for example.

Similarly, transportation networks use graphs to model road networks, railways, air transportation routes, and public transit networks. Nodes represent locations (e.g., cities, intersections, stations), while edges represent connections (e.g., roads, tracks, flight paths). Graph algorithms are then applied to optimize various operations, such as route planning (establishing connections between two locations).

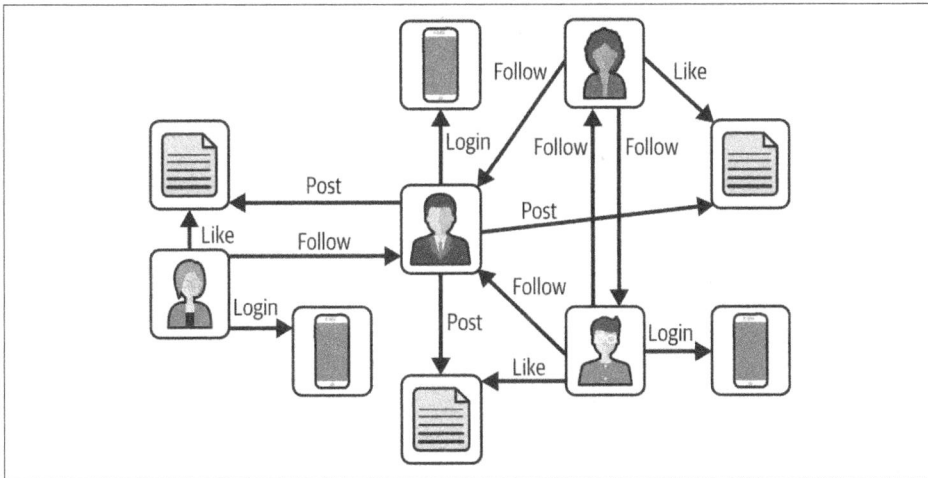

Figure 1-2. Simplified example of graph representation in social networks

The scenarios described here share a common feature: they all involve complex systems with complex relationships. When we refer to complex systems, we are talking about networks composed of numerous interconnected nodes that exhibit emergent behavior and nonlinear dynamics, making them challenging to predict or understand. These systems also feature complex relationships, characterized by multiple connections between nodes, further adding to their complexity. For example, in ecological food webs, various species interact through predation, competition, mutualism, and other ecological interactions. In this network, each species is connected to others by feeding relationships, forming a complex web of dependencies.

All these examples of graph applications highlight their inherent power. Another aspect of this power lies in the learning algorithms applied to these graphs. These algorithms, integral to graph learning, facilitate tasks such as suggesting new friendship connections or identifying optimal routes. Graph learning provides a comprehensive framework for solving problems represented graphically, which will be the focus of this book.

At the core of graph learning is the ability to distill complex relationships and structures. By representing data through nodes and edges, graphs facilitate the abstraction of complex details, allowing a focus on the essential connections that drive insights and understanding. Consequently, professionals across various fields can analyze large datasets more effectively and efficiently, uncovering patterns and trends that were once hidden by the overwhelming volume of data.

In the fast-paced, interconnected world of today, harnessing the power of graphs can significantly benefit businesses, governments, and individuals. This book delves into the significance of graph learning and inference at scale, employing graph-based algorithms and inference techniques to analyze vast datasets. We aim to show how these methods can transform data analysis, interpretation, and application, revealing their extensive potential.

For businesses, understanding complex data can lead to better decision making, streamlined processes, and increased revenue. For example, retail companies can utilize graph learning to craft targeted marketing strategies and offer personalized recommendations by deeply analyzing consumer behavior patterns and preferences. This nuanced understanding allows them to align their marketing efforts closely with customer expectations, enhancing the efficacy of their business operations. Similarly, financial institutions can leverage graphs to detect fraudulent transactions and assess credit risk with greater precision. By grasping the power of graphs, professionals can forge novel solutions to contemporary challenges, distinguishing themselves in their fields.

In scientific research, graph learning and inference enable the modeling of complex systems, such as protein interactions or ecological networks, opening the door to novel discoveries. By elucidating the connections between different components of these complex systems, scientists can create more accurate models, predict outcomes, and make informed decisions that propel human knowledge forward.

For governments and public entities, graph learning and inference are crucial in tackling some of today's most critical challenges. Whether it's tracking the spread of infectious diseases or understanding the dynamics of social unrest, graphs offer valuable insights that can guide policymaking.

As we edge toward the realization of artificial general intelligence (AGI),[1] the importance of graph learning and inference only grows. This increasing significance is clear in the remarkable increase of representation-learning research showcased at the International Conference on Learning Representations (ICLR) 2022, as highlighted by the keywords in Figure 1-3.

---

1 AGI refers to AI systems having human-like intelligence and adaptability, capable of understanding, learning, and performing a wide range of tasks across multiple domains. AGI is a more advanced form of AI, as opposed to specialized AI, which is designed to solve a specific problem, e.g., facial recognition. AGI remains a research goal.

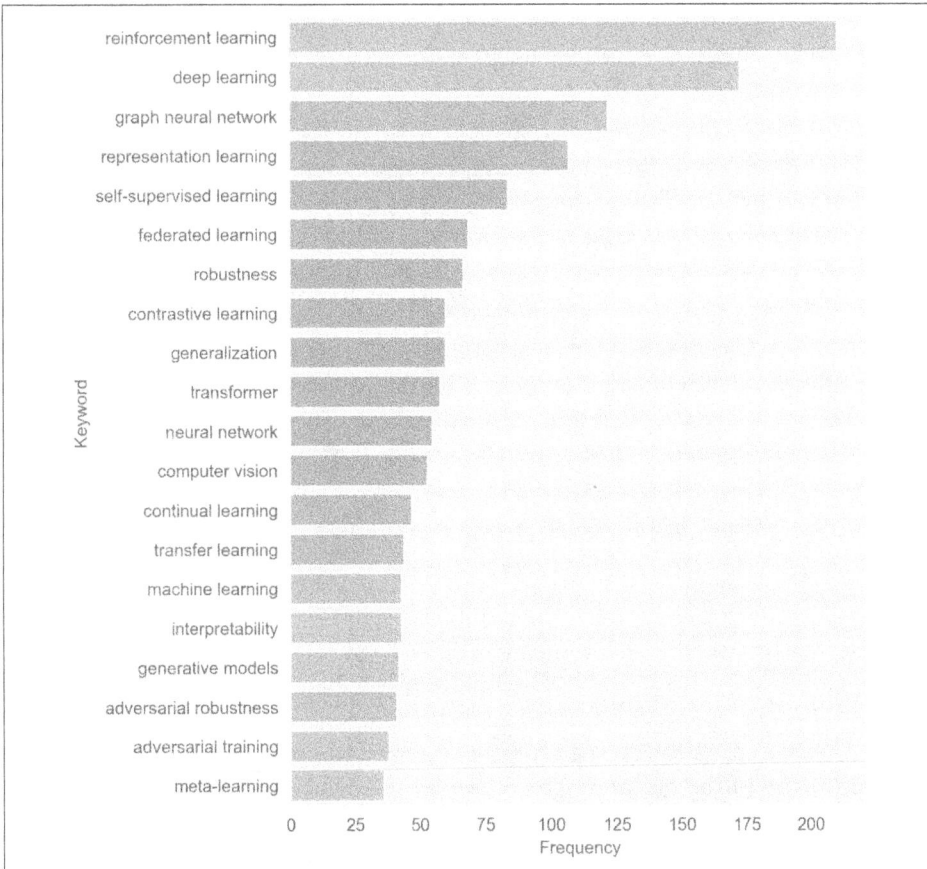

Figure 1-3. Top 20 keywords from work submitted to ICLR 2022: graph-based technologies are among the top active research areas (EdisonLeeeee/GitHub (https://oreil.ly/6MbJX))

In this book, we will explore both the theory and practice of enterprise graph learning and inference at scale, addressing the challenges involved in constructing end-to-end graph learning and inference pipelines capable of delivering both low latency and high throughput. We will lead you through the fundamentals of graph theory and introduce you to cutting-edge techniques and applications, all while providing a comprehensive framework to help you master the complex world of graphs.

One of the primary focuses of this book will be to tackle the scalability challenges in graph learning and inference. As data becomes larger and more complex—with potentially millions of nodes and edges, datasets expanding beyond terabytes in size, and the complexity of graphs escalating due to a variety of deep relationships—it becomes necessary to develop systems capable of efficiently managing these increases at scale. We will explore and cover various strategies and techniques to assist you in designing and implementing scalable graph learning and inference pipelines, ensuring that your solutions stay performant and effective as your data grows.

To accelerate the advancement of graph-based learning methodologies and inference systems, this book will introduce an open source package that leverages widely used open source tools, integrating best practices for the design and implementation of graph-based solutions. This package aims to not only save you time and effort but also to equip you with a robust foundation for developing advanced graph learning and inference systems customized to meet your unique needs.

By harnessing the power of graph learning and inference at scale, you will unlock the ability to tackle complex challenges and discover new opportunities for personal and professional development. Equipped with the knowledge and tools presented in this book, you will be prepared to navigate the challenges of an ever more connected world, transforming how you analyze, interpret, and leverage data in your endeavors.

A Bird's-Eye View: Navigating the Book's Chapters

If you're curious about what to expect from this book and how to navigate it, we've got you covered. Chapters 1, 2, and 3 are designed to familiarize you with the world of graphs. They will cover the fundamentals of graphs, the graph learning pipeline, and traditional approaches to graph learning with hands-on examples. Chapter 4 will introduce PyGraf,[2] an open source library, explaining its architecture, modules, and how it can be used. Chapters 5 through 9 cover advanced topics such as graph neural networks and constructing large-scale networks, leveraging the capabilities of PyGraf.

Chapter 10 will focus on federated learning and differential privacy, offering an in-depth exploration of these concepts for building privacy-preserving graph learning and inference pipelines. Following this, Chapter 11 will cover different inference strategies, providing deeper insights into this area. To conclude, Chapter 12 will guide you on how to effectively monitor and refine these processes via feedback loops.

So, let's continue with Chapter 1! This chapter is all about introducing you to the exciting world of graph learning in enterprise settings. We'll start by breaking down the concepts of graphs and graph learning, making sure we're all on the same page. After that, we'll explore the incredible benefits of graph machine learning (GML) across different applications. Trust us, you'll be amazed by the scope of its applications.

We'll also take a close look at real-world use cases that demonstrate the power and potential of graph learning. We'll emphasize why it's crucial for businesses to adopt these methods and techniques, and how they can drive success in various industries.

---

2 PyGraf is the tentative name of our open source library and is subject to change.

Towards the end of Chapter 1, we'll address an important aspect: the limitations of graph learning when applied at an enterprise scale. It's essential to understand these challenges, as they lay the groundwork for the subsequent chapters where we'll go deeper into how to proactively mitigate these challenges. So, hang tight as we pave the way for tackling those obstacles head-on.

Hope that gives you a clear idea of what lies ahead! Get ready for an exciting journey through the world of graph learning in enterprise environments.

Graphs and Graph Learning

Now that we've provided a bird's-eye view of the book's chapters, we'll embark on our journey by laying the basic foundations for understanding graph learning. To begin, let's explore the fundamental concepts of graphs and graph learning, exploring their applications, and addressing the challenges and potential solutions for implementing graph learning at an enterprise scale.

What Is a Graph?

In discrete mathematics, particularly within the field of graph theory, a graph is a structure that involves a collection of objects, where certain pairs of objects have a particular kind of association/relationship. These objects are represented as mathematical concepts known as *vertices* (also referred to as nodes or points), and the connections between pairs of vertices are termed *edges* (also known as links or lines).[3]

We can think of graphs as complex topographical structures with no fixed order or reference points. This implies that there's no inherent order or reference point governing the organization of graph nodes and edges. Consequently, graphs showcase complexity and variability in their structure. Their size and structure can vary. Graphs can be *static* or *dynamic* in structure. Static graphs have a fixed structure where nodes and edges do not change over time. One example of a static graph is a graph that represents a snapshot of road networks, where the road intersects represent nodes and the roads represent edges.

Dynamic graphs, on the other hand, have time-varying structures. This means that a node or an edge can be removed or added over time without losing the graph's structure. Many applications involve dynamic graphs. Social networks such as Facebook and X[4] are examples of dynamic graphs that evolve over time as new people join, existing people leave and remove their accounts temporarily or permanently, new friendships are formed, and old ones are deleted.

---

3 Trudeau, Richard J. (1993), *Introduction to Graph Theory*. Dover Publications.

4 Formerly known as Twitter (*http://www.twitter.com*).

Figure 1-4 represents a dynamic graph of a social network, where the temporal aspect is represented as an asynchronous stream of events. This means that the graph changes over time, and these changes are captured as a series of asynchronous events. The status of the network at $t = 0$ has only three people with two friendship connections existing between Person1 and Person2, and Person2 and Person3. At $t = 1$, Person4 joined the platform and its node was created and connected to Person3. At $t = 2$, Person4 follows Person2, and this creates a new edge linking the two.

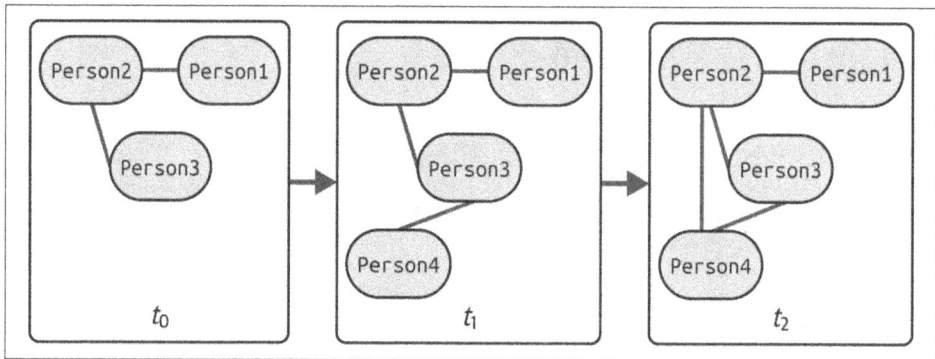

Figure 1-4. A dynamic graph representing a social network evolving over time

We refer to the data that is contained within the graph as *graph data*. It refers to the structured information that is represented as a graph, consisting of interconnected nodes and edges. Graph data spans various domains, such as transportation networks, social networks, biological networks, finance, linguistics, etc. The nature of data might vary, and we will go through this in the "Definition of Graph Data and Graph Data Levels" on page 28.

When discussing graph data and its characteristics, it's important to understand the specifics of the graph. Graphs can take different forms, including directed and undirected types, and may feature multiple edges between nodes. Let's cover these distinctions:

Directed versus undirected graphs
   Directed graphs have edges with a specific direction, meaning the relationship between nodes is one-way. Undirected graphs, on the other hand, lack edge directions, implying a two-way relationship between nodes.

Multiple edges between nodes
   Although we often simplify by assuming a single edge connecting a pair of nodes, it's possible for two nodes to share multiple edges. These graphs are termed *multigraphs*.

Edge labeling

> Edges within a graph can have a label, conveying additional information about the relationship between nodes. These labels might represent timestamps for friendship connections in a social network, distances or costs in a road network, or any other relevant properties associated with the edges.

Graph learning, on the other hand, refers to the process of extracting useful insights and patterns from graph-structured data using machine learning techniques. By leveraging the properties of graphs, graph learning algorithms can uncover hidden patterns and relationships within the data such as identifying tightly connected communities within a social network based on their interactions, interests, or affiliations, enabling more effective decision making and predictions.

Having established an introductory understanding of the concepts of graphs and graph data, "Graph Data Representation" focuses on exploring the methodologies involved in representing graph data.

Graph Data Representation

A graph is also a form of representation used to simplify a situation or problem. This mapping of any scenario to a graph representation is known as *graph data representation,* and it involves representing the problem's data as a graph, with nodes representing graph nodes (or entities) and edges (or links) representing relationships between those entities. The first step in this mapping process is to identify the entities that will be represented as nodes and their relationships (edges).

Once the nodes and edges have been identified, a visual representation of the problem can be created in the form of a graph (nodes connected by edges). This visual mapping is referred to as *graph modeling*. It is useful for intuitively understanding the problem and visualizing the relationships between different nodes. While this step is merely illustrative and hence optional, you can use various software tools to generate the visual representations. Popular software tools include Gephi (*https://gephi.org*), Cytroscape (*https://cytoscape.org*), and Graphviz (*https://graphviz.org*). Other text-to-graph tools include those designed to handle unstructured data (e.g., raw text) and utilize natural language processing (NLP) techniques to automatically generate a graph representation based on the identified nodes and edges in the text. Examples of such tools include Neo4j (*https://neo4j.com*) and IBM Watson Knowledge Studio (*https://oreil.ly/NHF5G*). However, for most of these tools, visualizing the graph is only applicable when the size of the nodes is manageable.[5]

---

5 There is a limitation on how many nodes and edges we can draw manually, and in most graph visualization software.

Figure 1-5 shows graph modeling or visualization of a simplified road network. Here the graph nodes are the road intersections, which are connected to one another by roads, which represent edges.

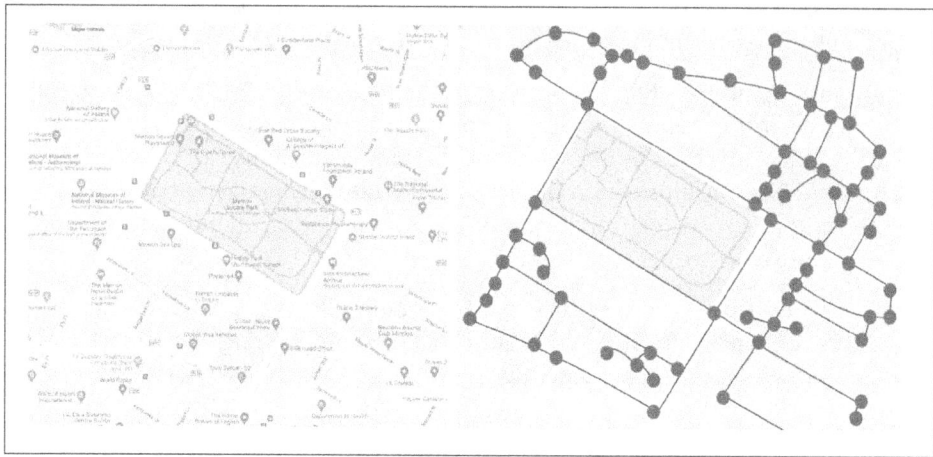

Figure 1-5. Representation of the road network as a graph: the image represents the map of "Merrion Square Park in Dublin, Ireland"

Using the nodes and edges that were identified in the previous step, the second step of graph representation requires finding a mathematical representation that captures the graph structure. This could mean modeling the structure using matrices or vectors, which then can subsequently be used for graph-based computations. In general, this mathematical representation can be done using traditional or advanced techniques. Traditional graph representation techniques include an *adjacency matrix* or an *adjacency list*. Adjacency matrices are square matrices that represent the relationships between nodes in a graph, where 1 indicates an edge between two nodes, and 0 indicates no edge. Adjacency lists represent each node and its neighbors as a list. You will learn more about this in Chapter 2.

In terms of advanced graph representation techniques, embeddings serve as the foundation. Graph embeddings are a way of representing nodes and edges in a graph as numerical vectors, which can be fed as inputs into machine learning algorithms. Their goal is to encapsulate the structural and semantic information of the graph in a way that can be easily processed by graph algorithms. There are various techniques for generating graph embeddings, and we'll cover how these techniques are implemented through interactive examples from Chapters 3 to 8.

Until this point, we've seen how graph representation can be used to map complex phenomena or a real-world network into a visual representation, and how these representations are then utilized to create a map of the geometrics of graph structure using traditional or advanced graph representation techniques. The latter representation is subsequently fed into machine learning (ML) models as input data. But how does this representation actually work within the machine learning model?

Well, once this representation is generated, we can apply a graph algorithm, which is a set of algorithms used to solve graph-related problems such as finding the shortest path in a transportation network as in Google Maps or predicting new nodes or edges, etc.[6] The relationships between different data points are important to consider when performing ML tasks. Using graph data representation allows machine learning models to directly incorporate this structural information into their predictions and decisions, which can improve performance and accuracy.

Now that you've learned about graphs and graph data representation, let's explore graph learning.

Graph Learning

Graph learning refers to the process of applying machine learning algorithms to analyze, learn, and make predictions on graphs. This can involve common GML tasks such as *node classification* (assigning labels to nodes), *link prediction* (predicting connections between nodes), and *clustering* (grouping nodes based on similarities). You'll explore these tasks further in Chapter 2, with an example in Chapter 3.

Once the graph data has been represented using graph representation as described in "Graph Data Representation" on page 9, we can apply graph learning, aka machine learning algorithms, to solve problems on graphs. For example, we can use *graph convolutional networks* (GCNs) (*https://oreil.ly/ICin8*) for model classification tasks.

The most recent approach in graph learning uses a more advanced representation of graph data, known as *graph representation learning*. Let's look at what this is and how it differs from graph data representation

Graph representation learning involves transforming the graph structure into a simplified, low-dimensional space—essentially a mathematical space with few dimensions. Imagine the nodes and edges of the graph as points and lines within this space. It serves as a method for visually and computationally representing the structure of a graph. This process, known as *embedding*, aims to capture information about individual nodes or edges within the graph by assigning them coordinates within a non-Euclidean space (*https://oreil.ly/cSrv6*). These embeddings encode core details about the graph's connectivity patterns, spanning both local and global aspects. For instance, they can illustrate the proximity of nodes and explain their roles within different *subgraphs*, which are smaller, self-contained segments of the larger graph.

---

6 These algorithms will be covered in greater detail throughout this book. Core graph algorithms and traditional GML will be reviewed in Chapter 2) and graph neural networks will be studied in Chapters 3 through 9.

A common methodology for graph representational learning is the employment of profound neural architectures—including but not limited to, GCNs, graph autoencoders (GAEs), graph attention networks (GATs), and graph isomorphism networks (GINs).[7] These methods learn embeddings by iteratively transforming the features of a node's neighbors, either via convolution or attention mechanism, until a fixed-size embedding is produced. These approaches will be covered in greater detail in Chapters 3 and 4.

Other graph representation learning techniques include random walk-based algorithms. These algorithms use the sequences of nodes visited during these walks to train node embeddings, effectively capturing the local and global structure of the graph. This will be covered in more detail in Chapter 2.

Once learned, node embeddings can be utilized for a multitude of machine learning tasks such as node/vertex classification, link prediction, and graph clustering. This means that node embeddings can serve as an input layer for the graph algorithms used to approach these tasks, such as PageRank[8] and shortest path algorithms.[9]

Overall, graph representational learning has become an important component of graph learning, as it allows for the efficient processing of large and complex graphs. Its quality also influences the ability of machine learning models to make accurate predictions on graph data.

Let's use social networks as an example to demonstrate how graph learning works at a high level. You might use graph learning to predict future interactions between users, such as a potential friendship connection, recommending content, or identifying communities the user might want to join. To apply ML, you'd need to encode the pairwise properties between nodes, such as the type and strength of the relationship between two people (nodes). The ML model might also need global positioning information about each node so that it can include the person's local neighborhood in the contextual information it captures about them.

> The difference between graph data representation and graph representation learning is that graph data representation is about structuring your data in the form of a graph, whereas graph representation learning is a machine learning task that learns a way to represent parts or all of your graph as low-dimensional vectors (embeddings) that can be used for various tasks.

---

7 You can read about the architectures of these networks (*https://oreil.ly/ICin8*).

8 Brin, S., and Page, L. (1998). "The Anatomy of a Large-Scale Hypertextual Web Search Engine" (*https://oreil.ly/co84t*). *Computer Networks and ISDN Systems*, 30(1-7), 107-117.

9 Cormen, T. H., Leiserson, C. E., Rivest, R. L., and Stein, C. (1989). *Introduction to Algorithms*. MIT Press.

Graph learning has made remarkable progress, as evidenced by its successful application in various use cases. Nevertheless, considering the importance of scalability in an enterprise context, scalable graph learning has been adopted to accommodate the growth associated with these environments.

Now that we grasped what graph learning is, let's look into *scalable graph learning* and its prerequisites.

Scalable Graph Learning: Addressing the Requirements

Because of the dynamic nature of the enterprise ecosystem, graph learning should ideally be scalable. Scalable graph learning refers to the ability to perform machine learning on large-scale graph datasets efficiently. It involves the development of algorithms and models capable of processing graphs containing millions or billions of nodes and edges, while effectively leveraging computational resources and memory utilization through distribution and parallelism. Here are some of the requirements for scalable graph learning:

Data quality and integration
  Enterprise-ready graph learning systems need to be able to handle and integrate data from a variety of sources—including structured and unstructured data—and ensure that the data is accurate, consistent, and up-to-date.

Graph storage
  Scalable graph learning requires efficient graph storage mechanisms that can handle large-scale graphs. By "large-scale graphs," we are referring to graphs at the enterprise level, characterized by an extensive number of nodes and edges, often representing a network of millions or even billions of connections.[10] Distributed graph storage systems such as Hadoop Distributed File System (HDFS) and Apache Cassandra are examples of storage solutions commonly used in this context.

Distributed computing
  Scalable graph learning requires distributed computing frameworks that can distribute both the graph data and the computation across multiple machines. An example of such a framework is Apache Spark, which is widely used for processing large-scale datasets across a cluster of machines.

Integration with other systems
  A scalable graph learning system should seamlessly integrate with existing enterprise infrastructures including data warehouses, business intelligence tools, and

---

10 Besta, M., and Hoefler, T. (2024). "Parallel and Distributed Graph Neural Networks: An In-Depth Concurrency Analysis" (*https://oreil.ly/1ciVz*). *IEEE Transactions on Pattern Analysis and Machine Intelligence.*

visualization platforms. It should offer compatibility, APIs, and connectors to easily ingest data from various sources.

Scalability

Graph learning systems often need to process and analyze large and complex graphs with millions or billions of nodes and edges. This requires the system to be able to handle such large graphs efficiently and effectively. It's actually one of the key challenges restricting graph-based industrial applications—which often need to deal with very large and multisourced data while maintaining low latency. The association between graph scalability and latency constraints is strong and varies by application and infrastructure settings. It restricts the potential of delivering offline-trained graph-based models into active or serving graph products.

Security and privacy

Graph learning systems designed for enterprise use—particularly those dedicated to handling sensitive data—need to prioritize data security as a means to prevent unauthorized breaches. This involves giving importance to measures such as implementing secure data pipelines, employing strong authentication methods, enabling auditing and logging functionalities, ensuring a secure infrastructure, and complying with relevant data protection regulations. Moreover, when scalability and privacy are key considerations, the adoption of federated learning techniques can be beneficial. By utilizing federated learning, graph learning models can be trained on decentralized data sources while maintaining data privacy and security. Chapters 8 and 9 will provide a more in-depth exploration of these techniques.

Hardware acceleration

Graph learning algorithms are usually computationally intensive. Therefore, hardware acceleration techniques play a crucial role in accelerating the computations of these algorithms. Graphical processing units (GPUs) or tensor processing units (TPUs) can significantly speed up the execution of these algorithms. By leveraging the specialized architectures of GPUs and TPUs, graph learning algorithms can be executed efficiently, leading to faster training on large-scale graph datasets.

Advantages of Scalable Graph Learning in Enterprise

In this section, we will explore in detail the benefits of employing scalable graph learning in enterprise settings and emphasize how this approach can drive significant advancements in various domains. By harnessing the unique capabilities of graph learning, businesses can tap into deeper data insights, enabling strategic advantages that are not readily achievable with traditional analytics techniques. Let's explore these benefits in two distinct categories: technical and business advantages.

From a technical standpoint, scalable GML offers several advantages. It enhances data representation, which enables a comprehensive and nuanced understanding of complex data structures. This capability allows graphs to capture higher-order interactions between entities in a graph, leading to improved predictive modeling and robustness. Moreover, it seamlessly integrates with existing data management systems. In terms of privacy and security, scalable graph learning can be combined with privacy-preserving techniques like federated learning and differential privacy, ensuring the confidentiality and protection of sensitive data. This is especially important for organizations that deal with confidential information and must comply with regulatory requirements.

These technical aspects translate into significant business benefits. They enhance business insights by revealing hidden patterns and relationships, resulting in more informed decision making and a competitive edge through the identification of market opportunities. Furthermore, they enable personalized offerings and more effective marketing strategies, which could lead to increased customer retention, higher revenue, and so on. By harnessing the power of scalable graph learning in enterprise environments, organizations can unlock new possibilities in data analysis, predictive modeling, and decision making, propelling them toward a more data-driven future.

As we transition to "Large-Scale Graphs in Real-World Enterprises: Use Cases", we will explore how these benefits of scalable graph learning manifest in practical applications. We will examine a range of breakthroughs and advancements in various industries that have leveraged large-scale graph learning to address complex challenges and drive innovation. By understanding these real-world use cases, you will gain a clearer perspective on the potential impact of scalable graph learning techniques and how they can be harnessed to transform enterprise operations across diverse domains.

Large-Scale Graphs in Real-World Enterprises: Use Cases

Graph technology is rapidly permeating various aspects of our daily lives, profoundly impacting the way we interact with the world around us. From utilizing Google Maps for seamless navigation between locations to engaging with others on social media platforms like X and Facebook, graph applications are transforming our experiences.

In the subsequent sections, we will cover a diverse range of large-scale graph applications across multiple domains, including geospatial analysis, drug discovery, and fraud detection within the financial industry. By exploring these examples, you will gain a deeper understanding of how graph-based solutions are revolutionizing different sectors and driving innovation.

Travel-Time Predictions on Google Maps

If you have used Google Maps, you've experienced firsthand how it utilizes graph theory and graph learning algorithms (*https://oreil.ly/8gbFy*) to model road networks and accurately predict travel times. By constructing a graph representation of the road network, with nodes representing interactions or points of interest, and edges representing roads or highways, Google Maps efficiently calculates travel times between two locations by finding the shortest path in this graph.

To achieve this, Google Maps employs a blend of graph search algorithms, such as Dijkstra's algorithm for finding the shortest path and A* search for efficient pathfinding. Additionally, it integrates machine learning techniques to consider control variables such as distance, speed limits, and traffic conditions, ensuring accurate and up-to-date results. These algorithms dynamically adapt to changing factors, giving users reliable navigation guidance. For deeper insights into these algorithms, you can explore resources like *Graph Algorithms* by Mark Needham and Amy E. Hodler (O'Reilly).

Drug Development: Halicin

Molecules are modeled as graphs with atoms as nodes and bonds as edges, with added properties to nodes and edges for detail. Graph learning algorithms are effective in analyzing these structures, leading to faster drug development by predicting molecular characteristics such as solubility and toxicity. Specifically, GCNs—a type of *neural network*, which we will visit in future chapters—are suited for graph data and have been used to predict the antibacterial properties of molecules, advancing antibiotic discovery.

Figure 1-6 presents the end-to-end pipeline for developing this transformative approach to antibiotic discovery by utilizing the power of graph neural networks. This method vastly accelerates the search for new antibiotics by computationally navigating through extensive chemical territories, which traditionally required laborious and costly experimental screenings.

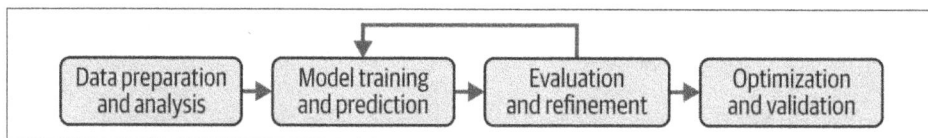

Figure 1-6. End-to-end pipeline used by MIT researchers to advance antibiotic discovery using graph learning algorithms (adapted from Stokes et al. (2020) (https://oreil.ly/Mav9O))

The pipeline includes the following high-level steps:

1. *Data preparation and analysis*

   A large dataset of chemical data, including molecular structures and properties effective against E. coli, is compiled. A GCN analyzes this data, representing molecules as graphs with atoms and bonds as nodes and edges, respectively.

2. *Model training and prediction*

   The GCN model is trained on the molecular data and then used to predict potential antibacterial molecules. These predictions are based on the model's ability to recognize patterns that indicate effectiveness against E. coli.

3. *Evaluation and refinement*

   Predictions are evaluated for accuracy, with the most promising candidates identified as "leads." The model is iteratively refined using this evaluation feedback to improve its predictive accuracy.

4. *Optimization and validation*

   Leads are optimized for increased antibacterial efficacy and safety, and the model's predictions are scaled up for larger datasets. The results of the machine learning approach are compared with those from traditional experimental methods.

The process demonstrates GML's role in accelerating drug discovery. A model trained on 2,335 molecules identified new antibiotics, and when applied to over 107 million molecules, it pinpointed compounds active against E. coli. Candidates were ranked by the model's predicted effectiveness. One standout candidate, Halicin, proved effective against various bacteria and safe for human cells, marking a significant step in combating antibiotic resistance. Though further research is needed to understand Halicin's mechanisms, its discovery is a notable breakthrough in the field.

Fraud Detection

GML is a powerful tool for detecting fraudulent transactions in real time. In financial institutions, transactions are often processed through complex networks of accounts, transactions, and relationships. These networks can be represented as graphs, with nodes representing accounts and the edges representing transactions or relationships between accounts. The labels for the nodes could include information about the account such as the account holder's name, account balance, and transaction history. Similarly, the labels for the edges could also include additional information about the transaction such as the amount, date, and type of transaction. It is also possible to include additional nodes in the graph to represent other entities, such as merchants or payment processors. Figure 1-7 depicts an example representation of this network. It provides a conceptual way to visualize complex transactions between different entities. Nodes represent interacting entities in the systems (such as *merchants or cardholders*) with additional information shared via labels (*location*), and the relationships between nodes indicate the occurrence of transactions with labels to highlight additional transaction properties (for instance, *amount* and *transaction type*).

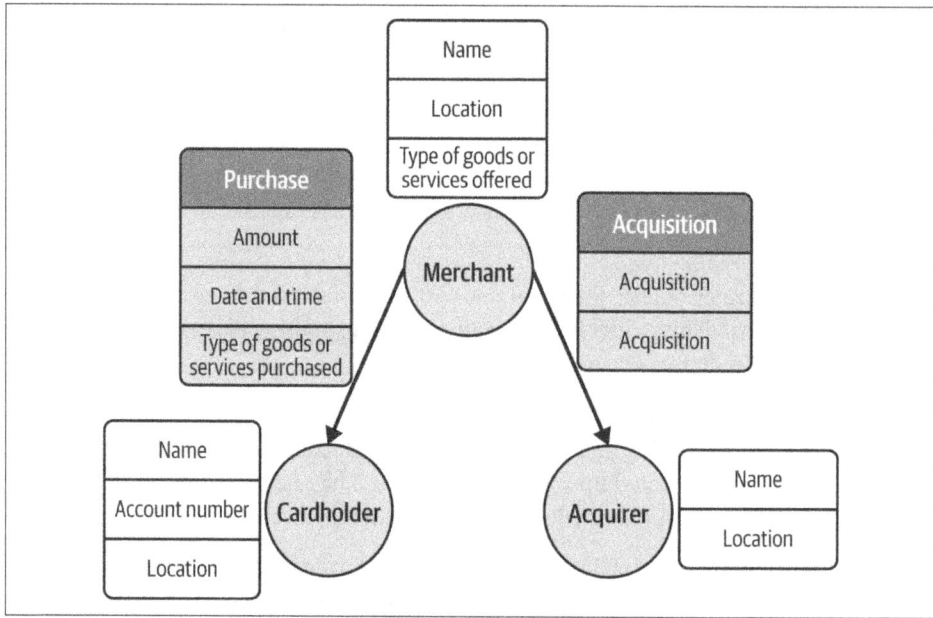

Figure 1-7. Illustration of a graph data model depicting a transaction network, allowing a visual representation of interactions between entities through labeled nodes and relationships

By analyzing these graphs, ML algorithms can identify patterns and anomalies that may suggest fraudulent activity: a cardholder suddenly making a large number of purchases in a short period of time, a high volume of transactions from a single cardholder to multiple merchants in a short period of time, a large number of transactions from a single merchant to multiple cardholders, or a merchant experiencing a high rate of chargebacks are all patterns of fraudulent activities. GML systems identify these patterns by analyzing the graph's edges and labels, and they are used to flag transactions for further investigation or to trigger fraud alerts.

GML can process enormous amounts of data in real time, even the hundreds of thousands of transactions that financial institutions typically process every day. This makes it excellent at quickly identifying suspicious transactions and alerting financial institutions, so they can take corrective action before any funds are lost. Graph ML can also learn and adapt over time. As an algorithm processes more data, its ability to detect fraudulent activities and eliminate false positives improves. In "The Evolution of Graphs and Graph Learning: From Early Beginnings to Modern Applications" on page 19, we'll show you how this works.

The Evolution of Graphs and Graph Learning: From Early Beginnings to Modern Applications

The field of graph learning has evolved significantly over the past several decades. In this section, we will explore the key milestones and breakthroughs that have shaped this evolution from its early beginnings to the present day. Figure 1-8 depicts snapshots of this evolution.

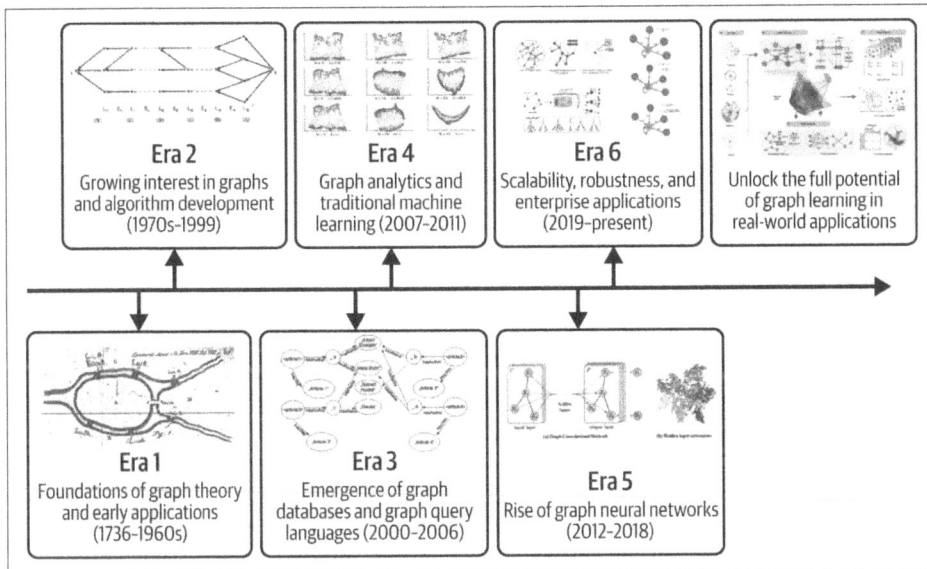

Figure 1-8. Evolution of graph learning systems (sources: era 1,[11] era 2,[12] era 3,[13] era 4,[14] era 5,[15] era 6,[16] top right image[17])

---

11 The Königsberg bridge problem. Euler, L. (1741). Solutio problematis ad geometriam situs pertinentis. *Commentarii academiae scientiarum Petropolitanae*, 128-140.

12 Hopcroft, J. E., and Karp, R. M. (1973). An n^5/2 algorithm for maximum matchings in bipartite graphs. *SIAM Journal on Computing*, 2(4), 225-231.

13 Castillo, R., Rothe, C., and Leser, U. (2010). "RDFMatView: Indexing RDF Data for SPARQL Queries" (*https://oreil.ly/9ENnS*).

14 Belkin, M., and Niyogi, P. (2003). "Laplacian Eigenmaps for Dimensionality Reduction and Data Representation" (*https://oreil.ly/k_0M2*). *Neural Computation*, 15(6), 1373-1396.

15 Kipf, T. N., and Welling, M. (2017). "Semi-Supervised Classification with Graph Convolutional Networks" (*https://oreil.ly/xwLNA*). arXiv preprint arXiv:1609.02907.

16 Karagiannakos, Sergios. "Best Graph Neural Network Architectures: GCN, GAT, MPNN, and More" (*https://oreil.ly/zI5yd*). September 23, 2021.

17 Weis, J. W., and Jacobson, J. M. (2021). "Learning on Knowledge Graph Dynamics Provides an Early Warning of Impactful Research" (*https://oreil.ly/M9p6J*). *Nature Biotechnology*, 39(10), 1300-1307.

Era 1: The Foundation of Graph Theory and Algorithms (1736-1970)

This era marks the birth of graph theory. It all began when Leonhard Euler introduced the concept of a graph and solved the Seven Bridges of Königsberg problem (*https://oreil.ly/_5tmn*). As time went on, lots of exciting developments took place in the graph space, most notably the creation of Dijkstra's algorithm, which became a powerful tool for finding the shortest path in graphs.

Era 2: More Advancement in Graph Algorithms and Technologies (1970-1999)

During this period, significant advances in graph technologies and algorithms occurred, including the development of graph-based data structures, graph traversal algorithms, graph coloring algorithms, and the establishment of graph theory as a foundational discipline in computer science.

This era also marks some very early work on graph storage capabilities with the introduction of *relational databases* as dominant technologies for data storage and querying. The relational database systematically arranges data using rows and columns, which collectively form a table. Typically, data spans across several tables, which can be joined together via a primary key or a foreign key.[18] This systemic configuration, inherent to a relational database management system (RDBMS), facilitates the seamless and efficient execution of relational operations, such as JOINs, enabling rapid retrieval and correlation of data. However, it struggles with modeling complex data relationships.

Furthermore, the *Resource Description Framework (RDF)* (*https://oreil.ly/ZuVfx*) was introduced in 1999, establishing the framework for describing data on the web in a graph-based structure, which later contributed to the emergence of linked data and the Semantic Web. Each RDF statement is a three-part structure, called a tuple, comprising three resources, each identified by a Uniform Resource Identifier (URI). Each tuple is represented as (Subject, Predicate, Object). The adoption of RDF as a data representation facilitates seamless identification, faster disambiguation, and interconnection of information by AI systems.

Similarly, the development of semantic graphs has witnessed significant progress. Semantic web technologies have evolved, giving rise to the concept of *knowledge graphs* (*https://oreil.ly/7Xk7J*), which serve as a more flexible and expressive form of a graph database. These knowledge graphs store structured data and knowledge about entities and their relationships. Knowledge graphs establish contextual relationships through the use of linking and semantic metadata, providing a structured approach to integrate, unify, analyze, and share data. At the core of a knowledge graph lies

---

18 "What Is a Relational Database?" (*https://oreil.ly/9kleL*). IBM, October 20, 2021.

a comprehensive knowledge model, comprising interconnected descriptions of concepts, entities, relationships, and events. A prime example of a knowledge graph is the Google Knowledge Graph (*https://oreil.ly/0eGi3*)—an expansive and contextually enriched data structure that semantically connects various informational elements.

Era 3: Emergence of Graph Databases and Graph Query Languages (2000-2006)

With the increasing importance of graphs in various domains, the need for efficient storage and retrieval mechanisms for graph data became apparent. This era saw the emergence of graph databases such as Neo4j, OrientDB, and ArangoDB, and the development of graph query languages like Cypher, SPARQL, and Gremlin. *A graph database (GDB)* is a database that is designed to store and manage data using graph structures with nodes, edges, and properties. It also enables semantic queries.[19] This graph-based structure facilitates the creation and execution of complex queries.

Era 4: Graph Analytics and Traditional Machine Learning (2007-2011)

Graph analytics frameworks such as Apache Giraph (*https://oreil.ly/nUcJR*) and GraphX (*https://oreil.ly/XWNrs*) emerged during this period, enabling large-scale graph processing and analysis. At the same time, researchers began to explore the application of traditional machine learning techniques to graph data, paving the way for graph analytics. These GML tasks include link prediction, node classification, and graph clustering became increasingly popular.

Era 5: Rise of Graph Neural Networks (2012-2018)

The introduction of GCNs marked a significant turning point in GML, as researchers started to leverage deep learning techniques for graph data. This era saw the development of various graph neural network architectures, including GraphSAGE,[20] graph attention networks (GATs),[21] and graph isomorphism networks (GINs).[22]

---

19 Bourbakis, Nikolaos G. (1998). *Artificial Intelligence and Automation.* World Scientific Publishing Co Pte Ltd.

20 Hamilton, W., Ying, Z., and Leskovec, J. (2017). "Inductive Representation Learning on Large Graphs" (*https://oreil.ly/n6B7y*). *Advances in Neural Information Processing Systems*, 30.

21 Velickovic, P. et al. (2017). "Graph Attention Networks" (*https://oreil.ly/3ifga*). arXiv:1710.10903.

22 Xu, K. et al. (2018). "How Powerful Are Graph Neural Networks?" (*https://oreil.ly/W3Fs5*) arXiv preprint arXiv:1810.00826.

Era 6: Scalability, Robustness, and Enterprise Applications (2019-Present)

The most recent era in the evolution of GML has focused on addressing the challenges of scalability, robustness, and privacy in graph learning, along with an increasing emphasis on real-world enterprise applications. Novel techniques such as graph partitioning and Cluster-GCN have emerged to handle large-scale graph learning problems.

Challenges of Enterprise-Ready Graph Learning Systems

Images and sequential data, such as text audio, have a linear structure, order, and point of reference. Graphs, on the other hand, have arbitrary dimensions, complex topology, and lack a reference point or concept of spatial location in networks. Furthermore, "graphs cannot be represented as a single entity" (*https://oreil.ly/7TKc9*) due to their inherent nature that consists of nodes and edges. This means that information on a graph can be missing or noisy, and the graph may become difficult to fully capture by a single representation. Also, enterprise graph networks tend to be dynamic and multimodal, which means they represent different data types: text, images, audio etc. All these characteristics present challenges for enterprise settings. Here, we'll look at a few of those challenges in more detail.

Data Harmonization Challenges

Enterprise-ready graph learning systems need to be able to handle and integrate data from a variety of sources and providers while ensuring that the data is consistent. This data comes in different data formats (unstructured, semi-structured, structured) and granularities. In the context of graph data representation, data harmonization can be a challenge since graph data frequently consists of a large number of interconnected entities and connections, which can be challenging to reconcile and standardize across multiple sources. Two examples of why data harmonization can be difficult are differences in schema and ontologies, and standardization across different data sources:

Differences in schemas and ontologies
> Different sources may use different schemas or ontologies to represent the same concepts. For example, one source may represent a person using a "name" and an "age" field, while another source may use "first_name" and "last_name" fields to represent the same information. To harmonize these data sources, the data must be transformed into a common format that can be understood by all of the sources (this is also called *reconciliation)* without introducing errors due to discrepancies in representation formats.

Differences in the applied standardizations

Different sources may use different data standards or conventions for representing data. For example, one source may use the ISO 8601[23] standard for representing dates, while another source may use a different standard. Thus, to use these data sources, all the data must be transformed into a common format that adheres to a single standard.

Computationally Intensive Workloads

Developing GML systems can be computationally and resource intensive. This is mainly because each stage in the GML pipeline requires a different set of resources, such as storage for graph data, computing power for data preparation and training, and memory for storing parameters. Here, we will discuss the computational challenges associated with graph data, graph complexity, and training procedures:

Graph data processing challenges

When working with graph data, two properties add additional challenges to its operational aspects. These characteristics are the volume and the high dimensionality of graph data. The complexity of storing and processing these massive and high-dimensional datasets is compounded by the constant problem of scaling the training process. To properly train a GML system, both of these factors would require more computing resources, ranging from memory storage to processing power.

Graph complexity challenges

Graphs can capture complex relationships between nodes and edges, which can be difficult to model and analyze. This can require the use of more sophisticated machine learning algorithms and techniques, which can be computationally intensive.

Training challenges

GML systems may require distributed training, which involves training the model across multiple machines or devices. This can be challenging to set up and manage, and it can also increase the computational resources required to train the model.

Dynamic Evolving Graphs

When it comes to complexity in graph systems, the dynamic evolving nature of graphs presents a unique challenge due to their ability to constantly change over time. This means that the graph structure and relationships between nodes can change frequently. Traditional algorithms that assume static graph structure are insufficient

---

23 ISO 8601 (*https://oreil.ly/wrgEr*) is an international standard for representing date and time-related data.

in these cases, hence there is a need for dynamic models that can accurately predict or classify based on the graph data. Building these models on dynamically evolving graphs can be challenging, as it requires a high level of adaptability, flexibility, and computational power to be able to accurately and efficiently analyze the constantly changing data. These aspects could be difficult to achieve at scale as models have to be responsive in learning and updating their predictions in response to changing data. Another challenge is the sheer volume of data generated; as the graph changes over time, new data is constantly being added, and the models must be able to handle and analyze this data in real time.

Some algorithms and techniques used to analyze dynamic evolving graphs include graph clustering, community detection, and centrality measures. These methods can be used to identify patterns and trends in the data and understand how the graph is evolving over time.

Active Monitoring and Drift Detection

For GML systems in production, active monitoring and drift detection present issues as they call for the system to continuously monitor the data and model performance and to identify when the models are no longer producing accurate predictions.

The primary hurdle lies in the need to continually process and analyze enormous volumes of data in real time, precisely evaluating the effectiveness of sophisticated models, and comparing present performance against historical performance to pinpoint plausible deviations or drifts in both data and model dynamics. This requires a robust and efficient system for storing and accessing historical data and model performance metrics, which can be difficult to design and implement in a production context. This will demand a significant amount of computational power and efficient data processing techniques, both of which can be challenging to produce at scale. Another associated difficulty here is the complexities of the models themselves. GML models often require complex processes and potentially have many parameters, making it challenging to effectively and timely assess their performance and detect when they are no longer making accurate predictions.

Real-Time Inference

When it comes to real-time predictions, GML models must be accurate with submillisecond latency. But this is no easy task. These models deal with complex operations that demand a lot of computing power, making it a challenge to achieve those submillisecond response times.

Several factors affect how quickly these models can make inferences in real time. Things like the size and complexity of the graph, the machine learning algorithms chosen, and the hardware and software infrastructure used for running the models all play a role. That's why it's crucial to optimize both the model design and the infrastructure to reduce the time needed for each prediction. This can involve techniques like model pruning, quantization, and parallelization. It also means fine-tuning the hardware and software infrastructure to minimize any extra time or effort involved in running the models.

Summary

In this chapter, we've laid the fundamentals for enterprise-ready graph learning, emphasizing the importance of scalable pipelines. These principles form the basis for the entire book's content, setting the stage for our exploration of graph learning's potential in the following chapters.

As we conclude this introductory chapter, let's preview the exciting journey ahead. Our book's overarching goal is to provide a comprehensive understanding of graph learning, its diverse applications across domains, such as healthcare, finance, biology, etc, and the unique challenges and opportunities it offers. We will start by delving into traditional machine learning for graphs, covering aspects like pipeline development, feature engineering, representation learning, semi-supervised node classification, and an introduction to our open source graph library.

In subsequent chapters, we'll dive into various graph pipelines, utilize traditional techniques to learn from graphs, cover deep learning and graph neural networks (GNNs), explore scalable node embeddings, discuss large-scale graph neural networks, investigate enterprise applications, and address privacy preservation. Finally, we'll cover graph inference strategies and the monitoring and feedback loop in GML systems. This roadmap promises an enriching exploration of graph learning and its potential impact on diverse industries and applications.

## CHAPTER 2

The Graph Machine Learning Pipeline

In Chapter 1, we gave you a glimpse into the world of graph learning in enterprise settings. We talked about its various use cases and wrapped up the chapter by highlighting the challenges it poses. As we move forward in the book, we're going to give you a high-level overview of the entire GML pipeline that we'll be exploring. From start to finish, this pipeline covers everything from collecting graph data to serving it for GML.

In this chapter, we'll start with the foundation stage: the *graph data pipeline*. This initial phase, crucial for the entire process, refers to a series of processes designed to efficiently handle, process, and analyze data structured in the form of graphs. It sets the groundwork for everything that follows. Next, we'll discuss the GML training pipeline, a series of steps designed to train and evaluate a chosen graph learning algorithm for a specific graph task, such as node classification or link prediction. Finally, we'll go through the graph inference pipeline, which tests whether the new model is ready for production promotion. If it is, the model is deployed to be utilized by downstream systems. For example, in building an ecommerce graph recommender system, the model is integrated into the bigger ecommerce solution to provide personalized recommendations for the platform's users. The three subpipelines are illustrated in Figure 2-1.

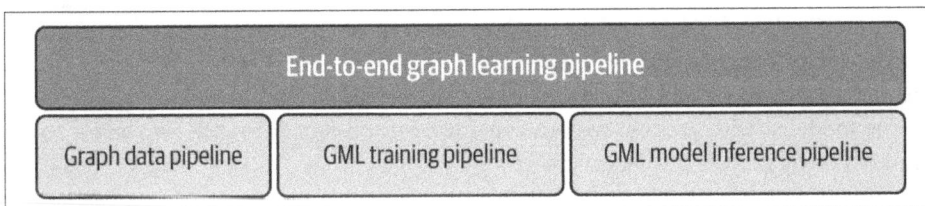

Figure 2-1. The graph learning pipeline is broken down into three stages: data, training, and inference

It's worth noting that, aside from the high-level overview of the graph data pipeline provided in this chapter, this book will not explore the data pipeline aspect in detail. There are excellent resources available that cover this topic, such as *The Practitioner's Guide to Graph Data* (O'Reilly), among others. Instead, this book will primarily focus on the graph training and inference pipelines.

The Graph Data Pipeline

In this section, we'll go into the first stage of the graph learning pipeline, which is the graph data pipeline (Figure 2-2). But before getting into the components of this pipeline, let's first define graph data and the graph data types.

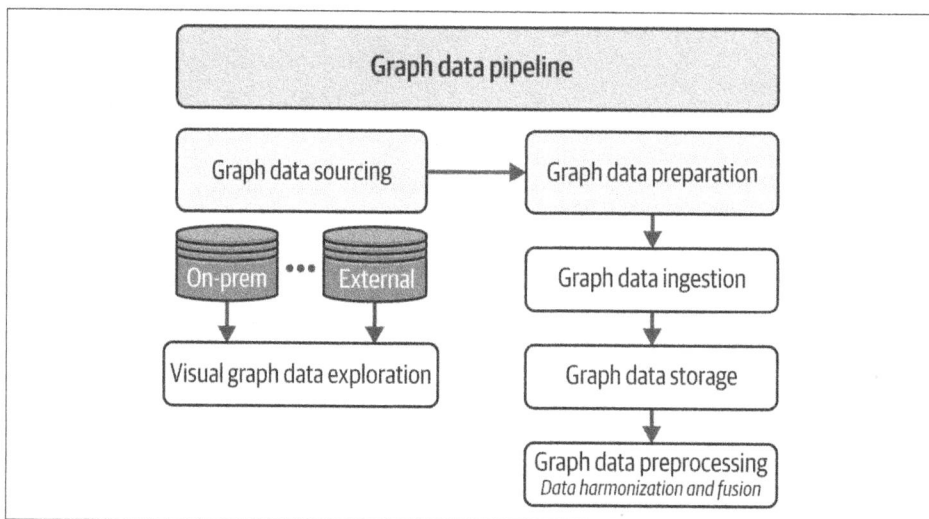

Figure 2-2. Simplified design of graph data pipeline components

Definition of Graph Data and Graph Data Levels

Graph data refers to data that is represented as a collection of nodes connected by edges. Graph data can represent a wide variety of data, including transportation networks, biological networks, social networks, recommendation systems, etc.

The graph data, which is widely used in modern applications, is characterized by high levels of connectivity between entities. Although social media network graphs are perhaps the most well-known examples, many other phenomena and applications can be modeled with graphs. We can categorize graph data into different levels based on the transformation needed to create a graph.

These levels are represented in Figure 2-3, which shows the four levels of a hierarchy organized according to readiness for graph modeling. These levels are:

- *Natural graph data* representing data that has a graph-like structure
- *Graphically represented phenomena* with dynamic structures
- *Structured data*
- *Unstructured data* that can be transformed into structured formats

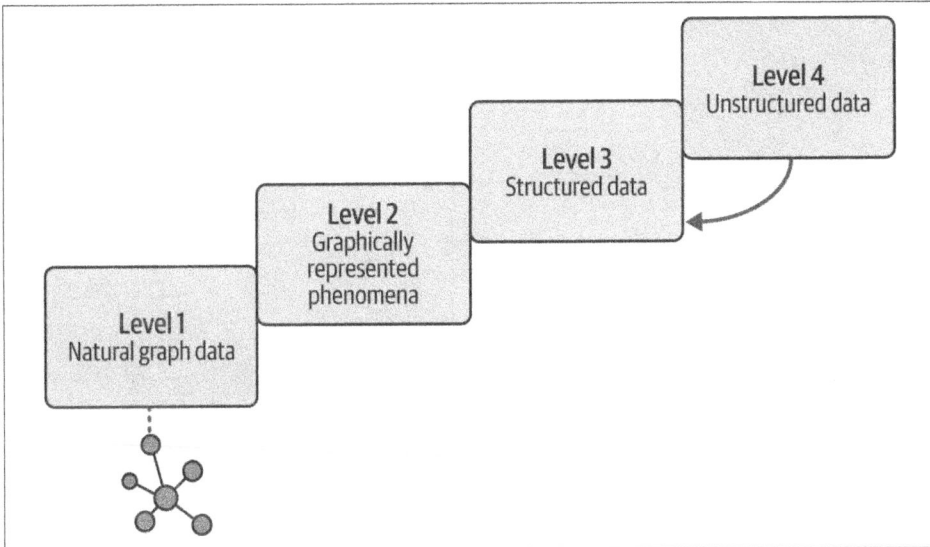

Figure 2-3. Four graph data levels based on the amount of work required to convert them to a graph structure (the arrow indicates the transformation's direction)

Natural graph data is level 1 in this hierarchy, indicating that data in this category has a graph-like structure already. Level 2 represents graphically represented phenomena that represent problems or phenomena with dynamic behavior that can be represented as a graph after performing graph data representation. Level 3 represents structured data, aka data with a structure like databases, and level 4 represents data without any structure, aka unstructured data such as text. The arrow beneath indicates the transformation's direction. For example, if we have unstructured data and want to represent it as a graph, we must first transform it into structured data. In the remaining part of this section, we will explore each category and cover them thoroughly.

Natural graph data

We've referred a few times now to graphable data found in nature, also known as "natural graphs" or "natural networks." In natural graphs, the underlying data is represented as graphs and meets its definition: that is, a network of nodes (entities) connected by edges (relationships). Therefore, natural graph data refers to data that occurs in nature and has a graph-like structure.[1]

Nature and its biological components are data, so one natural approach to represent them is through graphs. Interactions between and among animals, plants, and humans can be represented as a graph. One example of this interaction is a food web (*https://oreil.ly/XyeX4*), which depicts the natural interconnections of food chains and includes a graphical representation of what eats what in an ecological community.

Chemical molecules are yet another example of naturally occurring graph-like data, with atoms acting as nodes and bonds as edges. In general, there's a lot of naturally graphable data in biomedicine—genes and proteins regulate biological processes, and their interactions can be graphed (as in Figure 2-4).

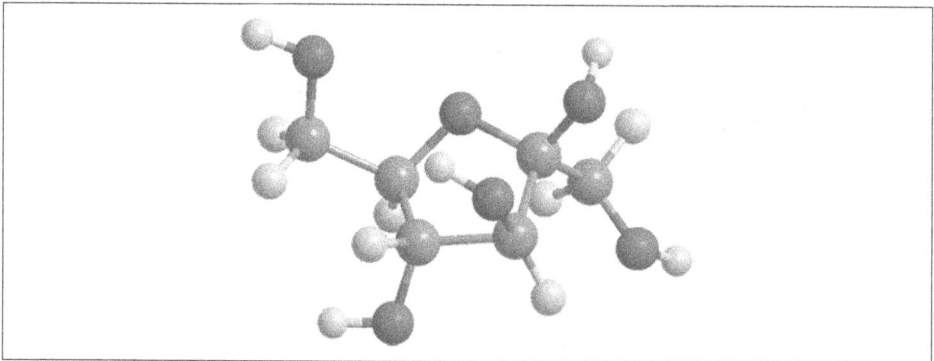

Figure 2-4. A fructose molecule (https://oreil.ly/nDO3W) exemplifies the intuitive graph-like structure wherein nodes correspond to atoms and edges represent the chemical bonds

The human nervous system can also be considered a complex graph. The connections between neurons in our brains essentially operate as a network, where receptors serve as nodes and neurons act as edges. Representing these massive systems as graph networks abstracts away many complications to make analysis easier.

---

1 In Chapter 1, we presented some examples of graphs found in nature.

Graphically represented phenomena

Graphs have huge representational power, which allows for the majority of problems to be represented and modeled in graph terms. Phenomena that reflect dynamic interactions between things can be modeled as graphs. What these phenomena have in common is that their underlying data satisfies the primary requirements of graph structure, namely nodes that are connected by edges, and the data is continuously evolving.

An example of this category is a road network: a collection of road segments and interactions (refer back to Figure 1-5). Social networks and societies are also ultimately collections of millions or billions of individuals (nodes) and their relationships (edges). Other examples are phone conversations, communications and transactions between electronic gadgets, and financial transactions.

Structured data

Structured data refers to data that has a well-defined structure that can be represented using a graph structure. Some examples include relational databases, ontology, and knowledge graphs. Despite their diverse representations (such as tables in a relational database or tuples in a Resource Description Framework[2]), most of these types of data can be conceived as a graph. In fact, one representation can be converted to another with some mapping.

Consider a relational database in which data is organized in tables, as shown in Figure 2-5. To represent relationally structured data as in a graph, you can start by identifying the *entities* (or *objects*) in the data and representing them as nodes in the graph. In Figure 2-5, the entity set is (groups, users, posts, comments). Then, you can identify the *relationships* between these entities and represent them as edges connecting the nodes (in Figure 2-5, the friendship and membership tables represent relationships between two entities). *Attributes* or labels are used to represent additional information about entities and relationships.

Think about a simple relational data structure representing a social network, where each record represents a person and includes information about their name, age, and the names of their friends. To represent this data in a graph, you could create a node for each person and connect them with an edge for each friendship relation. The graph would then consist of a set of nodes representing the people in the social network and a set of edges representing the friendships between them.

---

2 RDF (*https://oreil.ly/4re8C*) is the core data model of the Semantic Web. Data in this data model is represented as a 3-tuple (subject–predicate–object)

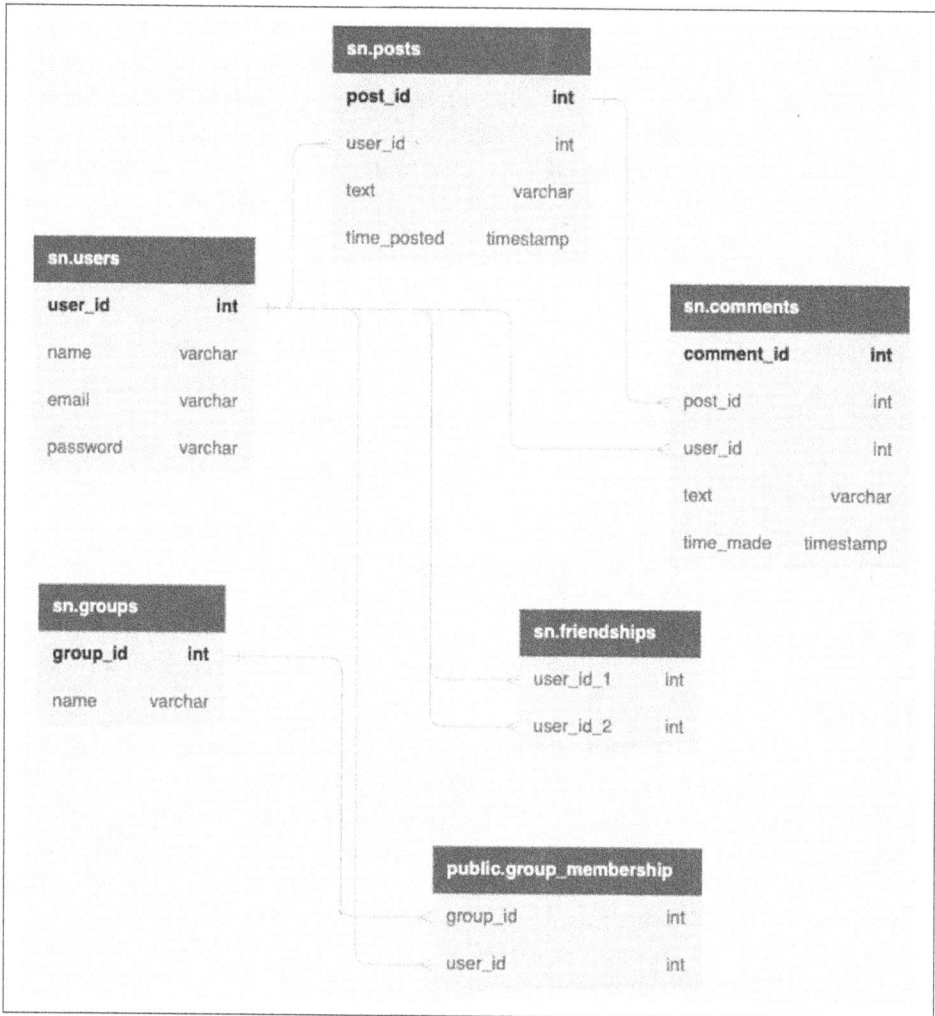

Figure 2-5. This relational data model, or entity-relationship diagram, displays the relationships of entity sets stored in the database

You can also use attributes or labels on the nodes and edges to represent additional information about the entities and relationships in the data. For example, you could label each node with the person's *name* and *age*, and label each edge with the type of relationship (e.g., *friendship, family*, etc.). Figure 2-6 shows how structured data can be smoothly mapped onto a graph representation. In the figure, tables representing entities in the relational structure become nodes and are depicted as circles; tables showing relationships between nodes are depicted with connecting lines labeled to describe the relationships.

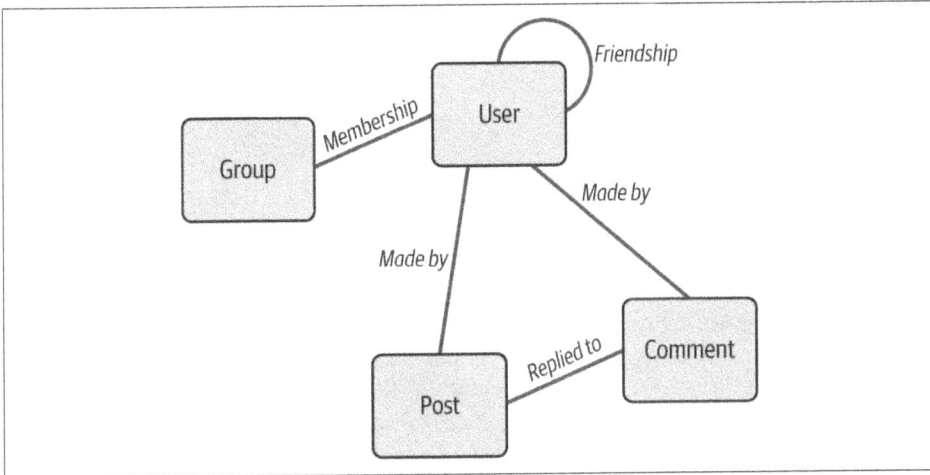

Figure 2-6. *The relationally structured data from Figure 2-5 is mapped in graph form*

Unstructured data

Unstructured data is not standardized—it does not have a well-defined structure, so it cannot be presented in a data model or a schema as it is. Textual data is an example of unstructured data. It needs to be transformed or tabulated to create a structured format. One common process to derive structure from textual data is to use natural language processing (NLP) to identify named entities.[3] Once extracted, these meaningful named entities from unstructured texts are then stored in databases or other types of structured formats. The resulting structured data can then be represented as a graph. To illustrate our approach, we created a conceptual illustration (Figure 2-7) of the main processes in converting unstructured data into graph data.

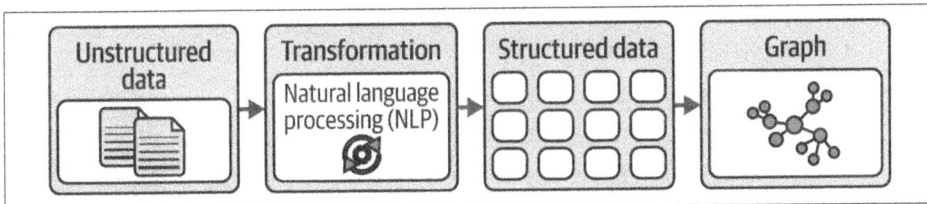

Figure 2-7. *A sample flow of converting unstructured data to graph data*

---

3 Named entities (NE) are real-world objects that are important to understanding text. They come under different predefined categories such as names, organizations, locations, quantities, etc. An example of a named entity would be Cairo (City). In NLP, the technique to identify and classify named entities is called named entity recognition (NER). NER automatically scans the entire text and extracts named entities.

Ultimately, the approach that is best suited for creating a graph representation of a company's data will depend on the specific needs and goals of the organization. It may be necessary to experiment with different approaches and tools to find the right one.

Graph Data Sourcing and Understanding

As we have seen, graph data can be produced from different data types. We can now dive into the process of using these types of data.

The first step towards building a graph data pipeline is to source and understand graph data. Both steps are essential for graph analysis. Graph data sourcing entails gathering data from a variety of sources, while the understanding step is delivered through visualization. The primary goal of graph visualization is to explore and analyze data using various tools to identify patterns, trends, and anomalies. Let's go over both steps in detail.

Graph data sourcing

Enterprise graph data sourcing refers to the process of acquiring graph data from various sources. It involves identifying relevant data sources. It is often followed by exploratory data extraction to determine whether the data is relevant before large-scale extraction. It is also linked to the succeeding steps (data preparation/data ingestion), where the data will be extracted and prepared for storage and integration into a graph database or knowledge graph. Graph data can be sourced from a variety of sources. Here are some high-level source:

Internal data sourcing
> This covers internal enterprise data sources such as proprietary databases, applications within the enterprise, and other enterprise repositories. This covers both offline storage and real-time or near-real-time data streaming.

External data sourcing
> This entails utilizing external data sources such as industry-specific data providers, public databases, open data, or any other data that is relevant to the enterprise's domain. This might also be expanded to use web scraping or data APIs (application programming interfaces) to access online data.

Enterprises address two important considerations when performing data sourcing: data governance and compliance, and data quality. From an enterprise standpoint, it is critical to ensure compliance with data governance policies, privacy regulations, and data security measures. Sourcing should be done under data quality processes to assure completeness, correctness, and relevance. To maintain high-quality sourcing, this may entail data profiling, which is the process of analyzing the graph data to understand its structure, content, and quality. This can reveal issues such as inconsistencies, duplicates, or missing values.

Once the graph data has been identified, we can begin exploring it to determine its suitability and quality. Visualization is a popular method for accomplishing this.

Understanding visual graph data

Graph visualization and exploration are optional, yet recommended and beneficial at various stages of the graph learning pipeline. In graph data understanding, visual graph exploration is used to have a more tangible and immediate understanding of the structure and the content of the graph data, without delving too much. This step usually includes visualizing the data and examining summary statistics about the structure and behavior of graph data, and identifying native connections, trends, correlations, and outliers in large graph data.

Visualization can also be used to identify clusters of data points connected by similar relationships. They are particularly useful for identifying anomalies or outlines in the data. In a social network, for example, an individual with a high number of connections could be a key influencer or a big potential risk.

There are several ways to store graph data for exploration and visualization, depending on the specific needs and constraints of your application. Graph visualization approaches, in general, are linked to the underlying data storage and the frontend used to generate the visuals/graphics. Based on those two dimensions, we divide graph visualization techniques into three groups based on how closely they adhere to the associated data storage and visualization language:

Graph database visualizers
> Graph databases are specialized databases designed primarily for storing and querying graph data. They are often optimized for fast traversal of the graph and support powerful querying capabilities, making them well-suited for exploring and visualizing large graphs. Neo4j (*https://neo4j.com*) and Amazon Neptune (*https://oreil.ly/9NlbY*) are two graph database examples. They are usually coupled with visualizers, such as Neo4j Bloom, to assist users in understanding various events and patterns in the graph data.

Graph visualization software
> There are many tools for visualizing graph data in this category. These tools are often delivered as prepackaged software that does not require any programming knowledge. Gephi (*https://gephi.org*) and Graphviz (*https://graphviz.org*) are examples of these tools. These tools often allow you to import graph data in various formats (e.g., CSV or JSON) and offer a variety of visualization options and interactive capabilities for exploring and analyzing the data.

Custom storage and visualization solutions

Depending on your specific requirements, you may also opt to develop a custom solution for storing and visualizing graph data. This could involve using a general-purpose database (such as MySQL or MongoDB) to store the data and using a programming language (such as Python or JavaScript) to build a custom visualization tool or integrate with an existing visualization library such as D3.js.

Each visualization category has its pros and cons. Thus, the best approach for storing and visualizing graph data will depend on the volume and complexity of your data, the application's defined needs, and the available resources and expertise.

Graph Data Preparation

Graph data processing typically involves some substeps that are designed to prepare the data for graph learning training. While the specific steps involved may vary depending on the characteristics of the graph data, and the goal of the graph learning, some common steps include graph data ingestion, graph data storage, and graph data preprocessing.

The primary goal of graph data preprocessing is to ensure that the data is accurate, complete, consistent, and consumable for the graph problem at hand. Let's review each of these common graph data preparation steps in the following sections.

Graph data ingestion

Graph data ingestion concerns deciding on data sources, extracting them, and standardizing them into a common format that the system can process. This requires careful consideration of the available datasets—including their formats, sizes, and structures. It also involves setting up a pipeline to pull data from internal or external sources, such as databases, files, website scraping, and API calls.

Graph data storage

Once you collect all the relevant data, you need to store it. The next activity, data storage, concerns where to store this extracted data. Depending on your system's requirements, this might involve a persistent storage solution or a system that is optimized for graph data, such as a graph database like Neo4j (*https://neo4j.com*) or a distributed graph processing system like Apache Giraph (*https://oreil.ly/nUcJR*).

Common graph data storage solutions in enterprise settings also include Amazon Neptune (*https://oreil.ly/9NlbY*), Dgraph (*https://dgraph.io*), and Microsoft Azure Cosmos DB (*https://oreil.ly/Oe5h6*).

Graph data preprocessing

Once we gain access to the graph data, the next step involves preprocessing, which is essential for refining the quality of the dataset. This process entails cleaning noisy data and normalizing data values to ensure consistency and accuracy in the analysis. The outcome of this preprocessing step is twofold:

A clean graph dataset
> This refers to a dataset where inaccuracies, irrelevant information, and anomalies have been removed or corrected. A clean graph dataset is crucial for GML as it ensures that the relationships and entities within the graph accurately represent real-world connections and attributes, without distortion by noise or errors. Cleaning a graph dataset might involve removing duplicate edges, ensuring that node labels are correctly applied, and discarding any data points that do not have relevance to the problem at hand.

A list of features
> Defining features is a critical process in preparing for GML model development. Features in a graph context refer to the attributes or properties associated with nodes and edges that the model will use to learn patterns. For example, in a social network graph, node features might include user demographics, activity metrics, or content preferences, while edge features could encompass the strength or frequency of interactions between users. The process of feature selection is guided by the specific objectives of the GML model, such as classification, recommendation, or clustering tasks. Properly defined features are instrumental in enabling the model to make accurate predictions or classifications based on the structure and properties of the graph.

As previously stated, large volume and varied sources variation are common aspects of graph data. The same is true in enterprise data: enterprise graph data typically combines on-premises data and third-party data. So, first, let's look at why integrating third-party data is important in such settings, and then at how this integration takes place.

Why enrich graph data with external data?

Integrating third-party data with enterprise graph data can provide a number of benefits for GML including improved accuracy and effectiveness, enhanced feature engineering, improved ability to handle missing or incomplete data, and increased scalability. Here we list the details of the contribution:

Enhanced precision and effectiveness of machine learning models
By integrating external data with enterprise data, machine learning models' accuracy and effectiveness can be improved. This is because the external data can provide additional context and information that can assist the model in gaining a deeper comprehension of the underlying patterns in the dataset and consequently provide accurate predictions.

Enhanced feature engineering
Integrating external data with enterprise data offers enhanced feature engineering capabilities, which allow for more comprehensive and informative features for your machine learning models. This can help the model more accurately capture the relationships and patterns in the data, leading to improved performance.

Improved ability to handle missing or incomplete data
Incorporating external data with enterprise data can help fill in gaps or missing data in the enterprise data, allowing the model to make more accurate predictions even when some data is missing.

Increased scalability
By integrating external data with enterprise data, you can create larger and more comprehensive datasets that can be used to train GML models. This can help increase the scalability of your models and enable them to handle larger and more complex datasets.

Now that we've explored the potential benefits of enriching enterprise graph data with other external data sources, let's see how this integration is facilitated at the data preparation layer. To begin, let's discuss the process of data harmonization.

Graph data harmonization

Data harmonization, also known as data cleansing or data normalization, is the process of integrating data from various sources into a common format and ensuring that data is consistent, clean, and of good quality before designing the graph schema and ingesting it into a graph database. This process often involves standardizing data formats, resolving data conflicts, and eliminating duplicates to facilitate seamless analysis and processing.

By graph schema, we mean the structure that defines the types of nodes and edges that can exist in a graph, and the properties or attributes associated with each node or edge type. Let's use our fraud detection example in Figure 1-7. To recap, our transaction network consists of accounts (*nodes*) and the relationships between these accounts are represented by transactions (*edges*). The accounts can be either *cardholder* or *merchant*. The *cardholder* node could have a *name, account number,* or *location*. The other type of account node, the *merchant*, may have a *name, location,* or the *types of goods or services offered*. The relationship between a cardholder and a merchant is a *purchase* relation, so the edge is labeled a *purchase*. This purchase edge has attributes such as the amount, the date and time, and the type of goods or services purchased.

Given this definition of the schema, the question now is how to design it. The first step towards designing a graph schema is to identify the most important entities and relationships in the graph data. This allows you to focus on the most important aspects of the data and avoid adding unnecessary complexity to the graph. The second step is to use clear and consistent naming conventions for nodes and edges, as well as to define consistent sets of attributes for each node or edge, which can help ensure that your graph schema is both readable and understandable by all users while remaining efficient in terms of scalability.

As the size of the graph grows—reflecting an increase in the complexity and volume of relationships and entities represented—it becomes imperative to address the challenges associated with the performance and scalability of the schema. This growth might result from accumulating more data over time, expanding the graph's scope to encompass new types of entities and relationships, or incorporating additional data sources. A larger graph can significantly impact query performance, leading to longer execution times due to the increased complexity of traversing more nodes and edges. Additionally, memory usage escalates as the graph expands, requiring more resources to store the additional nodes, edges, and their attributes, which can strain system performance.

To mitigate these potential performance bottlenecks and scalability challenges, several strategies can be utilized:

Refining the schema
> Simplify the graph structure by reducing the number of node and edge types where possible and eliminating unnecessary attributes. This streamlining can decrease the graph's complexity, leading to improved performance.

Graph partitioning
> Implementing graph partitioning to divide the graph into smaller, more manageable subgraphs allows for the distribution of the graph across multiple servers. This strategy helps in handling the graph's growth by distributing the load and facilitating horizontal scaling.

Indexing and caching
> Indexing frequently accessed nodes and edges can significantly enhance query execution times by making data retrieval processes more efficient. Similarly, caching frequently requested data reduces the need for repeated queries, improving response times.

Before deploying the graph schema in a production environment, it's crucial to test and validate it to ensure it meets the application's needs. This typically involves loading sample data into the graph and then executing various queries to verify that the schema delivers the expected performance and accuracy. For example, if the graph represents an ecommerce network with nodes for users and products, and edges for purchases, you might use a query[4] like:

```
MATCH (user:User)-[:PURCHASED]->(product:Product)
WHERE user.name = 'Ali'
RETURN product.name
```

This query helps check if the schema correctly identifies all products purchased by a user named Ali, effectively testing the schema's ability to handle real-world data retrieval scenarios.

Now back to data harmonization and its importance for better data use. Some of the key reasons data harmonization is necessary are:

Data quality
> Ensuring that data is consistent, aligned with any relevant standards and guidelines, and clean before ingestion can improve the quality of the data and reduce the risk of errors or inconsistencies in the graph.

Data integration
> Harmonizing data from multiple sources can help to ensure that the data is integrated in a consistent and standardized way, enabling the use of advanced graph learning techniques.

Performance and scalability
> Harmonizing data before ingestion can improve the performance and scalability of the graph database by reducing the complexity of the data and enabling the use of efficient data storage and processing techniques.

Figure 2-8 illustrates the common processes that are involved in data harmonization: data transformation, data cleaning and preprocessing, data storage, and data security. The data transformation step entails transforming the data to make it more suitable for analysis or integration with other datasets. This might include tasks such as joining data from multiple sources, aggregating data, or performing feature engineering. Data storage involves storing the harmonized data from the data cleaning process in a way that is accessible and efficient for further analysis or integration with other systems. This might involve saving the data as a file. Alternatively, the data could be stored in a database or data warehouse.

---

4 The example query provided is written in Cypher (*https://oreil.ly/JVLkV*), which is a query language specifically designed for working with graph databases, particularly Neo4j (*https://neo4j.com*).

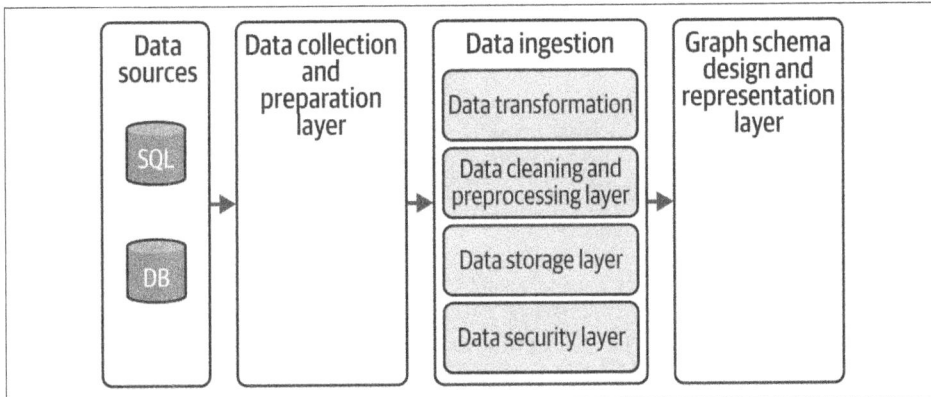

Figure 2-8. An overview of the data harmonization and representation process in graph learning

The Graph Training and Inference Pipelines

The enterprise graph training and inference pipeline is a framework for building and deploying machine learning models on graph data in enterprise settings. It is designed to handle large-scale complex graphs and provides a flexible and scalable platform for training and deploying graph-based models.

GML Training Pipeline Overview

Once the graph data is consumable, you'll move into the GML training pipeline of the process, illustrated in Figure 2-9, which is where you begin building the GML model to solve a particular graph learning task(s). This stage covers feature engineering and model-building activity.

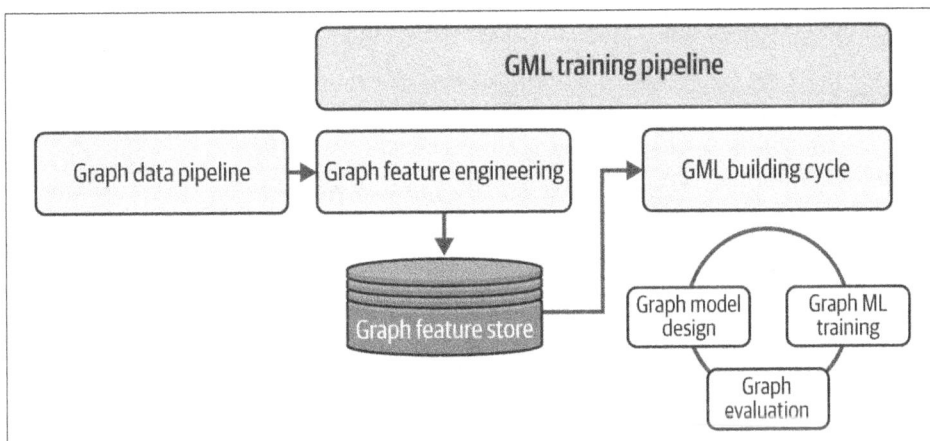

Figure 2-9. Simplified layout of GML training pipeline components

Graph feature engineering

Not all data features or characteristics are equally important for GML models. In this case, feature engineering is used to create and transform features of nodes or edges in a graph for use in machine learning models. The result of this step is a list of features, usually stored in a feature store, where the most contributing features are registered to the graph learning algorithms.

Graph model building cycle

After selecting the features, GML model building begins. The model-building cycle is an iterative process with three main components: model design, model training, and model evaluation. Let's see their internal steps:

1. *GML model design*

    In this step, you'll decide on a training algorithm, a model architecture, optimizers, a loss function, parameters, hyperparameters, and evaluation metrics. In the following chapters, we will demonstrate how to design a GML to address a particular task.

2. *GML model training*

    In this step, you'll need to identify a candidate graph learning algorithm that could be used for solving the specific task(s) in mind. You will need to choose a machine learning library or framework (such as TensorFlow (*https://tensor flow.org*) or PyTorch (*https://pytorch.org*)), set up a training pipeline, and begin training your model.

3. *GML model evaluation*

    Next, you'll evaluate the trained GML model for performance and accuracy. This step serves as a checkpoint to assess whether the model meets the business's usefulness threshold. If the model does not pass this threshold, several steps can be followed to enhance its performance, for example:

    Acquire more data

    Expanding the graph data can significantly improve model performance. Adding more nodes and edges can enrich the graph's structure, providing a more comprehensive dataset for the model to learn from.

    Include more node and edge attributes

    Incorporating additional attributes for nodes and edges can offer the model a deeper understanding of the relationships and entities within the graph. These attributes can serve as critical features that influence the model's ability to make accurate predictions or classifications.

Feature engineering

> Improving or adding new features can often lead to better model performance. For graph data, this could involve extracting more complex graph metrics (like centrality measures—refer to Chapter 3 for hands-on example) that might reveal new insights about the connections within the data.

Choose a different graph learning algorithm

> If performance issues persist, considering an alternative graph learning algorithm may be beneficial. Different algorithms have varying strengths and are suited to specific types of graph data and tasks. Experimenting with another algorithm could lead to better alignment with the problem at hand and improve overall model performance.

Once trained and the best-performing models are identified, the model artifacts are transferred for use in what are known as "production settings." This process, known as inference, involves deploying trained models to make predictions on freshly provided data. This occurs as part of the GML inference pipeline.

GML Inference Pipeline Overview

Once the "best" performing model is selected, it moves to a different computing environment (such as different Kubernetes (*https://kubernetes.io*) clusters) to go through the inference pipeline steps, illustrated in Figure 2-10. The model inference process consists of two major steps: GML model registration and GML model serving.

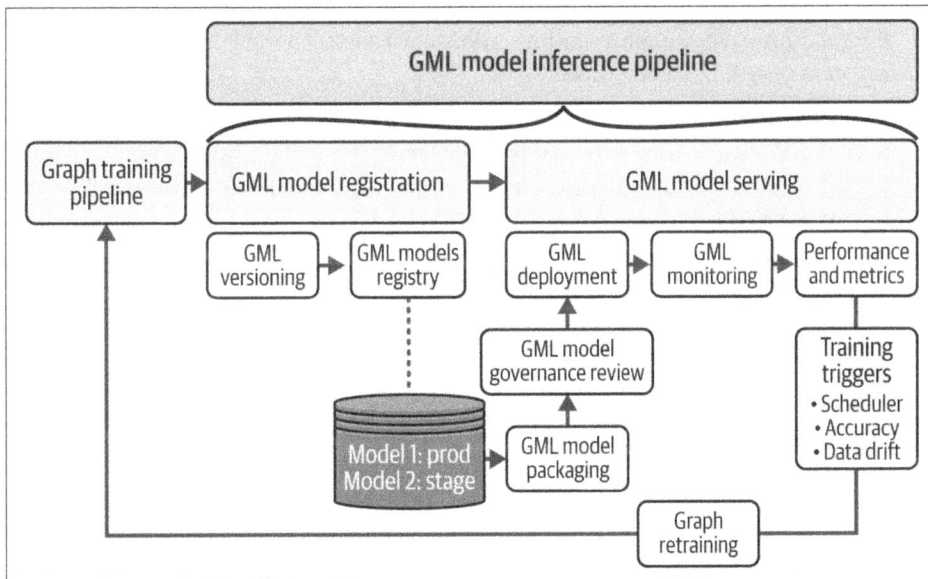

Figure 2-10. Simplified view of GML inference pipeline components

GML model registration

Once you're satisfied with your model's performance, you can begin the model promotion and registration step. This is where the model gets deployed to the production environment, which in most enterprises is different from the development environment where model building occurs. We start with *model versioning*, where you'll tag all of your models with labels about their status, such as `pass`, `fail`, `retrain`, `discard`, or `promoted to production`. You'll store your versioned models in a *model registry*, a repository you'll use to track their life cycles. Models with `pass` or `promotion to production` are then routed from the registry to a packaging step, where they will be subjected to a governance review. The audit will be conducted in accordance with the enterprise's deployment policy to ensure that the GML models, for example, are not biased.

GML model serving

Next, you'll submit models that passed the governance review to the deployment environment, where they'll go live in accordance with the deployment strategy[5] you have chosen. This step can also involve setting up a serving infrastructure, such as TensorFlow Serving (*https://oreil.ly/AOQUh*) or Seldon (*https://seldon.io*); integrating the model into an application or workflow. For example, in the case of building a graph recommender system for ecommerce:

- You develop a RESTful API around your model serving infrastructure. This API acts as the interface through which the ecommerce platform can query the recommender system, sending user data and receiving personalized product recommendations in response.

- The development team then integrates this API into the ecommerce platform's backend. When a user browses the platform, the system automatically fetches personalized recommendations by querying the graph recommender system through the API.

- The recommender system is also integrated into the ecommerce platform's email marketing tools. This allows for personalized product recommendations to be included in marketing emails, enhancing user engagement and sales.

---

5 ML deployment strategy specifies how models or their updated versions will be deployed. There are various strategies, such as shadow, canary, A/B testing, and so on. You'll learn more about these strategies in Chapters 10 and 11.

Monitoring and feedback loop

Once the models are deployed in the production environment, close monitoring of their performance throughout their life cycles is essential for ensuring smooth operation. This process, known as *model monitoring*, involves several key activities:

Tracking model inference performance
Compare the model's predictions to actual outcomes. In an ecommerce application, for example, analyze what the customer ultimately purchased and whether it was among the recommended products.

Identifying serving skew
Detects any signs of serving skew, which occurs when changes in the data negatively impact the deployed model's accuracy.

Initiating model retraining
Depending on performance metrics, model retraining may be necessary. Training triggers for launching the training pipeline to retrain and evaluate models include:

Scheduler based
Retrains models periodically.

Accuracy based
Monitors accuracy and initiates model training when it falls below a certain threshold.

Data drift based
Starts training based on significant changes in the data.

All retrained models, regardless of the scenario, will undergo the same GML model serving pipeline before being updated in the production environment.

Moreover, the feedback loop is a critical component of maintaining and enhancing the performance of graph learning applications. It involves collecting data on the application's performance in real-world scenarios and using this information to inform future model training and deployment strategies. This cycle of feedback ensures that the model remains effective over time, adapting to new data and evolving patterns in user behavior.

Once you've completed all of these steps, your GML system will be ready for use in real-world applications.

It's important to note that the pipeline contains an active data update. Because graphs are constantly evolving as data is updated (including adding or removing nodes or edges), your data pipeline will need to be updated, too. This means that data pipeline and feature engineering steps are carried out continuously to obtain the most up-to-date and recent data. As a result, you'll need to set up processes for updating the data periodically and trigger the rest of the graph learning pipeline, as usual, to get newly trained models on new data and roll it out for production.

Summary

In this chapter, we've looked at the primary phases of the GML pipeline and emphasized their significance in establishing the foundation for a highly scalable system. Given that graph data can incorporate various data types and sources, it becomes imperative to establish a robust data pipeline that effectively handles and prepares the data for the subsequent stages.

Moving forward, Chapter 3 will explore graph feature engineering by looking into traditional machine learning approaches for graph learning.

Traditional Machine Learning for Graphs

In this chapter, we will explore both traditional and nontraditional machine learning approaches applied to graphs. Then, we will dive into traditional graph-based machine learning, building upon the foundational concepts introduced in Chapter 2. We'll start by exploring the nuances of graph data representation, transitioning from general methods to a focused case study on the Amazon copurchasing network. As we navigate through, we'll uncover the diverse tasks that can be tackled using this dataset.

The heart of our exploration lies in graph feature engineering—a pivotal step that can make or break the performance of machine learning models. Here, we'll unravel the importance of this process, the challenges encountered, and the different types of features that can be derived from graphs. Our hands-on approach will guide you through feature extraction, culminating in the integration of graph-derived metrics to enrich product attributes such as price and product category, among others. For example, we'll demonstrate how these metrics can enhance product attributes like customer preferences, providing insights for decision making and product improvement.

Moving forward, we'll harness these graph features to empower traditional machine learning models. You'll gain insights into various tasks such as node classification, link prediction, and graph clustering. Through practical examples, we'll demonstrate the process of building and validating prediction models, specifically focusing on predicting high-rated products.

As we approach the chapter's finale, you'll be introduced to the concept of feature learning with node embeddings. By leveraging algorithms like random walks, you'll be guided to generate embeddings for the Amazon copurchasing dataset and discern their potential applications.

By the end of this chapter, you'll have a comprehensive understanding of how graph features can be effectively used in traditional machine learning tasks, and how they can provide an edge in solving complex problems. Let's embark on this exciting journey!

Approaches to Graph Machine Learning

Drawing on the emergence of deep learning as a reference point, we can categorize graph machine learning (GML) approaches into two distinct periods: pre-deep learning, characterized by traditional methods, and post-deep learning, encompassing nontraditional techniques.

Traditional Graph-Based Machine Learning

This category of algorithms, known as traditional graph-based machine learning, predates the widespread adoption of deep learning methods. It refers to the use of established algorithms and techniques for conducting machine learning tasks on graph-structured data. These methods typically involve the manual crafting of features based on graph properties such as node degree or centrality measures.

Traditional graph-based algorithms often employ techniques like PageRank, random walk-based approaches, or graph clustering algorithms for tasks such as node classification or link prediction. Due to their reliance on handcrafted features, they may encounter scalability issues and necessitate manual intervention for feature updates. However, one advantage of these algorithms is their interpretability. Because they rely on predefined features and rules, their inner workings are often more understandable compared to more complex methods like deep learning.

Nontraditional Graph-Based Machine Learning

This category of graph algorithms refers to newer approaches that leverage deep learning, including techniques like GNNs, GCNs, GATs, and graph embeddings. These methods operate directly on graph structures, allowing them to automatically learn representations from raw data.

These techniques have gained popularity due to their ability to handle large-scale graphs and achieve state-of-the-art performance across various tasks. However, one potential drawback is that they may sacrifice some level of interpretability compared to traditional methods.

In this chapter, we will revisit traditional approaches to comprehend how graph tasks used to be engineered. The nontraditional approaches will be revisited throughout future chapters—starting from Chapter 4. But first, let's explore the differences between these two approaches through Table 3-1, which summarizes the distinctions between them in terms of the number of dimensions.

Table 3-1. A comparison of traditional and nontraditional graph ML approaches across three dimensions: representation learning, interoperability, and scalability

Graph aspect	Traditional graph-based ML	Nontraditional graph-based ML
Representation learning	Relies on handcrafted features.	Learns representations directly from the graph data.
Interpretability	Offer interpretability in both features and algorithms enables a clear understanding of how predictions are made.	May sacrifice interpretability for improved performance.
Scalability	May struggle to scale to large graphs, as they require manual interventions to handcraft the features.	Those based on deep learning and implemented on computational frameworks like GPUs or TPUs can take advantage of parallel computing architectures.

Representing Graphs for Traditional ML

Let's start this journey on how to represent graphs for traditional machine learning! When it comes to working with graphs, it's all about understanding how to represent them in a way that traditional ML algorithms can digest. In this section, we're going to take a deep dive into graph representation. But, we will go beyond theory—we're going to get hands-on with a popular dataset from Amazon (the Amazon copurchasing network (*https://oreil.ly/spRIh*)). We'll explore how to extract graph representations from this dataset, and by the end of this, you'll have a solid grasp of how to represent graphs and make them ready for our next hands-on examples.

Graph Representation

In Chapter 1, we dug into the concept of *graph data representation*, which is the process of encoding or mapping data as a graph structure, with nodes representing entities and edges representing relationships between those entities. This representation is particularly useful when dealing with data that's all tangled up in complex relationships, such as molecules, social networks, or even road networks.

Now, here's the cool part. When you've organized your data in this graph representation, you can use graph algorithms to analyze, uncover hidden insights, and eventually make predictions on top of it. It's all about making sure we capture the data correctly before use in graph ML (GML).

When it comes to graph representation, there are a number of commonly used data structures for representing graph data, each with its advantages and disadvantages. Let's review two of the most common representations: the *adjacency list* and *adjacency matrix*.

The adjacency list and adjacency matrix are two common data structures utilized to represent graphs. To illustrate these two techniques, we will utilize Figure 3-1, which shows an example graph with a walk-through on deriving these representations.

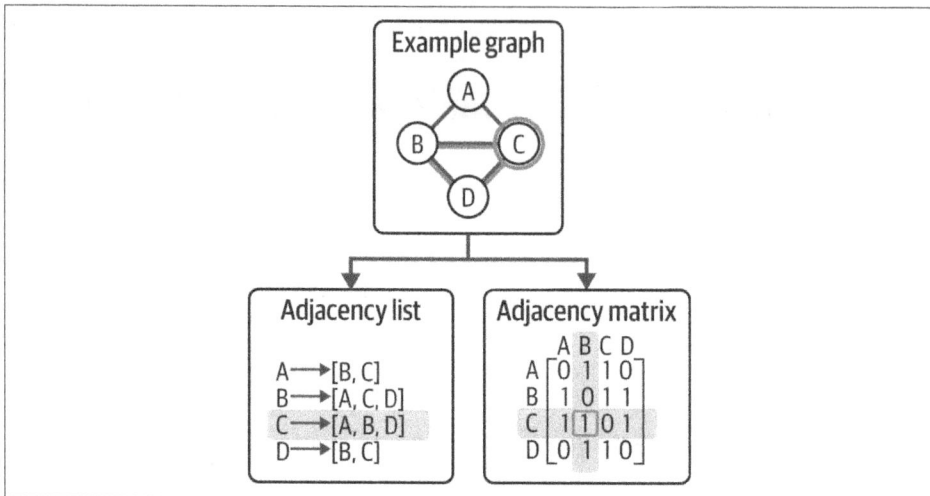

Figure 3-1. An example graph of four nodes and five edges and the calculation of two graph representation techniques (adjacency list and adjacency matrix)

The two common data structures used for representing graphs are as follows:

Adjacency list

A collection of lists that serves as a graph representation method. Each list is associated with a node in the graph and contains references or identifiers of adjacent nodes that are directly connected by edges. Adjacency lists are useful for representing sparse graphs, where the number of edges is much smaller than the number of nodes. They are also useful for representing large graphs that don't fit in memory. In such cases, the adjacency list can be stored on disk and accessed as needed.

Adjacency matrix

A way to represent a graph as a 2D matrix. The matrix has dimensions $n \times n$, where n is the number of nodes in the graph. Each entry (i, j) in the matrix represents an edge between the ith and jth nodes. If there is an edge between the ith and jth nodes, the entry (i, j) is set to 1. If there is no edge between the ith and jth nodes, the entry (i, j) is set to 0. Adjacency matrices are often used to represent graphs because it's simple to perform fast matrix operations on them. However, they can be inefficient when the graph is sparse, because a large number of entries in the matrix will be 0.

Representing Amazon Copurchasing Networks as Graphs

To effectively harness the power of graph representations, it's crucial to begin by pinpointing the essential nodes, edges, and attributes inherent in our dataset. By methodically structuring this information, we pave the way for deeper insights and a richer understanding of the data. In this section, we'll explore this graph-building process using the Amazon copurchasing dataset as our canvas. We chose this dataset because of its richness and ease of interpretation in terms of graph features. This quality facilitates the extraction of valuable insights from the graph structure, making it particularly relevant to a common use case: predicting customer behavior and shopping preferences.

The Amazon copurchasing network dataset (*https://oreil.ly/spRIh*)[1] encapsulates relationships between products based on the purchasing patterns of customers. Each product in this dataset can be represented as a node, and the copurchasing behavior between two products can be represented as an edge between their corresponding nodes. This naturally lends itself to a graph representation, where products are nodes and copurchasing relationships are edges.

It's a popular dataset that captures complex relationships as products don't exist in isolation. Their purchasing patterns reveal intricate relationships that are best represented in a graph. One important thing to mention about this dataset is that it represents a directed graph as per the data instructions. Based on the "Customers Who Bought This Item Also Bought" feature of the Amazon website, the presented dictionary operates under the assumption that "if product A is frequently copurchased with product B," the graph includes a directed edge from A to B. However, it's worth noting that this interpretation might diverge from the typical understanding of copurchasing, which is often considered a symmetric relationship. In other words, the statement "A is purchased together with B" is usually equivalent to "B is purchased together with A." In this context, we can consider the relation as unidirectional (no arrows) or bidirectional (two-way arrows).

However, despite the typical understanding of bidirectionality in such relationships, we will adhere to the instructions provided by the released data and consider it as a directional relationship (one way). In a directed graph, edges are represented with arrows indicating the flow and direction of interactions between nodes. This concept can be likened to a map with one-way streets, where the direction of travel is explicitly indicated.

Let's examine the components of this dataset. We've extracted and presented selected information in Table 3-2. We can see that the dataset primarily revolves around products, each associated with various categories, with Books representing the largest proportion within this category.

---

1 This dataset was accessed October 19, 2023. Please note that information may have changed since.

Table 3-2. Overview of the Amazon copurchasing dataset

Dataset statistics	Count
Products	548,552
Reviews	7,781,990
Products by product group	-
Books	393,561
DVDs	19,828
Music CDs	103,144
Videos	26,132

Let's break the dataset down into graph components such as nodes, edges, and attributes. A general guideline is that, typically, nouns[2] (or entities/actors) are represented as nodes, while verbs /actions are depicted as edges. Both entities and actions can have additional details known as attributes. So, with this basic insight, we can cluster our data's columns according to their function:

Amazon copurchasing nodes and their attributes
> The dataset primarily revolves around products, which are essentially entities or nouns. Therefore, we can consider them as potential key nodes within the dataset. In this context, each product is represented as a node. When we examine the metadata associated with each product, we observe that it typically includes details such as the product's title, ASIN (Amazon Standard Identification Number), sales rank, category, average rating, reviews, and more. These various descriptions provide valuable attributes for our identified nodes, enhancing our understanding and analysis of the dataset.

Amazon copurchasing edges and their attributes
> Having identified the key nodes as products, the next step is to uncover the relationships between pairs of these products. Upon close examination of the dataset, we find that there is primarily one type of relationship between two products: copurchasing. In cases where product A and product B are commonly purchased together, we establish a connection between these two nodes. This connection, represented as an edge, indicates the presence of a copurchasing relationship between the two products. Edges also come with their own associated attributes, which can include metadata such as the frequency of copurchases or a weight that signifies the strength of the relationship between two products.

---

2 Noun is a word (excluding pronouns) employed to identify a class of people, locations, or things. Here, a noun can be a common noun that refers to general things (e.g., "a city" or "a country") or a proper noun that refers to specific named things (e.g., "Dublin: name for a city" and "Libya: name for a country")

Now that we've identified the various components of the graph's representation, let's see how they integrate. Figure 3-2 illustrates a graphical representation generated from the Amazon copurchasing dataset. The arrow pointing from the book *Patterns of Preaching: A Sermon Sampler* to *Candlemas: Feast of Flames* signifies that purchasing the former implies purchasing the latter, but not vice versa.

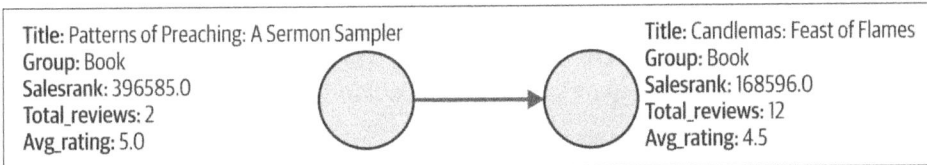

Figure 3-2. *Graphical illustration of two nodes and their connection from the Amazon copurchasing dataset*

Navigating Graph Tasks in the Amazon Copurchasing Dataset

Graphs offer us a powerful tool to visualize and analyze data, uncovering valuable insights and hidden patterns. Now that we've grasped the process of obtaining a graph representation from the dataset, let's dive into the dataset's dynamics and consider the range of tasks we can perform on top of it:

Recommendation systems
> Graphs are powerful tools for recommendation systems. If a customer purchases a product, one can traverse the graph to find closely copurchased products and recommend them. This is similar to Amazon's "Customers Who Bought This Item Also Bought" feature.

Community detection
> One can identify clusters or communities of products that are frequently bought together. This can reveal insights into customer segments or product bundles.

Centrality analysis
> By identifying products that are most central in the copurchasing network, businesses can pinpoint key products in their inventory that influence purchasing decisions.

Let's dig into the exciting hands-on section, where we'll construct a graph. We will use Python 3.8. You will also need to install the NetworkX (3.2) (*https://net workx.org*), Matplotlib (*https://matplotlib.org*), and pandas (2.1.1) libraries (*https:// oreil.ly/yXqGw*).

Upon downloading the dataset, you will find a single file *amazon-meta.txt*, which contains the data in a semi-structured format. To use the data, we will need to parse it. Our parsing script will create three files. The first file, *products.csv*, represents nodes (products) and contains product information such as ASIN, title, similar (which indicates similar items), total reviews, etc. The second file, *reviews.csv*, represents the reviews and contains the review date, customer, rating, votes, etc. The third file, *amzn_directed_graph.csv*, represents the edges. You will work with all of these files, except the *reviews.csv* file. Let's start with our coding steps:

Loading data

First, we will load two CSV files—one containing the edges (or relationships) between products (*amzn_directed_graph.csv*) and the other containing metadata about the products (*products.csv*)—into DataFrames edges_df and products_df, respectively.

Data cleaning

We will perform some data cleaning by dropping any rows in products_df that contain missing values using the dropna() method. This ensures that the graph doesn't have nodes with incomplete information.

Graph initialization

Now, let's initiate a directed graph object (G) using NetworkX by calling nx.DiGraph(). A directed graph means that the relationships (edges) have a direction, i.e., they go from one product (source) to another product (target):

```
import networkx as nx
import pandas as pd

# Load CSV files
edges_df = pd.read_csv('amzn_directed_graph.csv')
products_df = pd.read_csv('products.csv')

# Dropping NAs in the data
products_df = products_df.dropna()

# Create a directed graph
G = nx.DiGraph()
```

Adding nodes

Our graph object (G) is ready, and next we need to attach nodes to it. The code then iterates over each row in the products_df DataFrame and adds a node to the graph for every product. Each node is assigned several attributes like its ASIN, title, group, salesrank, and more.

Adding edges

After adding nodes, the code adds edges based on the edges_df DataFrame. For each row in this DataFrame, an edge is added from FromNodeID to ToNodeID, indicating a copurchasing relationship between two nodes (aka products):

```
# Add nodes from the products DataFrame
for idx, row in products_df.iterrows():
    G.add_node(row['Id'],
               ASIN=row['ASIN'],
               title=row['title'],
               group=row['group'],
               salesrank=row['salesrank'],
               similar=row['similar'],
               categories=row['categories'],
               total_reviews=row['total_reviews'],
               avg_rating=row['avg_rating'])

# Add edges from the edges DataFrame
for idx, row in edges_df.iterrows():
    G.add_edge(row['FromNodeId'], row['ToNodeId'])
```

Once the graph is constructed, you can visualize it to gain insights and comprehend the relationships among products. The provided code utilizes the NetworkX and Matplotlib libraries to visualize a subset of the generated graph:

```
import matplotlib.pyplot as plt

# Figure size
fig = plt.figure(figsize=(14, 8))

# Draw a subset of the graph
H = G.subgraph(list(G.nodes)[:5])

pos = nx.spring_layout(H, iterations=50)

node_colors = plt.cm.Pastel1(range(len(H)))

# Draw nodes and edges
nx.draw_networkx_nodes(H, pos, node_size=500, node_color=node_colors,
                       edgecolors='black', linewidths=0.5)
nx.draw_networkx_edges(H, pos, edge_color='gray', alpha=0.6, width=1.5)

# Offset labels
label_pos = {node: (x, y+0.) for node, (x, y) in pos.items()}

# Draw labels
labels = {node: split_label(H.nodes[node]['title']) for node in H.nodes()}
nx.draw_networkx_labels(H, label_pos, labels, font_size=10, font_family='Arial',
                        font_weight='bold')

plt.axis('off')
plt.show()
```

The visualization result is shown in Figure 3-3.

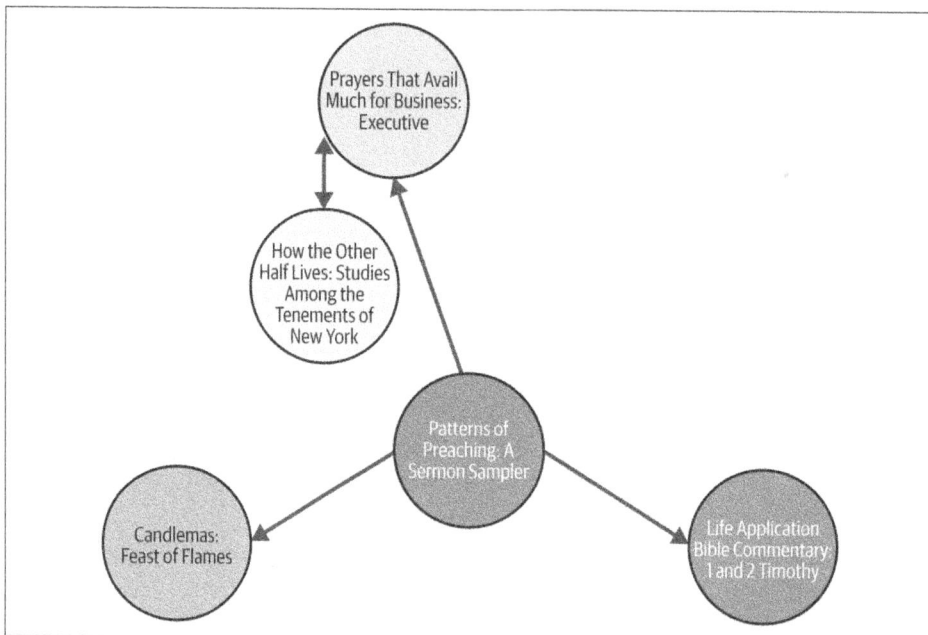

Figure 3-3. Graph visualization example on a subset of Amazon copurchasing dataset Using NetworkX and Matplotlib

In the visualization in Figure 3-3, we can see some relationships between books based on Amazon's copurchasing patterns. Each node represents a book, and the connecting lines, or edges, indicate that customers often buy those books together. An example from this graph is the bidirectional connection between *Prayers That Avail Much For Business: Executive* and *How the Other Half Lives: Studies Among the Tenements of New York*. This suggests that many Amazon customers purchased these two books together.

> You can access the fully functional example (notebook 3) on our GitHub repository (*https://github.com/gl4ebook/py-graf*).

Graph Feature Engineering

So far, we've got our graph data ready, and we've even represented it as an adjacency matrix. Now, we can dive into the feature phase. We take this graph representation and encode/transform it into features that our machine learning model can digest. Figure 3-4 shows the flow that lays out this whole process and how everything talks to each other.

For graph learning, there are two approaches to feature creation. There's the traditional way, which we call *graph feature engineering*. With this approach, you will manually decide how to extract the features. For instance, you can predefine an approach to extract all node features. Alternatively, there's a more advanced approach called *graph representation learning*. In graph representation learning, features are learned during the model training, not extracted separately. The model automatically learns meaningful features, typically node or graph embeddings. These embeddings are obtained from the last layer of the neural network and used for downstream tasks. Graph representation learning is like teaching your model to understand the essence of the graph data and figure out the features itself.

In this chapter, we're going to walk you through traditional graph feature engineering. But, as we move forward in the upcoming chapters, we'll dive deeper into graph representation learning and explore how neural networks come into the mix. So, get ready!

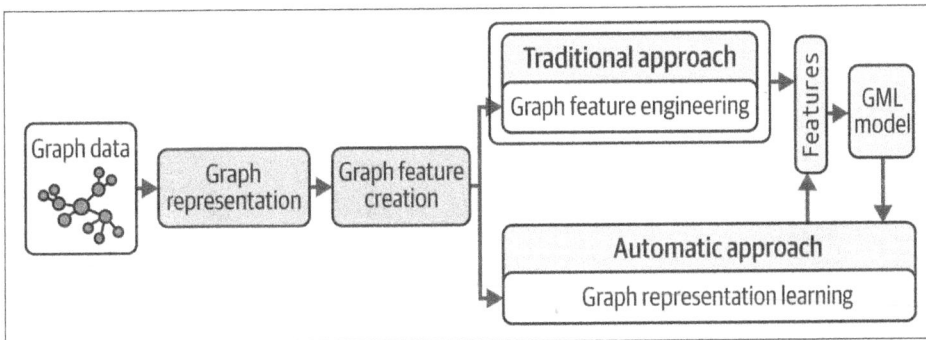

Figure 3-4. A schematic of the graph learning process

Importance and Challenges

The importance of understanding the features at your disposal cannot be overstated. Graph feature engineering resembles the process of transforming raw data into a format that is digestible by your machine learning model. It is crucial, because well-crafted graph features enable your model to capture complex relationships within a graph—leading to more accurate predictions.

Nevertheless, we equally need to acknowledge the formidable challenges associated with this process, such as determining feature generation and ensuring relevance. Noise and outliers further complicate this process and require careful handling. Graphs can exhibit considerable complexity, making it challenging to determine which features to generate, as well as to how to create them effectively and ensure that they encapsulate the relevant information. Furthermore, working with massive graphs poses a computational challenge, requiring substantial resources such as large memory and GPU/TPU power, and efficient algorithms to engineer features effectively, thereby adding another layer of complexity to the step.

Types of Graph Features

Now that we've understood why these features matter, let's dive into what they actually are. Graph features are grouped into three main categories based on the graph component (node, edge, full graph) that they describe. First, there are *node features*, which describe the characteristics of the node within the graph, like a person's name in a social network. Second, there are *edge features*, which pertain to the relationship between these nodes, like how strong a connection is between two users. Lastly, graph features give us a bird's-eye view of the entire graph, revealing overarching properties such as the overall connectivity or density of the network.

Node-level features

Node-level features, in the context of graph structures, encompass the unique attributes or characteristics linked to each node. These attributes serve to encapsulate information about the entities represented by the nodes. For instance, when examining diverse applications like social network analysis or road networks, nodes symbolize entities such as users or intersections. In the Amazon copurchasing network dataset, products will be the nodes. The features capture information about those entities, encompassing attributes like title or sales rank.

Let's talk about the different types of features we can dig up for nodes in GML. We'll take a closer look at what each of them means:

Node degree
    A fundamental node-level feature that represents the number of edges connected to a particular node. In a social network example, a node degree tells you how many friends or neighbors that node has right next to it. In directed graphs like the copurchasing graph, the degree can be split into *in-degree* (number of incoming edges) and *out-degree* (number of outgoing edges).

Node centrality
    Node centralities, as a concept, encompass a range of different metrics that provide insights into individual nodes within a network. Think of them as toolkits we use to figure out what the most important node is in the graph. We will review three centrality measures: *degree*, *betweenness*, and *closeness*. There are actually more centrality measures, but we'll focus on these three for now. If you're curious about the others, you can check out *Graph Algorithms* by Mark Needham and Amy E. Hodler.

    Degree centrality measures a node's importance based on the number of connections it has. A highly central node is typically seen as the most influential in the graph. *Betweenness centrality*, on the other hand, quantifies how often a node acts as a bottleneck between other nodes, whereas *closeness centrality* tells you how close a node is to all others in the graph. High centrality indicates quick connections, whereas low centrality indicates isolation.

We will use Figure 3-5 to demonstrate the calculation of these three nodes' centrality measures. In Figure 3-5 is a graph with four nodes, A, B, C, and D, and the following edges: (A, B), (A, C), (B, C), (C, D). The degree centrality of the nodes is as follows: A = 2 because it has two edges connected to it, and similarly B = 2, C = 3, and D = 1). The closeness centrality of node C is 3/6 = 0.5, because it lies on three of the six shortest paths between pairs of vertices (A, B), (A, D), and (B, D).

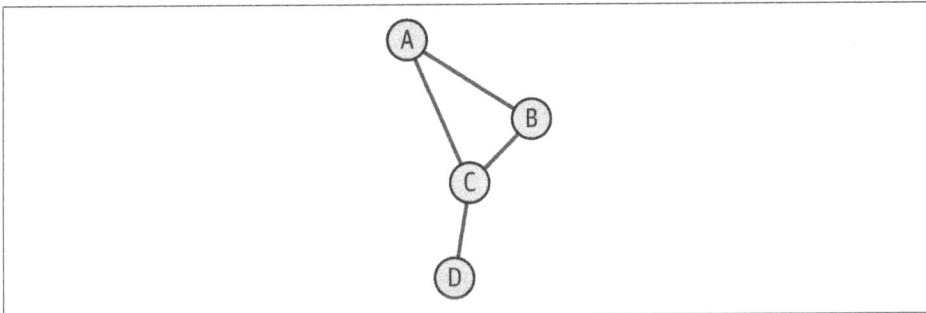

Figure 3-5. Node centrality example

Edge-level features

When we talk about *edge-level* (or *relation-level*) features, we're referring to the characteristics or attributes of edges that connect two nodes. In the context of our Amazon copurchasing dataset example, various types of these features can be employed to predict if two products are likely to be bought together. Example edge features may include:

Edge weight
It's a measure of the strength or importance of the edge between two nodes, often represented by a numerical value or weight. In this dataset, the weight of an edge connecting two products could represent the frequency or strength of their copurchasing relationship. Higher weights would suggest a stronger tendency for these products to be bought together—possibly derived from factors such as sales rank or the frequency of their joint appearances.

Edge type
This is a categorical feature that indicates the type of relationship between two nodes. In this dataset example, the edge type is labeled as "similar to," denoting a copurchasing relationship. This indicates products that are commonly bought together due to their similarities.

Timestamps

These are time-based features that indicate when an edge was created or last updated. Although not included in the dataset, if available, such features could be valuable for tracking the timing of product interactions. For instance, timestamps could reveal when two products are frequently bought together. These timestamps could potentially be derived from product reviews, providing insights into customer purchase and review times.

Edge attributes

These are any other characteristics or attributes of the edges that might be relevant to the machine learning task at hand. In this dataset, edge attributes could include product categorization, the frequency of copurchases between two products, and average ratings. Product categorization serves as an edge attribute to provide further context regarding the relationship between two products. For instance, if two products share the same category, it could strengthen their copurchasing association. Additionally, attributes derived from product reviews, such as the number of votes, can serve as indicators of average ratings, capturing both popularity and sentiment. Products with higher ratings are more likely to be purchased together, thus providing valuable insights as edge attributes.

Graph-level features

When we talk about *graph-level* features, we're basically discussing the characteristics or attributes of the entire graph. To clarify, let's use a hypothetical fintech application scenario. Imagine we've got a graph that represents all the financial transactions happening between customers of a bank. Now, what if we want to come up with some features for a machine learning model that can predict the chances of a customer defaulting on a loan? Well, in that case, we might think about some graph-level features like:

Graph density

This is a measure of the number of edges in the graph relative to the number of possible edges. A dense graph has many edges, while a sparse graph has few edges. In the fintech example, a dense graph might indicate a high level of financial activity and a higher risk of default, since there are more potential connections and interactions between customers.

Graph diameter

This is the greatest length of all shortest paths between any two nodes in the graph. A graph with a large diameter has nodes that are more spread out and disconnected, while a graph with a small diameter has more closely connected nodes. In a transaction network, a large diameter might indicate that some customers are more isolated and less connected, which could be a risk factor for default.

Graph average degree
> This is the average number of edges per node in the graph. The higher a graph's average degree, the more closely its nodes are connected. In the transaction network example, a high average degree might indicate that customers are generally well connected and have a strong support network, which could be a protective factor against default.

Graph clustering coefficient
> This measure tells us how many nodes in the graph like to cluster together and form little groups. If a graph has a high clustering coefficient, it means there are lots of these tight-knit groups of nodes. On the other hand, if it has a low clustering coefficient, there are fewer of these groups, and they're more likely to spread out. Now, back to our transaction graphs example. If there is a high clustering coefficient, it could mean there are close-knit groups of customers who support each other financially. This kind of unity might also help protect against fraud.

Let's take a step back and try some of these features on our Amazon copurchasing dataset.

Hands-on: Extracting Features for the Amazon Copurchasing Graph

We saw that graphs encode relationships between nodes, and that their structure can provide rich information that can be transformed into features for machine learning tasks. These graph-derived features can augment existing attributes, enriching the data and potentially improving the performance of machine learning models. So, in the upcoming section, we'll go ahead and extract the features from our example dataset.

Graph feature derivation

Features can be derived from various graph metrics and properties. We'll give an example of two commonly used features and how to derive them:

Node degree
> In the context of the copurchasing dataset, a product's degree represents how many other products are frequently bought with it. A high degree indicates that the product is often copurchased with many other products, suggesting its popularity or versatility.

Node clustering coefficient
> In the context of the copurchasing dataset, a high clustering coefficient for a product would mean that customers who buy this product also tend to buy its copurchased products together. This could indicate product bundles or items that are commonly used together.

Back to our previous coding example. Here, we will leverage features from the NetworkX library. The following code snippet calculates the preceding two features for the Amazon copurchasing graph. It calls the degree and clustering coefficient functions and attaches them to the nodes as attributes:

```
import networkx as nx

# Degree of each node
degree = dict(G.degree())

# Clustering coefficient of each node
clustering_coefficient = nx.clustering(G)

# Add these as node attributes
nx.set_node_attributes(G, degree, 'degree')
nx.set_node_attributes(G, clustering_coefficient, 'clustering')
```

When you run this code, you'll get nodes with some extra info—their degree and coefficient. We call these things "features" because they're like additional characteristics that we figure out based on the graph's context. For instance, the product's node degree can tell us how popular that product is in our dataset.

Leveraging graph-derived metrics to enrich product attributes

Having extracted graph-based features like degree and clustering coefficient, it's time to leverage them to enhance our existing dataset. These features can provide additional context and information that might not be evident from the original attributes alone. By integrating graph-derived features with the primary dataset, we can offer a richer representation of each product, capturing both its inherent attributes and its role within the broader copurchasing network.

The following code merges original product attributes with the driven graph features:

```
# Extracting graph features into a DataFrame
graph_features_df = pd.DataFrame({
    'Id': list(G.nodes),
    'degree': list(degree.values()),
    'clustering': list(clustering_coefficient.values())
})

# Merging with original product features
merged_df = pd.merge(products_df, graph_features_df, on='Id')
```

Graph Features in ML Modeling

Now that we've got a handle on what these graph features are and how to put them into our graph setup, it's time to jump into the exciting part—using these features in a machine learning model. But, before we get into this, let's discuss an overview of the tasks and techniques that come into play when dealing with graphs. To keep things clear, we'll pick one of these tasks, node classification, and use it as our demo example.

Task and Techniques Overview

Just like any machine learning problem, graph problems are tackled through specific tasks. These tasks formalize the problem and guide how we handle it. There are several common graph tasks, and we'll go over some of them here. Figure 3-6 shows a visual of what each task means. Think of the question mark and dashed line in the figure as your map legend. They're like little hints about what the task is all about. For instance, in node classification, those nodes with question marks are the ones our ML model is trying to figure out—it's like a puzzle to decide if they should be labeled as a dark or light shade.

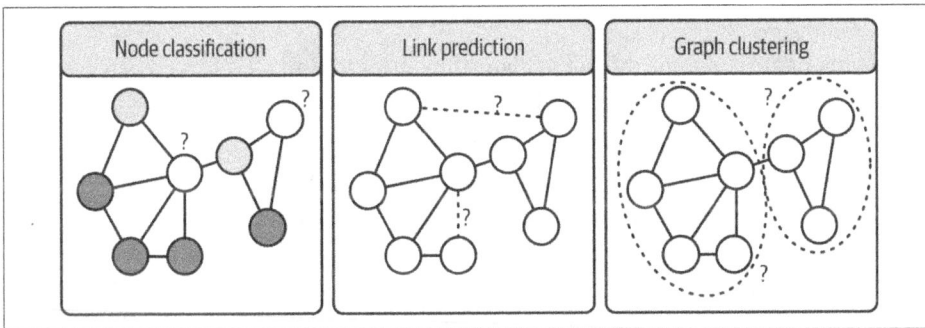

Figure 3-6. Illustration of three graph tasks

Node classification

Node classification is all about giving nodes in a graph their *identity* or *label*. We're essentially trying to figure out which group a node belongs to by looking at its features and what its neighbors are labeled as. One common technique for this task is *random walk*, which is an algorithm that traverses or walks around the graph, gathering information about nodes and their context, and then applying what it has learned to classify nodes.

Link prediction

In this task, we will try to predict the edge joining a pair of nodes in a graph. In essence, we will be attempting to figure out which nodes should be connected. One of the techniques is the *Jaccard coefficient* (*https://oreil.ly/I7YrG*). It is a simple yet effective measure. It computes the similarities between two sets by dividing the size of their intersection by the size of their union. In link prediction, you can use it to estimate the likelihood of an edge/link forming between two nodes based on the common neighbors they share.[3] A high Jaccard coefficient suggests a stronger likelihood of a link between these nodes. Other techniques for calculating link predictions include the *Adamic–Adar Index* and *neighborhood calculation*. If you're keen to explore further, we would recommend checking out the link prediction chapter in Niyati Aggrawal and Adarsh Anand's book *Social Networks: Modeling and Analysis*.

Graph clustering

Graph clustering involves categorizing nodes in such a way that nodes within the same cluster are more alike compared to nodes outside their group. Two common techniques for this task are:

Spectral clustering (https://oreil.ly/0gcvq)
> This algorithm uses a graph's eigenvalues to create clusters.

Community detection algorithms
> As the name suggests, this set of algorithms tries to find closely connected groups of nodes (communities) within the graph.

Now that we've enriched our dataset by integrating original product metadata with graph-derived features, we're in a stronger position to leverage this comprehensive data for enhancing the decision-making capabilities of machine learning models.

Predicting High-Rated Products with a Prediction Model

Businesses can benefit immensely from predicting the potential success or reception of a product. By forecasting whether a product is likely to receive a high average rating, businesses can make informed decisions regarding marketing tactics and inventory management.

For instance, products predicted to have high ratings could be promoted more aggressively, stocked in higher quantities, or even bundled with other products for sales promotions. Conversely, products anticipated to have lower ratings could undergo further quality checks, and improvements, or be marketed differently.

To build our ML model, we will use scikit-learn (often called sklearn), a popular Python library for machine learning. It offers a wide range of tools for building and validating models, from simple linear regressions to complex ensemble methods.

Before we dive in, let's get clear on what we're tackling and what we're working with in terms of data. So, let's outline a summary of the machine learning task we're about

---

3 Bhuvaneswari, A., and Jijina, K. K. (2023). A novel friend recommendation system using link prediction in social networks. In N. Hoda and A. Naim (Eds.), *Social Capital in the Age of Online Networking: Genesis, Manifestations, and Implications* (pp. 28-40). IGI Global.

to tackle, along with a clear description of the inputs and what we expect the model to produce as output:

Task definition

Our task is node classification. Essentially, we're trying to predict whether a product will score high or not.

Target definition

Also known as *output label*. The target variable, high_rating, is defined based on the avg_rating column using a threshold value. If a product has an average rating greater than 4.5, it's labeled as having a high rating (1); if it has a lower rating, it will not (0).

Input features

The features used for prediction include both the original product metadata (salesrank and total_reviews) and the graph-derived features (degree, betweenness, and clustering).

Data splitting

We will adopt the conventional ML approach. The dataset will be divided into training and test subsets, allocating 80% for training purposes and the remaining 20% for testing. We will use sklearn's function train_test_split to perform this.

Model training

For training, we will choose sklearn's RandomForestClassifier. It's a versatile and commonly used ensemble learning method. It works by training multiple decision trees and aggregating their outputs for prediction, making it robust and less prone to overfitting. For this, we will use our train portion of the data.

So, let's put all this in a snippet:

```
from sklearn.model_selection import train_test_split
from sklearn.ensemble import RandomForestClassifier
from sklearn.metrics import accuracy_score, classification_report

# Define our target variable based on avg_rating
merged_df_cleaned['high_rating'] = merged_df_cleaned['avg_rating']
                    .apply(lambda x: 1 if x > 4.5 else 0)

# Splitting data into training and test set
X = merged_df_cleaned[['degree', 'clustering', 'salesrank', 'total_reviews']]
y = merged_df_cleaned['high_rating']
X_train, X_test, y_train, y_test = train_test_split(X, y, test_size=0.2,
                                                    random_state=42)

# Training a random forest classifier
clf = RandomForestClassifier()
clf.fit(X_train, y_train)
```

Once our classifier `clf` is trained, let's evaluate its performance on unseen data to understand its predictive capabilities. This ensures that our model isn't just memorizing the training data (overfitting) but is genuinely identifying patterns that generalize well to unseen data. To do this, we'll utilize the testing portion of our data split:

```
# Predictions
y_pred = clf.predict(X_test)

# Evaluation
accuracy = accuracy_score(y_test, y_pred)
report = classification_report(y_test, y_pred)

print(f"Accuracy: {accuracy}")
print(report)
```

Output:

```
Accuracy: 0.6951206405502713
              precision    recall  f1-score   support

           0       0.77      0.81      0.79     52619
           1       0.48      0.41      0.44     21817

    accuracy                           0.70     74436
   macro avg       0.62      0.61      0.62     74436
weighted avg       0.68      0.70      0.69     74436
```

The preceding code snippet is predicting product ratings using the trained random forest model on the test set, then evaluating and displaying the model's accuracy and detailed performance metrics (precision, recall, F1-score) for each class.

Let's build the same model, excluding the graph features:

```
# Splitting data into training and test set
X = merged_df_cleaned[['salesrank', 'total_reviews']]
y = merged_df_cleaned['high_rating']
X_train, X_test, y_train, y_test = train_test_split(X, y, test_size=0.2,
                                                    random_state=42)

# Training a random forest classifier
clf = RandomForestClassifier()
clf.fit(X_train, y_train)
```

Now, let's produce predictions for the test set and display the corresponding accuracy report:

```
# Predictions
y_pred = clf.predict(X_test)

# Evaluation
accuracy = accuracy_score(y_test, y_pred)
report = classification_report(y_test, y_pred)
```

```
print(f"Accuracy: {accuracy}")
print(report)
```

Output:

```
Accuracy: 0.6744720296630663
              precision    recall  f1-score   support

           0       0.77      0.77      0.77     52619
           1       0.44      0.43      0.44     21817

    accuracy                           0.67     74436
   macro avg       0.61      0.60      0.60     74436
weighted avg       0.67      0.67      0.67     74436
```

Incorporating graph-derived features into our model resulted in a notable performance boost. Specifically, accuracy increased from 67.4% to 69.5%—a 2.1% improvement. This highlights the significant value of meshing graph insights with traditional data features, leading to enhanced predictive capabilities. Integrating such graph metrics can be a strategic move for achieving more accurate machine learning outcomes.

Feature Learning with Node Embeddings

In graph theory, nodes represent entities, and edges represent relationships or interactions between these entities. Just as images have pixels and natural language texts have word vectors as their features, graphs need a mechanism to convert their structural information into a format suitable for machine learning. This is where node embeddings come into play.

Node embeddings are vector representations of nodes in a graph. These embeddings capture the topology of the graph, the node's position, and its neighborhood information. The idea is to represent nodes with similar graph structures by using vectors that are close to each other in the vector space. By learning such representations, we can utilize these embeddings in various machine learning tasks, such as node classification, link prediction, and recommendation.

Node embeddings can be learned using various techniques. One popular method is node2Vec (*https://oreil.ly/JbF7V*), which utilizes random walks to generate sequences of nodes, akin to sentences in natural language processing. These sequences are then fed into a word2Vec-like model (*https://oreil.ly/pdRhq*) to learn the embeddings.

Vector representations are numerical representations of objects or data in a multidimensional space, with each dimension corresponding to a specific attribute of the node. This allows for mathematical operations and comparisons to be performed between vectors. It's important here to distinguish between learning embeddings and extracting vectors from the graph. Learning embeddings involves training a model to generate vectors that encode meaningful information about the data. Extracting vector representation, on the other hand, involves directly deriving vectors from the data or graph without any explicit learning, often by considering specific features or properties of the data (for instance, defining the length of the vector based on the maximum number of neighbors a node could have) In this case, each dimension represents a neighbor node.

Random Walk Algorithm

A random walk on a graph is a path that starts from a particular node and then moves from the current node to a randomly chosen neighbor. This process is repeated for a specified number of steps or until a termination condition is met.

Here's a simple way to describe the random walk:

1. Start at a node.
2. Randomly choose an adjacent node and move to it if the graph is undirected. For directed graphs choose nodes that are reachable via outgoing edges from the current node, and move to them.
3. Repeat step 2 for a specified number of steps, or until there are no further outgoing edges from the current node.

Consider the graph in Figure 3-7.

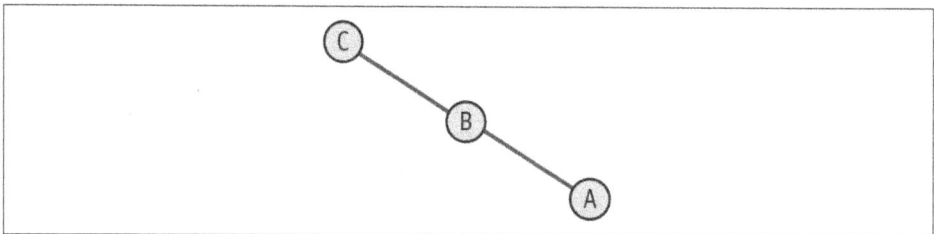

Figure 3-7. A demonstration graph for the random walk algorithm

The steps are as follows:

1. Start at node B.

2. Possible moves: A or C (because both are neighbors of B).

3. Let's say we randomly choose to move to A.

4. From A, the only move is back to B (since A has only one neighbor in this graph).

5. If our walk length is 3, we'd move back to B and stop there.

Amazon Copurchasing Dataset and Node Embeddings

Back again to our Amazon copurchasing dataset, let's see how node embeddings can be relevant and beneficial. But first, let's learn to generate them.

Node embeddings use case for Amazon copurchasing dataset

Now, let's set the stage for how we can make the most of these node embeddings. To start, since each node here represents a product, we'll create embeddings for every single one of them—think of it as giving each product a unique ID in the form of vectors. The cool part is, since these embeddings are essentially vectors, we can do some basic math with them. We can calculate how similar or different they are from one another.

One of the initial applications in our dataset is using node embedding to capture product similarities. By generating node embeddings for products, we can capture implicit similarities between products based on their copurchasing patterns. Products that are frequently copurchased would have embeddings closer in the vector space, which could be used for a variety of use cases:

Recommendation systems
> Given a product, find the most similar products using the cosine similarity of their embeddings. This can be the basis for a recommendation system.

Product classification
> Use embeddings as features to classify products into categories or to predict their sales rank.

Anomaly detection
> Find products that have embeddings significantly different from their peers, indicating unusual purchasing patterns.

Let's start using the node2vec library to generate node embeddings based on the Amazon copurchasing dataset.

Generating node embeddings

From our previous example, we have a graph representation of the Amazon copurchasing dataset. Here, we will use off the shelf node2Vec (*https://oreil.ly/JbF7V*) to generate the node embeddings. Although the chapter primarily delves into traditional graph ML, the incorporation of node2vec—a versatile and widely adopted technique for learning representations of nodes in networks—enhances the traditional Graph ML approach, enabling it to better capture complex relational structures and patterns within the data.

The recipe for generating node embeddings is as follows:

1. We will use the node2Vec algorithm to generate the random walks on the copurchasing graph.

2. Then, we will train the famous skip-gram model (*https://oreil.ly/pdRhq*) (a component of word2Vec) on these random walks to generate embeddings.

3. Once trained, each product (node) will have an associated vector (embedding) capturing its context in the copurchasing graph.

Let's implement these steps with a practical code example. We can categorize the steps outlined here into three groups: one that pertains to the initialization of node2Vec, the second that involves training the model, and the third relating to extracting the features:

Step 1: node2Vec initialization

1. We will install and import node2Vec. We install node2Vec using the Python package (*https://oreil.ly/PUF-s*) by calling `!pip install node2vec`.

2. Then, we will instantiate node2Vec algorithm with the following parameters:

   - Our Amazon copurchasing graph (G).

   - The size or the dimension (`dimension`) of the node2Vec embeddings (the default is 64).

   - The random walk parameters. Each random walk on the graph will cover a distance of 30 nodes (`walk_length=30`) and will perform a total of 200 random walks for each node (`num_walks=200`).

Step 2: Model training

1. For the training part, we call the `fit()` method on the `node2Vec` object. This will essentially train a skip-gram model in the background using the random walks we generated in step 1.

2. The context window size is set to 10 (`window=10`), meaning it will consider 10 neighboring nodes in the random walk sequence to predict the current node.

3. The model will consider all nodes for training, even if they appear only once in the random walks, as indicated by `min_count=1`:

```
!pip install node2vec

from node2vec import Node2Vec

node2vec = Node2Vec(G, dimensions=64, walk_length=30,
                    num_walks=200, workers=4)
model = node2vec.fit(window=10, min_count=1)
```

Now that we've successfully trained the model for embeddings, let's explore how we can link these embeddings to the nodes in our example.

Step 3: Feature extraction and merging

1. We initiate a `node2vec_features` dictionary to store the node embeddings.

2. We loop through the node (products) in our graph (G) and extract its corresponding embedding (vector representation) from the trained model (the result from step 2). Then we store it in the `node2vec_features` dictionary with the node as the key:

```
node2vec_features = {}
for node in G.nodes():
    node2vec_features[node] = model.wv[node]
```

To improve the representation of products and capture more nuanced relationships, the learned node embeddings can be combined with the original product metadata, such as `salesrank`. This enhanced feature representation is expected to capture both the inherent characteristics of a product (such as its sales rank) and its relationships with other products from the embeddings.

The following code snippet combines the node2vec feature with selected original product metadata:

```
# Convert node2vec function dictionary to DataFrame
features_df = pd.DataFrame.from_dict(node2vec_features, orient='index')

# Join features_df with products_df
features_df = features_df.join(products_df.set_index('Id'), on=features_df.index)

# Only use 'node2vec' column from features_df
# and salesrank from the original products metadata
X = list(features_df['node2vec'])
X = pd.DataFrame(X)
X['salesrank'] = features_df['salesrank']
```

To cluster the products, we can use the following code snippet where:

- A k-nearest neighbors (KNN algorithm (*https://oreil.ly/CGdKT*)), a clustering technique, is trained on the combined feature set.
- The KNN model uses the cosine distance metric, which is particularly suited for high-dimensional data like embeddings, to find similarities between products:

```
from sklearn.neighbors import NearestNeighbors

model_knn = NearestNeighbors(metric='cosine', algorithm='brute',
                             n_neighbors=20, n_jobs=-1)
model_knn.fit(X)
```

The trained model `model_knn` can then be used to make recommendations where:

- A `get_recommendations(..)` function is defined to retrieve the top K similar products for a given `product_id`.
- Given a `product_id`, the function finds its index (`product_index`) in the feature DataFrame `features_df`.
- Using the trained KNN model (`model_knn`), it identifies the nearest neighbors (most similar products) for the given product.
- The function returns the IDs of the top K products:

```
def get_recommendations_with_titles(product_id, k=5):

    product_index = features_df.index.get_loc(product_id)

    # Running the trained model against the given product
    distances, indices = model_knn.kneighbors(
                                    X.iloc[product_index, :]
                                    .values.reshape(1, -1),
                                    n_neighbors=k+1)

    # Getting the IDs of the recommended similar products
    recommended_ids = features_df.index[indices[0]].tolist()[1:]

    # Getting the titles of the recommended IDs
    recommended_titles = products_df[products_df['Id']
                      .isin(recommended_ids)]['title'].tolist()
    return list(zip(recommended_ids, recommended_titles))

# Generate recommendations
product_id_test = features_df.index[10]
recommendations_with_titles =
                        get_recommendations_with_titles(product_id_test)

# Print output
print("Given the input product ID:", product_id_test, "titled:",
```

```
        products_df[products_df['Id'] == product_id_test]['title'].iloc[0])
    print("\nThe recommended products based on copurchasing patterns are:")
    for id_, title in recommendations_with_titles:
        print("- Product ID:", id_, "titled:", title)
```

Output:

```
Given the input product ID: 5 titled:
"Prayers That Avail Much For Business: Executive"

The recommended products based on co-purchasing patterns are:
- Product ID: 352954 titled: "Entrepreneurship"
- Product ID: 200336 titled: "Executive Temping : A Guide for Professionals"
- Product ID: 42322 titled: "Chaos or Creativity?"
- Product ID: 387069 titled: "A Handbook of Model Letters for the Busy Executive"
- Product ID: 117493 titled:
  "Balancing Your Body : A Self-Help Approach to Rolfing Movement"
```

You can access the fully functional example (notebook 3_4) on our
GitHub repository (*https://github.com/gl4ebook/py-graf*).

Summary

In this chapter, we navigated the nuances of representing graphs for traditional
machine learning. We began by exploring foundational graph representations,
including adjacency matrices and lists. The Amazon copurchasing dataset served
as our primary example, enabling us to practically showcase the process of graph
creation and representation.

Diving into graph feature engineering, we highlighted its significance and the challenges it poses. We explained various types of graph features, including node-level,
edge-level, and graph-level features. A hands-on approach demonstrated the extraction of features from the Amazon copurchasing graph, revealing the power of graph-
derived metrics in enriching product attributes. As we transitioned into the domain
of graph features in ML modeling, we introduced key tasks such as node classification, link prediction, and graph clustering. The chapter also presented a practical use
case: predicting high-rated products. We explored the steps of building and validating
predictive models, leveraging both graph features and traditional ML techniques.

To conclude our exploration, the chapter introduced the concept of feature learning
with node embeddings, emphasizing the random walk algorithm used by node2Vec.
Through the lens of the Amazon copurchasing dataset, we demonstrated the generation and application of node embeddings, underscoring their potential in enhancing
machine learning models.

## CHAPTER 4

PyGraf: End-to-End Graph Learning and Serving

Now that you've grasped the graph pipeline and its traditional ML approaches, this chapter introduces our open source graph machine-learning library, PyGraf (*https://github.com/gl4ebook/py-graf*). It serves as our framework for constructing robust graph learning ecosystems at an enterprise level.

Throughout this chapter, we'll walk you through the library's architecture and its core modules. We'll also showcase the library's capabilities by reworking an example presented in Chapter 3 using this library.

By leveraging this library, you, as a reader, will not only solidify your understanding of concepts from earlier chapters, but also learn how to practically apply them in common tasks. You will also be able to experience graph representation, and explore different ways to utilize this process. Additionally, the library encompasses an entire GML pipeline, featuring a range of algorithms, metrics, and connectors. This facilitates the seamless creation of custom pipelines with precision and ease. With these resources readily available, you will have comprehensive guidance to navigate and follow along in the upcoming chapters.

Let's delve into this chapter by exploring the library and uncovering its purpose.

Graph Libraries Overview

The emergence of graph learning and serving technologies has opened new frontiers in data analytics, particularly for enterprises dealing with large-scale, complex datasets. With this open source and prosperity GML libraries have emerged such as PyTorch Geometric (PyG) (*https://pyg.org*), Deep Graph Library (DGL) (*https://www.dgl.ai*) and StellarGraph (*https://oreil.ly/Eg-hd*). These libraries offer comprehensive toolsets and efficient implementations of graph neural networks. However, current open source graph learning solutions often present challenges, especially for enterprise-level applications. These challenges stem mainly from the need for manual specification and low-level coding, which can be both time-consuming and technically demanding. In exploring graph libraries, we highlighted the challenges that work as our driving force to create an open source library that serves as a demonstration for readers in how to build an enterprise-level graph learning pipeline.

Challenges of Open Source Graph Libraries: PyGraf Opportunities

You may have encountered the aforementioned libraries, and while many of them boast well-established communities, they still face certain challenges. Let's explore the challenges encountered by existing open source graph libraries and how PyGraf steps in to tackle them. These challenges primarily arise in two areas: learning and applicability. Users often desire a structured learning path for grasping graph concepts, followed by the ability to apply this knowledge in a scalable enterprise environment without being constrained by specific use cases. Here's an overview of these challenges:

Addressing the manual specification challenge
  As you may have already experienced, traditional graph learning frameworks often require users to manually specify a multitude of parameters and settings. This extensive customization can pose a significant obstacle, especially for organizations lacking in-house technical expertise. It significantly hampers the deployment of graph learning solutions at scale.

The complexity of low-level implementations
  Many existing graph learning tools demand interaction with low-level implementations. This means grappling with complex algorithms and data structures, slowing down development and increasing the risk of errors. It makes these tools less accessible to nonspecialists.

Lack of integrated E2E pipeline
  There is another noticeable gap in the current landscape—the absence of a comprehensive tool or library seamlessly connecting the entire end-to-end (E2E) pipeline of graph learning and serving. Enterprises often have to use multiple disjointed tools for different stages of the graph learning process, leading to inefficiencies and inconsistencies.

To tackle these challenges and create a more engaging and seamless experience, we introduce PyGraf.

PyGraf: A Solution for Streamlined Graph Learning and Serving

In response to these challenges, and those associated with enterprise settings such as development speed and scaled deployment, we present PyGraf. PyGraf distinguishes itself as an advanced open source library specifically designed for enterprise-level end-to-end (E2E) graph learning and serving. It encompasses not only the learning phase involving data and model building but also extends to the serving phase where the graph model is actively deployed. PyGraf streamlines the process for practitioners to leverage graph learning technologies by abstracting away low-level complexities and providing a cohesive pipeline.

PyGraf integrates four core modules—which we will learn about in the rest of this chapter—into a unified and user-friendly library. This integration enables businesses to streamline their graph learning workflows, leading to faster deployment times and more reliable results. Moreover, the library's emphasis on user-friendly APIs and modular architecture further democratizes access to advanced graph analytics, empowering a wide range of professionals within an enterprise to leverage the capabilities of graph learning.

As a reader, from this chapter, you will notice the value of this library in introducing the concepts from previous chapters and laying the ground for implementation for future chapters. Let's now explore its architecture and structure.

Introduction to PyGraf

At this stage, we can introduce PyGraf as an end-to-end graph learning and serving library that simplifies both development and deployment by offering the four key pillars of a graph AI system within a modular architecture. These pillars form the cornerstone of building a production-ready graph system. They include data management, model training, serving, and auxiliary functionalities.

Ready to dive into PyGraf? Let's explore its features and learn about its architecture to unlock the full potential of graph data in enterprise settings. Let's get started!

PyGraf Key Features

PyGraf focuses on streamlining both the development and deployment of a graph learning system. How does it achieve this? In the following outline the key features and provide explanations of each:

Scalable and modular architecture
> PyGraf is designed to scale horizontally, making it suitable for accommodating large datasets and high-throughput scenarios commonly encountered in enterprise environments. Its modular design facilitates seamless integration with existing data pipelines and ML workflows.

Comprehensive graph operations

PyGraf emphasizes versatility by supporting a wide range of graph libraries, including NetworkX (*https://networkx.org*), Graph-tool (*https://oreil.ly/IhoOQ*),[1] and others. This broad support ensures comprehensive coverage of graph operations, providing users with a versatile toolkit for graph analytics.

Seamless machine learning integration

PyGraf effortlessly integrates with popular machine learning frameworks such as TensorFlow (*https://tensorflow.org*) and PyTorch (*https://pytorch.org*), empowering the implementation of advanced graph learning algorithms and AI techniques.

Privacy and security

PyGraf incorporates privacy-preserving methods like federated learning to safeguard sensitive data. It has a dedicated module for this feature.

Monitoring and logging

PyGraf allows for the continuous tracking and logging of various metrics related to the performance of graph models. This includes monitoring aspects such as model accuracy, training time, resource utilization, and any errors or anomalies encountered during execution.

Intuitive interface

Despite its technical depth, PyGraf remains accessible to users across different proficiency levels through its intuitive interface and user-friendly APIs (*https://oreil.ly/XfvVs*).

Scalable deployment options

PyGraf incorporates principles for large-scale deployment, offering containerization support with Docker (*https://docker.com*) and Kubernetes (*https://kubernetes.io*) to ensure scalable deployment in production environments.

PyGraf Purposes: Empowering Dynamic Environments

PyGraf is engineered to be a versatile, scalable, and adaptable framework for processing, analyzing, and modeling graph data. In the realm of enterprise data analytics and machine learning, PyGraf plays a crucial role in optimizing the graph learning and serving pipeline. Its overarching purpose encompasses several key objectives:

Facilitating end-to-end graph learning pipelines

At its core, PyGraf facilitates end-to-end graph learning pipelines by seamlessly integrating with diverse data sources through its array of connectors, which span

---

1 Graph-tool is a Python library renowned for its efficient performance in graph manipulation and analysis. It stands out for its speed due to its algorithms being implemented in C++.

traditional databases, files, and cloud storage solutions. Furthermore, PyGraf empowers advanced graph analytics with its comprehensive suite of tools, allowing for detailed "slicing and dicing" into graph data to extract specific insights from complex structures. This robust functionality enables organizations to enhance decision-making and operational efficiency by leveraging the wealth of information contained within their graph data.

Empowering scalable and efficient model training
PyGraf's architecture includes distributed computing support, crucial for training models on large datasets, while its integration with state-of-the-art open source GML frameworks enables the implementation of efficient graph learning algorithms.

Streamlining model serving and deployment
PyGraf streamlines model serving and deployment by offering deployment readiness tools and frameworks—including support for containerization technologies like Docker and Kubernetes, ensuring swift transition of models from development to production environments. Additionally, its API-driven serving mechanism enables easy access to model outputs, facilitating integration and sharing with enterprise applications and decision-making workflows.

Ensuring compliance-driven learning
PyGraf incorporates federated learning as a core feature to enhance data security and privacy in enterprise environments. This approach enables model training across decentralized datasets without data sharing, ensuring confidentiality. Especially in sensitive sectors such as healthcare or finance, federated learning ensures compliance with data protection regulations while leveraging ML capabilities.

Best practices in model training and selection
PyGraf optimizes model training and selection for large, dynamic graph datasets. It supports incremental and batch training methods, ensuring adaptability to changing data for accuracy. Additionally, PyGraf employs advanced algorithms to select models based on graph structure nuances, ensuring optimal performance for specific analytics tasks.

Now that you have a grasp of PyGraf's features and purposes, let's delve into its architecture and core modules.

Architecture and Core Capabilities

PyGraf's architecture adopts a multilayered approach, offering both flexibility and robustness. Illustrated in Figure 4-1, PyGraf's architecture consists of a modular design allowing for seamless expansion and integration with external tools and technologies.

The architecture comprises three essential layers: the core components, which form the foundation of the library; adaptation and integration, which enhance its functionality; and lastly the implemented best practices, ensuring efficiency and reliability in its operation. Let's take a quick look at these three layers to get a better sense of the entire library.

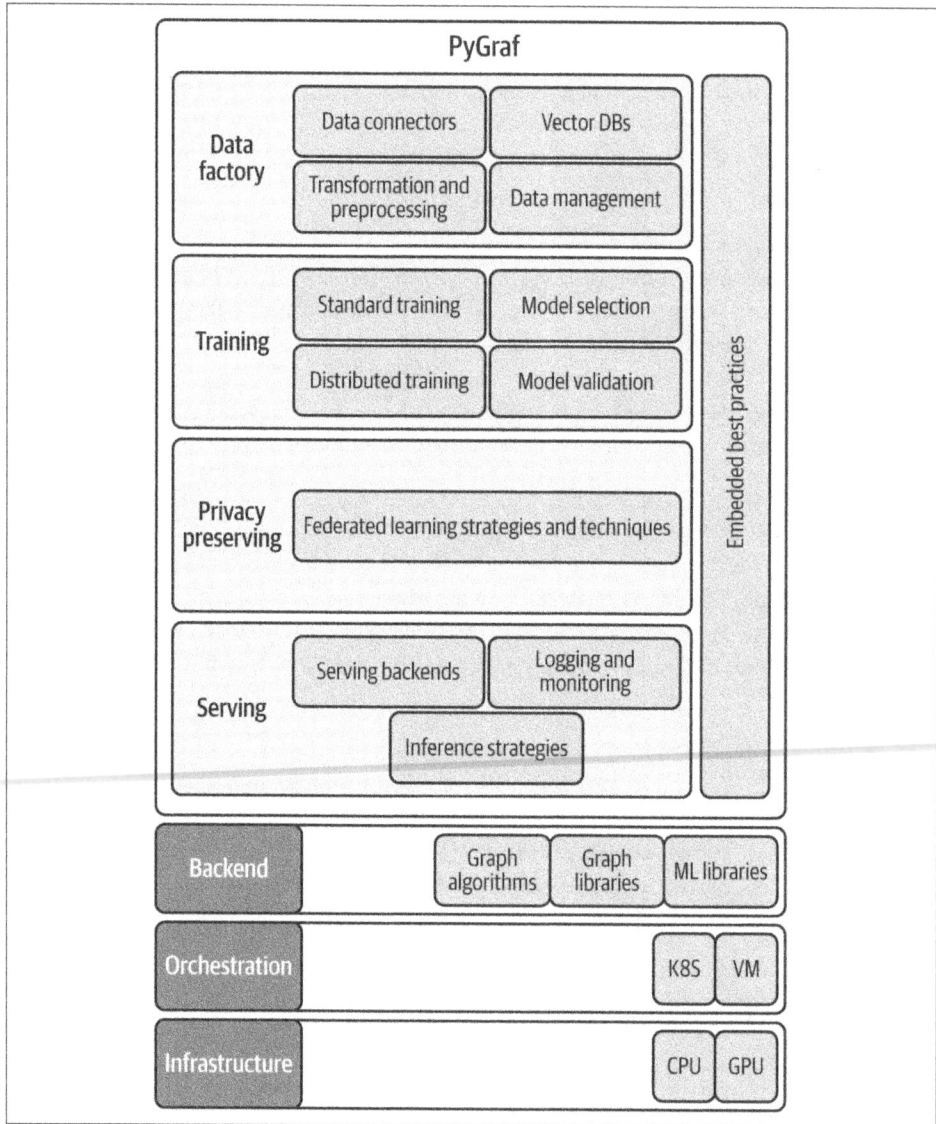

Figure 4-1. PyGraf architecture

Core Components Layer

At the heart of this library are the "core components," serving as PyGraf's engine room. This is where the real value of the library resides. Within this layer, we find four cores: data management, training, privacy preservation, and serving. Let's delve into the function of each component:

Data

This component is designed for efficient data ingestion and preprocessing. It seamlessly connects with both SQL and NoSQL databases, adeptly processes real-time data streams, and efficiently handles batch processing tasks for large datasets. This adaptability ensures PyGraf's seamless integration into various data ecosystems.

Training

PyGraf's core features a robust training engine, leveraging diverse open source graph libraries to provide extensive graph algorithms and processing capabilities.This engine is optimized for memory efficiency and computational speed, effortlessly managing large-scale graph data. Additionally, PyGraf's training engine accommodates both standard and distributed computing environments, facilitating parallel processing across multiple computing resources for enhanced efficiency and scalability.

Serving

The last component of PyGraf's core layer revolves around deploying and serving graph models. PyGraf offers tools for containerization, API management, and scalable deployment strategies. This ensures that the insights generated by PyGraf can be integrated into applications and decision-making processes effectively and securely.

From this layer, let's take a quick look at the other two layers: adaptation and integration and best practices.

Adaptation and Integration Layer

As you may have guessed, this layer is all about connecting PyGraf with custom solutions tailored to your backend, infrastructure, and orchestration options. This layer allows you to add additional functionality to PyGraf to meet your specific operational needs and requirements. With this layer, PyGraf offers flexibility, whether it's integrating new state-of-the-art graph algorithms, extending the library with additional ML capabilities, or customizing orchestrational aspects using Kubernetes or virtual machines. It also supports communication with various physical infrastructures such as CPUs or GPUs. This enables seamless customization and extensibility, empowering you to optimize PyGraf for your unique use cases and workflows.

Best Practices Layer

PyGraf's best practices layer encompasses guidelines for optimizing GML work-flows—including graph data preprocessing, feature transformation and engineering, scalable model training, and evaluation. These practices ensure data quality, algorithm suitability, and model performance for effective graph analytics. They are specifically tailored for enterprise environments, addressing critical aspects such as data governance, scalability, and compliance. By adhering to industry standards and regulations, these practices ensure that GML workflows and artifacts are compliant and seamlessly integrate into enterprise ecosystems.

Now that we've explored the three layers of PyGraf, let's dive deeper into its core component layer and learn how to use it through an example towards the end of this chapter. As for the adaptation and integration layer, we'll revisit it in future chapters, where we'll showcase various scenarios depicting the library's use in different operational settings. Regarding the best practices layer, we'll progressively incorporate and reflect on them, starting from this chapter and showcasing different examples in subsequent chapters to provide practical insights.

In-Depth Exploration of Core Library Components

Let's dive into the core components of PyGraf. In essence, our architecture revolves around four main components: data, training, serving, and privacy preservation.

Data Component

As you may have guessed, PyGraf's first and cornerstone component is the data component. It is designed to channel and enhance the preliminary stages of graph data analysis and preparation. The module is engineered with the flexibility to connect to a wide range of data sources, enabling users to seamlessly integrate their graph data into the graph pipeline.

Following are the key features of this foundational component:

Pre-integrated datasets
> PyGraf provides access to popular datasets, saving users time otherwise spent searching and downloading. With this feature, users can focus on their core work instead of dataset acquisition.

Data connectors
> These connectors are designed to facilitate importing graph data from various sources.

Advanced transformations and preprocessors

This part of the component is responsible for preprocessing and transforming the graph data into a representation suitable for model learning. It also provides graph data optimization through various transformations, allowing you to slice and dice your data for a more in-depth subgraph understanding.

Pre-integrated datasets

PyGraf comes with a collection of pre-integrated datasets that are readily available for graph data analysis and training. These datasets can be easily imported and utilized within your projects to facilitate the development and testing of graph-based models.

PyGraf's dataset handling module, `pygraf.datasets`, provides two convenient methods for accessing data:

Access and select

PyGraf provides access to numerous datasets through its `pygraf.datasets` module. Users can explore the available datasets by importing the list class and invoking the `list_datasets()` function. It will provide the names of all datasets available for use. An example of how to start is shown in the following code snippet.

Shortcut datasets

In machine learning, repositories like the Stanford Large Network Dataset (*https://oreil.ly/KrdHY*) provide well-documented datasets commonly used in popular ML tasks. PyGraf simplifies access to such repositories by dedicating a class to each, such as `StanfordLargeNetworkDataset()`. By importing this class and initializing its object, you can easily load the dataset by simply passing its name to the object. In the following example snippet, we are loading the `AmazonCoPurchase` dataset:

```
from pygraf.datasets
            import StanfordLargeNetworkDataset, list as list_datasets

# 1. List all available datasets
available_datasets = list_datasets()
print("Available Datasets:", available_datasets)

# 2. Initialize a popular pre-configured dataset
dataset = StanfordLargeNetworkDataset('AmazonCoPurchase')
```

Extending with new datasets

PyGraf is built with an open source ethos and designed to be easily extensible. That means it welcomes contributions from both the community and companies. If you want to extend the range of datasets available, you can do so by creating a new dataset class. Just make sure that your new class follows the structure outlined in the abstract

Dataset class. This way, we can keep expanding the library and making it more versatile for everyone to use.

Here is a basic template for the Dataset abstract class, which you can use as a guide to create your own dataset classes:

```python
from abc import ABC, abstractmethod

class Dataset(ABC):
    """
    Abstract class for datasets in PyGraf.
    """

    def __init__(self, name):
        self.name = name
        self.data = None

    @abstractmethod
    def load(self):
        """
        Load the dataset into memory. This method should be implemented by all
        subclasses and is responsible for actually loading the dataset data.
        """
        pass

    def preprocess(self, preprocessor):
        """
        Optionally preprocess the dataset. This method can be overridden by
        subclasses if specific preprocessing steps are needed.
        """
        self.data = preprocessor.preprocess(self.data)

# Example subclass implementation
class YourCustomDataset(Dataset):
    def __init__(self, name):
        super().__init__(name)

    def load(self):
        # Implement dataset loading logic here
        self.data = "your dataset loading logic"
```

How do we use this template? Well, to add a new dataset, simply create a new class that inherits from Dataset and implement the load method with the logic to load your specific dataset. Optionally, you can also override the preprocess method if your dataset requires special preprocessing steps.

Connectors in PyGraf

Connectors in PyGraf play a pivotal role as the pipeline for data ingress into the system. These connectors function like adept translators, converting diverse data formats into a standardized structure that PyGraf can efficiently process. This adaptability allows PyGraf to interact with a wide range of data sources, which is essential for managing the various data environments typically found in enterprise settings.

To use the connectors, we begin by importing the `pygraf.connectors` module. Within this module, you'll find various connectors tailored to link with different data sources like databases and files. To import a specific connector, you simply import the class that represents it:

```
# Import the data connector module from the library
import pygraf.connectors
```

Here we will overview the various categories of connectors used in PyGraf:

Graph database connectors

These connectors are designed to interface with graph databases like Neo4j, enabling PyGraf to directly query and fetch graph data. To demonstrate the simple process of utilizing Neo4j with our library, consider the following example. It illustrates how to establish a connection to a Neo4j database and retrieve graph data using a simple Cypher query (*https://oreil.ly/N_0Cu*). This example is particularly helpful if you're looking to integrate Neo4j graph data into your analysis or preprocessing workflows.

To initiate a connection to graph DB, we import the `GraphDBConnector` class and initiate the object by providing the URI along with the Neo4j credentials. After initializing the object, we execute the `fetch_graph_data` method with the Cypher query. Now you have the fetched data stored in the `graph_data` variable:

```
# Import the GraphDBConnector from our library
from pygraf.connectors import GraphDBConnector

# Initialize a connector for a Neo4j database
# Ensure that you replace "password" with your actual Neo4j database password
connector = GraphDBConnector(uri="bolt://localhost:7687", user="neo4j",
                             password="password")

# Fetch graph data using a Cypher query
# This example query retrieves all nodes and relationships between them
graph_data = connector.fetch_graph_data(query=
                                "MATCH (n)-[r]->(m) RETURN n, r, m")
```

SQL database connectors

With SQL connectors, PyGraf can use relational databases. This comes in handy for extracting relational data that can then be transformed into graph structures. To showcase this, let's use PostgreSQL as an example.

In the following code snippet, we set up the database connection by importing the `SQLDBConnector` class and creating the connection object with specified parameters such as database name, username, password, and host. Then, we use the `fetch_data` method to execute a SQL query and store the retrieved relational data in the variable `relational_data`:

```
from pygraf.connectors import SQLDBConnector

# Initialize a connector for a PostgreSQL database
connector = SQLDBConnector(db_name="postgres", user="user",
                           password="password", host="localhost")
relational_data = connector.fetch_data(query="SELECT * FROM my_table")
```

File-based connectors

In addition to the database, PyGraf features connectors for file-based data sources, allowing for the ingestion of graph data from file formats such as CSV, JSON, or XML. To demonstrate this, we will read a CSV file as an example.

In the following code snippet, we establish a connection to a file-based data source by importing the `FileConnectors` class and creating an object with the filepath and the file type specified. Once you have this object, you start reading the file by calling the `read_file()` method:

```
from pygraf.connectors import FileConnector

# Initialize a connector for a CSV file
connector = FileConnector(file_path="path/to/graph_data.csv",
                          file_type="csv")
file_data = connector.read_file()
```

Vector database connectors

So, with PyGraf, we've got vector databases sorted out. Think of them as these treasure chests where you can interact, store, and retrieve all sorts of rich and multidimensional data representations. Having these connectors is super important for graph learning because they let you tap into a wide variety of databases.

To make this connection happen, first, you need to import `VectorDatabase` from the `connectors` module. Then, you just need to initialize it by passing on the type of vector database you're using—in this case, we're going with `"Faiss"`—and the dimensions of the vector (128). Once you've got that sorted, you can easily kickstart the connection. The following code snippet shows these steps:

```
# Example: Integrating with a vector database
from pygraf.connectors import VectorDatabase

# Initialize and connect to a vector database
vector_db = VectorDatabase(type="Faiss", dimensions=128)
vector_db.connect()
```

Now that we've covered the fourth connector in PyGraf—the vector database—we've got access to a set of different data sources all sorted out. The next step in our data component is processing and transforming all that data we've gathered from the connectors. Let's dive into this phase and break it down step by step.

Preprocessors and Transformation in PyGraf

The next phase in PyGraf's data component is preprocessing and transformation. This is where raw data undergoes refinement, becoming ready for graph analysis and machine learning tasks. This stage holds significant importance as it greatly influences the quality of insights from the data. Typically, this stage can be quite challenging if approached with standard code. PyGraf offers a suite of standard preprocessors within the `preprocessors` module, specially designed to work effectively with graph data. These preprocessors ensure that the data fed into the system is clean, consistent, and structured optimally for graph processing.

Examples of modules under this subcomponent include a graph feature extractor, missing data imputer, and edge weight standardizer. These preprocessors can also be combined and customized to the specific requirements of your graph data and analytical tasks. The following material outlines how to use each one:

Graph feature extractor
> As you remember from Chapter 2, having features at both the node and edge levels is super important for machine learning models dealing with graph data. This class makes it easy to extract and generate these crucial features.

> To extract features from any of the graph data read through the `connectors` module, we utilize the `GraphFeatureExtractor` class. After initializing its object, we apply it to an input graph (`input_graph`). Feature extraction is initiated by calling the `extract_features` method. The extracted features are then stored in the variable `feature_enriched_graph`:

```
from pygraf.preprocessors import GraphFeatureExtractor

feature_extractor = GraphFeatureExtractor()
feature_enriched_graph = feature_extractor.extract_features(input_graph)
```

Missing data imputer
> In real-world enterprise scenarios, data isn't always perfect. Sometimes, information might be missing. The `MissingDataImputer` class is all about tackling those missing bits in graph attributes. It can either fill in those missing values or apply strategies to handle incomplete data gracefully.

> To use it, you need to import the class and initialize it with the preferred strategy: in the following example we use the `'mean'` value strategy, but you could also use `'median'`, `'most_frequent'`, etc. To apply it to the input graph, all you need to do is call the `impute_data` method:

```
from pygraf.preprocessors import MissingDataImputer

# Other strategies could be 'median', 'most_frequent', etc.
imputer = MissingDataImputer(strategy='mean')
imputed_graph = imputer.impute_data(input_graph)
```

Edge weight standardizer

This class standardized or normalizes the weights of the edges in the graph, crucial for algorithms that are sensitive to edge weight variations. By using EdgeWeightStandarizer, we can ensure that all edge weights use a consistent scale or distribution. This, in turn, helps prevent any undesired influence on algorithm performance caused by variations in edge weight magnitude or range across the graph. For example, consider a graph with 100 edges, where 20% of the edges have a weight of 10k, while the rest are under 100.

In the standard procedure, we import the EdgeWeightStandarizer class, initialize its object, and then call the standardize_weights method on the input_graph:

```
from pygraf.preprocessors import EdgeWeightStandardizer

standardizer = EdgeWeightStandardizer()
standardized_graph = standardizer.standardize_weights(input_graph)
```

You've now seen how these useful preprocessors can be called with just a few lines of code and without the need to write lengthy code from multiple libraries. Everything is neatly packaged for easy reading and calling. Moreover, integrating these preprocessors into PyGraf's workflow is smooth, making it simple for you as a user to construct your workflow and apply them to your graph data.

Training Component

Now that we've delved into the data components—including connectors and preprocessing—it's time to shift our focus to the training aspect. The training component in PyGraf serves as the powerhouse of the library, engineered with resilience and adaptability for training graph-based machine learning models. In this section, we'll dive into the practical aspects of leveraging PyGraf for training, highlighting both standard and distributed environments. We'll illustrate these concepts using a repository of open source datasets from the Stanford Large Network Dataset Collection (*https://oreil.ly/KrdHY*).

Within this component, we'll explore three phases: actual training (learning), including standard and distributed training methods, fine-tuning, and validation.

Graph learning (Training)

PyGraf offers two training approaches: standard and distributed. Standard training utilizes either a CPU or a single GPU, while distributed training involves the use of multiple GPUs for parallel computing.

The core training module for PyGraf is `pygraf.training`, which has two classes, `GraphTrainer` and `DistributedGraphTrainer`, corresponding for the two training approaches, standard and distributed, respectively.

For both approaches, we create an object specifying the `model` and `dataset`. In distributed training, we additionally specify the number of GPUs required (`num_gpus`). Once the object is constructed, we call the `train` method on the perspective object, and we officially initiate the training process. Only one parameter, the number of epochs, is required for this operation. Here are examples of both approaches:

Standard training approach

Following is the code snippet to initiate standard training using the Cora dataset, a citation network, and the GCN (graph convolutional network) algorithm trained over 50 epochs with the `GraphTrainer`:

```
from pygraf.training import GraphTrainer
from pygraf.datasets import StanfordLargeNetworkDataset

# Example: Using the 'Cora' dataset for graph convolutional network (GCN)
dataset = StanfordLargeNetworkDataset('Cora')

# Initialize the standard graph trainer with a GCN model
trainer = GraphTrainer(model='GCN', dataset=dataset)
trainer.train(epochs=50)
```

Distributed training approach

For handling larger datasets, PyGraf supports distributed training using the `DistributedGraphTrainer` class in order to distribute the workload across multiple GPUs—in this example, four GPUs:

```
from pygraf.training import DistributedGraphTrainer

# Using the same 'Cora' dataset for distributed training
dist_trainer = DistributedGraphTrainer(model='GCN', dataset=dataset,
                                       num_gpus=4)
dist_trainer.train(epochs=50)
```

These examples show how easy it is to train models using the trainer model, making the whole process quite straightforward and intuitive. After the model is trained, fine-tuning becomes necessary to enhance its performance. Let's explore this phase next.

Fine-tuning

PyGraf also supports fine-tuning, but before delving into PyGraf's approach, let's clarify what fine-tuning entails. Fine-tuning is a pivotal step in machine learning, closely related to the training phase. It entails further training a pre-trained model on a particular task or dataset to improve its performance. This process involves adjusting the model's parameters—such as learning rate and weight decay—to better suit the new data, often by refining its weights through additional training iterations.

In PyGraf, `fine_tune` can be initiated using the `trainer` object, focusing on adjusting two primary parameters: learning rate and weight decay. Following is a code snippet illustrating this process:

```
# Fine-tuning the GCN model
trainer.fine_tune(learning_rate=0.01, weight_decay=0.0001)
```

Model selection and validation

In any task, various algorithms can be applied—each with its own performance and requirements. In applications, it's common to train multiple models such as GCN or GraphSAGE, or different variations of the same model. For example, you could use multiple GCNs with different learning rates, layers, etc. These variations help explore different configurations in order to find the optimal model for your specific task and dataset. Subsequently, you'll compare the performance of these variations and select the one with the best performance. To quantify performance, validation metrics are used, with accuracy being one of the most common metrics.

Using PyGraf's `validation` module, you can select models by initializing a `Model Selector` and specifying the `models` and `dataset`. On the `selector` object, you can use `select_model` to focus on a specific `metric`, such as `'accuracy'`. You can validate the model using the `validate_model` method with a specific `metric`—`'accuracy'` here:

```
from pygraf.validation import ModelSelector

# Initialize model selector with different graph models
selector = ModelSelector(models=['GCN', 'GAT', 'GraphSAGE'], dataset=dataset)

# Select the best model based on accuracy
best_model = selector.select_model(metric='accuracy')
print(f"Selected best model: {best_model}")

# Validate the performance of the selected model
validation_accuracy = selector.validate_model(best_model, metric='accuracy')
print(f"Validation accuracy of the model: {validation_accuracy}")
```

Serving Component

Now that the model is validated, the next natural step in the pipeline is serving. PyGraf includes a dedicated component for this purpose, designed to seamlessly transition models from the training stage to real-world applications. In this section, we will explore the essential aspects of deploying models efficiently and scaling them for production use. Special emphasis will be placed on integration with advanced serving engines like NVIDIA Triton (*https://oreil.ly/_wFUa*),[2] meeting enterprise-level requirements.

Serving mechanisms: Scaling and optimizing for production

PyGraf's approach to serving mechanisms is focused on ensuring scalability and optimizing performance for production environments. This segment delves into how PyGraf facilitates these objectives, with an emphasis on the flexibility in backend selection. We will also provide a practical example using NVIDIA Triton Inference Server.

One of PyGraf's key strengths in serving mechanisms is its ability to dynamically scale with demand. This scalability is crucial for handling varying load conditions efficiently, ensuring that resources are optimally utilized without compromising performance. PyGraf achieves this through:

Dynamic load balancing
PyGraf automatically adjusts resource allocation based on incoming request volume, ensuring consistent performance even under high demand.

Backend versatility
PyGraf's architecture allows for the selection of different backends for model serving, catering to specific needs of the use case, whether that involves prioritizing low-latency responses or handling large batch processes.

NVIDIA Triton Inference Server example

NVIDIA Triton offers a robust and efficient serving platform, well-suited for enterprise-level applications. It supports multiple frameworks and provides features like model versioning, which are vital for production environments.

Now, with PyGraf, we can easily set up Triton Inference Server for serving our model. First we initialize the `TritonServer` by specifying the model name, version, and the URL where Triton is running. We can then tweak the deployment configurations

---

2 NVIDIA Triton is an inference serving software by NVIDIA that enables the deployment and scaling of AI models in production environments.

such as `batch_size` and `request_timeout` to fine-tune how our model gets served. All these steps are listed in the following code snippet:

```
from pygraf.serving import TritonServer

# Initialize the Triton server for model serving
triton_server = TritonServer(model_name='example_graph_model',
                             model_version='1', url='triton-server-url')

# Deploying the model with Triton
triton_server.serve(batch_size=32, request_timeout=100)
```

Without PyGraf, setting up serving with Triton could've been a real headache. We're talking potentially pages of deployment instructions! But thanks to PyGraf's Triton Server class, all that complexity is abstracted away. It's just four simple lines of code to deploy and serve models with Triton. This showcases how PyGraf's serving component makes it easy to tap into the powerful features of NVIDIA Triton, like support for various frameworks, dynamic batching, and making the most out of GPU resources. It's about simplicity and efficiency!

Privacy Preserving Component

In today's data-centric world, protecting sensitive information is crucial, particularly in domains handling large-scale graph data. PyGraf's Privacy Preserving Component, with its focus on federated learning, is designed to meet these challenges head-on—providing effective solutions for preserving data privacy during the graph learning process.

Federated learning: Principles and implementation in PyGraf

In the context of graph learning, privacy preservation is a paramount concern, especially for enterprises handling sensitive or proprietary data. Federated learning emerges as a key technique in this regard, offering a means to train models on decentralized data. PyGraf's privacy preserving component focuses on integrating federated learning principles to enable secure and private model training.

Federated learning represents a privacy-preserving machine learning training strategy, wherein the training of the model is executed over a network of decentralized devices or servers, each possessing distinct local data samples, without the need for data interchange. This approach is relevant in environments where the preservation of data privacy is required or in circumstances where the centralization of data is hindered by privacy laws or logistical limitations:

Data privacy
　　By training models on local datasets without transferring data, federated learning ensures a high level of data privacy.

Compliance with regulations
Federated learning aids in compliance with data protection regulations like the General Data Protection Regulation (GDPR), as sensitive data does not leave its original location.

Efficient use of bandwidth
Since only model updates are exchanged, not the data itself, federated learning is bandwidth efficient.

Leveraging distributed data
Federated learning allows for the utilization of a comprehensive list of data sources, which can lead to more robust and generalizable models.

Implementing federated learning in PyGraf

PyGraf simplifies the implementation of federated learning, offering a straightforward approach without compromising privacy protection. This is possible through the FederatedGraphTrainer module. The following is an example illustrating how to create a federated model:

```
from pygraf.federated import FederatedGraphTrainer

# Example: Federated learning with PyGraf
trainer = FederatedGraphTrainer(model='GCN', dataset='Cora', num_clients=5)

# Training the model in a federated manner
trainer.federated_train(epochs=50, aggregation_method='FedAvg')
```

In the preceding example, FederatedGraphTrainer is used to train a GCN model on the Cora dataset in a federated manner. The num_clients parameter specifies the number of decentralized nodes (clients), and the aggregated_method denotes the technique used to aggregate the updates from different clients, with 'FedAvg' (federated averaging) being a common choice.

Now that we've grasped the core components of PyGraf, let's put this knowledge into practice. In the remainder of this chapter, we'll revisit the example from Chapter 3, but with a twist—we'll leverage the core components of the library for a deeper understanding and application.

End-to-End Example Using PyGraf: Amazon Copurchasing Dataset

In this section, we'll walk you through a complete graph learning workflow using PyGraf, leveraging the Amazon copurchasing dataset from the Stanford Large Network Dataset Collection. In this demonstration, we'll be tracking the same task showcased in Chapter 3—link prediction. We'll illustrate this task using the standard GCN algorithm.

Preprocessing and Transformation

The Amazon copurchasing dataset we're using for this demonstration is the same one we presented in Chapter 3. So, let's dive straight into how to use it. For more detailed exploration of this dataset, please revisit Chapter 3. First, we'll load and preprocess the dataset, transforming it into a format suitable for the GCN algorithm. To do so, we'll import the necessary modules from the library. The two relevant modules here are `pygraf.datasets` and `pygraf.preprocessors`.

The `pygraf.datasets` module is responsible for wrapping datasets, including providing functionality for loading and handling various datasets. In the following code snippet, `StandfordLargeNetworkDataset` is a class from this module specifically designed to handle datasets from the Stanford Large Network Dataset Collection. By importing and initiating this class, we create an object dataset that can access and work with the Amazon copurchasing dataset.

To transform this dataset object, we import the `pygraf.preprocessors` module, which is responsible for handling preprocessing steps and transforming the data into a suitable format. First, we initiate `GraphDataPreprocessor` object and pass the `dataset` object/variable. It will preprocess and transform the Amazon copurchasing dataset using the `preprocess` method of the `GraphDataPreprocessor`:

```
from pygraf.datasets import StanfordLargeNetworkDataset
from pygraf.preprocessors import GraphDataPreprocessor

# Load the Amazon co-purchasing dataset
dataset = StanfordLargeNetworkDataset('AmazonCoPurchase')

# Preprocess and transform the dataset
preprocessor = GraphDataPreprocessor()
processed_data = preprocessor.preprocess(dataset)
```

> To check out which datasets are available and what collections there are, you can simply import, initialize, and print out the `list_dataset` class from the `datasets` module.

We can check the result of this transformation by printing out the `processed_data` variable. With the graph data transformed and prepared within the `processed_data` variable, we can proceed to the next step: training.

Model Training

Moving forward, our next step involves constructing our training pipeline using the processed_data generated from the previous step. Here, you will notice the high level of abstraction provided by the library, where only high-level parameters need to be configured.

We'll conduct our training using pygraf.training[3] module, which encompasses all the necessary functionality for setting up the model. In our example we will use the following setup:

1. From pygraf.training, import the GraphTrainer class.

2. Initialize a GraphTrainer object with two parameters. The first one specifies the model type—which in this case is 'GCN' (graph convolutional network)—and the second parameter, dataset, concerns the preprocessed dataset processed_data. We will store this in the trainer.

3. Now the trainer object—which represents the model—is fully set up and prepared for training. By invoking the train method on the trainer object, we officially initiate the training process. Only one parameter, the number of epochs, is required for this operation—in this example it is set to 50.

4. The trainer model can be saved by calling the save() function and specifying the model name and the location.

All this is encapsulated in the following code snippet. After writing it, let's execute the code and check the output:

```
from pygraf.training import GraphTrainer

# Initialize the graph trainer
trainer = GraphTrainer(model='GCN', dataset=processed_data)

# Train the model
trainer.train(epochs=50)

# Save the model
trainer.save(model_name='amazon_co_purchase_gcn',path='//local/saved_models/')
```

After successfully running the code, you'll have the model represented by the trainer object. At this stage, you're abstracted from all low-level details, with only visibility of the model. To obtain more information about the model as an artifact, call the trainer.info() method.

---

3 To view the algorithms available within this module, you can use the following command: training.models.

In machine learning, trained artifacts cannot be used blindly without evaluation. Therefore, our next step is to evaluate the model.

Evaluation and Model Selection

Now, we will evaluate the model with metrics and select the best-performing model. For this part, we will leverage the `validation` module from PyGraf:

```
from pygraf.validation import ModelEvaluator

# Initialize the model evaluator
evaluator = ModelEvaluator(dataset=processed_data)

# Evaluate the model
evaluation_results = evaluator.evaluate(trainer.model,
                                        metrics=['accuracy', 'f1_score'])
print(f"Evaluation Results: {evaluation_results}")

# Model selection based on evaluation
best_model = evaluator.select_best_model(metric='accuracy')
```

Deployment and Monitoring

Now that we have the module trained and ready for inference (also known as serving), let's demonstrate how to deploy the trained model for this purpose. To do this, we'll utilize two modules from PyGraf: `deployment` and `serving`.

First, let's address deployment. We'll proceed with the following code snippet, which handles the deployment process:

1. From `pygraf.deployment`, import the `ModelDeployer` class.

2. Initialize a `ModelDeployer` object (`deployer`) by specifying the type of the model (`best_model`), and the deployment `environment`. In this example we specify `triton`, which is a common inference server for deploying deep learning models.

3. The next step is to activate the deployment by calling `deploy_to_triton` method on the `deployer` object by specifying the `model_name` and `version`, which in our example are `'amazon_co_purchase_gcn'` and `'1'`, respectively:

```
from pygraf.deployment import ModelDeployer

# Deploy the model using Triton Inference Server
deployer = ModelDeployer(model=best_model, environment='triton')
deployer.deploy_to_triton(model_name='amazon_co_purchase_gcn', version='1')
```

With a deployment, monitoring comes into play. We will leverage the monitoring server by following these steps:

1. From `pygraf.serving`, import the `TritonServer` class.
2. Initialize a `TritonServer` object with one parameter (`url`) that specifies the URL of the Triton Server. The resulting object will be stored in `triton_server`.
3. Now, we can enable monitoring with a specified logging path (`log_path`) by calling the `enable_monitoring` method on the `triton_server` object.

All these steps are illustrated in this code snippet:

```
from pygraf.serving import TritonServer

# Set up monitoring for the deployed model
triton_server = TritonServer(url='triton-server-url')
triton_server.enable_monitoring(log_path='/var/logs/pygraf')
```

With this example, we showcased the end-to-end pipeline of utilizing PyGraf. It involves training a GCN model on the Amazon copurchasing dataset, deploying the model on the Triton Inference Server, and enabling monitoring for performance tracking and operational insights.

Summary

In this chapter, we dove into PyGraf, a high-level library tailored for end-to-end graph learning and serving in an enterprise context. We started by exploring its architecture, features, and how it handles scalable data and graph analytics. Then, we looked deeper into how PyGraph manages, processes, and prepares graph data for learning, focusing on training methodologies and fine-tuning.

Moving on to deployment, we discussed how PyGraf efficiently serves and scales graph models, especially with its integration with NVIDIA Triton Inference Server. We also touched on the importance of privacy preservation, showcasing how PyGraf implements federated learning.

Finally, we wrapped up with a hands-on demo using the Amazon copurchasing dataset, showing how the library streamlines everything from data preprocessing to deployment and giving a practical view of its capabilities. With this conclusion, we highlighted PyGraf's potential for insightful decision-making and operational efficiency in enterprise scenarios. This sets the stage nicely for our Chapter 5, where we'll dive into graph neural networks. Prepare for hands-on learning with practical examples of using PyGraf.

Graph Neural Networks

In this chapter, we will explore *graph neural networks* (GNNs), an essential class of neural-based architectures within our graph learning journey. GNNs are distinctively designed to process graph-structured data, enabling them to leverage the inherent relationships and interconnections embedded within such datasets. Their ability to operate on graph-structured data is different from that of conventional neural networks—which are not inherently designed to interact directly with data that lacks a regular, grid-like structure. Unlike standardized data formats, such as images or sequential text that fit neatly into these traditional models, graph data is inherently complex and irregular, consisting of nodes (or vertices) and edges that represent a diverse range of relationships and attributes.

GNNs have the ability to model and interpret these complex relationships in graph data such as social networks, knowledge graphs, and recommendation systems. Through a process of iterative message passing—in which nodes exchange information and encode these interactions through multiple layers in a manner similar to traditional deep learning models—GNNs are capable of learning detailed and new representations of not just individual nodes and edges but also for the entire graph. The representations derived from GNNs can be used for a wide range of downstream graph learning tasks such as node classification, where each node receives a specific label; link prediction, which forecasts the potential of a relation/connection between two nodes; and graph classification, which categorizes entire graphs. As we progress further into this chapter, we will cover the foundational principles of GNNs, focusing on their core operations of message passing and aggregation. These processes are crucial as they allow GNNs to dynamically learn from and adapt to graph structures. Additionally, we will present practical implementations and real-world use cases, demonstrating the application of these theoretical concepts to tackle complex challenges in graph data analysis. Let's start this exciting journey with a high-level introduction to GNNs.

Introduction to Graph Neural Networks

GNNs are a class of deep neural-based models tailored for conducting various graph learning tasks on data represented as graphs. Unlike traditional neural networks that assume the data to be in regular structures like grids (images) or sequences (text), GNNs thrive on data with complex relationships and irregular formats, such as social networks, molecular structures, or any system that can be represented as nodes (entities) and edges (relationships).[1]

At their core, GNNs leverage the connections between nodes to propagate and update node features, enabling the aggregation of neighborhood information. This process allows GNNs to learn powerful representations that capture both the properties of individual entities and their relationships, as shown in Figure 5-1, which provides a high-level overview of a vanilla GNN architecture. The ability to directly process graph-structured data makes GNNs a powerful tool for a wide spectrum of applications, from recommendation systems to drug discovery.

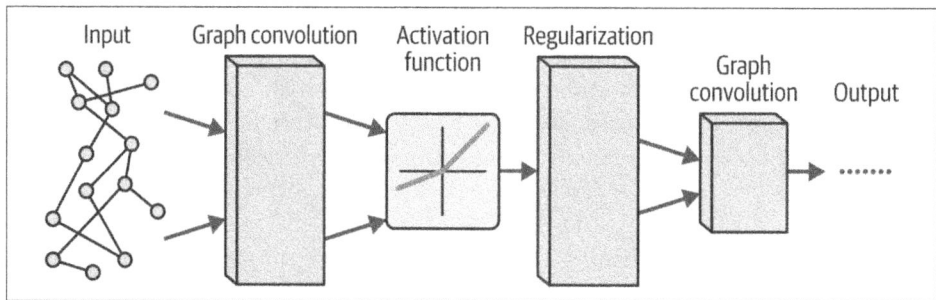

Figure 5-1. High-level overview of a typical GNN architecture

The Significance of GNNs in Graph Learning

Graph structures are a dominant form of data representation in many real-world domains. Traditionally, machine learning on graphs required extensive feature engineering and preprocessing to convert graph data into a format that can work with conventional algorithms. This process not only added computational complexity but also frequently led to the erosion of critical relational information.

GNNs revolutionize this approach by directly operating on graph structures, therefore preserving the inherent topology and connectivity patterns of the graph data.

---

1 Wu, Z. et al. (2020). "A Comprehensive Survey on Graph Neural Networks" (*https://oreil.ly/QgTwl*). *IEEE Transactions on Neural Networks and Learning Systems*, 32(1), 4-24.

Overview of GNN Applications

The unprecedented advantage of GNNs and the ability to operate directly on graph structure has allowed for remarkable advancements in a broad spectrum of fields and applications,[2] demonstrating the technology's impact and potential. Here are some key areas where GNNs have made significant contributions:

Social network analysis

 GNNs can predict user behavior, recommend content, and identify influential users within social networks by analyzing the complex web of social interactions.[3]

Bioinformatics

 In drug discovery and genomics, GNNs analyze molecular structures and genetic networks to identify potential drug candidates and understand genetic diseases.[4]

Recommendation systems

 By representing users and items as nodes in a graph, GNNs can uncover complex patterns of interaction, leading to more accurate and personalized recommendations.[5]

Computer vision

 GNNs are used to process non-Euclidean data, such as 3D shapes and point clouds, enabling advancements in fields like autonomous driving and robotics.[6]

Natural language processing (NLP)

 GNNs enhance traditional NLP tasks by capturing the relational information in language, such as syntactic structures and semantic relationships.[7]

Cybersecurity

 Analyzing network traffic as a graph, GNNs can detect anomalies and predict vulnerabilities, offering a robust tool against cyber threats.

---

2 Wu, Z. et al. "A Comprehensive Survey on Graph Neural Networks" (*https://oreil.ly/QgTwl*).

3 Hamilton, W., Ying, Z., and Leskovec, J. (2017). "Inductive Representation Learning on Large Graphs" (*https://oreil.ly/lLhzd*). *Advances in Neural Information Processing Systems*, 30.

4 Duvenaud, D. K. et al. (2015). "Convolutional Networks on Graphs for Learning Molecular Fingerprints". (*https://oreil.ly/hPox3*) *Advances in Neural Information Processing Systems*, 28.

5 Ying, R. et al. (2018). "Graph Convolutional Neural Networks for Web-Scale Recommender Systems" (*https://oreil.ly/IGTbx*). In *Proceedings of the 24th ACM SIGKDD International Conference on Knowledge Discovery and Data Mining* (July), 974-983.

6 Battaglia, P. et al. (2016). "Interaction Networks for Learning About Objects, Relations and Physics" (*https://oreil.ly/ukmWc*). *Advances in Neural Information Processing Systems*, 29.

7 Yao, L., Mao, C., and Luo, Y. (2019). "Graph Convolutional Networks for Text Classification" (*https://oreil.ly/70DQC*). In *Proceedings of the AAAI Conference on Artificial Intelligence*, 33(1) (July), 7370-7377.

Infrastructure and network analysis

From optimizing logistics to predicting network failures, GNNs analyze the complex relationships in infrastructure networks, improving efficiency and reliability.

This wide-ranging applicability underscores the transformative potential of GNNs across industries and scientific domains, marking them as a pivotal development in the field of AI.

Foundations of GNNs

GNNs represent a significant advancement in the ability to work with data in the form of graphs. This section explores the core principles and methodologies that GNNs utilize in their graph learning process.

GNNs operate on these graphs by applying the principle of message passing, where nodes communicate with their neighbors by exchanging information. Through iterative rounds of message passing, nodes update their states based on their own features and the aggregated information from their neighbors. This process allows GNNs to capture both local structures (the immediate neighborhood of nodes) and global graph properties.

Message passing in GNNs

The concept of message passing in GNNs allows nodes in a graph to update their features by aggregating and processing information from their neighbors, as shown in the simplified example in Figure 5-2, which demonstrates aggregating the features of the neighboring nodes of a node labeled "1." This capability is foundational in enabling GNNs to leverage the graph structure effectively.

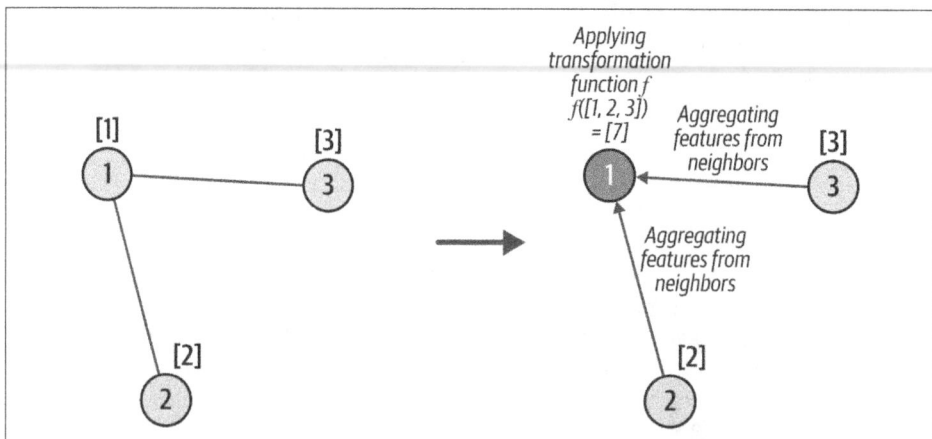

Figure 5-2. Simplified example demonstrating aggregating the features of the neighboring node of a node labeled "1"

This process is mathematically represented as:

$$\mathbf{x}_v^{(\ell+1)} = f_\theta^{(\ell+1)}\Big(\mathbf{x}_v^{(\ell)}, \big\{\mathbf{x}_w^{(\ell)} : w \in \mathcal{N}(v)\big\}\Big)$$

where:

$\mathbf{x}_v^{(\ell)}$

Feature vector v of node at layer l. This vector contains all the information (attributes) that the network knows about node v up to layer l.

$\mathcal{N}(v)$

Set of neighboring nodes of v. These are the nodes directly connected to v via edges in the graph.

$\big\{\mathbf{x}_w^{(\ell)} : w \in \mathcal{N}(v)\big\}$

The set of feature vectors of the neighbors of v at layer l.

$f_\theta^{(\ell+1)}$

A parametric function (often a neural network) that combines the node's features and the aggregated features from its neighboring nodes into a new feature vector for the next layer $l + 1$. This function is typically learned during training.

Learning process

The learning process in GNNs involves several key steps:

1. Feature extraction

Initially, GNNs can work with raw node features or simple attributes that are directly available from the data. Unlike traditional methods that require complex feature engineering at the start, GNNs can use these straightforward inputs effectively. More details on how GNNs drive their features and don't require manual crafting are reviewed in an upcoming section.

2. Message passing

This core step involves nodes aggregating features from their direct neighbors. The aggregation function, which can be as simple as a weighted sum or as complex as a neural network, allows GNNs to dynamically learn how to effectively aggregate features from a specific node's local neighborhood based on the task.

3. Update mechanism

Each node updates its features based on the aggregated information and its current state. This step typically involves neural networks that can learn complex patterns from aggregated features, thus adapting to the specificities of the graph structure.

4. Readout phase

Finally, GNNs use the updated node features to generate embeddings for nodes, edges, or entire graphs. These embeddings could then be used for various graph learning tasks like classification, prediction, or clustering, directly leveraging the learned features without additional engineering.

Graph Convolutional Networks

Graph convolutional networks (GCNs) are a pivotal development in the GNN family, introducing the concept of convolution to graph-structured data.[8] The intuition behind GCNs is to generalize the convolution operation from grid data (such as images) to graphs. This involves aggregating neighbor information to update node representations, analogous to how convolutional filters aggregate local pixel information in images.

The convolution operation

The convolution operation extends this message passing mechanism by not only aggregating information from the neighbors but also including the node's own features in the aggregation. This method ensures that each node's updated feature vector reflects both its own properties and the collective attributes of its neighborhood. The aggregation typically involves a weighted sum where the weights might include the degrees of the nodes involved, or other properties specific to the graph's structure.

The GCN layer operation

Now let's dive into one of the core building blocks of a GCN architecture: the GCN layer. Using matrix notation to present how the features of a node at specific layer $l + 1$ can be derived from the node features at layer l, a single layer of a GCN can be represented as:

$$H^{(l+1)} = f\left(H^{(l)}, A\right)$$

where:

- $H^{(l)}$ is the matrix of a specific node's features at layer l, with $H^{(0)} = X$, where X is a node features matrix. For example, consider a graph with N nodes where each node i has a feature vector/list x_i. These feature vectors for all nodes can be compressed in a $N \times D$ feature matrix X, where N represents the total number of nodes, and D denotes the number of features per node.

---

8 Kipf, T. N., and Welling, M. (2016). "Semi-Supervised Classification with Graph Convolutional Networks" (*https://oreil.ly/DiGC7*). arXiv preprint arXiv:1609.02907.

- A is the adjacency matrix: the structure of the graph is represented using an adjacency matrix A, which is an $N \times N$ matrix. In A, entry A_{ij} is 1 if there is an edge from node i to node j, and 0 otherwise.

Combining these concepts, a single layer of a GCN can be represented as:

$$f\left(H^{(l)}, A\right) = \sigma\left(AH^{(l)}W^{(l)}\right)$$

where:

- $W^{(l)}$ is the weight matrix for layer l, which is learned during training based on the graph structure and the task at hand.
- $\sigma(\cdot)$ is a nonlinear activation function, like tanh or ReLU.

Let's address two limitations with the preceding formulation to come up with the final mathematical formulation of this layer.

First, multiplication with A means that the node's new features would be solely based on its neighbors, neglecting its own attributes. Enforcing self-loops allow a node to consider its own features during the aggregation process.

The second limitation is that the feature aggregation step could scale the features up or down significantly, depending on the number of connections (degree) a node has. High-degree nodes could overshadow the influence of lower-degree nodes, or vice versa. We can eliminate this problem by normalizing the adjacency matrix A with self-loops, let's call it $\widehat{A}$. The purpose of symmetric normalization is to balance the influence of nodes with varying degrees. The normalization is performed using the degree matrix $\widehat{D}$, where $\widehat{D}_i$ is the sum of the ith row of $\widehat{A}$. In practice, symmetric normalization such as the following works better as it helps in maintaining the magnitude of feature vectors through the layers of a GCN:

$$\widetilde{D}^{-1/2}\widetilde{A}\widetilde{D}^{-1/2}$$

This ensures that the feature vectors do not grow too large or diminish to insignificance, which could hinder the learning process.

Combining these two solutions, a single layer of a GCN can be represented as:

$$H^{(1)} = \sigma\left(\widetilde{D}^{-1/2}\widetilde{A}\widetilde{D}^{-1/2}H^{(0)}W^{(0)}\right)$$

Let's strengthen your understanding of this core component of GCN by considering the following simple example.

Simple example

Imagine a very simple graph with three nodes, where node 1 connects to nodes 2 and 3, while nodes 2 and 3 have no direct connection to each other. Each node has a single feature to start. For simplicity, let's consider the identity matrix as the initial features, meaning $H^{(0)} = I_3$ (the 3×3 identity matrix represents 3 nodes with an initial feature value of 1 for simplicity).

The original adjacency matrix A (without self-loops) for this graph is:

$$A = \begin{bmatrix} 0 & 1 & 1 \\ 1 & 0 & 0 \\ 1 & 0 & 0 \end{bmatrix}$$

Adding self-loops, we get $\tilde{A} = A + I_3$:

$$\tilde{A} = \begin{bmatrix} 1 & 1 & 1 \\ 1 & 1 & 0 \\ 1 & 0 & 1 \end{bmatrix}$$

The degree matrix D for A would simply count the connections each node has, but for $\tilde{A}$, we also count the self-loops, resulting in $\tilde{D}$:

$$\tilde{D} = \begin{bmatrix} 3 & 0 & 0 \\ 0 & 2 & 0 \\ 0 & 0 & 2 \end{bmatrix}$$

For the GCN calculation, we need $\tilde{D}^{-1/2}$, which involves taking the inverse square root of each diagonal element:

$$\tilde{D}^{-1/2} = \begin{bmatrix} 1/\sqrt{3} & 0 & 0 \\ 0 & 1/\sqrt{2} & 0 \\ 0 & 0 & 1/\sqrt{2} \end{bmatrix}$$

Assume a simple weight matrix $W^{(0)}$ (for the first layer) that is just 1×1 for simplicity, and we'll keep it as 1 to focus on the transformation process.

Applying the formula:

$$H^{(1)} = \sigma\left(\tilde{D}^{-1/2}\tilde{A}\tilde{D}^{-1/2}H^{(0)}W^{(0)}\right)$$

Substituting the matrices and simplifying (with $W^{(0)} = 1$ and σ as the identity function), we perform the matrix multiplications to update the feature representation. This results in a new feature representation for each node, $H^{(0)}$, which incorporates information from its neighbors and itself, effectively smoothing the features across the graph based on the connectivity.

This example simplifies several steps for clarity, especially around matrix dimensions and the choice of σ. The actual process involves matrix multiplication that considers the dimensions of $H^{(l)}$ and $W^{(l)}$ for feature transformation. The key takeaway is that through this operation, each node updates its features by combining information from its neighboring nodes (and itself), weighted by the connectivity and the learnable parameters in $W^{(l)}$.

This allows the network to learn complex relationships and patterns in the graph structure over multiple layers. Specifically, by aggregating neighbor features, each node's representation becomes a reflection not only of its own attributes but also of its local neighborhood's structure and features. This is crucial for tasks where the context provided by a node's connections can significantly impact the output, such as classifying nodes based on their role in a social network or identifying clusters of similar nodes within a larger graph.

Also, the choice of the activation function, σ, in the GCN formulation is pivotal. After each layer's linear transformations (via the weight matrices and the adjacency-based aggregation), the activation function introduces nonlinearity into the model. This nonlinearity is essential for the network to model and learn complex and nonlinear relationships in the data.

Now let's understand the impact of transitioning from the traditional graph learning techniques (some of which we covered in Chapter 3) and understand how GNNs and particularly GCNs help in removing most of the complexities around crafting features.

Transition from Traditional Graph Learning to GCNs

In traditional graph learning approaches, a significant amount of effort is dedicated to feature engineering. This process involves crafting features manually from graph data, which can be both complex and time-consuming. These features might include node degree, clustering coefficients, or more sophisticated structures such as graphlets. The quality and effectiveness of these manually engineered features heavily depend on domain expertise and the specificities of the task at hand.

GCNs, on the other hand, revolutionize this approach by learning to extract features automatically. This capability of GCNs to learn from raw data mitigates the need for complex feature engineering tasks, which hugely depend on the domain understanding of the data—making them highly adaptable and efficient for a broad range of applications. By leveraging the inherent structure of the graph and node attributes, GCNs apply convolution operations that aggregate and transform features from a node's local neighborhood.

How GCNs Simplify Feature Engineering

GCNs simplify the feature extraction process through their unique architecture, which integrates the following aspects:

Local neighborhood aggregation
> Each layer of a GCN aggregates features from the immediate neighbors of a node, blending local information to learn more comprehensive node representations.

Layered transformation
> Through successive layers, these features are transformed, enabling the model to learn complex patterns over larger neighborhoods incrementally.

End-to-end learning
> The entire process from raw input features to task-specific outputs is learned end-to-end without the need for manual feature selection or transformation.

This approach not only enhances the learning capability of the model but also significantly reduces the preprocessing steps required in traditional methods. The automation of feature learning allows GCNs to focus on higher-level patterns in the data, which can be crucial for tasks such as community detection, node classification, and link/relation prediction.

Now that we understand the core components of GCNs as well as their advantages when operating on graph structures, let's dive into some practical applications. We'll use one of the most popular open source libraries and encapsulate and abstract key details through the PyGraf library API interface for quick prototyping and embedded best practices that can help you easily navigate the graph journey and apply it to your company.

Hands-on E2E Example Using PyG and the PyGraf Interface

In this section we are going to introduce one of the widely used open source libraries developed by researchers in Stanford, as well as go through a couple of examples that illustrate how to build GCN architectures and evaluate them on validation and held-out datasets.

PyG: Karate Club Example

PyG is a library built on top of PyTorch that provides easy-to-use interfaces and tools for working with graph structured data. To utilize this library, you'll need to install several dependencies that enable the manipulation of graph data and the application of neural network models on graphs. Following is a step-by-step guide to installing PyG for PyTorch version 1.11.0+cu113.

PyG installation

Before installing the required packages, it's helpful to set an environment variable to specify the version of PyTorch you're using. This helps in fetching the correct versions of the dependencies that are compatible with your PyTorch installation:

```
import os
import torch
os.environ['TORCH'] = torch.__version__
print(torch.__version__)
```

This code sets the TORCH environment variable to your installed PyTorch version.

Next, we need to install `torch-scatter`, which is a dependency that provides support for scatter and segment operations that are often required in GNN computations, such as summing node features within a neighborhood:

```
!pip install -q torch-scatter -f https://data.pyg.org/whl/torch-${TORCH}.html
```

Then we need to install `torch-sparse`, which provides efficient sparse matrix operations. These matrix operations are crucial for handling large and sparse graphs typically encountered in graph neural networks:

```
!pip install -q torch-sparse -f https://data.pyg.org/whl/torch-${TORCH}.html
```

Finally, install PyG itself. This library includes a variety of graph neural network layers and utility functions that make it easier to develop GNN models:

```
!pip install -q git+https://github.com/pyg-team/pytorch_geometric.git
```

PyG graph data representation

Let's further our understanding of PyG and explore the world of GNNs using a basic graph-structured example. We'll start by examining Zachary's Karate Club network, a well-known graph representation. This network describes social interaction among 34 members of a karate club and highlights connections between club members who interacted or have some relationship outside of the club. Here, our focus is on identifying communities that arise from the members' interactions.

PyG provides easy access to various datasets via its `datasets` subpackage:

```
from torch_geometric.datasets import KarateClub
# Load the Karate Club dataset
dataset = KarateClub()
print(f'Graph Dataset Object: {dataset}:')
print(f'Number of graphs: {len(dataset)}')
print(f'Number of classes: {dataset.num_classes}')
print(f'Number of features: {dataset.num_features}')
```

Output:

```
Dataset: KarateClub():
Number of graphs: 1
Number of classes: 4
Number of features: 34
```

After initializing the Karate Club dataset, we can first inspect some of its key properties. It contains a single graph with each node characterized by a 34D feature vector, uniquely representing the karate club members. Another important property is that the graph comprises four distinct classes, representing the community to which each node belongs.

Now, let's look closely at the underlying representation of the graph object:

```
# Analyze the dataset
karate_data = dataset[0]

print(karate_data)

# Gather some statistics about the graph
print(f'Number of nodes: { karate_data.num_nodes}')
print(f'Number of edges: { karate_data.num_edges}')
print(f'Average node degree: { karate_data.num_edges /
                              karate_data.num_nodes:.2f}')
print(f'Number of training nodes: { karate_data.train_mask.sum()}')
print(f'Training node label rate: {int(karate_data.train_mask.sum()) /
                              karate_data.num_nodes:.2f}')
print(f'Has isolated nodes: { karate_data.has_isolated_nodes()}')
print(f'Has self-loops: { karate_data.has_self_loops()}')
print(f'Is undirected: { karate_data.is_undirected()}')
```

Output:

```
Data(x=[34, 34], edge_index=[2, 156], y=[34], train_mask=[34])
Number of nodes: 34
Number of edges: 156
Average node degree: 4.59
Number of training nodes: 4
Training node label rate: 0.12
Has isolated nodes: False
Has self-loops: False
Is undirected: True
```

Each PyG graph is encapsulated within a single Data object, which holds all the necessary information for its representation. By calling `print(karate_data)`, we can obtain a concise summary of the object's attributes and their shapes:

```
Data(edge_index=[2, 156], x=[34, 34], y=[34], train_mask=[34])
```

The graph object encompasses four key properties or attributes:

`edge_index`
> This attribute holds the connectivity information of the graph. It is represented by a tuple of source and destination node indices for each edge, detailing the links between nodes.

`x`
> This represents the feature vectors of the nodes. Each of the 34 nodes in the dataset is characterized by a 34-dimensional feature vector, encapsulating the node-specific data.

`y`
> This attribute assigns a label to each node, categorizing every node into one of several predefined classes.

`train_mask`
> This indicates which nodes have known community affiliations. Currently, the dataset includes ground-truth labels for only four nodes—one for each community—which necessitates the task of inferring the community assignments for the remaining nodes.

Additionally, the graph object includes several utility functions that provide essential insights into the graph's structure. These functions allow us to identify isolated nodes (those without any connections), detect self-loops (edges that connect a node to itself), and verify if the graph is undirected.

Let's explore the `edge_index` property of the Karate Club graph in more detail:

```
# Inspect the edge_index property for graph connectivity
edge_index = karate_data.edge_index

print('Edge Index - List of graph connections:')
print(edge_index.t())
```

Output:

```
Edge Index - List of graph connections:

tensor([[ 0,  1],
        [ 0,  2],
        [ 0,  3],
        [ 0,  4],
        ...
```

```
...
[33, 31],
[33, 32]])
```

Looking at edge_index, we can further understand how PyG represents graph connectivity under the hood. In this representation we have a tuple of two node indices for each edge. The first value represents the index of the source node, and the second value represents the index of the destination node of an edge. This representation, known as *Coordinate Format* (COO), was mainly invented to help in representing sparse matrices where the majority of values are zeros.

In case of undirected graphs, PyG represents them as a special case of directed graphs where we'll have a reversed edge for every tuple in the edge_index. For visualization purposes, we convert the graph data into the NetworkX format, enabling us to use its extensive graph visualization functionality:

```
# Convert to NetworkX format for visualization
from torch_geometric.utils import to_networkx

karate_nx_graph = to_networkx(karate_data, to_undirected=True)
```

Now let's define a function that uses the draw_networkx module of the networkx library to visualize this graph:

```
import networkx as nx
import matplotlib.pyplot as plt

def visualize_graph(Graph, color):
    plt.figure(figsize=(7,7))
    plt.xticks([])
    plt.yticks([])
    nx.draw_networkx(Graph, pos=nx.spring_layout(Graph, seed=42),
                     with_labels=False, node_color=color, cmap="Set2")
    plt.show()
```

Now let's call this function on the converted networkx graph format karate_nx_graph. The output of this operation is visually represented in Figure 5-3:

```
visualize_graph(karate_nx_graph, color= karate_data.y)
```

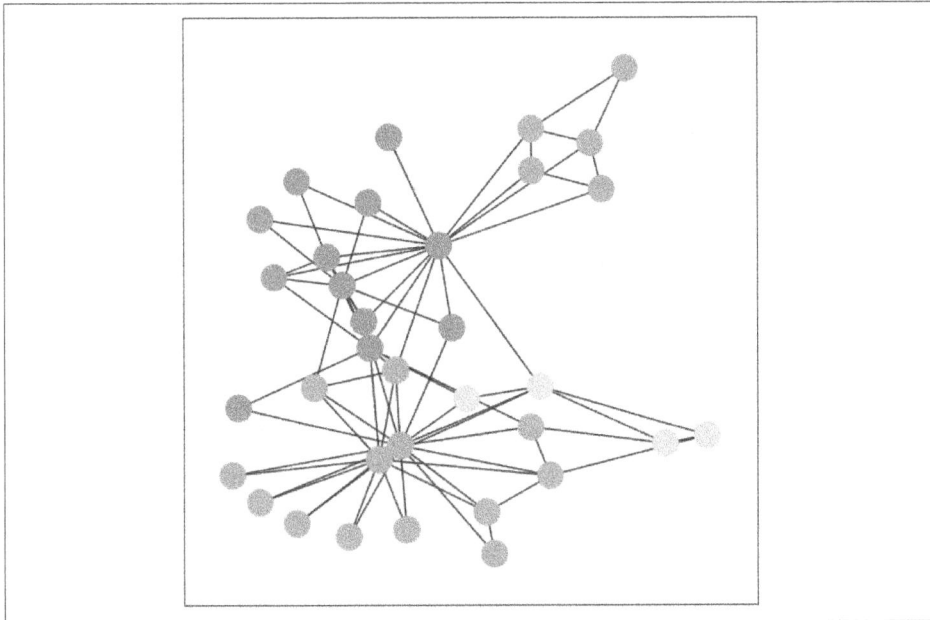

Figure 5-3. Graph visualization of Karate Club graph data

PyG GCN API interface

Now that we've learned about PyG's graph data handling, let's proceed to implement our first GNN using the GCN layer for the Karate Club graph data. The equation that we mentioned earlier for the GCN layer uses the matrix notation to represent the update operation for the entire graph's node features at once.

Rather than adopting a holistic perspective that considers the simultaneous updating of features across all nodes in the graph, let's focus on the detailed process of how the features of an individual node are updated within a GCN layer. The node-specific update equation will be defined as:

$$\mathbf{x}_v^{(\ell + 1)} = \mathbf{W}^{(\ell + 1)} \Sigma_{w \in \mathcal{N}(v) \cup \{v\}} \frac{1}{c_{w,v}} \cdot \mathbf{x}_w^{(\ell)}$$

where:

Node-specific update
> This equation focuses on the update of the feature vector for a specific node v in the graph. It explains how the new features $\mathbf{x}_v^{(\ell + 1)}$ for node v at layer $\ell + 1$ are computed.

Aggregation

The sum $\Sigma_{w \in \mathcal{N}(v) \cup \{v\}}$ indicates that the features of node v and its neighbors w are aggregated. The set $\mathcal{N}(v)$ includes all neighbors of v, and $\{v\}$ ensures that the node's own features are also included (self-loop).

Normalization

The term $\frac{1}{c_{w,v}}$ is a normalization factor applied to the features of each neighbor w and the node itself before aggregation. This normalization typically depends on the degrees of the nodes involved. $c_{w,v}$ could, for instance, be $\frac{1}{\sqrt{d_v d_w}}$ where d_v and d_w are the degrees of nodes v and w, respectively.

Weight matrix

$\mathbf{W}^{(\ell+1)}$ is a learnable weight matrix of shape [num_output_features, num_input_features] that is specific to layer $\ell + 1$ that transforms the aggregated feature vector.

In PyG, the essential GCN layer is implemented as GCNConv. This layer can be easily utilized by providing it with two key inputs: the node feature representation, which encapsulates the attributes of each node, and the edge_index, which details the graph's connectivity in COO format.

Now, we're prepared to construct the first GNN by defining the network architecture within a torch.nn.Module class. In the following example, we define a GNN architecture tailored for the Karate Club dataset with its 34-dimensional feature vector and 4 classes. This GNN architecture utilizes three GCN layers followed by a classifier, specifically designed to analyze and classify nodes into one of these 4 classes/communities.

Let's explain the architecture choices we have made in detail:

- Architecture overview

  — Three GCN layers: Sequential graph convolutional layers that transform node features, capturing local neighborhood structures progressively.

  — First layer: Takes the 34-dimensional input features and reduces them to 4 features, integrating information from each node's immediate neighbors.

  — Second and third layers: Further refine and compress the node features, preparing them for classification, with each layer outputting 4 and then 2 features respectively.

  — Classifier: A linear transformation layer that maps the final node embeddings to the number of classes (4 communities). This layer is crucial for predicting the community membership of each node based on its learned features.

- Initialization method (__init__)

  — Layer setup: Initializes the graph convolutional layers and the classifier.

  — GCNConv(dataset.num_features, 4): Configures the first GCN layer to accept the initial node features.

  — GCNConv(4, 4) and GCNConv(4, 2): Sequential layers for feature transformation.

  — Linear(2, dataset.num_classes): Final classifier that outputs predictions for the 4 classes.

- Forward method (forward)

  — Data flow: Defines how data passes through the network, including activation functions:

  — Input features and graph structure: Accepts node features and the graph connectivity structure (edge_index).

  — Activation functions: Each GCNConv layer is followed by a tanh activation function to introduce nonlinearity, enhancing the network's ability to learn complex patterns.

  — Output: The method returns both the logits (class scores before softmax) from the classifier and the final node embeddings, providing insights into node classification and the learned feature representations.

The code is as follows:

```
import torch
from torch_geometric.nn import GCNConv
from torch.nn import Linear


class GCN(torch.nn.Module):
    def __init__(self):
        super().__init__()
        torch.manual_seed(1234)
        self.conv1 = GCNConv(dataset.num_features, 4)
        self.conv2 = GCNConv(4, 4)
        self.conv3 = GCNConv(4, 2)
        self.classifier = Linear(2, dataset.num_classes)

    def forward(self, node_features, edge_index):
        node_embeddings = self.conv1(node_features, edge_index)
        node_embeddings = node_embeddings.tanh()
        node_embeddings = self.conv2(node_embeddings, edge_index)
        node_embeddings = node_embeddings.tanh()
        node_embeddings = self.conv3(node_embeddings, edge_index)
        node_embeddings = node_embeddings.tanh()  # Final GNN embedding space.
```

```
    # last layer will be the linear classifier
    out = self.classifier(h)

    return out, node_embeddings


# Initialize and print the model
model = GCN()
print(model)
```

Output:

```
GCN(
  (conv1): GCNConv(34, 4)
  (conv2): GCNConv(4, 4)
  (conv3): GCNConv(4, 2)
  (classifier): Linear(in_features=2, out_features=4, bias=True)
)
```

Now that we have defined our GCN architecture, let's embed the dataset using the untrained model and see if we can draw anything interesting based on this.

Embedding the Karate Club network

Now that we have the untrained GNN-generated embeddings, the next step is to visualize them. We'll input two parameters to the model: the initial node features represented by the embeddings param, and the graph connectivity structure edge_index. Afterwards, we'll call the function visualize_embedding to visualize its projected 2D embedding. Let's define a method called visualize_embedding, which will help to visualize the embeddings in two-dimensional space:

```
# Function to visualize node embeddings
def visualize_embeddings(embeddings, colors, current_epoch=None,
                         current_loss=None):
    plt.figure(figsize=(7,7))
    plt.axis('off')
    embeddings = embeddings.detach().cpu().numpy()
    plt.scatter(embeddings[:, 0], embeddings[:, 1], s=140, c=colors, cmap="Set2")
    if current_epoch is not None and current_loss is not None:
        plt.xlabel(f'Epoch: {current_epoch}, Loss: {current_loss:.4f}',
                   fontsize=16)
    plt.show()
```

Now let's call this method with an untrained model and color the dots as per the classes we have in the Karate Club dataset:

```
model = GCN()

_, node_embeddings = model(karate_data.x, karate_data.edge_index)
print(f'Embedding shape: {list(node_embeddings.shape)}')

visualize_embedding(node_embeddings, color=karate_data.y)
```

Output:

```
Embedding shape: [34, 2]
```

It's quite remarkable that even before we start training our model, it can already produce node embeddings that closely reflect the community structure of the graph, as shown in Figure 5-4.

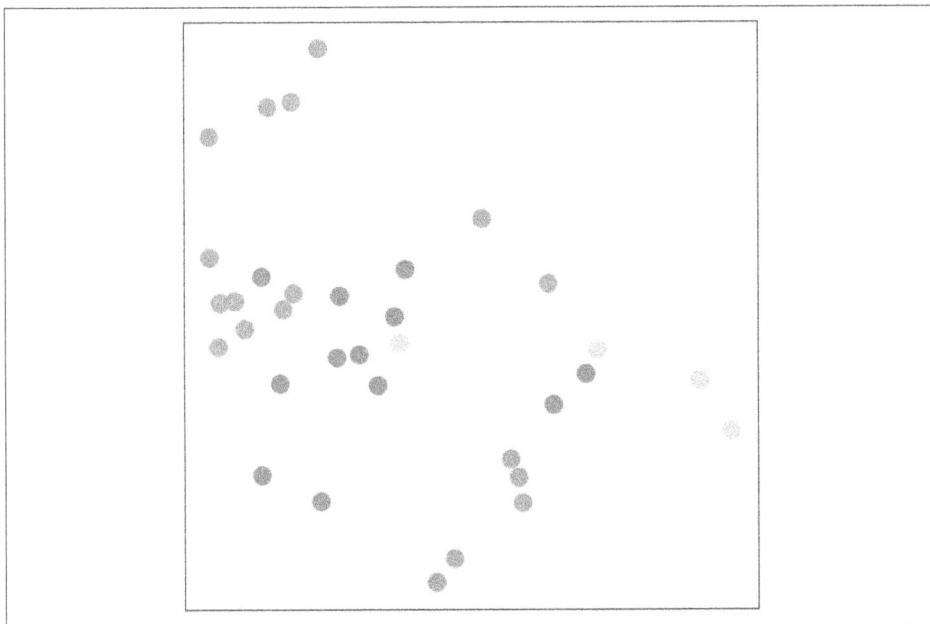

Figure 5-4. Visualization of the 2D projection of embeddings from an untrained GCN model, based on randomly initialized model parameters

This means that nodes belonging to the same community tend to cluster together in the embedding space, despite the model's weights being randomly initialized and no training having taken place yet! This demonstrates the fact that GNNs possess a strong *inductive bias* (*https://oreil.ly/vLEsv*), which naturally encourages the model to produce comparable embeddings for nodes that are close to one another in the graph—effectively capturing the inherent structure of the graph data right from the start. Let's explore how these initial node embeddings could be refined further to better represent the community structure of the graph after the training process and adjusting the randomly initialized network parameters.

Our model is designed to be fully differentiable and parameterizable, which allows us to incorporate specific labels, train the model, and then observe how the node embeddings adapt based on this training. We utilize a semi-supervised or transductive learning approach, where the model is trained using just one labeled node per class but benefits from the entire graph structure. This method leverages the comprehensive connectivity information contained within the graph to enhance learning, even from a minimal set of labeled examples.

Let's go through the process of training the GCN model defined here. Training any neural-based model mainly requires two things: a loss function (in this case we use CrossEntropyLoss) and initialization of a stochastic gradient optimizer (in this case we use the Adam optimizer).

During the training phase, PyG executes multiple optimization cycles, each consisting of a forward pass to calculate predictions and a backward pass to determine the gradients of the GCN model parameters relative to the computed loss. This sequence facilitates the adjustment of model parameters to minimize the loss over iterations. For a deeper understanding of this process, the PyTorch documentation (*https://oreil.ly/8ghYe*) provides a comprehensive explanation of how these operations contribute to the model's learning.

We can execute the semi-supervised learning process using:

```
loss = criterion(out[karate_data.train_mask],
                 karate_data.y[karate_data.train_mask])
```

While node embeddings are computed for all nodes in the graph, the loss calculation is selectively performed using only those nodes designated for training. This selective approach is implemented by filtering the classifier's output and the corresponding ground-truth labels to include only those nodes identified by karate_data.train_mask. This method ensures that the training process focuses on a specific subset of the graph, optimizing the model based on the available labeled data.

In the following code snippet, we define a training loop for GCN tailored to process and learn from our graph data. This setup involves initializing the model, setting up a loss criterion and optimizer, defining the training function, and executing the training process across multiple epochs:

Training setup
- Model initialization: Instantiates the GCN model, which is structured to handle node feature transformations and classification tasks within graphs.

- Loss criterion and optimizer:

  CrossEntropyLoss: Utilized to measure the discrepancy between the predicted class probabilities (from the GCN model) and the actuals.

  Adam optimizer: Chosen for its adaptive learning rate capabilities, which helps to optimize the GCN model parameters effectively. The learning rate is set to 0.01.

Training function (train) flow
- Zero gradients: Clears old gradients from the previous step, which is necessary to prevent accumulation of gradient values across epochs.

- Model forward pass: Computes the logits (out) and node embeddings (h) by passing node features (karate_data.x) and the graph structure (karate_data.edge_index) through the model.

- Loss computation: Calculates the loss using only the training nodes (nodes for which the training mask is true), focusing the learning process on a subset of the graph's nodes.

- Backpropagation: The gradients are computed with respect to the loss and back propagated through the model.

- Optimizer step: Updates and optimizes the model parameters as per the calculated gradients.

Training loop
- Execution over epochs:

The model undergoes training for 401 epochs, with the train function being called each epoch to perform the training step described earlier.

- Visualization and timing:

Every 10 epochs, the embedding of nodes (h) is visualized using the visualize_embedding function, which plots the 2D embedding space colored by the node's community/class.

A pause (time.sleep(0.3)) is introduced to slow down the loop, potentially to allow time for visualizations to be generated and viewed:

```python
import time

model = GCN()
criterion = torch.nn.CrossEntropyLoss()  # Define loss criterion.
# Define optimizer.
optimizer = torch.optim.Adam(model.parameters(), lr=0.01)

def train(data):
    optimizer.zero_grad()  # Clear gradients.
    out, node_embeddings = model(karate_data.x, karate_data.edge_index)

    # Compute the loss solely based on the training nodes.
    loss = criterion(out[karate_data.train_mask],
                    karate_data.y[karate_data.train_mask])
    loss.backward()  # Derive gradients.
    optimizer.step()  # Update parameters based on gradients.
    return loss, node_embeddings

for epoch in range(401):
    loss, node_embeddings = train(karate_data)
    if epoch % 10 == 0:
        visualize_embedding(node_embeddings, karatae_data.y, epoch, loss)
        time.sleep(0.3)
```

As you can see in Figure 5-5, which shows the embedding visualization for different epochs during the training process, the visualization from epoch 400 demonstrates that the 3-layer GCN network architecture achieved very good separation of the four communities and accurately classified most of the nodes.

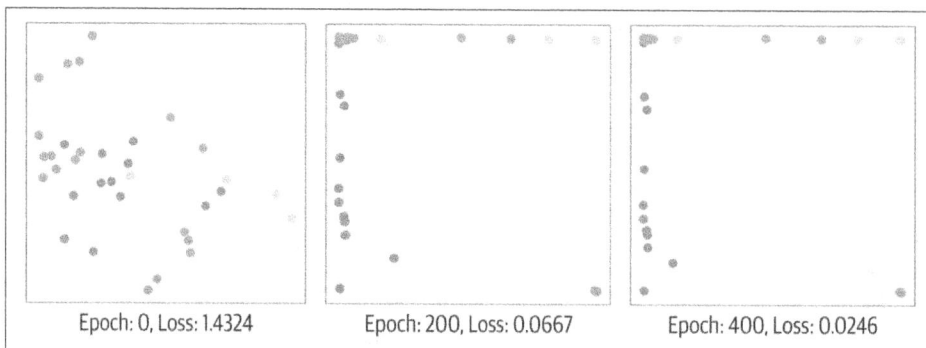

| Epoch: 0, Loss: 1.4324 | Epoch: 200, Loss: 0.0667 | Epoch: 400, Loss: 0.0246 |

Figure 5-5. Visualization of the 2D projection of embeddings for different epochs during the model training process

As you may have observed, we accomplished this with minimal code, largely owing to the PyG library's efficient handling of data management and GNN implementations. Going through this simple Karate Club network helped in understanding the building blocks of a GCN architecture as well as building one using PyG library. Next up, we'll go through a more sophisticated example using the Cora dataset and see how to evaluate and test the model based on a held-out test set.

Cora Node Classification

This example will guide you on how to utilize GNNs for node classification tasks. The dataset includes the ground-truth labels for only a limited subset of nodes, and our objective is to infer the labels for all the remaining nodes (transductive learning).

Data preparation

The structure of the Cora dataset is quite like the Karate Club network previously discussed. It contains 2,708 nodes and 10,556 edges, resulting in an average node degree of 3.9. The dataset includes ground-truth classifications for 140 nodes, with 20 nodes per class, which equates to a training node label rate of just 5%. This setup illustrates the limited labeled data available for training, typical of many real-world scenarios.

In contrast to Zachary's Karate Club, this graph holds the additional attributes val_mask and test_mask, which denote which nodes should be used for validation and testing. Furthermore, we make use of data transformations via transform= NormalizeFeatures(). Transforms can be used to modify your input data before inputting them into a neural network, e.g., for normalization of data augmentation. Here, we row-normalize the bag-of-words input feature vectors:

```
from torch_geometric.datasets import Planetoid
from torch_geometric.transforms import NormalizeFeatures

dataset = Planetoid(root='data/Planetoid', name='Cora',
                    transform=NormalizeFeatures())

print()
print(f'Dataset: {dataset}:')
print(f'Number of graphs: {len(dataset)}')
print(f'Number of classes: {dataset.num_classes}')
print(f'Number of features: {dataset.num_features}')


# Get the first graph object.
cora_data = dataset[0]

print(cora_data)

# Gather some statistics about the graph.
print(f'Number of nodes: {cora_data.num_nodes}')
print(f'Number of edges: {cora_data.num_edges}')
print(f'Average node degree: {cora_data.num_edges / cora_data.num_nodes:.2f}')
print(f'Number of training nodes: {cora_data.train_mask.sum()}')
print(f'Training node label rate: {int(cora_data.train_mask.sum()) /
                                   cora_data.num_nodes:.2f}')
print(f'Has isolated nodes: {cora_data.has_isolated_nodes()}')
print(f'Has self-loops: {cora_data.has_self_loops()}')
print(f'Is undirected: {cora_data.is_undirected()}')
```

Output:

```
Downloading...
Processing...
Done!

Dataset: Cora():
Number of graphs: 1
Number of classes: 7
Number of features: 1433

Data(x=[2708, 1433], edge_index=[2, 10556], y=[2708], train_mask=[2708],
     val_mask=[2708], test_mask=[2708])
Number of nodes: 2708
Number of edges: 10556
Average node degree: 3.90
Number of training nodes: 140
Training node label rate: 0.05
Has isolated nodes: False
Has self-loops: False
Is undirected: True
```

GCN model architecture

Building upon the first Karate Club example of this chapter, we'll use the GCNConv module for the GCN layers:

```
from torch_geometric.nn import GCNConv

# Define a graph convolutional network (GCN) model
class GCN(torch.nn.Module):
    def __init__(self, hidden_channels):
        super().__init__()
        torch.manual_seed(1234567)
        self.conv1 = GCNConv(dataset.num_features, hidden_channels)
        self.conv2 = GCNConv(hidden_channels, dataset.num_classes)

    def forward(self, x, edge_index):
        x = self.conv1(x, edge_index)
        x = x.relu()
        x = F.dropout(x, p=0.5, training=self.training)
        x = self.conv2(x, edge_index)
        return x


# Instantiate the GCN model
model = GCN(hidden_channels=16)
print(model)
```

Output:

```
GCN(
  (conv1): GCNConv(1433, 16)
  (conv2): GCNConv(16, 7)
)
```

Embedding the Cora network

As we did for the Karate Club example, let's visualize the node embeddings of the GCN network without any training and only rely on the randomly generated parameters of the model.

For visualization, we use a technique called t-distributed stochastic neighbor embedding (t-SNE) (*https://oreil.ly/e9lV-*) to embed the 7D node embeddings onto a 2D plane. Let's first define the visualize function:

```
def visualize(embeddings, color):
    z = TSNE(n_components=2).fit_transform(embeddings.detach().cpu().numpy())

    plt.figure(figsize=(10,10))
    plt.xticks([])
    plt.yticks([])

    plt.scatter(z[:, 0], z[:, 1], s=70, c=color, cmap="Set2")
    plt.show()
```

Now let's visualize the embeddings of the untrained model, as shown in Figure 5-6:

```
model = GCN(hidden_channels=16)
model.eval()

embeddings = model(data.x, data.edge_index)
visualize(embeddings, color=cora_data.y)
```

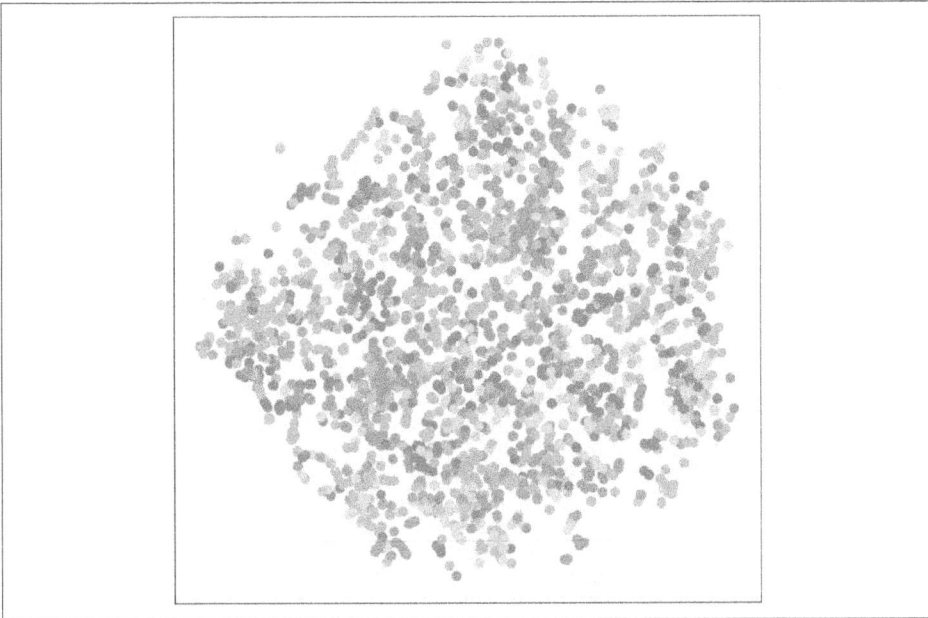

Figure 5-6. Visualization of the 2D projection of embeddings of the untrained GCN model

Model training and evaluation

Now let's try to do a better job by training the GCN model. Unlike the Karate Club example, the model's accuracy is evaluated on a test set. Also, this example will integrate a slightly different optimization setup by including one of the parameters of Adam optimizer, called *weight decay*, which is a regularization technique used to prevent overfitting. It leads to better generalization by penalizing larger weights, thereby encouraging the model to learn simpler patterns that are presumably more generalizable:

```
model = GCN(hidden_channels=16)

optimizer = torch.optim.Adam(model.parameters(), lr=0.01, weight_decay=5e-4)
criterion = torch.nn.CrossEntropyLoss()


# Define the training procedure
```

```
def train():
    model.train()
    optimizer.zero_grad()
    out = model(cora_data.x, cora_data.edge_index)
    loss = criterion(out[cora_data.train_mask],
                     cora_data.y[cora_data.train_mask])
    loss.backward()
    optimizer.step()
    return loss

def evaluate(mask):
    model.eval()
    with torch.no_grad():
        out = model(cora_data.x, cora_data.edge_index)
        pred = out.argmax(dim=1)
        correct = pred[mask] == cora_data.y[mask]
        acc = int(correct.sum()) / int(mask.sum())
    return acc

best_val_acc = 0
best_model_state = None

for epoch in range(1, 101):
    train_loss = train()
    val_acc = evaluate(cora_data.val_mask)
    if val_acc > best_val_acc:
        best_val_acc = val_acc
        best_model_state = model.state_dict()
    print(f'Epoch: {epoch:03d}, Loss: {train_loss:.4f}, Val Acc: {val_acc:.4f}')
```

Output:

```
Epoch: 001, Loss: 1.9463, Val Acc: 0.2880
Epoch: 002, Loss: 1.9409, Val Acc: 0.2580
Epoch: 003, Loss: 1.9343, Val Acc: 0.2560
...
Epoch: 098, Loss: 0.5989, Val Acc: 0.7800
Epoch: 099, Loss: 0.6021, Val Acc: 0.7720
Epoch: 100, Loss: 0.5799, Val Acc: 0.7780
```

Model testing

After training the model, we can check its test accuracy:

```
# Load the best model state
model.load_state_dict(best_model_state)
test_acc = evaluate(cora_data.test_mask)
print(f'Test Accuracy: {test_acc:.4f}')
```

Output:

```
Test Accuracy: 0.8150
```

We can also verify that by once again looking at the output embeddings of our trained model, which now produces a far better clustering of nodes of the same category:

```
model.eval()

# Visualize the embeddings
embeddings = model(cora_data.x, cora_data.edge_index)
visualize(embeddings, color= cora_data.y)
```

Figure 5-7 presents a significantly improved representation of the node embeddings, showing a more accurate representation of the community structure within the graph.

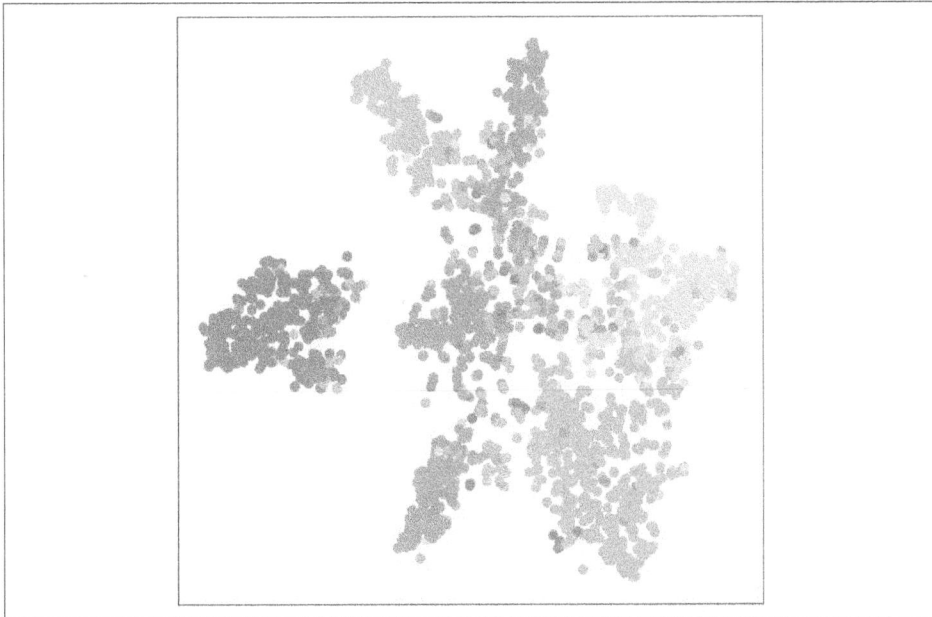

Figure 5-7. Visualization of the 2D projection of embeddings of the trained GCN model

Now that we've learned how to build our GCN model using PyG, let's explore how we can utilize the GCN model from the PyGraf library, which offers a higher level of abstraction on top of PyG.

PyGraf API Interface

In this section, we will demonstrate the use of the PyGraf API interface to build a comprehensive end-to-end training and evaluation pipeline for graph neural networks. The code is organized into several distinct sections, each highlighting a crucial step in constructing this pipeline.

Initializing modules and dependencies

First, we import the necessary modules from PyGraf along with other essential Python libraries:

```
# Import necessary modules from pygraf
from pygraf.graph_models import GCN
from pygraf.graph_utils import visualize_embeddings
# Assuming data handling is part of pygraf
from pygraf.data_loader import DataLoader
from pygraf.trainer import Trainer
from pygraf.evaluator import Evaluator

import torch
```

Data loading and preprocessing

We initialize the `DataLoader` module, which simplifies the task of loading and optionally preprocessing graph data:

```
# Initialize DataLoader
# Users can specify the dataset, where it's stored,
# and any transformations to apply to the features.
data_loader = DataLoader(dataset_name='Cora', root='data',
                         feature_transforms=None)

# Retrieve the graph data, number of classes, and feature counts
data, num_classes, num_features = data_loader.get_data()
```

Model initialization

With the data loaded, we proceed to initialize the GCN model from PyGraf's `model` module. This setup allows users to switch between different models or adjust model parameters such as the number of layers, hidden channels, and classes in order to explore various architectures or optimize performance:

```
# Initialize the GCN model
model = GCN(num_features=num_features, hidden_channels=16,
            num_classes=num_classes)
print("Initialized Model:", model)
```

Setting up the training components

Next, we configure the optimizer and loss criterion, providing flexibility to experiment with different optimization techniques and loss functions:

```
# Set up optimizer and loss criterion for training
optimizer = torch.optim.Adam(model.parameters(), lr=0.01, weight_decay=5e-4)
criterion = torch.nn.CrossEntropyLoss()
```

Training logic

We then initialize the `Trainer`, which encapsulates the training logic, allowing for easy adjustments without altering the core model code:

```
# Initialize the Trainer
trainer = Trainer(model=model, optimizer=optimizer, criterion=criterion)
```

The training loop is straightforward, offering detailed insights into the process. Here, validation loss and accuracy are printed to monitor progress:

```
# Training loop
for epoch in range(100):
    loss = trainer.train(data)
    val_acc = Evaluator.evaluate(model, data, data.val_mask)
    print(f'Epoch {epoch+1}, Loss: {loss:.4f}, Val Acc: {val_acc:.4f}')
```

Model evaluation

Towards the end of the pipeline, we evaluate the model using a held-out test set from the Cora dataset:

```
# Evaluate the model using the test set
test_acc = Evaluator.evaluate(model, data, data.test_mask)
print(f'Test Accuracy: {test_acc:.4f}')
```

Visualization of embeddings

Finally, we visualize the embeddings produced by the trained model to assess how well it has learned to cluster different nodes:

```
# Visualize the output embeddings
embeddings = model(data.x, data.edge_index)
visualize_embeddings(embeddings, data.y, title='GNN Embeddings from pygraf')
```

This comprehensive and high-level E2E setup provided by the PyGraf API facilitates efficient and effective training and analysis of graph neural network models, streamlining the development and experimentation process and making it easy to quickly prototype with different architecture params as well as optimization methods.

In Chapter 6, you will unlock the full potential of PyGraf, where users can easily try out different GNN architectures and design flavors, which can help guide them on choosing the right architecture for their use case.

Limitations of GCN-Based Architecture

GCNs have significantly advanced the field of graph learning, providing effective means to handle graph-structured data. Despite their successes, several inherent limitations exist within the standard GCN architecture, leading to the development of various other GNNs to address these issues. Here are the primary limitations of GCN and the motivations for other GNN variations:

Oversmoothing

As the number of layers in a GCN increases, node features tend to converge to similar values, a phenomenon known as oversmoothing. This makes it challenging for the model to distinguish between nodes in deeper networks, leading to a loss of useful information and a decrease in performance. This issue has prompted the development of architectures designed to limit the depth of the network or to introduce mechanisms to retain node-specific information across layers.

Limited scope of receptive field

Standard GCNs aggregate information from a node's immediate neighbors. With increasing layers, although the receptive field grows, it remains inherently limited by the number of layers. This can be insufficient for capturing wider graph structures in large graphs or for tasks requiring global graph properties. Variations like *graph attention networks* (GATs) allow dynamic weighting of neighbor contributions, expanding the effective scope dynamically based on the task's requirements.

Scalability issues

GCNs involve matrix multiplications that are computationally expensive and not well-suited for very large graphs due to quadratic growth in memory and computational requirements with respect to the number of nodes and edges. This limitation has led to the development of more scalable GNN architectures—such as GraphSAGE—which sample a fixed number of neighbors, thereby reducing the computational load.

Handling of directed graphs

GCNs typically treat edges as undirected, which can be a limitation when the direction of edges carries important semantic information (e.g., in citation networks where direction indicates the flow of information). This has motivated the creation of directional GNNs that can explicitly account for edge directionality in their convolutional processes.

Homophily assumption

GCNs assume that connected nodes are likely to belong to the same class (homophily). This assumption does not hold in heterophilic graphs, where connected nodes might have different labels. Newer GNN models, such as heterogeneous GNNs (HetGNNs), are designed to handle heterophily more effectively by considering different types of nodes and edges in the graph.

Dynamic graphs

Standard GCNs are typically designed for static graphs but in reality many real-world graphs are evolving over time and dynamic, where nodes and edges can change over time. This has spurred interest in developing dynamic GNNs that can update their embeddings in response to changes in graph structure over time.

Node feature dependence

GCNs heavily rely on the availability and quality of node features. In scenarios where node features are sparse or noisy, GCNs might struggle to perform effectively. This challenge has led to the exploration of GNN variants that can work with little or no initial node features, focusing more on the structure of the graph itself.

Summary

In this chapter, we explored the foundational concepts and practical applications of GNNs, focusing particularly on GCNs. We delved into the significant advancements that GNNs bring to processing graph-structured data, allowing them to effectively capture both local and global graph properties through the mechanism of message passing. This capability enables GNNs to learn powerful node representations that are crucial for tasks such as community detection, node classification, link/relation prediction, and graph classification.

We began by introducing the architecture of GCNs, which adapt the traditional convolutional operations to the irregular structure of graphs by aggregating and transforming neighbor information. This approach was illustrated through the hands-on example using PyG, where we embedded the well-known Zachary's Karate Club network. The practical steps included data preparation, model training, evaluation, and deployment, demonstrating how to implement and utilize GCNs in a typical workflow.

Despite their strengths, we acknowledged the limitations of the GCN architecture, such as oversmoothing, limited receptive fields, scalability issues, and assumptions of homophily, which can hinder their applicability to more complex or dynamic graph structures. These limitations underscore the necessity for more advanced or specialized GNN variants.

In Chapter 6, we will address the limitations highlighted hereby exploring different variations and families of GNN models. This exploration will include models like GATs, which adapt attention mechanisms to graph structures, allowing for more flexible and powerful node feature aggregation. We'll also cover more scalable solutions or techniques such as neighborhood sampling to tackle the scalability challenges faced by GCNs, making GNNs feasible for large-scale graphs. And equally importantly we'll discuss how to handle dynamic graphs and how GNNs can be adapted or designed to manage dynamic graphs where the graph structure evolves over time. We'll be able to support heterogeneous graph models that can handle different types of nodes and edges, addressing the challenges posed by heterophily and complex relational data.

## CHAPTER 6

Advanced Techniques in Graph Learning

Working with complex and dynamic graph-structured data requires some advanced techniques in graph learning. These techniques, like knowledge graph embeddings and attention mechanisms, are great at handling tasks that need a deep understanding of graph structures and scale well for unseen nodes of these graphs.

In this chapter, we'll go deeper in defining different types of graphs, like homogeneous graphs, heterogeneous graphs, and temporal graphs. Knowing about these different kinds of graphs is important because each one comes with its own challenges and opportunities, making advanced graph learning techniques even more useful.

We'll also cover some advanced graph learning architectures to overcome the limitations of the models we navigated in Chapter 5. We'll explain the graph attention network (GAT) from the paper "Graph Attention Networks" (*https://oreil.ly/9zLQ9*) by Veličković et al. This model uses *attention mechanisms* in graph learning, which means it can give different importance to different nodes in the graph. This is a big step up from the models in Chapter 5 that treated all connections the same. With GAT, graph neural networks can be more aware of context and more effective in various situations.

Different Types of Graphs

Graphs play a crucial role in modeling complex systems. As we've covered in earlier chapters, a graph consists of nodes and edges connecting them. These basic structures let us represent and analyze many real-world scenarios, from social networks to biological systems. However, not all graphs are the same. Here, we'll discuss three important categories of graphs: *homogeneous*, *heterogeneous*, and *temporal* graphs.

Grasping the differences between these types of graphs is key to using graph theory effectively across various fields. Homogeneous graphs offer a simpler, more uniform framework, while heterogeneous graphs provide a richer and more detailed representation of complex systems. Temporal graphs add another layer by incorporating the dimension of time, allowing us to track changes and dynamics within the network. This chapter will define these three types of graphs, explore their characteristics, and discuss their applications.

Homogeneous Graphs

Homogeneous graphs, also known as *uniform graphs*, are graphs where all nodes and edges are of the same type. In a homogeneous graph, each vertex is indistinguishable from others in terms of type, and each edge represents the same kind of relationship or interaction between nodes.

Properties of homogeneous graphs include:

Uniformity
Every node is of the same type, and every edge represents the same kind of connection.

Simplicity
These graphs are easier to analyze and visualize due to their uniform structure.

Regularity
Often, homogeneous graphs exhibit regular patterns and properties, such as degree regularity (where every node has an equal number of connections).

Some examples of homogeneous graphs include:

Social networks
In a basic social network graph, each node represents an individual, and each edge represents a friendship between two individuals. Here, both nodes and edges are homogeneous.

Communication networks
Nodes represent devices, and edges represent direct communication links between devices.

Heterogeneous Graphs

On the other hand, heterogeneous graphs contain different types of nodes and/or edges. These graphs, also known as multigraphs or heterogeneous information networks, can capture more complex and diverse relationships within a system.

Properties of heterogeneous graphs include:

Diversity

    Nodes and edges can represent different types of entities and relationships, allowing for a richer representation of the system.

Complexity

    The analysis of heterogeneous graphs is more complex due to the diversity of node and edge types.

Flexibility

    These graphs can model more complex systems and interactions compared to homogeneous graphs.

Some examples of heterogeneous graphs include:

Academic networks

    Nodes can represent researchers, papers, and conferences, while edges can represent authorship, citations, and participation in conferences.

Biological networks

    Nodes represent genes, proteins, and metabolites, while edges represent various biological interactions, including gene regulation, protein–protein interactions, and metabolic reactions.

Temporal Graphs

A temporal graph is a graph in which the edges are active only at certain times. Unlike static graphs where edges represent permanent relationships, temporal graphs capture the dynamic nature of connections that change over time.

Properties of temporal graphs include:

Temporal dynamics

    Edges have a temporal component, indicating when interactions occur.

Event-based representation

    Relationships between nodes are defined by specific events or time intervals.

Order and timing

    The order and timing of edges can significantly influence the properties and behavior of the graph.

Some examples of temporal graphs include:

Communication networks

    Nodes represent individuals, and temporal edges represent phone calls or messages exchanged at specific times.

Transportation networks
> Nodes represent locations, and temporal edges represent the availability of transportation links at particular times.

Temporal graphs are widely used in scenarios where the timing and sequence of interactions are critical. They are particularly useful in:

Epidemiology
> Modeling the spread of diseases where the timing of contacts between individuals affects transmission dynamics

Social network analysis
> Understanding the evolution of social interactions and influence over time

Infrastructure management
> Analyzing the usage patterns and reliability of infrastructure such as transportation and communication networks

Graph Embedding Models

Graph embedding models are representation learning models that aim to learn efficient vector representations of graph components (edges and nodes) to utilize them for different graph learning objectives. These methods operate on both homogeneous and heterogeneous graphs, where their most common application is modeling homogeneous information graphs, i.e., knowledge graphs.

How Do Knowledge Graph Embeddings Work?

Knowledge graph embedding models learn low-dimensional representations of nodes and edges in the graph and use these embeddings to make predictions on the graph data. These predictions can be inferring new links (edges) in the graph, classifying entity types, and more.

The core idea behind the knowledge graph embeddings method is modeling facts using their embedding interactions, where the interaction is a function of the embedding of different components that computes a factuality score of a single fact in the graph. For example, let's assume that we have the fact that London is the capital of England modeled in a graph with two nodes "London" and "England" and an edge "IsCaptialOf" that connects these two entities. Knowledge graph embedding models operate by modeling an interaction between the embeddings of the subject node "London", the object node "England," and the predicate "IsCapitalOf," where the result of this interaction is considered the score of this fact. The objective of these models is then to maximize the score of the true graph node-edge-node combination and minimize the other negative combination.

Knowledge graph embedding models use different types of interaction methods, where the interaction method combined with the objective loss function is the core difference between these models. In the following sections, we discuss the different types of embedding methods and objective loss functions utilized in knowledge graph embedding models. We also discuss the training pipeline of these methods and provide different insights on how to optimize the training of knowledge graph embedding in terms of both performance and predictive accuracy

Training Knowledge Graph Embedding Models

Training knowledge graph embeddings is a multiphase pipeline that is executed to learn efficient vector representations of graph components. We start with initializing the embedding vectors of the graph edges and nodes with random values. This initialization is often done using a customized uniform random initialization, which is often attributed to a faster learning process.[1] The training process then operates iteratively on all the known graph facts as shown in Figure 6-1. Let's take a simple example of an instance of graph triplet (fact) and see how it is processed through the training process of knowledge graph embedding models.

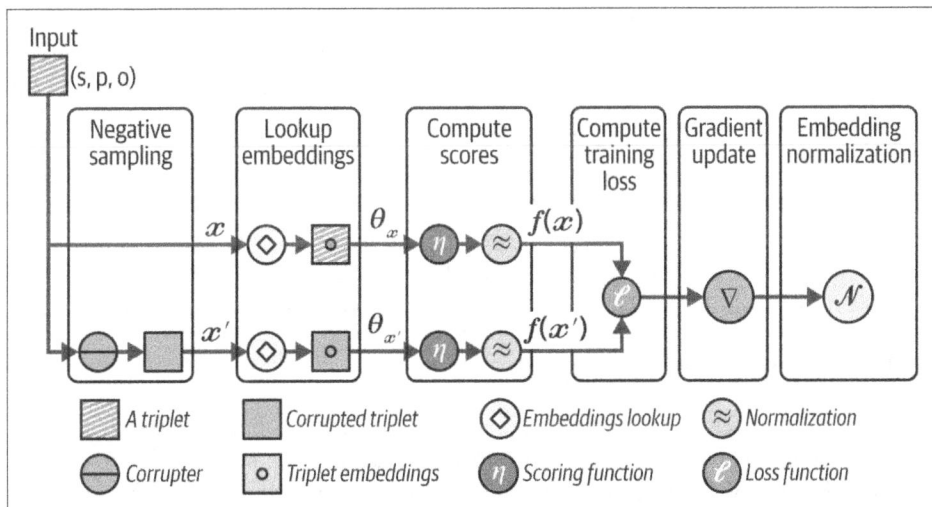

Figure 6-1. An illustration of the training pipeline of knowledge graph embedding models (Mohamed et al. (2021))

---

1 Mohamed, S.K., Muñoz, E., and Novacek, V. (2021). "On Training Knowledge Graph Embedding Models." *Information* 12(4), 147.

Let's assume that we are operating on a general information graph, and we have initialized the embedding of all the graph components with uniform random values. We are now going to operate on the triplet/fact (London, isCapitalOf, England) to train the model. This fact is a positive example as it is a true, known fact in the graph.

The first step in knowledge graph embedding training models is to sample negative example facts. This happens by corrupting either the subject or the object entities to generate a corrupted version of the fact. For example, a corruption of our example could be (Facebook, isCapitalOf, England), where Facebook is the entity for Facebook, the company. Note that the corruption procedure is totally random, which can theoretically yield another true example, especially in many-to-many relationships. However, this rarely happens in reality; graphs are often very sparse and the probability of sampling another true entity is negligible.

The next step is to look up the embeddings of both the negative and positive examples; these embeddings are then fed to the embedding interaction/scoring function to compute the score of the fact. The embedding interaction function in this context is the main differentiator between different knowledge graph embeddings models, where different models have different interaction functions. The output of the interaction function is a score for each fact instance, which is passed to the loss objective step to compute the model training loss. The loss is then used to update the model parameters (the embeddings). Some models apply normalization to the embeddings after each update to ground the model and apply some constraints to the embeddings.

In "Embedding Interaction Methods", we discuss in more detail the embedding interaction functions and training objectives of knowledge graph embedding models and how different knowledge graph embedding models use different strategies in their training pipelines in order to learn graph embeddings efficiently and accurately.

Embedding Interaction Methods

Knowledge graph embedding models compute interactions between graph components' embeddings using various techniques such as *distance-based*, *similarity-based*, and *complex* interactions. In the following, we discuss these different techniques and give a detailed description of popular examples of each technique.

In the following context (Figure 6-2), we refer to a graph fact (node-edge-node) as a subject, predicate, object triplet. We also refer to the embeddings of these components as e_s, w_p, and e_o and respectively, where e is an embedding of a subject/object node and w is an embedding of a predicate edge, and $e, w \in \mathcal{R}^k$, where k is the size of the embedding vector. In this context, we denote the embedding interaction function of a (s, p, o) triplet by $f(e_s, w_p, e_o)$.

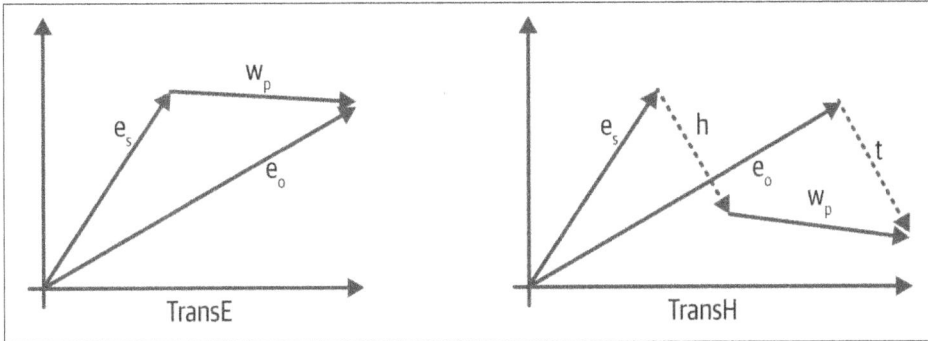

Figure 6-2. An illustration of the distance-based embedding interaction

Distance-based embedding interactions

Here we study an embedding interaction technique where the interaction between the graph components is modeled as a translation in the embedding space. The earliest and simplest example of this approach is the *translating embedding* (TransE) model,[2] which models the interaction according to the following formula:

$$e_s + w_p = e_o$$

The intuition behind this formulation is modeling the relationship between two objects as a simple additive translation in the embedding space, where the embedding of the predicate (edge) acts as the translation between the subject and object nodes. The scoring function of this model is then defined as follows:

$$f_{TransE_s}\big(e_s, w_p, e_o\big) = \big\|e_s + w_p - e_o\big\|_{L1/L2}$$

where $L1$ and $L2$ are the embedding norms of rank 1 and 2, and $e_s + w_p - e_o = 0$ for true fact instances and higher values for other false fact instances.

Other variations of this method include the TransH[3] model, which resembles TransE with the subject and object embeddings projected to another hyperplane. The embedding interaction function is then defined as follows:

$$f_{TransH_s}\big(e_s, w_p, e_o\big) = \big\|\big(e_s - w_p^\top h_p\big) + d_p - \big(e_o - w_p^\top t_p\big)\big\|_{L2}$$

2 Bordes, A. et al. (2013). "Translating Embeddings for Modeling Multirelational Data" (*https://oreil.ly/DcPUa*). *Advances in Neural Information Processing Systems*, 26.

3 Wang, Z. et al. (2014). "Knowledge Graph Embedding by Translating on Hyperplanes" (*https://oreil.ly/Qs4M_*). *Proceedings of the AAAI Conference on Artificial Intelligence* 28 (1).

where h and t are extra vectors that are used to project the embeddings of the subject and object entities (nodes).

Another method called TransR[4] uses a more sophisticated projection method that utilizes projection matrices instead of vectors; however, these methods utilize very similar approaches that are focused on modeling the interaction between the graph components as translation in the embeddings space.

Factorization-based embedding interactions

Another embedding interaction technique models embedding interactions using factorization as a product of the different interacting components. The simplest form of these interactions is the *DistMult model*,[5] which models the interactions of fact components as the product of their embedding vectors. Its scoring function is then defined as follows:

$$f_{DistMult_s}\left(e_s, w_p, e_o\right) = \Sigma_k e_{sk} w_{pk} e_{ok}$$

where $\Sigma_k e_{sk} w_{pk} e_{ok}$ denotes the summation of the resulting embedding vector of size k. This summation performs the same job as the $L1$ and $L2$ norms in the TransE model, which is to convert vector form embeddings to a single scalar value that is then used as a score of the subject, predicate, object fact. The idea behind this method is very simple: interactions of embeddings are the multiplication of all their values. However, this embedding multiplication approach is symmetric, which means that the score of the fact (London, isCapitalOf, England) is equal to the score of the fact (England, isCapitalOf, London). This problem is solved in later factorization-based approaches such as the ComplEx model,[6] where each graph component is represented with two vectors that represent the real and imaginary parts of a complex vector.

In general, factorization-based approaches are known to yield better predictive accuracy in complex learning tasks on graphs when compared to translation-based approaches. They are also as scalable as translation-based approaches, as they rely on the same training pipeline and optimization objectives.

4 Lin, Y. et al. (2015). "Learning Entity and Relation Embeddings for Knowledge Graph Completion" (*https://oreil.ly/r3DW2*). *Proceedings of the AAAI Conference on Artificial Intelligence* 29(1).

5 Yang, B. et al. (2014). "Learning Multirelational Semantics Using Neural-Embedding Models" (*https://oreil.ly/Cz4sF*). arXiv preprint arXiv:1411.4072.

6 Trouillon, T. et al. (2016). "Complex Embeddings for Simple Link Prediction" (*https://oreil.ly/C6P6j*). *Proceedings of the 33rd International Conference on Machine Learning*, PMLR 48, 2071-2080.

Training Objectives

The main objective of knowledge graph embedding models is to learn efficient representation for the graph nodes and edges. They start from randomly generated embeddings and update these embeddings to reach an optimal state of the embeddings that efficiently model information in the graph. In the training processes of knowledge graph embedding models, the training process is modelled as a ranking task where the objective is to rank graph triplets (potential facts) such that known true triplets have higher scores than other triplets. In this context, the loss objective of the models is defined in different ways as follows:

Pairwise losses

The objective in this loss type is to maximize the score of positive samples and minimize the scores of negative samples by maximizing the difference between the two samples, a positive and negative one. This means that the model weights are going to be updated to increase the score for the positive sample and decrease the score of the negative sample for the difference between the two scores to increase. Examples of this type of loss are *pairwise hinge loss* and *pairwise square loss*.

Pointwise losses

A type of loss that compares the model score to labels (0, 1) such that the objective is to minimize the distance between the model score and the sample assigned label. The positive samples are compared to label 1 and other samples are compared to label 0. This approach is identical to binary classification losses where we could use logistic loss and squared error loss to model this type of objective.

Multiclass losses

There are other types of loss that model the objective as a multiclass loss approach where the positive sample is compared to negative samples generated by corrupting facts using the whole vocabulary of entities. This approach is superior in terms of predictive accuracy compared to previously mentioned approaches; however, it is less scalable due to its quadratic space complexity.

Strengths of Graph Embedding Models

Graph embedding models are popular for their high scalability and performance. They excel at tasks such as link prediction, graph completion, and link classification.[7] These models have many strengths that make them ideal for learning over large

---

7 Wang, Q. et al. (2017). "Knowledge Graph Embedding: A Survey of Approaches and Applications" (*https://oreil.ly/LoDR7*). *IEEE Transactions on Knowledge and Data Engineering* 29(12), 2724-2743.

complex graphs. In the following list, we discuss some of their main strengths and benefits compared to other approaches:

Scalability
> Knowledge graph embedding models are highly scalable and flexible, making them suitable for large-scale knowledge graphs. Popular and performant models such as the DistMult and ComplEx models have linear time and space complexity, which makes them excel in terms of scalability compared to other methods for learning on graphs. Combined with their high predictive accuracy, this makes knowledge graph embedding models the go-to method for learning on large scale heterogeneous graphs.

Capturing complex relationships
> One of the primary strengths of knowledge graph embedding models is their ability to capture complex relationships between entities and their attributes. Traditional methods, such as random walks and similarity models, are limited in their ability to model complex relationships, as they rely on simple methods. In contrast, knowledge graph embedding models can capture complex relationships by learning vector representations of entities and their attributes that preserve the structural properties of the knowledge graph.

Improved performance
> Knowledge graph embedding models have been shown to outperform traditional methods in various applications, including link prediction, entity disambiguation, and question answering. That made them very popular in multiple academic and industrial applications where they are used to infer new knowledge on graphs.[8]

Robustness to noise and incompleteness
> These models are also robust to noise and incompleteness in the data, making them suitable for real-world applications where data quality issues are common. These models can learn to ignore noisy or missing data and focus on the underlying patterns and relationships in the data.

Example: Learning on Freebase Dataset

In the following example, we will give an example of how to train knowledge graph embedding models on a graph dataset, and how to use the trained model to perform different learning tasks on the dataset graph. Our example works on the freebase "FB15k_237" dataset, which is a general knowledge dataset that contains information about locations, music content, movies, sports content, and other general knowledge

---

8 Mohamed, S., Nounu, A., and Nováček, V. (2021). "Biological Applications of Knowledge Graph Embedding Models." *Briefings in Bioinformatics* 22(2), 1679-1693.

concepts. We are going to use the preprocessed form of the dataset offered by PyG, which has the data indexed in numeric format so it is ready for use. However, when building your own graph dataset, you will need to encode your data into the COO index format (*https://oreil.ly/FXQ7o*), which is supported by PyG.

Loading and exploring data

First, we start by loading the dataset using the PyG `datasets` module as follows:

```
from pathlib import Path

import torch
from torch_geometric.datasets import FB15k_237

device = 'cuda' if torch.cuda.is_available() else 'cpu'

data_dirpath = Path() / 'data'

train_data = FB15k_237(data_dirpath, split='train')[0].to(device)
val_data = FB15k_237(data_dirpath, split='val')[0].to(device)
test_data = FB15k_237(data_dirpath, split='test')[0].to(device)
```

This will download the dataset with its training, validation, and testing splits into a local `data` directory, and it will always load it into memory.

We can examine the dataset to explore the statistics of its contents and the different types of information that it contains. We can explore the number of relations (edges), entities (nodes), and facts (triplets) included in FB15k_237 as follows:

```
# Print information about the dataset
print(f'Dataset: FB15k_237')

print(f'Number of triples (train): {train_data.num_edges}')
print(f'Number of triples (val): {val_data.num_edges}')
print(f'Number of triples (test): {test_data.num_edges}\n')

print(f'Number of entities (train): {train_data.num_nodes}')
print(f'Number of relations (train): {train_data.num_edge_types}\n')

print(f'Number of entities (val): {val_data.num_nodes}')
print(f'Number of relations (val): {val_data.num_edge_types}\n')

print(f'Number of entities (test): {test_data.num_nodes}')
print(f'Number of relations (test): {test_data.num_edge_types}')
```

Output:

```
Dataset: FB15k_237
Number of triples (train): 272115
Number of triples (val): 17535
Number of triples (test): 20466
```

```
Number of entities (train): 14541
Number of relations (train): 237

Number of entities (val): 14541
Number of relations (val): 237

Number of entities (test): 14541
Number of relations (test): 237
```

Initializing the model and training configuration

Now, we can initialize our model and training configuration. For our example, we are going to use the ComplEx model, which is one of the most capable knowledge graph embedding models. The code for loading the model and the training configurations is as follows:

```python
from torch_geometric.nn import ComplEx
import torch.optim as optim

embedding_size = 64

model = ComplEx(
    num_nodes=train_data.num_nodes,
    num_relations=train_data.num_edge_types,
    hidden_channels=embedding_size,
).to(device)

# Model data loader
loader = model.loader(
    head_index=train_data.edge_index[0],
    rel_type=train_data.edge_type,
    tail_index=train_data.edge_index[1],
    batch_size=1024,
    shuffle=True,
)

optimizer = optim.Adam(model.parameters(), lr=0.0001, weight_decay=1e-6)
```

This code initializes the ComplEx model using the number of entities and relations from the training dataset as the vocabulary for its node and relation embeddings. The embedding size in our examples is 64; however, in a real application the recommended embedding size is often around 200. This is because larger embedding sizes allow for capturing more complex relationships and interactions between entities and relations, leading to better model performance, especially in large-scale knowledge graphs. We have also initialized an instance for an Adam optimizer with a specific learning rate and weight decay. In a real application, the best practice is to learn these configurations using a hyperparameter tuning exercise.

Defining and executing the training loop

The next step is to execute the training procedure, where we define the training loop and the validation test step. This step can be implemented as follows:

```
BATCH_SIZE = 20000
NUM_EPOCHS = 100
def train():
    model.train()
    total_loss = total_examples = 0
    for head_index, rel_type, tail_index in loader:
        optimizer.zero_grad()
        loss = model.loss(head_index, rel_type, tail_index)
        loss.backward()
        optimizer.step()
        total_loss += float(loss) * head_index.numel()
        total_examples += head_index.numel()
    return total_loss / total_examples

@torch.no_grad()
def test(data):
    model.eval()
    return model.test(
        head_index=data.edge_index[0],
        rel_type=data.edge_type,
        tail_index=data.edge_index[1],
        batch_size=BATCH_SIZE, k=10,)

# The model training loop
for epoch in range(1, NUM_EPOCHS):
    loss = train()
    print(f'Epoch: {epoch:03d}, Loss: {loss:.4f}')
    if epoch % 20 == 0:
        rank, mrr, hits = test(val_data)
        print(f'Epoch: {epoch:03d}, Val Mean Rank: {rank:.2f},
                    Val MRR: {mrr:.4f}, Val Hits@10: {hits:.4f}')

rank, mrr, hits_at_10 = test(test_data)
print(f'Test Mean Rank: {rank:.2f}, Test MRR: {mrr:.4f},
            Test Hits@10: {hits_at_10:.4f}')
```

This code creates a training loop with 100 epochs and loads the training data in 20,000 samples per batch. The training loop will also evaluate the model on the validation set every 20 epochs.

The output of executing the training loop and then testing the model on the testing dataset split should look like the following:

```
Epoch: 001, Loss: 0.4317
Epoch: 002, Loss: 0.4292
Epoch: 003, Loss: 0.4271
....
....
```

```
Epoch: 018, Loss: 0.3854
Epoch: 019, Loss: 0.3829
Epoch: 020, Loss: 0.3805

100%|████████████████████| 17535/17535 [01:30<00:00, 192.97it/s]

Epoch: 020, Val Mean Rank: 451.32, Val MRR: 0.1955, Val Hits@10: 0.3372
....
....
....
....

Epoch: 097, Loss: 0.1811
Epoch: 098, Loss: 0.1791
Epoch: 099, Loss: 0.1780

100%|████████████████████| 20466/20466 [01:53<00:00, 180.60it/s]
Test Mean Rank: 464.18, Test MRR: 0.1588, Test Hits@10: 0.3103
```

Now we have our trained model and the model embeddings have a good representation of the graph components (edges and nodes).

The next step is to use the trained model to learn on the graph. One of the most common learning objectives for knowledge graph embedding models is *learn prediction*, where the objective is to find the right target of a specific relation. For example, a question such as "What is the hometown of the Arsenal football club?" could be answered using a query on a trained knowledge graph model that contains information about the Arsenal team. This is done by scoring all the triplets in the format of (Arsenal FC, hometown, ??), where we score all possible object entities to find the highest scoring entity, which is then considered the model's recommended answer.

In our example, let's take a sample of known, true facts and see how we can generate scores for them. For this we will use the testing set, get the first five triplets, and score them using our now trained model. The code is as follows:

```
num_samples = 5
subs = test_data.edge_index[0][:num_samples]
preds = test_data.edge_type[:num_samples]
objs = test_data.edge_index[1][:num_samples]

scores = model.forward(head_index=subs, rel_type=preds, tail_index=objs)
print(scores)
```

Output:

```
tensor([ 1.9491,  1.9998,  4.3225, -0.5076,  0.8754], grad_fn=<SubBackward0>)
```

We could then change the combination of triplets so that we score to learn different objects on the graph, as the embedding models will rank the triplets and give the most likely to be true a higher score compared to other methods.

Furthermore, the model embeddings can be used to cluster the entities and perform further types of learning on them by using the embedding vector of entities or relations as a modeling representation for them. This is a similar method to other graph learning approaches that use vector representation of graph components, such as node2vec (*https://oreil.ly/Kl8R1*) or DeepWalk, which learn embeddings for nodes in a graph for tasks such as node classification, link prediction, or clustering. Similarly, these embeddings can be used for downstream tasks such as recommendation systems, anomaly detection, or graph-based search.

Another powerful approach is leveraging attention mechanisms, which have proven highly effective in various machine learning domains. By applying attention mechanisms to graph structures, we can further enhance the model's ability to focus on the most important connections within the graph. This leads us to the concept of attention mechanisms on graphs.

Attention on Graphs

Attention mechanisms have become standard in many sequence-based tasks. They allow for variable-sized inputs and focus on the most relevant parts to make decisions. When used to compute representations of single sequences, this is referred to as self-attention or intra-attention. Recent work has shown that self-attention alone can construct powerful models, achieving state-of-the-art performance in tasks such as machine translation.

Graph attention networks (GATs) utilize the attention mechanism to determine the importance (attention) of nodes within the graph structure. The concept involves computing hidden representations of each node by focusing on its neighbors through a self-attention strategy. This method provides several benefits:

Efficiency
    The process can be parallelized across node–neighbor pairs.

Flexibility
    It can be applied to nodes with varying degrees by assigning arbitrary weights to neighbors.

Inductive learning
    The model can generalize to completely unseen graphs.

Feature Vectors

Each node v in the graph has an associated feature vector $h_v \in \mathbb{R}^F$ where F is the number of features. These feature vectors serve as the input to the model and encapsulate the information relevant to each node, such as attributes or characteristics of the entities the nodes represent. For example, in a social network graph, the feature vector of a node might include attributes like age, location, or interests of a person. In a knowledge graph, the feature vector might contain semantic or categorical properties of an entity.

These feature vectors form the basis for the learning process, enabling models to perform tasks like node classification, link prediction, and clustering by leveraging both the node attributes and the structure of the graph. In GNNs, feature vectors are often transformed and propagated through the network layers, allowing the model to iteratively refine node representations by considering both the node's own features and the features of its neighbors. This aggregation process helps the model learn more nuanced and context-aware representations.

Attention Mechanism

The core idea of GATs is to compute attention coefficients for the edges of the graph. For each node i, we compute a shared attention mechanism a, which is then used to compute the coefficients e_{ij} for each neighboring node j of i:

$$e_{ij} = \text{LeakyReLU}\left(a^T\left[Wh_i \parallel Wh_j\right]\right)$$

where:

- W is a weight matrix.
- $\parallel$ denotes concatenation.
- a^T is a learnable weight vector.

These coefficients are then normalized across all neighbors j using the softmax function:

$$\alpha_{i,j} = \frac{\exp\left(e_{i,j}\right)}{\Sigma_{k \in \mathcal{N}(i)} \exp\left(e_{i,k}\right)}$$

Finally, the node features are updated as a weighted sum of the features of neighboring nodes:

$$h_i' = \sigma\left(\Sigma_{j \in \mathcal{N}(i)} \alpha_{ij} Wh_j\right)$$

where:

- σ is a nonlinear activation function.

Multihead Attention

GAT uses *multihead attention*, which means instead of having just one attention mechanism focusing on neighbors, the model runs multiple attention mechanisms (called *heads*) in parallel. Each head looks at the neighboring nodes slightly differently, learning diverse patterns or relationships from the provided data representation.

Once these heads have processed the data, the outputs from all the attention heads are combined by either concatenating (stacking the outputs together) or averaging (taking the average of the outputs). Averaging helps smooth out the differences between the heads, which can stabilize the learning process and lead to better generalization:

$$h'_i = \|_{k=1}^{K} \sigma\left(\Sigma_{j \in \mathcal{N}(i)} \alpha_{ij}^k W^k h_j\right)$$

Example: Citation Network

Imagine a citation network where nodes represent research papers and edges represent citations between papers. Each paper (node) has a number of features, such as the number of citations, publication year, and the research field. Let's walk through the steps of how a GAT uses the attention mechanism.

Feature combination

Consider a target node (Paper i) and its neighbors j (Papers j). Each paper has a feature vector h. For simplicity, let's assume the feature vectors are only the number of citations and publication year, represented as follows:

- $h_i = [2,5]$ for Paper i
- $h_1 = [3,4]$ for Paper 1
- $h_2 = [1,6]$ for Paper 2
- $h_3 = [4,3]$ for Paper 3

Now let's combine the feature vectors of Paper i with each of its neighbors using the concatenation operation:

- $h_{i,1} = [2,5] \,\|\, [3,4] = [2,5,3,4]$
- $h_{i,2} = [2,5] \,\|\, [1,6] = [2,5,1,6]$
- $h_{i,3} = [2,5] \,\|\, [4,3] = [2,5,4,3]$

Score calculation

Next, we calculate a score for each combination using a learned weight vector and a nonlinear function (LeakyReLU). For instance, let's assume that $a = [0.1, 0.2, 0.3, 0.4]$. The scores e_{ij} are calculated as follows:

- $e_{i,1} = LeakyReLU(a^T \cdot h_{i,1}) = LeakyReLU(0.1 \cdot 2 + 0.2 \cdot 5 + 0.3 \cdot 3 + 0.4 \cdot 4)$
  $= LeakyReLU(3.1)$

- $e_{i,2} = LeakyReLU(a^T \cdot h_{i,2}) = LeakyReLU(0.1 \cdot 2 + 0.2 \cdot 5 + 0.3 \cdot 1 + 0.4 \cdot 6)$
  $= LeakyReLU(3.0)$

- $e_{i,3} = LeakyReLU(a^T \cdot h_{i,3}) = LeakyReLU(0.1 \cdot 2 + 0.2 \cdot 5 + 0.3 \cdot 4 + 0.4 \cdot 4)$
  $= LeakyReLU(3.9)$

Now we have calculated the score based on this combined information where the higher score represents how relevant this paper is to the target one (Paper i).

Normalization (softmax)

After calculating the scores, they are then normalized using the softmax function in order to get the attention weights α_{ij}. Now let's calculate for our specific scores:

$$\alpha_{i,1} = \frac{\exp{(3.1)}}{\exp{(3.1)} + \exp{(3.0)} + \exp{(2.9)}}$$

After calculating, let's assume the normalized weights are:

- $a_{i,1} = 0.34$
- $a_{i,2} = 0.33$
- $a_{i,3} = 0.33$

Weighted sum

Before updating the feature vector information of Paper i, we use the calculated attentions from before in order to calculate the weighted sum of the neighbor's features, using this equation:

$$h_i' = \sigma\left(\Sigma_{j \in \mathcal{N}(i)} \alpha_{ij} W h_j\right)$$

For now let's assume that W is the identity matrix (i.e., no transformation). The new feature vector for Paper i is as follows:

- $h'_i = 0.34 \cdot [3,4] + 0.33 \cdot [1,6] + 0.33 \cdot [4,3]$
- $h'_i = [2.68,3.36] + [0.33,1.98] + [1.32,0.99]$
- $h'_i = [4.33,6.33]$

Update paper *i* information

Finally the updated feature vector for Paper i incorporates information from its neighbors, weighted by their relevance:

- $h'_i = [4.33,6.33]$

The entire process, from combining the feature nodes to updating the features of the target node, is illustrated in Figure 6-3.

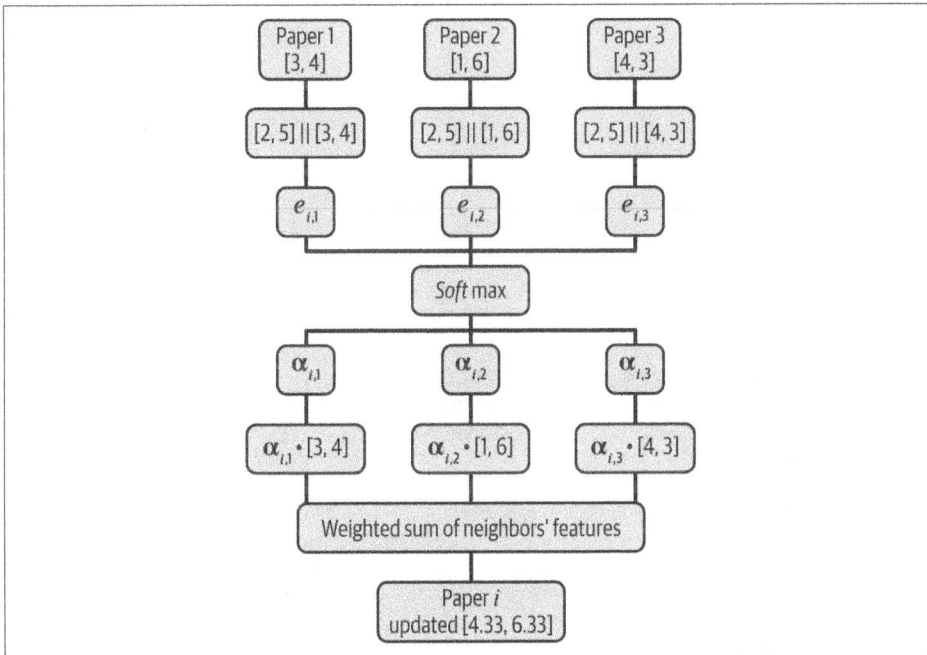

Figure 6-3. An illustration of the use of attention mechanisms on graphs

Now that we have covered the reasoning behind how GATs work to attend to the most relevant parts of the graph, let's see this in action using the following example.

CiteSeer Use Case Example

In this section, we will take a more hands-on approach by using the PyG API interface, specifically the GATv2Conv module, to build a GAT architecture for the CiteSeer use case described in the following.

The CiteSeer database (*https://oreil.ly/r-7kr*) is a well-known citation network used in the evaluation of machine learning algorithms for graph-based data. In this dataset, nodes represent research papers, and edges represent citations between these papers. Each paper (node) has a set of features, which typically include word occurrences from the paper's abstract or title. The goal is often to classify each paper into one of several predefined categories based on its content and citation links. Let's start this section by going through the required data preprocessing and getting more insights and understanding of the graph-structured data through some visualizations.

Data Preprocessing and Visualization

Let's start this section by understanding some statistics about the dataset and its graph-structured properties:

```
from torch_geometric.datasets import Planetoid

# Import dataset from PyTorch Geometric
dataset = Planetoid(root=".", name="CiteSeer")

data = dataset[0]

# Print information about the dataset
print(f'Dataset: {dataset}')
print('------------------')
print(f'Number of graphs: {len(dataset)}')
print(f'Number of nodes: {data.x.shape[0]}')
print(f'Number of features: {dataset.num_features}')
print(f'Number of classes: {dataset.num_classes}')

# Print information about the graph
print(f'\nGraph:')
print('------')
print(f'Edges are directed: {data.is_directed()}')
print(f'Graph has isolated nodes: {data.has_isolated_nodes()}')
print(f'Graph has loops: {data.has_self_loops()}')
```

Output:

```
Downloading...
Processing...
Dataset: CiteSeer()
------------------
Number of graphs: 1
Number of nodes: 3327
```

```
Number of features: 3703
Number of classes: 6

Graph:
------
Edges are directed: False
Graph has isolated nodes: True
Graph has loops: False
Done!
```

Now let's start by understanding the graph representation of this data and look at some properties of its nodes and edges. Let's start with the number of isolated nodes in the graph that don't have connection to any of the other nodes:

```
from torch_geometric.utils import remove_isolated_nodes

isolated = (remove_isolated_nodes(data['edge_index'])[2] == False)
                                  .sum(dim=0).item()
print(f'Number of isolated nodes = {isolated}')
```

Output:

```
Number of isolated nodes = 48
```

Let's gain some more insights into the clusters or communities within the graph using NetworkX:

```
# Visualization
import networkx as nx
import matplotlib.pyplot as plt

from torch_geometric.utils import to_networkx

G = to_networkx(data, to_undirected=True)
plt.figure(figsize=(18,18))
plt.axis('off')
nx.draw_networkx(G,
                 pos=nx.spring_layout(G, seed=0),
                 with_labels=False,
                 node_size=50,
                 node_color=data.y,
                 width=2,
                 edge_color="grey"
                 )
plt.show()
```

Figure 6-4 shows the overall structure and identifies patterns, such as isolated nodes and low-degree nodes.

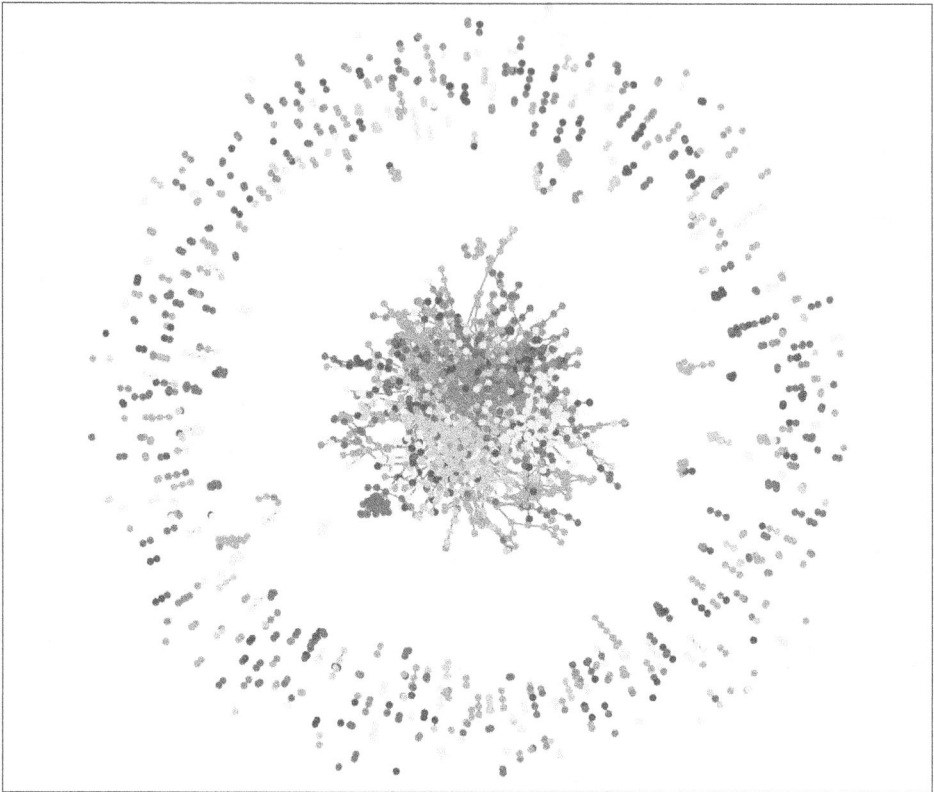

Figure 6-4. NetworkX visualization of the CiteSeer dataset

To better understand the graph data, let's analyze the distribution of node degrees:

```python
from torch_geometric.utils import degree
from collections import Counter

# Get a list of degrees for each node
degrees = degree(data.edge_index[0]).numpy()

# Count the number of nodes for each degree
numbers = Counter(degrees)

# Bar plot
fig, ax = plt.subplots(figsize=(18, 7))
ax.set_xlabel('Node degree')
ax.set_ylabel('Number of nodes')
plt.bar(numbers.keys(),
        numbers.values(),
        color='#0A047A')
```

The plot in Figure 6-5 shows some kind of a *long tail distribution*, where a few nodes have a very high degree, indicating they are highly connected within the

graph. Additionally, the majority of nodes have a low degree, with one, two, or three connections. This shows that most papers in the CiteSeer dataset either cite very few other papers or are cited by very few papers.

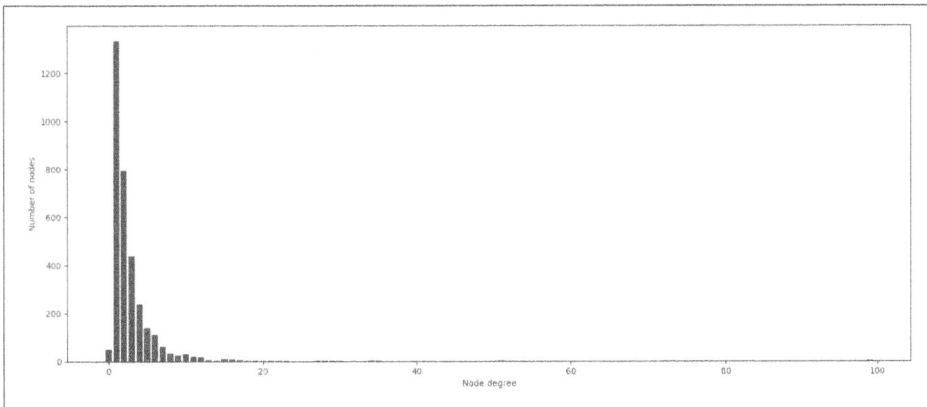

Figure 6-5. Visualization of the distribution of node degrees

Model Training Using PyG

Now, let's use the different PyG modules implemented for the GAT architecture to define our model and start the training process. Let's start with defining the GAT architecture that would be used:

```python
import torch.nn.functional as F
from torch.nn import Linear, Dropout
from torch_geometric.nn import GATv2Conv


class GAT(torch.nn.Module):
    """Graph Attention Network"""
    def __init__(self, dim_in, dim_h, dim_out, heads=8):
        super().__init__()
        self.gat1 = GATv2Conv(dim_in, dim_h, heads=heads)
        self.gat2 = GATv2Conv(dim_h*heads, dim_out, heads=1)
        self.optimizer = torch.optim.Adam(self.parameters(),
                                           lr=0.005,
                                           weight_decay=5e-4)

    def forward(self, x, edge_index):
        h = F.dropout(x, p=0.6, training=self.training)
        h = self.gat1(x, edge_index)
        h = F.elu(h)
        h = F.dropout(h, p=0.6, training=self.training)
        h = self.gat2(h, edge_index)
        return h, F.log_softmax(h, dim=1)
```

Now that we have our architecture defined, we can start defining the train function as well as the accuracy function that would be used to evaluate the model:

```python
def accuracy(pred_y, y):
    """Calculate accuracy."""
    return ((pred_y == y).sum() / len(y)).item()


def train(model, data):
    """Train a GNN model and return the trained model."""
    criterion = torch.nn.CrossEntropyLoss()
    optimizer = model.optimizer
    epochs = 200

    model.train()
    for epoch in range(epochs+1):
        # Training
        optimizer.zero_grad()
        _, out = model(data.x, data.edge_index)
        loss = criterion(out[data.train_mask], data.y[data.train_mask])
        acc = accuracy(out[data.train_mask].argmax(dim=1),
                       data.y[data.train_mask])
        loss.backward()
        optimizer.step()

        # Validation
        val_loss = criterion(out[data.val_mask], data.y[data.val_mask])
        val_acc = accuracy(out[data.val_mask].argmax(dim=1),
                       data.y[data.val_mask])

        # Print metrics every 10 epochs
        if(epoch % 10 == 0):
            print(f'Epoch {epoch:>3} | Train Loss: {loss:.3f} | Train Acc: '
                  f'{acc*100:>6.2f}% | Val Loss: {val_loss:.2f} | '
                  f'Val Acc: {val_acc*100:.2f}%')

    return model
```

Now let's start the training process:

```python
# Create GAT model
gat = GAT(dataset.num_features, 8, dataset.num_classes)
print(gat)

# Train
train(gat, data)

Output:

GAT(
  (gat1): GATv2Conv(3703, 8, heads=8)
  (gat2): GATv2Conv(64, 6, heads=1)
)
Epoch   0 | Train Loss: 1.792 | Train Acc:  14.17% | Val Loss: 1.80 |
```

```
Val Acc: 16.40%
Epoch  10 | Train Loss: 0.122 | Train Acc:  96.67% | Val Loss: 1.04 |
Val Acc: 66.00%
Epoch  20 | Train Loss: 0.026 | Train Acc:  99.17% | Val Loss: 1.14 |
Val Acc: 66.00%
  .
  .
  .
Epoch 190 | Train Loss: 0.006 | Train Acc: 100.00% | Val Loss: 1.16 |
Val Acc: 67.00%
Epoch 200 | Train Loss: 0.008 | Train Acc: 100.00% | Val Loss: 1.14 |
Val Acc: 68.00%
```

The training output of the GAT model shows accuracy improvements over 200 epochs and highlights how efficiently GAT captures complex patterns within the graph data.

Model Testing

Now let's test the model against the unseen data:

```
def test(model, data):
    """Evaluate the model on test set and print the accuracy score."""
    model.eval()
    _, out = model(data.x, data.edge_index)
    acc = accuracy(out.argmax(dim=1)[data.test_mask], data.y[data.test_mask])
    return acc

# Test
acc = test(gat, data)
print(f'\nGAT test accuracy: {acc*100:.2f}%\n')
```

Output:

```
GAT test accuracy: 68.70%
```

Embeddings Visualization

Now that we have the model trained, let's use t-distributed stochastic neighbor embedding (t-SNE) (*https://oreil.ly/0uT-e*) to visualize the trained GAT model embeddings and see how good it did on solving this task:

```
from sklearn.manifold import TSNE

# Get embeddings
h, _ = gat(data.x, data.edge_index)

# Train TSNE
tsne = TSNE(n_components=2, learning_rate='auto',
            init='pca').fit_transform(h.detach())

# Plot TSNE
```

```
plt.figure(figsize=(10, 10))
plt.axis('off')
plt.scatter(tsne[:, 0], tsne[:, 1], s=50, c=data.y)
plt.show()
```

As shown in Figure 6-6, which visualizes the 2D projections of the trained GAT model embeddings, the visualization effectively highlights the model's ability to distinctly separate various groups or communities within the graph.

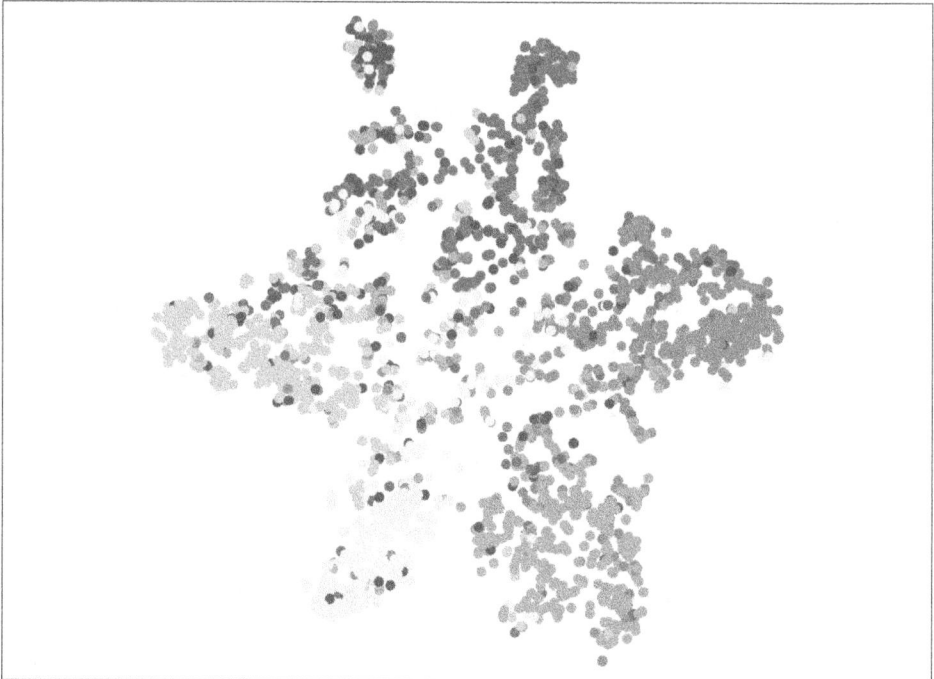

Figure 6-6. Visualization of the trained GAT model embeddings

Summary

This chapter explored some of the advanced graph learning techniques, mainly touching on knowledge graph embeddings and attention mechanisms on graphs. It also covered the fundamental concepts and methods behind knowledge graph embeddings, which create low-dimensional vector representations of nodes and edges to facilitate tasks such as link prediction and entity classification. Many embedding interaction methods, including distance-based approaches such as TransE and factorization-based methods such as DistMult, were discussed to illustrate how these interactions are modeled and utilized.

It also addressed the attention mechanisms employed in GATs. GATs use self-attention mechanisms to calculate attention coefficients for each node and its neighbors, allowing the model to consider the most relevant parts of the graph. GAT models enhance the efficiency and flexibility of graph neural networks, enabling them to manage nodes with varying degrees and generalize to unseen graphs. The implementation of multihead attention further stabilizes learning and enhances performance. We also highlighted practical applications of these advanced techniques across various domains, demonstrating their scalability and effectiveness.

In Chapter 7, we will explore the methods and techniques required to scale GNNs for large-scale graph learning tasks. As graphs grow in size and complexity, several challenges emerge, including computational limitations, memory constraints, and data management complexities. This chapter will cover key strategies for addressing these issues, such as mini-batching, memory-efficient training techniques like gradient checkpointing and subgraph sampling, and distributed computing approaches.

## CHAPTER 7

Scalable Graph Neural Networks

In the fast-paced world of machine learning, graph learning models are becoming a game changer for understanding and making sense of data that's structured like a graph. These models are super powerful and are being used in a variety of areas, from analyzing social networks to modeling biological data. Their strength lies in their ability to uncover complex patterns in data that's interconnected, which traditional machine learning methods might struggle with. However, as these graphs get bigger and more complicated, scaling graph learning models to handle these large-scale, real-world datasets becomes technically challenging. The challenges grow alongside the graphs—making it tough to maintain the efficiency and effectiveness of these models. As researchers and developers work on pushing the boundaries, finding ways to tackle these scaling challenges is key to unlocking the full potential of graph learning models in various practical applications.

Scalability is not merely an optional feature in graph learning; it is a fundamental requirement. The essence of graph learning methods lies in their ability to leverage the structure of graphs, where nodes represent entities and edges signify relationships. The value derived from graph models grows exponentially with the size and richness of the graph. For instance, social media networks, web graphs, and protein interaction networks often consist of millions or potentially billions of nodes and edges. To harness the full potential of graph learning models in these contexts, models must be capable of handling extensive and complex graph data efficiently. In smaller graphs, traditional graph learning models' architectures may perform adequately well. However, as the scale increases, several critical issues arise, necessitating innovative approaches to ensure that these models remain practical and effective. Scalable graph learning models can unlock vast amounts of untapped potential in massive datasets, providing faster insights and more accurate predictions.

Let's navigate the challenges that come with scaling graph learning models. As we progress through this chapter, we will explore strategies to address computational, memory, and data complexity issues.

Challenges in Scaling Graph Learning Models

When scaling graph learning methods, we face three main types of challenges: computational efficiency, memory constraints, and challenges related to data complexity and size. In this section, we shed some light on each of these challenges and discuss the problems and implications related to them. We also mention some potential techniques to tackle these challenges that we discuss in later sections in this chapter.

Computational Challenges

Scaling up graph learning methods substantially increases computational demands, similar to how running a marathon with a backpack full of rocks becomes exponentially more challenging. As the number of nodes and edges in a graph expands, tasks such as training and inference become significantly more time-consuming and resource-intensive. For example, consider a social network graph with millions of users (nodes) and their connections (edges). As the network grows, simple operations like node classification or link prediction require far more computational power. This increase in complexity often necessitates upgrading to more powerful and expensive hardware to handle the additional computational load. Without such upgrades, the efficiency of these algorithms suffers, leading to slower processing times and reduced performance.

Moreover, the increased computational burden also impacts the energy consumption and carbon footprint of data centers, raising environmental and sustainability concerns (*https://oreil.ly/3EBlB*). Advanced techniques like parallel processing and distributed computing are often employed to mitigate these challenges, but they come with their own set of complexities and overheads.

Memory Constraints

Larger graphs also present substantial memory challenges. The sheer volume of data that needs to be stored and processed can quickly exceed available memory resources. For instance, a graph representing a large transportation network, with cities as nodes and routes as edges, can become unwieldy as more cities and routes are added. Storing all this information in memory can be akin to trying to fit an entire library into a single bookshelf.

To manage these large datasets, graph learning techniques often employ strategies such as sampling or mini-batching. Sampling involves selecting a subset of the graph for processing at a time, which can reduce memory requirements but might miss important connections. Mini-batching, on the other hand, involves breaking down the data into smaller, more manageable pieces for sequential processing. While these methods help in handling large graphs, they introduce additional complexity. For instance, ensuring that sampled subsets maintain the overall structure and properties of the original graph can be challenging. Furthermore, these techniques might still struggle with extremely large graphs, necessitating even more innovative solutions like hierarchical graph processing (*https://oreil.ly/TUaKo*) or external memory algorithms (*https://oreil.ly/suzfP*).

Data Complexity and Size

Graph data is inherently complex due to the intricate relationships between data points, and this complexity escalates as the graph size increases. For example, in a biological network graph representing protein interactions, each protein (node) interacts with multiple other proteins (edges), creating a highly interconnected and intricate web. As more proteins and interactions are added, the graph becomes even more complex, akin to untangling a massive ball of yarn where each tug affects multiple strands simultaneously.

Handling this complexity requires more sophisticated models capable of managing the intricate web of relationships. *Advanced graph neural networks* (GNNs) and other graph-based learning models have been developed to address these challenges, but they require significant computational and memory resources. Additionally, as the size of the data grows, the likelihood of encountering noisy, incomplete, or irrelevant information increases. For instance, in a recommendation system graph, user interactions might include irrelevant or spammy data, complicating the training process. Models must be robust enough to handle these challenges, often necessitating complex preprocessing steps to clean and curate the data.

Furthermore, large and complex graph data can lead to *overfitting*, where models learn the noise in the data rather than the underlying patterns. This requires careful regularization and validation strategies to ensure that models generalize well to new, unseen data. Techniques such as graph augmentation, dropout for GNNs, and advanced training regimes are often employed to address these issues, but they add to the overall complexity of the graph learning process.

Now that we've navigated some of the main complexities and challenges in graph learning for enterprises dealing with massive graph datasets, let's explore some of the techniques widely used to address these challenges.

Mini-Batching in Graph Neural Networks

Mini-batching is a must-have strategy for scaling the training of GNNs to large data volumes. Unlike in traditional data structures like images or sequences, where examples are easily batched by resizing or padding, graph data presents unique challenges due to its complex and variable structure.

Definition and Importance of Mini-Batching

Mini-batching is a mechanism used to split a large dataset into smaller, more manageable batches of data during the training process. In traditional machine learning, mini-batching involves dividing a dataset into smaller subsets so that the model can be trained on these subsets rather than bigger batches or the entire dataset at once. This helps reduce memory usage and speeds up training.

In the context of graph neural networks, mini-batching is more challenging because graphs inherently contain a variable number of nodes and edges, making it difficult to apply the straightforward mini-batching approaches used in other domains like images or text. For efficient training on large graph datasets, it's crucial to process multiple graphs or subgraphs simultaneously without excessive memory overhead. Mini-batching allows the model to generalize better by learning from different parts of the graph in smaller batches, rather than requiring the entire graph to be loaded into memory at once.

Techniques for Effective Mini-Batching

PyG offers a sophisticated batching system that combines multiple graphs into a single large "batch graph" without the need for padding nodes or edges. This is achieved by:

Diagonal adjacency matrices
> Adjacency matrices are stacked diagonally, forming a block diagonal matrix that represents all batched graphs as isolated subgraphs within one larger graph.

Concatenating features
> Node and edge features are concatenated along their respective dimensions. This maintains the integrity and independence of each graph's data.

Sparse representation
> The use of sparse matrices for storing adjacency data ensures that only nonzero entries (actual edges) are kept, minimizing memory usage.

Implementation with PyG DataLoader

PyG utilizes the `DataLoader` class, which is an extension of PyTorch's `torch.utils`
`.data.DataLoader`. It customizes the `collate()` function to handle graph objects
properly:

```
from torch_geometric.loader import DataLoader
```

The `DataLoader` automatically adjusts the `edge_index` tensors for each graph, ensuring that node indices in edge lists correctly refer to the new node indices in the
batched graph.

For special cases, such as graph pairs or bipartite graphs (*https://oreil.ly/hs5zq*), PyG
allows for further customization:

Incremental indexing (__inc__)
Adjusts how node indices are incremented in batched graphs

Concatenation dimension (__cat_dim__)
Defines how different graph attributes are concatenated:

```
from torch_geometric.data import Data

class CustomData(Data):
    def __inc__(self, key, value):
        if 'index' in key:
            return self.num_nodes
        else:
            return 0

    def __cat_dim__(self, key, value):
        if 'index' in key:
            return 1
        else:
            return 0
```

Example: Batching pair and bipartite graphs

Here's how you might implement custom batching for complex scenarios such as
paired graphs of bipartite graphs:

```
class PairData(Data):
    def __inc__(self, key, value)  :
        if key.endswith('_s'):
            return self.x_s.size(0)
        elif key.endswith('_t'):
            return self.x_t.size(0)
        return 0

x_s = torch.randn(5, 3)  # Source nodes
x_t = torch.randn(4, 3)  # Target nodes
edge_index_s = torch.tensor([[0, 1], [1, 2]])
```

```
edge_index_t = torch.tensor([[0, 1], [1, 2]])

data = PairData(x_s=x_s, edge_index_s=edge_index_s, x_t=x_t,
                edge_index_t=edge_index_t)
loader = DataLoader([data], batch_size=2, follow_batch=['x_s', 'x_t'])
```

Memory-Efficient Training Techniques

As graph learning models continue to grow in size and complexity in order to tackle increasingly challenging tasks, the need for memory-efficient training techniques becomes paramount. These techniques are essential for researchers and practitioners working with large-scale graph data, as they enable the training of more sophisticated models on limited hardware resources. In this section, we will explore three key approaches that have shown great promise in reducing memory requirements while maintaining model performance: gradient checkpointing, subgraph sampling methods, and layer-wise relevance propagation.

Gradient Checkpointing

Gradient checkpointing is a technique that trades computation time for memory savings during the training of deep neural networks, including GNNs. The core idea behind this approach is to store only a subset of activations during the forward pass, and recompute the missing activations on demand during the backward pass. In the context of graph learning models, this technique can be particularly effective due to the often dense and memory-intensive nature of graph representations. By strategically selecting which activations to store and which to recompute, gradient checkpointing allows for training larger models or processing larger graphs that would otherwise exceed available memory. For example, Figure 7-1 gives an example of training forward and backward passes where specific computation nodes are stored as a checkpoint and later used in further pass updates.

The implementation of gradient checkpointing in graph learning models requires careful consideration of the graph structure and the specific operations involved in message passing and aggregation—which includes analyzing the graph's often irregular and sparse structure to optimize memory access during recomputation, strategically planning checkpointing within the computationally intensive message passing steps (perhaps checkpointing aggregated messages rather than individual ones), and understanding the computational cost of different aggregation functions. Researchers have developed various strategies for optimal checkpoint placement in GNNs, taking into account the connectivity patterns and computational costs associated with different layers and operations.

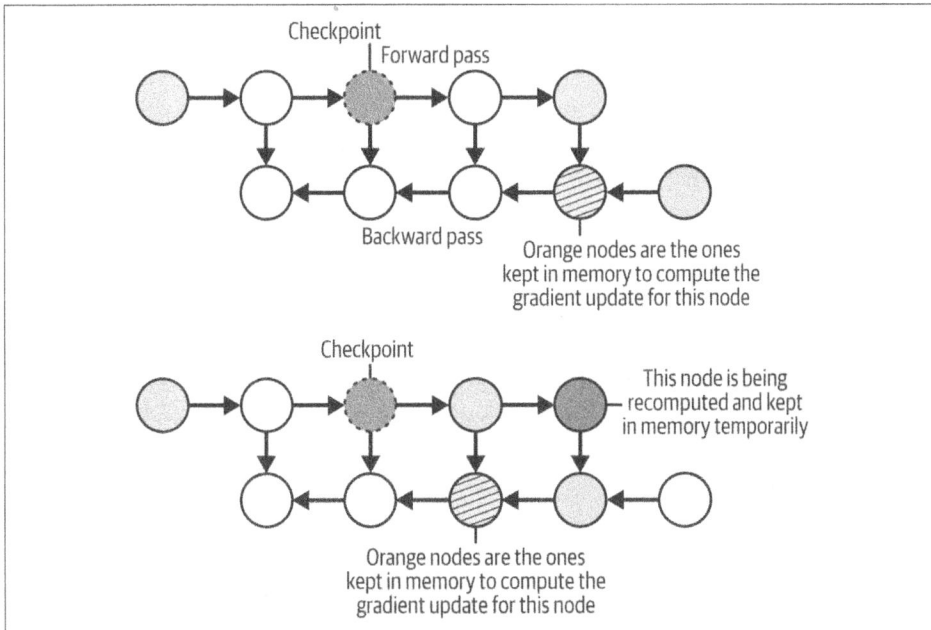

Figure 7-1. Illustration of gradient checkpointing on a training propagation graph (adapted from an image from Gradient Checkpointing Demo on GitHub (https:// oreil.ly/f0mZR)); orange nodes appear in solid light gray in print book

In the context of training deep GCNs using PyG, the CLASSDeepGCNLayer provides an option for gradient checkpointing through its ckpt_grad parameter:

```
DeepGCNLayer(..., ckpt_grad=True # Enable gradient checkpointing for each layer)
```

> This GitHub repository (*https://oreil.ly/qiP20*) provides a comprehensive framework for gradient checkpointing in general deep learning models that can be very useful in the context of training scalable graph models.

Subgraph Sampling Methods

Subgraph sampling methods offer a strategic approach to managing memory constraints in graph learning models by training on smaller subgraphs extracted from the original, larger graph instead of handling the entire structure at once. This method proves particularly useful for graphs that surpass the system's memory capacity. By working with smaller portions or subgraphs, the method helps circumvent the limitations posed by large data sizes.

There are several strategies for subgraph sampling, each catering to different aspects of graph structure:

Node-wise sampling
This strategy selects a subset of nodes and their immediate neighborhoods, focusing on local connectivity and the features of the chosen nodes.

Edgewise sampling
In contrast to node-wise sampling, this technique selects edges and their associated nodes, emphasizing the relationships within the graph.

Layer-wise sampling
This method varies the subgraphs sampled for each layer of the GNN, allowing for diverse exposure to the graph's features across the network's depth.

Subgraph sampling methods are typically applied stochastically during the training process. This variability allows the model to encounter different facets of the graph with each training iteration, serving two main purposes:

Reduction in memory usage
By managing only parts of the graph at any given time, memory usage is significantly reduced.

Regularization effect
Sampling acts as a form of regularization, potentially enhancing the model's predictability to generalize from training data to unobserved data.

However, there are important considerations to keep in mind when implementing subgraph sampling:

Maintenance of graph structure
It is crucial to ensure that the structural integrity and key properties of the original graph are preserved in the subgraphs. This preservation is vital for maintaining the quality and reliability of the learning process.

Avoidance of bias
The sampling process must be carefully designed to avoid introducing significant biases that could skew model training and affect performance.

PyG offers a variety of sampling techniques to efficiently handle large-scale graph datasets, such as the `NeighborSampler` for node-wise sampling among others:

```
from torch_geometric.loader import NeighborSampler

sampler = NeighborSampler(data.edge_index, num_neighbors=[10, 10],
                          replace=False, directed=True)

for subset_data in sampler(data):
    # Training your model on the subset_data
```

In the statement NeighborSampler(data.edge_index, num_neighbors=[10, 10], replace=False, directed=True) from PyG, the [10, 10] determines a 2-hop neighbor sampling strategy for creating mini-batch subgraphs: the first 10 specifies sampling up to 10 direct (1-hop) neighbors for each central node, while the second 10 dictates sampling up to 10 neighbors of those first-hop neighbors (2-hop neighbors) without replacement (replace=False) and considering edge directionality (directed=True); these dimensions define the local neighborhood size and receptive field captured in the sampled subgraphs for efficient training of graph neural networks on large datasets.

The book's GitHub repository (*https://github.com/gl4ebook/py-graf*) includes complete end-to-end examples that demonstrate how to implement these sampling techniques in practical scenarios.

Layer-Wise Relevance Propagation

Layer-wise relevance propagation (LRP) is a technique originally developed for explaining the predictions of deep neural networks, but it has found applications in memory-efficient training of graph learning models as well. In the context of GNNs, LRP can be used to identify the most relevant nodes, edges, or features for a particular prediction or task. This information can then be leveraged to prioritize the allocation of computational resources and memory during training. By focusing on the most relevant parts of the graph, LRP allows for more efficient use of available memory without significantly compromising model performance.

Additionally, LRP can be combined with other memory-saving techniques, such as subgraph sampling, to further optimize the training process. For instance, relevance scores obtained through LRP can guide the sampling process, ensuring that the most important subgraphs are selected for training. This approach not only reduces memory requirements but can also lead to faster convergence and improved model quality.

The implementation of these memory-efficient training techniques in graph learning models often requires careful consideration of the specific architecture and task at hand. For example, different GNN architectures may benefit more from certain techniques than others. Models with many layers or those processing graphs with high-degree nodes may see significant improvements from gradient checkpointing, while models dealing with extremely large graphs may rely more heavily on subgraph sampling methods. Moreover, the choice of technique may also depend on the available hardware resources and the desired balance between memory usage, computational cost, and model performance.

It's worth noting that these techniques are not mutually exclusive and can often be combined for even greater memory savings. For instance, a training pipeline might use subgraph sampling to reduce the overall size of the input, apply gradient checkpointing within the model to further reduce memory requirements, and utilize LRP to guide both the sampling process and the allocation of computational resources. Such a multifaceted approach can enable the training of increasingly large and sophisticated graph learning models on limited hardware.

As the field of graph learning continues to advance, we can expect to see further developments in memory-efficient training techniques. These may include novel sampling strategies that better preserve graph properties, more efficient implementations of gradient checkpointing for graph-specific operations, and advanced relevance propagation methods tailored to the unique challenges of graph data. Additionally, the integration of these techniques with emerging hardware accelerators like NVIDIA's Blackwell (*https://oreil.ly/3aaOh*) and distributed computing frameworks will likely play a crucial role in scaling graph learning models to even larger and more complex datasets.

Distributed Data and Compute Strategies

In this section, we will discuss how to tackle scalability challenges in graph learning related to both high computational complexity and large data size using distributed data and compute. We will discuss how to distribute data and compute in graph learning in order to scale it to highly complex graphs. We discuss some challenges that arise when trying to distribute data and compute in graph learning and how to address them. We will also discuss some of the tools and libraries that can be used to distribute data and compute in graph learning.

Distributed Execution Strategies

When it comes to large-scale graph learning, efficiently handling and processing data is key to ensuring that things run smoothly and quickly. One popular technique to achieve this is *distributed mini-batching*. This means splitting the data into smaller chunks (mini-batches) and processing them in parallel across multiple workers. Let's dive into different ways to do this, using the diagram in Figure 7-2 to guide us.

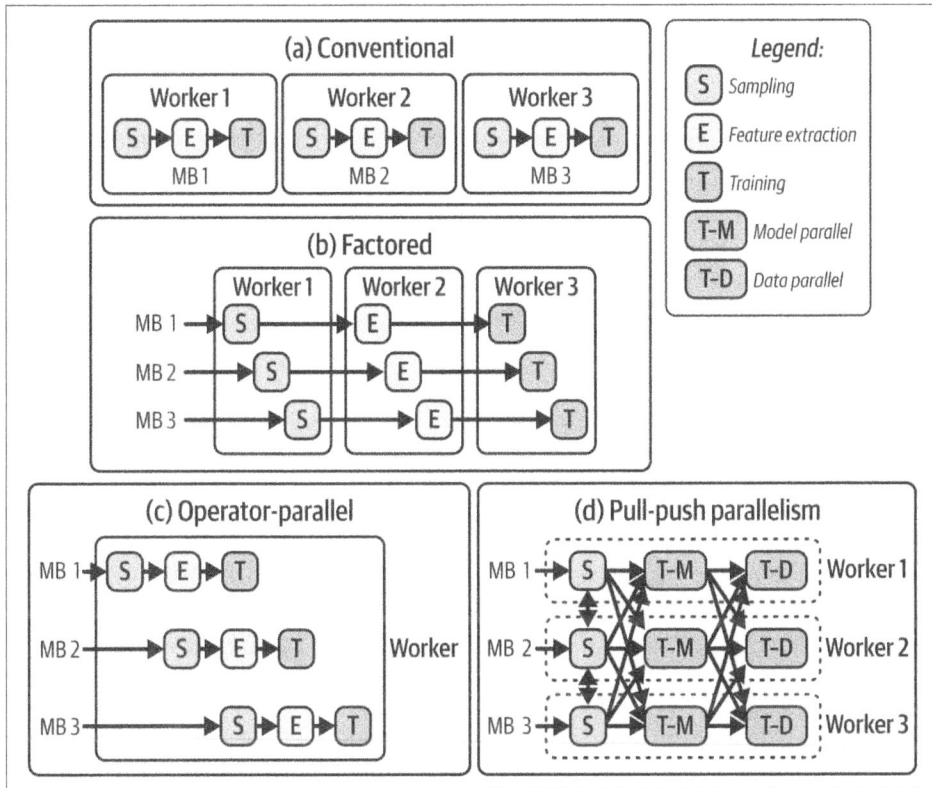

Figure 7-2. Different mini-batch execution strategies for data and compute parallelization in GNNs (Shao, Y. et al (2024))[1]

Conventional mini-batching

In the conventional approach, shown in Figure 7-2(a), we split the dataset into several mini-batches, with each worker handling one mini-batch from start to finish. This includes sampling (S), feature extraction (E), and training (T).

Each worker works independently, running the full pipeline on its assigned mini-batch. This method is straightforward and easy to manage, making it a popular choice. However, it doesn't take full advantage of parallel processing within each step, which can limit overall efficiency and scalability.

---

1 Shao, Y. et al. (2024). "Distributed Graph Neural Network Training: A Survey." *ACM Computing Surveys* 56(8), 1-39.

Factored mini-batching

The factored mini-batching approach, seen in Figure 7-2(b), splits the workload by assigning different tasks to different workers. For example, one set of workers handles all the sampling (S), another set does the feature extraction (E), and a third set takes care of training (T).

This method allows for more efficient use of resources; each stage of the process can be run in parallel and optimized separately. However, it adds complexity because workers need to communicate intermediate results to the next stage, which can create bottlenecks and increase data transfer overhead.

Operator-parallel mini-batching

Operator-parallel mini-batching, illustrated in Figure 7-2(c), aims to parallelize tasks within a single worker. Each mini-batch goes through the sampling (S), feature extraction (E), and training (T) steps concurrently.

This method maximizes the use of computational resources within a worker by running multiple mini-batches simultaneously, reducing idle times, and speeding up the process. However, managing dependencies and synchronization within a worker can be challenging and may require advanced scheduling techniques.

Pull-push parallelism

Pull-push parallelism, shown in Figure 7-2(d), combines both *model parallelism* and *data parallelism*. Here, the sampling step (S) is distributed across multiple workers. After that, the process splits into two parallel streams: model parallelism (T-M) and data parallelism (T-D).

Model parallelism splits the model across workers, allowing each to process different parts of the model at the same time. Data parallelism, on the other hand, replicates the model across workers so each can process different subsets of data simultaneously.

This hybrid approach leverages the strengths of both model and data parallelism, providing a scalable solution for large-scale graph learning. The pull-push mechanism ensures efficient data flow and synchronization between stages, minimizing bottlenecks and maximizing resource use.

Comparing the approaches

Each mini-batching strategy has its pros and cons. The conventional approach is easy to implement but may not use resources efficiently. Factored mini-batching introduces parallelism but requires careful management of worker communication. Operator-parallel mini-batching maximizes parallelism within a worker but can be complex to implement. Pull-push parallelism balances model and data parallelism for better scalability but also requires sophisticated data flow management.

When choosing a mini-batching strategy, consider:

Graph size and complexity
Larger, more complex graphs may benefit from advanced parallelism techniques.

Resource availability
The availability and configuration of computational resources, like CPUs and GPUs, can influence the choice.

Implementation complexity
Simpler methods may be easier to implement and maintain, while more complex strategies can offer better performance.

By weighing these factors and understanding the trade-offs, you can choose the best mini-batching strategy to achieve scalable and efficient graph learning.

Graph Partitioning Strategies

Graph partitioning is a crucial technique in scaling GML models, especially in a distributed setting where the graph's sheer size can overwhelm a single machine's memory and processing capabilities. The objective of graph partitioning is to segment a vast graph into smaller, manageable subgraphs that can be processed independently and concurrently across multiple machines or nodes. As illustrated in Figure 7-3, two fundamental strategies in graph partitioning are *node splitting* and *edge splitting*.

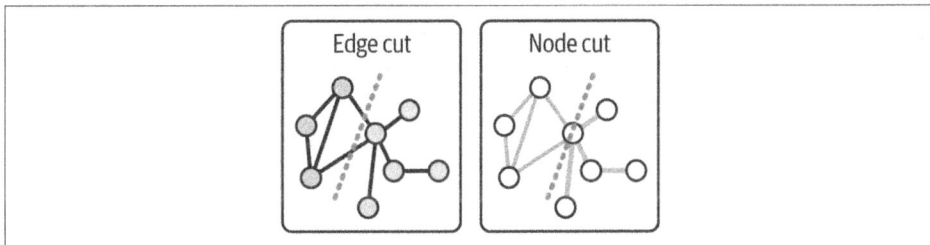

Figure 7-3. Graph partitioning techniques

Node splitting

Node splitting, also known as *vertex partitioning*, focuses on dividing the graph's nodes into distinct subsets. Each subset, or partition, contains a unique set of nodes and the edges that connect them within the same partition. The main challenge in the node splitting approach lies in minimizing the number of edges that traverse partitions—termed as *cut edges*—as these edges require inter-machine communication during distributed processing.

To achieve efficient node splitting, several heuristics and algorithms can be employed:

Min-cut partitioning
This algorithm aims to minimize the number of cut edges. The Kernighan–Lin algorithm (*https://oreil.ly/ZasjI*) and its variants are commonly used approaches. By iteratively swapping nodes between partitions to reduce the cut size, these algorithms achieve relatively balanced partitions with minimal communication overhead.

Multilevel partitioning
This approach involves coarsening the graph by consolidating nodes and edges, subsequently partitioning the condensed graph, and then refining the partitioning as the graph is expanded back to its original form. METIS[2] and Scotch[3] are popular tools that utilize multilevel partitioning. This multistage process aims to achieve efficient and high-quality graph partitioning, particularly for large graphs, by initially working with a smaller, coarser representation to quickly find a good initial split and then refining it on the original graph to optimize metrics like balanced partition sizes and minimized edge cuts, crucial for parallel processing and reducing communication overhead.

Spectral partitioning
This technique uses the graph's Laplacian matrix to find an optimal cut. By solving for the eigenvectors of the Laplacian, the nodes can be partitioned based on the sign of the components in the second smallest eigenvector.

Node splitting proves exceptionally effective in scenarios where the graph exhibits community structure, with nodes within the same community being more densely interconnected than those in differing communities. In such cases, partitions can organically conform to these community boundaries, hence reducing the number of cut edges and minimizing inter-machine communication.

Edge splitting

Edge splitting, or *edge partitioning*, takes a different approach by focusing on dividing the graph's edges rather than its nodes. Each partition in edge splitting consists of a unique set of edges, and nodes may appear in multiple partitions if they are incident to edges in different partitions.

The key considerations in edge splitting include:

---

2 Karypis, G., and Kumar., V (1997). "METIS: A Software Package for Partitioning Unstructured Graphs, Partitioning Meshes, and Computing Fill-Reducing Orderings of Sparse Matrices" (*https://oreil.ly/QAFyI*).

3 Chevalier, C., and Pellegrini., F. (2008). "PT-Scotch: A Tool for Efficient Parallel Graph Ordering" (*https://oreil.ly/aJ18M*). *Parallel Computing* 34(6-8), 318-331.

Edge-cut minimization

Similar to node splitting, edge partitioning aims to minimize the number of edges that need to be replicated across partitions. Algorithms such as *random edge assignment* (*https://oreil.ly/ptgBj*), *greedy edge assignment* (*https://oreil.ly/jvBYR*), and *hypergraph partitioning* (*https://oreil.ly/9GIhU*) can be used. Hypergraph partitioning, in particular, models the graph as a hypergraph where edges (hyperedges) can connect multiple nodes, allowing more sophisticated partitioning strategies.

Vertex replication

In edge partitioning, nodes are often replicated across partitions to maintain edge connectivity. The challenge is to minimize the replication factor, which is the average number of partitions a node is present in. High replication factors can lead to increased memory usage and inter-machine communication.

Load balancing

Ensuring that each partition has a roughly equal number of edges is crucial for balanced workload distribution. Imbalances can lead to some machines being overburdened while others are underutilized, reducing overall system efficiency.

Edge splitting is advantageous in scenarios where the graph is edge-heavy, and the computational tasks primarily involve edge operations, such as in certain types of link prediction and edge classification problems.

Both node splitting and edge splitting are essential techniques for scaling GML models in distributed environments. The choice between them depends on the specific characteristics of the graph and the nature of the machine learning tasks. Effective graph partitioning can significantly enhance the performance and scalability of distributed graph learning systems, enabling the processing of massive graphs that would otherwise be infeasible to handle. By carefully balancing the partitions and minimizing inter-machine communication, these techniques ensure efficient parallel processing and pave the way for advanced graph-based insights and applications.

Distributed Graph Learning Tools

Distributed computing involves dividing large tasks across multiple computers to enhance efficiency and processing speed. Instead of a single computer handling a massive job alone, distributed computing spreads the workload, making it easier to manage large datasets and complex computations. This approach not only accelerates processing but also helps avoid issues such as memory overload. It's akin to having a team work on different parts of a project simultaneously, rather than relying on one individual. In the realm of graph learning—which deals with extensive networks of interconnected data points—distributed computing is particularly valuable. Frameworks like PGL (*https://oreil.ly/RnyIl*) utilize these techniques to process graphs with billions of nodes and edges, enabling the analysis and extraction of insights from vast datasets. Such scalability is crucial for applications ranging from social network analysis to bioinformatics.

PyTorch Geometric

Distributed PyTorch Geometric (*https://oreil.ly/a32rS*) is a popular extension to PyTorch Geometric that leverages PyTorch's distributed package and can significantly speed up the training process. The following explores the key concepts and strategies for leveraging distributed PyTorch Geometric in multi-GPU and multinode environments:

Multi-GPU training

Utilizing multiple GPUs on a single machine can significantly accelerate the training process of graph learning models. PyG seamlessly integrates with PyTorch's native distributed computing capabilities, allowing for efficient data parallelism. In this approach, the input graph is partitioned across available GPUs, with each GPU processing a subset of the data. The model is replicated on each GPU, and gradients are synchronized across devices to update the model parameters.

PyG provides specialized data loaders and samplers that handle graph partitioning and distribution across GPUs. These tools ensure balanced workloads and minimize communication overhead between devices. Additionally, PyG offers distributed implementations of popular GNN layers, such as GraphSAGE and GCN, which are optimized for multi-GPU scenarios.

Multinode training

For extremely large-scale graph learning tasks, a single machine may not suffice. Multinode training extends the distributed paradigm across multiple compute nodes, each potentially equipped with multiple GPUs. This multinode training setup facilitates the processing of massive graphs that surpass the memory capabilities of a single machine and allows for linear scaling of computational resources.

PyG leverages PyTorch's distributed communication backend to facilitate multinode training. It supports various communication protocols, including *Transmission Control Protocol* (TCP) (*https://oreil.ly/Y4vvF*) and *Message Passing Interface* (MPI) (*https://oreil.ly/DdgUo*), to handle internode data transfer and synchronization. The library also provides abstractions for node-level operations, allowing seamless distribution of graph data and model computations across the cluster.

PaddlePaddle: Paddle Graph Learning (PGL)

PGL (*https://oreil.ly/RnyIl*) is a tool built by Baidu that offers various graph learning methods, including distributed training of graph models. It is a powerful graph learning tool designed to tackle the unique challenges of analyzing and learning from graph-based data.

Let's review some of the key features of PGL:

Efficient graph computation
> PGL is optimized for performance, with efficient graph computations that handle large datasets well. It includes fast sparse matrix operations and quick data loading, essential for working with big graph structures without slowing down.

Comprehensive graph utilities
> PGL provides a rich set of tools for graph data processing, including construction, transformation, sampling, and visualization. These utilities streamline the workflow from raw graph data to model training and evaluation, making it easier to manage and work with graph datasets.

Scalability and distributed training
> PGL is built for scalability, capable of handling large graph datasets through distributed training. By leveraging PaddlePaddle's distributed training capabilities, PGL can scale computations across multiple GPUs or entire clusters, ensuring efficient processing and training of large-scale graphs.

Scalable graph learning with PGL
> PGL's scalability makes it perfect for handling large and complex graph datasets found in both industry and research. Here are some ways to use PGL for scalable graph learning:

Distributed graph training
> PGL supports distributed training, allowing users to spread graph computations across multiple GPUs or machines. This parallelism reduces training time for large graphs, making it feasible to work with datasets containing millions of nodes and edges.

Graph data parallelism
> PGL enables *graph data parallelism*, where different parts of a graph are processed simultaneously. This approach is especially useful for extremely large graphs, maximizing resource use and minimizing data processing bottlenecks.

Efficient memory management
> PGL uses efficient memory management techniques to handle large graph structures without exhausting system resources. These optimizations ensure that even the largest graphs can be processed within available memory limits.

PGL is a robust, efficient, and flexible framework for scalable graph learning. Its integration with PaddlePaddle, support for a wide range of GNN models, and advanced features for distributed training and memory management make it a powerful tool for researchers and developers. Whether working with social networks, biological networks, recommendation systems, or other graph-based applications, PGL provides the necessary capabilities to manage, analyze, and learn from large-scale graph data effectively.

Distributed Training with PyG

The `torch_geometric.distributed` module offers a robust framework for distributed training of GNNs, exclusively utilizing PyTorch and PyG technologies. This system supports deployment across clusters of any size and utilizes multiple CPUs, with GPU compatibility currently in development and anticipated for future release.

Designed to streamline the training of large-scale GNNs, this solution incorporates *distributed data parallelism (https://oreil.ly/_qul2)* to manage model training and remote procedure call (RPC) (*https://oreil.ly/wrspR*) in order to facilitate the efficient sampling and retrieval of features from distant nodes. Key components of this architecture include:

`DistNeighborSampler`
> This class is responsible for implementing CPU-based sampling algorithms. It extracts features from both local and remote data sources while maintaining a consistent output data structure.

`DistLoader`
> This tool ensures the reliable management of RPC connections between samplers, handling the opening and closing of these connections securely.

`Partitioner`
> Employing a METIS-based strategy, this component efficiently divides the graph data among the nodes.

To effectively manage the complexities of distributed graph learning, the architecture employs a strategic approach to data preparation and distribution. The subsequent steps detail how the graph data is prepared and partitioned across the nodes in the cluster, a crucial phase that sets the stage for efficient distributed training.

Prepare and Partition the Graph Data

In the distributed training framework, each node within a cluster manages a specific portion of the graph data. Prior to initiating training, the dataset is segmented into multiple partitions. Each partition is specifically allocated to a corresponding training node.

The `partition_dataset` function in the following is designed to prepare and parti-tion graph data for distributed training. It handles the entire process from loading the dataset, applying necessary transformations, creating partitions for distributed nodes, and saving labels:

```
import os
import os.path as osp
import torch
from torch_geometric.distributed import Partitioner

# Function to partition dataset and save partitions and labels
def partition_dataset(data, dataset_label_col: str, dir: str, num_parts: int,
                      recursive: bool = False, use_sparse_tensor: bool = False):

    # Set up directory for saving partitions
    save_dir = osp.join(dir, 'graph_partitions', f'{num_parts}-parts')
    partitions_dir = osp.join(save_dir, 'graph_partitions')

    # Initialize and generate data partitions
    partitioner = Partitioner(data, num_parts, partitions_dir, recursive)
    partitioner.generate_partition()

    # Set up directory and save labels
    print('-- Saving label ...')
    label_dir = osp.join(save_dir, 'graph_label')
    os.makedirs(label_dir, exist_ok=True)

    # Label extraction
    label = data['dataset_label_col']

    # Save labels to file
    torch.save(label, osp.join(label_dir, 'label.pt'))

    # Get index splits and save respective partitions
    split_idx = get_idx_split(dataset, dataset_name, data)
    save_partitions(split_idx, dataset_name, num_parts, save_dir)
```

When training a model in a distributed environment using multiple nodes, the coordination and communication between these nodes are crucial. After partitioning the data, as discussed previously, you can either manually execute commands on each node or automate the process with a script. Let's focus on the manual execution method for simplicity.

Manual Execution of Distributed Training

In manual execution, you need to run a command on each node of your cluster. Each node requires specific configurations to identify its role and communicate effectively with others. Here's what you generally need to do:

Set the master address

The IP address of the node designated as the master (node#0) needs to be set on all nodes. This address is crucial as it serves as the main communication hub for all nodes during training.

Specify the node rank

Each node in the cluster must have a unique rank. Typically, the master node (where you might coordinate or initiate the training process) is assigned rank 0. Each additional node is assigned a subsequent rank (1, 2, 3, etc.). The node rank is critical because it identifies the node within the distributed system, allowing proper message passing and data synchronization.

Point to the dataset partition directory

Each node must know where to find its corresponding data partition. The path to this directory should be specified accurately to ensure that each node works with the correct subset of data.

Key Components of Distributed Training with PyG

The following are the key components that you need to consider while doing distributed training with PyG:

Initialization of distributed context

Establishing a distributed context is crucial for defining the communication and coordination mechanisms among the different nodes. In the code, this is done using `DistContext`, which configures settings such as `world_size`(number of nodes), `rank`, `global_world_size`, and `group_name`. This context is essential for managing the distributed environment and ensuring that each node knows its role within the overall system:

```
current_ctx = DistContext(
    world_size=num_nodes,
    rank=node_rank,
    global_world_size=num_nodes,
    global_rank=node_rank,
    group_name='distributed-ogb-sage'
)
```

`DistributedDataParallel` *setup*

The model is wrapped in `DistributedDataParallel` (DDP). This is a key component that enables the parallelization of data processing across multiple nodes. DDP synchronizes the gradients across the different nodes, ensuring that each node contributes to the learning process:

```
model = DistributedDataParallel(model)
```

Data loading with distributed neighbor loaders

`DistNeighborLoader` is used to distribute data across nodes. This loader ensures that each node only works with its partition of the data—which is crucial for large datasets where each node cannot hold the entire dataset in memory. It also handles neighbor sampling for graph neural networks—which is critical for the scalability of training on large graphs:

```
train_loader = DistNeighborLoader(
    ...
)
```

Training and testing functions

Both functions incorporate checks to ensure that operations are only performed on the data relevant to a specific node. This is guided by the node's rank within the distributed context. Progress and accuracy calculations are also localized to each node, and results are logged per node.

Synchronization points

The code uses `torch.distributed.barrier()` at various points to synchronize all nodes. These barriers ensure that no node moves ahead in the training or testing process without the others, which is crucial for maintaining consistency across the training epochs:

```
def train(model, loader, optimizer, dist_context, device, epoch):
    # ... training logic here
    torch.distributed.barrier()
```

In the GitHub repository (*https://github.com/gl4ebook/py-graf*), you can find complete end-to-end examples of training and testing code for several datasets, including both distributed CPU and GPU training. Each of the provided examples highlights best practices for setting up distributed training frameworks and optimizing performance across different hardware configurations.

Advanced Architectures for Scaling Graph Neural Networks

As GNNs continue to demonstrate their effectiveness in various domains, researchers and practitioners face the challenge of scaling these models to handle increasingly large and complex graph structures. This section explores advanced architectures and techniques that address the scalability issues inherent in GNNs, focusing on three key areas: sparsity exploitation, approximation techniques, and the use of external memory.

Sparsity Exploitation

Sparsity exploitation is a fundamental approach to scaling GNNs, leveraging the inherent sparsity often present in real-world graph data. Many large-scale graphs, such as social networks or molecular structures, exhibit sparse connectivity patterns where most nodes are connected to only a small fraction of the total graph. By exploiting this sparsity, we can significantly reduce the computational and memory requirements of GNN operations. One effective method is the use of sparse matrix representations and operations, which allow for efficient storage and manipulation of graph structures. These sparse representations can be combined with specialized hardware accelerators designed to handle sparse computations, further improving performance. Additionally, techniques like graph sampling and node clustering can be employed to focus computational resources on the most relevant parts of the graph, reducing overall complexity while maintaining model accuracy.

Approximation Techniques

Approximation techniques offer another avenue for scaling GNNs by trading off some degree of accuracy for improved efficiency and scalability. These methods aim to approximate the full graph convolution operation with less computationally intensive alternatives. One popular approach is the use of *graph coarsening*, where the original graph is progressively simplified into a hierarchy of smaller graphs. This allows for efficient computation at different scales, with information propagating between levels. Another promising technique is the application of random walk–based methods, which approximate the neighborhood aggregation process by sampling a subset of paths through the graph. These approaches can significantly reduce the computational complexity of GNN operations—especially for large graphs—while still capturing essential structural information. Researchers have also explored the use of low-rank approximations (*https://oreil.ly/eoaG0*) and dimensionality reduction techniques (*https://oreil.ly/IB5wr*) to compress the graph representation and accelerate computations.

Use of External Memory

The use of external memory has emerged as a powerful strategy for scaling GNNs beyond the limitations of GPU memory. As graph sizes continue to grow, it becomes increasingly challenging to fit entire graph structures and their associated feature representations into the limited memory of accelerator devices. External memory architectures like *distributed external memory architectures* (*https://oreil.ly/umVBN*) allow GNN models to operate on graphs that exceed available GPU memory by intelligently managing data movement between fast but limited GPU memory and larger, slower storage systems such as CPU RAM or even solid-state drives. This approach often involves partitioning the graph into manageable subgraphs and implementing efficient caching and prefetching mechanisms to minimize data transfer overhead. Some advanced architectures employ hierarchical memory systems, where different levels of the memory hierarchy are utilized for storing and processing graph data at various granularities. By carefully orchestrating data movement and computation, these external memory approaches enable the training and inference of GNNs on massive graphs that would otherwise be intractable.

The combination of sparsity exploitation, approximation techniques, and external memory usage forms a powerful toolset for scaling GNNs to handle increasingly large and complex graph structures. However, the effective integration of these approaches often requires careful consideration of trade-offs between accuracy, computational efficiency, and memory usage. Researchers continue to explore novel architectures that combine these techniques in innovative ways, such as hybrid models that adaptively switch between exact and approximate computations based on graph characteristics or available resources. Furthermore, the development of specialized hardware accelerators designed to efficiently handle sparse graph operations and manage complex memory hierarchies promises to further push the boundaries of GNN scalability.

As we look to the future of scaling graph learning models, several promising directions emerge. The integration of these advanced architectures with other machine learning paradigms, such as transformer models or neural ordinary differential equations, may lead to more powerful and flexible graph learning systems. Additionally, the development of distributed and federated learning approaches for GNNs could enable the processing of massive, geographically distributed graph datasets while addressing privacy and communication constraints. The continued advancement of these scaling techniques will be crucial in unlocking the full potential of graph neural networks across a wide range of applications, from analyzing large-scale social networks to simulating complex physical systems and beyond.

Summary

In this chapter we explored essential strategies and challenges associated with scaling GNNs to handle large and complex graph datasets. We discussed scalability fundamentals, emphasizing the need for efficient processing and distributed training and testing of large-scale graphs with millions of nodes and edges.

Key challenges such as computational demands, memory limitations, and data management complexities were covered. Techniques such as mini-batching, which adapt traditional batching to graph structures, and advanced memory-efficient methods such as gradient checkpointing and subgraph sampling were explored to optimize resource use and performance.

We also covered distributed data and compute strategies, which are crucial for managing high computational complexity and large data volumes. This included an examination of distributed training mechanisms in PyG, graph partitioning strategies like node and edge splitting, and practical case studies to illustrate these strategies in action.

## CHAPTER 8

Enterprise Applications of Graphs

Graphs have transformed the way that enterprises model and analyze complex relationships and interconnected systems. Unlike traditional tabular data structures, graphs excel at capturing the rich, multifaceted relationships that exist between entities within an organization. This distinctive capability empowers enterprises to derive more profound insights, enhance decision-making processes, and optimize operational efficiencies in ways that were previously challenging to attain.

One of the primary advantages of graph technology lies in its ability to represent relationships between entities. For instance, in *customer relationship management* (CRM) systems, graphs can effectively model the relationships between customers, their purchases, and their interactions with the company. This rich data can then be leveraged to identify patterns and trends, such as determining which products are most popular with specific customer segments or which marketing campaigns yield the highest return on investment. Similarly, graphs are well-suited for representing complex systems such as supply chains or IT networks. By modeling these systems as graphs, organizations can better understand their operations, identify potential bottlenecks, and pinpoint areas for improvement, ultimately leading to enhanced efficiency and reduced costs.

Scalability is another critical advantage of graph technology in enterprise environments. As businesses expand, the volume and complexity of their data grow in tandem. Graphs are uniquely equipped to handle large-scale data and can be scaled to meet the demands of even the most data-intensive applications. Furthermore, the efficiency of graph technology ensures that even complex queries like "Identify all customers who purchased product X in the last quarter, are connected to customers who have a high lifetime spending, and whose network of friends shows a positive sentiment towards our brand on social media" are processed quickly, allowing organizations to gain the insights they need in a timely manner.

In this chapter, we will explore how graphs are being applied in various enterprise contexts today, highlighting their impact and potential for driving business success in domains such as customer insights, security and risk analysis, and healthcare.

Customer and Market Insights

In the modern data-driven business environment, organizations are persistently exploring methods to secure a competitive advantage and stimulate business growth. Graphs have surfaced as a robust tool for extracting valuable insights from customer and market data (*https://oreil.ly/OExKe*). By harnessing the capability of graphs to model complex relationships and interconnected systems, enterprises can gain a more profound understanding of their customers, uncover new opportunities, and make well-informed decisions.

A key advantage of utilizing graphs for business intelligence is their capacity to illustrate customer behavior and preferences as well as incorporate the 360 view of other connected neighboring customers in the graph. By presenting the relationships among customers, their purchases, and their interactions with the company, businesses can uncover insights into customer journeys, pinpoint key influencers, and enhance the precision of their marketing strategies. For instance, a retail organization might leverage a graph to identify customers who regularly buy a specific product and subsequently suggest complementary items based on their purchasing patterns.

Graphs can also serve as a powerful tool for uncovering new growth opportunities. By examining the interconnections between customers, products, and competitors, businesses can detect market gaps and innovate new products or services to address these unmet needs. For example, a technology firm might utilize a graph to identify customers currently using a competitor's product and subsequently design a new offering that remedies the deficiencies of the competitor's product.

Beyond analyzing customer behavior and identifying growth opportunities, graphs can significantly enhance decision making. By modeling the interdependencies among various factors—such as customer demand, supply chain constraints, and financial performance—businesses can simulate different scenarios and make well-informed decisions regarding resource allocation and operational optimization. For instance, a manufacturing company might utilize a graph to assess the impact of various production schedules on both customer satisfaction and profitability. In the following, we will discuss applications of graph learning models in the context of customer segmentation, social networks, and recommendation engines.

Customer Segmentation

Customer segmentation is a critical component of CRM, entailing the division of customers into discrete groups based on common characteristics, behaviors, or preferences. Conventional methods of customer segmentation typically depend on static attributes, such as demographics or purchase history. In contrast, graphs facilitate a more dynamic and nuanced analysis by incorporating the relationships among customers and their interactions with the company, thereby offering deeper insights into customer behavior and connections.

For instance, a graph can be constructed with customers and products as nodes and their purchase history as edges. Analyzing this graph using clustering algorithms can reveal groups of customers with similar purchasing behaviors. This analysis enables the development of targeted marketing campaigns, personalized recommendations, and tailored loyalty programs. While traditional customer segmentation methods often rely on static attributes like demographics or purchase history, offering a limited view of customer behavior, graphs provide a more dynamic understanding by incorporating the relationships and interactions among customers and the company.

A huge advantage of utilizing graphs for customer segmentation is their ability to uncover hidden relationships and patterns within customer data. By examining the connections between customers, graphs can reveal underlying structures and communities that might remain obscured with traditional segmentation methods. This deeper insight enables the creation of targeted marketing campaigns, personalized recommendations, and loyalty programs that are finely tuned to the distinct needs and preferences of each customer segment.

In practice, graphs can be constructed using a variety of techniques. Here are a few examples of real-world companies and solutions that utilize graph-based customer segmentation:

- Airbnb customer segmentation (*https://oreil.ly/rlF3N*)

  Use case

  Airbnb leverages graph-based machine learning models to analyze the relationships among users, listings, and bookings. This analysis enables Airbnb to identify various customer segments, such as frequent travelers, luxury seekers, and budget-conscious users, by uncovering patterns and connections within the data.

  Solution

  Airbnb employs graph databases and algorithms to cluster users based on shared booking patterns, preferences, and behaviors. This helps them personalize the user experience and improve recommendations.

- Netflix content segmentation (*https://oreil.ly/gfRB2*)

    Use case

    Netflix leverages graph-based segmentation to recommend content to its users. By creating a graph of users and the shows or movies they watch, Netflix can identify clusters of users with similar viewing habits.

    Solution

    Netflix uses these graphs to segment users into different categories, allowing them to recommend content that is more likely to resonate with a particular user segment.

- LinkedIn user segmentation (*https://oreil.ly/Hjqz_*)

    Use case

    LinkedIn uses graph-based algorithms to segment its users based on their professional networks, interests, and activities. This segmentation allows LinkedIn to provide personalized content, job recommendations, and networking opportunities.

    Solution

    By analyzing the connections between users, companies, and groups, LinkedIn creates segments that help in targeting specific content or ads to relevant user groups.

Social Network Analysis

Social network analysis (SNA) is a method for examining the structure and dynamics of social networks. In the context of customer behavior, SNA helps to understand how customers interact with one another and with the company. This analysis can uncover key influencers, track the dissemination of information, and inform the development of targeted marketing campaigns.

For instance, we can create a graph with customers as nodes and their social media connections as edges, similar to the Facebook graph shown in Figure 8-1. SNA algorithms can then identify the most influential customers and the communities they belong to. This information is instrumental in crafting marketing campaigns that capitalize on social influence.

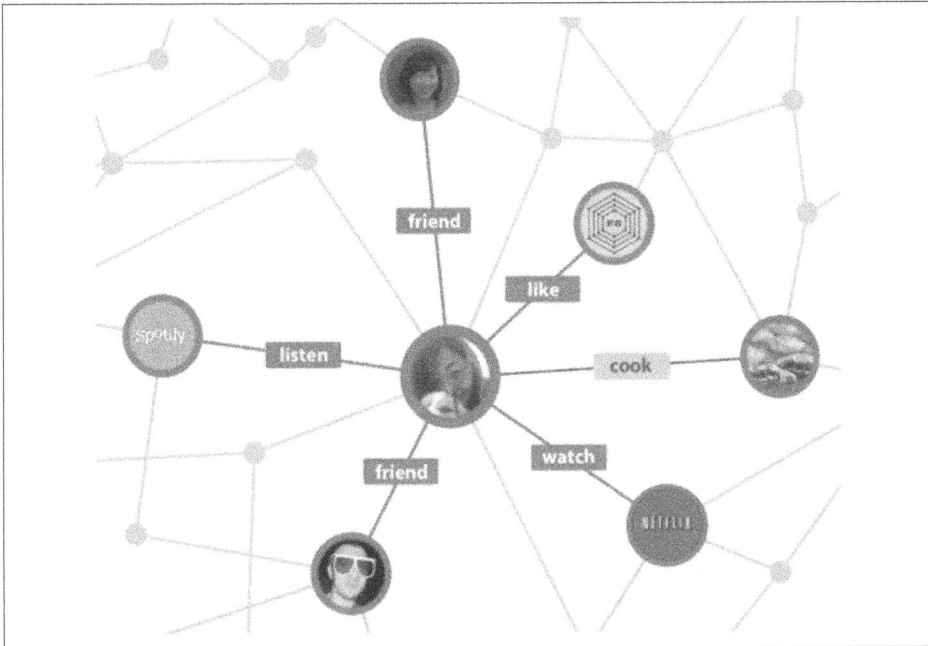

Figure 8-1. Illustration of Facebook social media graph data (TechCrunch (2012) (https://oreil.ly/9WZax))

SNA is a powerful technique for uncovering the structure and dynamics of social networks. In a customer context, SNA provides valuable insights into interactions both among customers and between customers and the company. This analysis offers several practical benefits:

Identification of influential customers
    SNA can pinpoint highly influential customers within a network who, due to their extensive connections, significantly impact the opinions and behaviors of others. Understanding these key individuals allows companies to tailor marketing strategies to engage them more effectively.

Tracking information dissemination
    SNA tracks the flow of information through the network, revealing how customers learn about new products and services and share their experiences. This insight helps in understanding information spread and influence and planning product strategies.

Tailoring marketing campaigns

By analyzing customer connections, SNA enables the development of targeted marketing campaigns that resonate more strongly with specific customer segments. This focused approach improves campaign effectiveness and engagement.

One common way to apply SNA to customer data is to construct a social network graph. In this graph, customers are represented as nodes, and the edges between nodes represent their social connections. SNA algorithms can then be used to analyze the graph and identify the most influential customers, as well as the communities that exist within the network.

This information can be leveraged to refine marketing strategies. For example, companies can direct exclusive offers or promotions towards their most influential customers and design campaigns tailored to the unique needs of each community within the network.

Recommendation Engines

Recommendation engines are sophisticated systems designed to provide personalized suggestions to users based on their historical behavior and preferences. Graphs are exceptionally effective for constructing these engines, as they adeptly model the complex relationships between users, items, and their interactions. We experience graph-based recommendations regularly through search engines, which deliver relevant results to our queries, and social networks, which tailor content to our interests.

For example, a graph can be created with users and items as nodes, and their ratings as edges. Graph-based algorithms can then recommend items to users by evaluating their similarity to items previously rated highly by the user. These recommendation engines enhance the customer experience, boost sales, and drive engagement.

Recommendation engines are systems designed to offer personalized suggestions based on users' historical behavior and preferences. They are essential for various online platforms, including ecommerce sites, streaming services, and social media. By leveraging data and machine learning algorithms, recommendation engines analyze user interactions to identify patterns and predict future preferences.

Figure 8-2 illustrates the information associated with Google (the company) in its knowledge graph. Graphs are particularly effective for developing recommendation engines (*https://oreil.ly/D7cQj*) due to their ability to model the complex relationships between users, items, and their interactions.

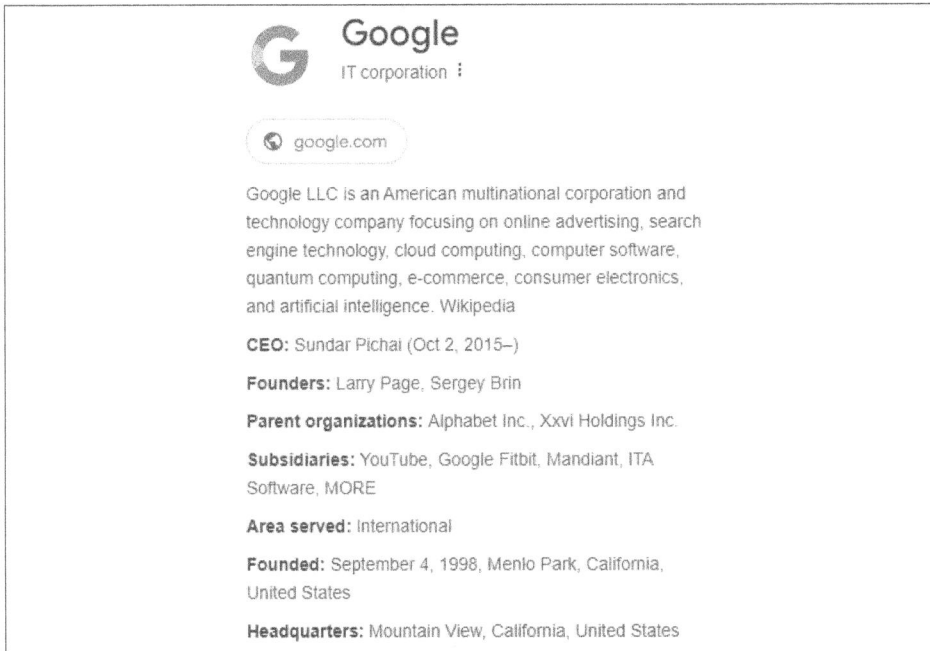

Figure 8-2. Example of Google search content retrieved from the Google Knowledge Graph

To enhance recommendation engines further, we can integrate additional data sources (such as user demographics, item attributes, and contextual information). This integration helps to capture a more subtle understanding of user preferences and deliver more precise recommendations. To maintain and improve the effectiveness of recommendation engines, it is essential to continuously monitor and assess their performance, tracking metrics such as click-through rates, conversion rates, and user engagement. Based on these evaluations, the recommendation engine can be iteratively refined and optimized.

This can be executed in multiple domains including product recommendation for ecommerce applications or content recommendation for streaming services, etc. Figure 8-3 provides a basic illustration of the use of graphs in the context of movie recommendations. This example shows a simple recommendation based on connected entities where the most connected content to the user in the graph is recommended to him. In practice, this is usually done with embeddings similarity or is treated as a link prediction problem. Graphs have proven to be a versatile tool, finding applications in diverse domains such as product recommendations for ecommerce and content recommendations for streaming services. Their ability to model complex relationships and interconnectedness makes them ideally suited for recommendation tasks.

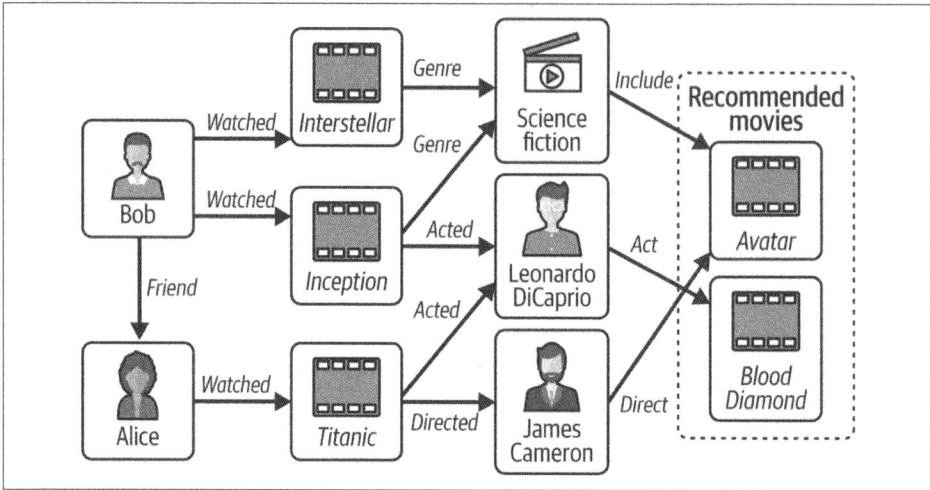

Figure 8-3. Illustration of a movie recommendation engine based on graphs (Liu, J., and Duan, L. (2021))[1]

The most straightforward approach to movie recommendations based on this graph is to identify the movies that are most connected to a user in the graph. These movies are assumed to be the ones that are most relevant to the user and are, therefore, recommended.

However, in practice, more sophisticated methods are typically employed. One approach is to use embedding similarity. Here, each user and movie is represented as a vector of numbers, known as an embedding. The similarity between two embeddings reflects the similarity between the corresponding user or movie. This allows for more fine-grained recommendations, as it takes into account the specific preferences and characteristics of each user and movie.

Another approach is to frame movie recommendations as a link prediction problem. Here, the objective is to forecast whether a user will view a particular movie based on their historical behavior and the relationships between users and movies within the graph. Various machine learning techniques, such as matrix factorization and graph neural networks, can be employed to tackle this challenge.

---

1 Liu, J., and Duan, L. (2021). "A Survey on Knowledge Graph-Based Recommender Systems" (*https://oreil.ly/9yzd8*). *2021 IEEE 5th Advanced Information Technology, Electronic, and Automation Control Conference (IAEAC)*, 2450-2453.

These advanced methods allow for the integration of additional factors into the recommendation process. They can incorporate elements such as movie genre, release year, actors, and the user's ratings of other films. This comprehensive approach results in more personalized and precise recommendations, thereby enhancing the user experience and boosting engagement with the platform. Here are a few real-world examples of companies and their graph-based recommendations:

- LinkedIn: "People You May Know" and job recommendations
  - *Company*: LinkedIn
  - *Solution*: LinkedIn employs a graph database, internally known as *Galene* (*https://oreil.ly/aR23f*), to fuel its "People You May Know" feature. This graph-based recommendation engine utilizes the relationships between users, including shared work experiences, educational backgrounds, mutual connections, and other platform interactions. By analyzing these connections, LinkedIn can recommend new professional connections or job opportunities that are highly relevant to the user.
  - *Graph database*: LinkedIn initially used a custom-built graph processing engine called *Li-Graph*. They also utilize Apache Giraph, an open source graph processing framework.
- Pinterest: Content and user recommendations
  - *Company*: Pinterest
  - *Solution*: Pinterest uses a graph-based recommendation system to suggest pins, boards, and other users that a person might be interested in. The graph here consists of users, pins, boards, and the interactions between them (e.g., saving a pin, following a board). By analyzing this graph, Pinterest recommends content based on what similar users engage with, or by finding similar items within the same board.
  - *Graph database*: Pinterest uses Apache Giraph and other custom graph processing solutions.
- Amazon: Product recommendations
  - *Company*: Amazon
  - *Solution*: Amazon's recommendation engine is famously robust and uses a variety of techniques, including graph-based algorithms. One of the ways Amazon uses graphs is to create a product recommendation graph, where nodes represent products and edges represent interactions such as copurchases, views, or customer ratings. By analyzing these relationships, Amazon can recommend products that are often bought together or are of interest based on similar customer profiles.

— *Graph database*: Amazon utilizes several tools, including *Neptune* (*https://oreil.ly/q9xOj*), its proprietary managed graph database service. Neptune supports both property graph and Resource Description Framework (RDF) graph models, offering flexibility for various graph-based applications.

- Uber: Restaurant recommendations for Uber Eats

  — *Company*: Uber

  — *Solution*: Uber Eats uses graph databases (*https://oreil.ly/FSblL*) to enhance their restaurant recommendation system. The graph connects users with their food preferences, order histories, and restaurant locations. The recommendation engine analyzes this graph to suggest new restaurants or dishes based on what similar users have ordered, and what is trending in certain areas.

  — *Graph database*: Uber has used Neo4j, a popular graph database, in different parts of its infrastructure, though they also develop custom solutions.

Operations and Supply Chain Management

Graph applications play a crucial role in optimizing enterprise operations and managing supply chains. By representing different components of operations and supply chains as nodes and the relationships between them as edges, businesses can solve complex problems more efficiently. Here we explore how graphs are applied in enterprise operations and supply chain management, followed by a discussion on specific applications.

Network Optimization in Supply Chains

Supply chains typically involve complex networks involving suppliers, manufacturers, distribution centers, and retail outlets, as illustrated in Figure 8-4. Graphs can effectively model these networks, with nodes representing entities such as factories, warehouses, and retail stores, and edges depicting the connections between them, such as transportation routes.

Suppliers, often located globally, provide raw materials and components to factories. These factories then produce finished goods, which are transported to distribution centers. Distribution centers manage inventory and distribute products to retail stores, which sell them to consumers. The efficiency of a supply chain hinges on the seamless coordination of these diverse entities, each with its own objectives and requirements. This coordination can be complex, given the varying goals and operational constraints of each participant.

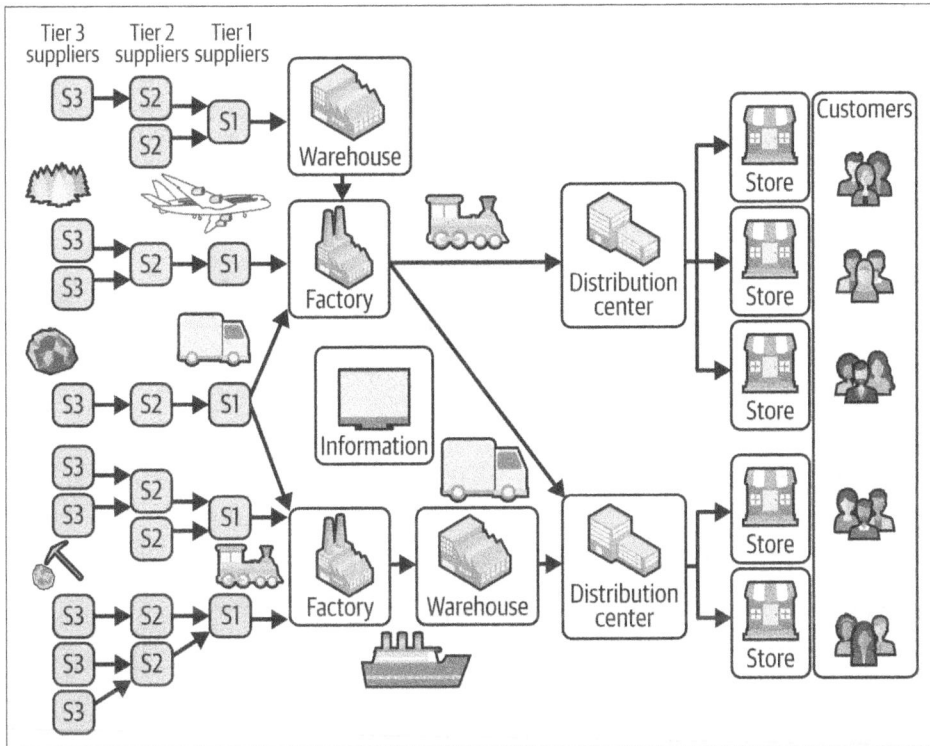

Figure 8-4. Illustration of supply chain network connections (adapted from LinkedIn day-to-day (2023) (https://oreil.ly/c3wuM))

For example, suppliers may want to minimize their costs, while factories may want to maximize their output. Distribution centers and stores may have different inventory levels and customer service requirements:

Shortest path problems

One common application is finding the shortest path in the supply chain network to minimize transportation costs or time. Algorithms like Dijkstra's or the Bellman–Ford algorithm (*https://oreil.ly/3Js1R*) can efficiently find the shortest path between nodes, ensuring goods move from suppliers to consumers as quickly and cost-effectively as possible.

Maximum flow problems

In situations where resources must be distributed through the network (like product distribution), the maximum flow problem determines the maximum amount of goods that can be transported through the network without exceeding the capacity of any path. The Ford–Fulkerson algorithm is often used for this purpose.

Inventory Management

Graphs enhance inventory management by representing warehouses and distribution centers as nodes, with edges illustrating the flow of goods between them. Utilizing graph-based methods allows companies to optimize stock levels, minimize holding costs, and ensure timely restocking:

Cycle detection (https://oreil.ly/tnL7_)
   This technique identifies recurring patterns, like seasonal demand spikes for certain products every holiday season (e.g., toys in December, gardening supplies in spring), in inventory replenishment, helping to prevent overstocking or understocking by recognizing cyclical ordering trends.

Graph clustering (https://oreil.ly/XsUNA)
   By clustering items within a graph, companies can more effectively manage product categories. Grouping products with similar demand patterns enables the refinement of inventory policies for each cluster, thus improving overall inventory management.

Risk Management and Supply Chain Resilience

Supply chains are susceptible to disruptions from events such as supplier failures, natural disasters, or political instability. Graphs play a crucial role in risk management by identifying critical nodes and edges within the supply chain network:

Graph centrality
   Metrics such as degree centrality, betweenness centrality, and eigenvector centrality are utilized to identify the most critical nodes, such as suppliers or distribution centers, within a network. These metrics help determine which nodes are most likely to cause substantial disruptions if they fail, thereby highlighting their significance in maintaining the network's stability.

Resilience analysis
   Graph theory enables the simulation of various disruption scenarios and supports the design of more resilient supply chains. By incorporating redundancy, such as alternative routes or backup suppliers, companies can enhance their ability to withstand and recover from potential disruptions.

Supplier selection and relationship management

Selecting the right suppliers is vital for a smooth supply chain. Graphs can represent the network of potential suppliers, with edges indicating the quality, cost, and reliability of relationships. In the following, we discuss some graph concepts that we have discussed in the previous chapters and describe how they can be used in the context of supplier selection and management:

Bipartite graphs
> These are used to model relationships between two distinct sets, such as suppliers and manufacturers. They help in evaluating and selecting suppliers based on multiple criteria, ensuring the optimal match between supply needs and available options.

Weighted graphs
> Suppliers can be ranked and selected based on weights assigned to edges, which represent factors like cost, quality, and delivery time. The aim is to minimize costs while maximizing reliability and quality.

Demand forecasting and distribution planning

Graphs help in demand forecasting by analyzing historical sales data, represented as time-series graphs, and identifying trends:

Time-series graphs
> These graphs can identify patterns and cycles in demand over time, which are then used to predict future demand. This prediction is crucial for planning production and distribution.

Graph matching
> This technique can be used to align supply with demand by matching distribution capabilities with forecasted demand across different regions.

Transportation and logistics optimization

Logistics involves the movement of goods, often across vast networks. Graph theory helps optimize these operations by solving routing and scheduling problems:

Traveling salesman problem (TSP)
> This well-known graph problem is employed in logistics to determine the most efficient route for a delivery vehicle that must visit a set of locations, with the goal of minimizing the total travel distance or time.

Vehicle routing problem (VRP)
> A more sophisticated extension of the TSP, the VRP involves optimizing routes for multiple vehicles tasked with delivering goods to various destinations. It incorporates additional constraints, such as vehicle capacity and delivery time windows, to ensure efficient and feasible routing.

Real-World Applications

Several leading companies across various industries have successfully implemented graph-based solutions to optimize their enterprise operations and supply chain management. Following are examples of real-world applications.

Amazon: Supply chain and logistics optimization

Amazon operates one of the most complex and extensive supply chain networks globally, involving thousands of suppliers, distribution centers, and delivery routes. The company uses graph theory extensively to optimize its logistics and supply chain operations:

Dynamic routing
> Amazon leverages graph-based algorithms to address the VRP for its delivery fleet. The company must determine the most efficient routes for thousands of delivery vehicles each day, factoring in delivery windows, traffic conditions, and vehicle capacities. Graph algorithms enable Amazon to minimize delivery times and costs while ensuring timely deliveries.

Supply chain resilience
> Amazon utilizes graph-based resilience analysis to identify critical nodes and pathways within its supply chain. By pinpointing vulnerable suppliers or transportation routes, the company can implement proactive measures, such as sourcing from alternate suppliers or rerouting shipments, to mitigate the impact of potential disruptions.

Walmart: Inventory management and supplier relationships

Walmart, one of the world's largest retailers, leverages graph theory to manage its vast inventory and supplier network efficiently:

Supplier network optimization
> Walmart uses bipartite graphs to model relationships between its numerous suppliers and the products they provide. This helps the company evaluate suppliers based on criteria such as cost, quality, and reliability, enabling Walmart to select the best suppliers for each product category. This approach has allowed Walmart to maintain low costs and high efficiency across its supply chain.

Inventory optimization
> Walmart utilizes graph clustering techniques to group products with similar demand patterns, enhancing its inventory management strategies. By identifying clusters of products that exhibit comparable sales behaviors, Walmart can optimize stock levels more effectively. This approach allows for more efficient allocation of resources and improved inventory control across its vast product offerings.

UPS: Transportation and logistics

United Parcel Service (UPS), a leading company in logistics and package delivery, extensively leverages graph theory to optimize its operations:

On-Road Integrated Optimization and Navigation (ORION) system
> UPS developed the ORION system, a cutting-edge tool that applies graph theory to solve the TSP for its delivery drivers. ORION calculates the most efficient delivery routes each day by considering variables such as traffic patterns, customer delivery time preferences, and road conditions. This system has enabled UPS to save millions of miles annually, significantly reducing fuel consumption and operational costs while improving delivery efficiency.

Network optimization
> UPS also uses graph theory to model its global transportation network, optimizing the flow of packages through various hubs and distribution centers. By identifying the most efficient routes and hubs, UPS ensures that packages move through its network as quickly and cost-effectively as possible.

Security and Risk Management

In the rapidly evolving era of cybersecurity, enterprise organizations encounter increasingly complex challenges that require adaptive and resilient strategies. Graph technology has become a vital tool in security and risk management, offering advanced capabilities for detecting, analyzing, and mitigating threats. By harnessing the strengths of graph databases and algorithms, enterprises can achieve a deeper understanding of their security infrastructure, predict emerging risks, and implement proactive defenses to safeguard critical assets.

Threat Detection and Analysis

Traditional security tools often struggle to detect sophisticated, multistage attacks that evolve over time. Graphs, however, excel at modeling and analyzing relationships, making them ideal for uncovering hidden connections that may indicate a threat. For instance, a graph-based security system can map out relationships between various entities such as users, devices, IP addresses, and domains. By applying graph algorithms, such as community detection or anomaly detection, these systems can identify unusual patterns that may signify an ongoing attack, such as lateral movement within a network or the presence of an advanced persistent threat (APT).

There are multiple products that offer threat detection services using graph learning methods, such as Palantir Foundry. Palantir's platform integrates graph technology to provide real-time insights into security data. By correlating vast amounts of data from disparate sources, it helps enterprises detect and investigate potential security threats more effectively.

In the next few sections, we'll review several tools involving security and risk management, then cover some related enterprise products.

Identity and Access Management

Identity and Access Management (IAM) is the framework of policies and technologies used to ensure that the right people and systems have the appropriate access to resources and information, at the right times and for the right reasons. Essentially, it's about managing who can do what within an organization's digital environment.

Effective IAM is essential for ensuring enterprise security. Graph technology allows organizations to model relationships between users, roles, permissions, and resources. This relational framework ensures that users are granted the appropriate level of access based on their roles, responsibilities, and real-time context, thereby enhancing security while maintaining operational flexibility.

Graphs can also enhance IAM by enabling real-time monitoring and alerting of access patterns. For example, if a user attempts to access a resource that is not typically within their scope, a graph-based system can quickly flag this behavior as potentially malicious, triggering further investigation or automated responses. Related enterprise products include:

Microsoft Entra ID
Entra ID incorporates graph technology to manage and visualize the relationships between users, groups, and permissions. This allows for more sophisticated and dynamic management of access rights, reducing the risk of unauthorized access.

Neo4j Graph Data Science for IAM
Neo4j's platform allows enterprises to model complex IAM scenarios, such as role hierarchies and access privileges, using graph structures. This provides a more intuitive and flexible approach to managing identities and access, as well as detecting anomalies in access patterns.

Fraud Detection

Fraud detection is another critical area where graphs have made a significant impact. Fraudulent activities often involve complex networks of actors and transactions that are challenging to detect using traditional methods. Graphs can represent these networks as interconnected nodes and edges, enabling the detection of corner cases of fraud schemes, such as money laundering, insurance fraud, or credit card fraud.

By analyzing relationships and patterns within networks, enterprises can more accurately identify suspicious behavior in real time. Graph-based systems offer the ability to capture new signals in the data and cope with new fraud tactics by continuously learning from new data, ensuring that detection mechanisms remain effective over time. This dynamic approach enhances the ability to respond to emerging threats and maintain security integrity. Related enterprise products include:

Linkurious Enterprise

This graph analytics platform is designed specifically for fraud detection and investigation. It allows enterprises to explore and visualize complex networks of transactions and relationships, making it easier to uncover fraudulent activities.

TigerGraph for Fraud Detection

TigerGraph's platform leverages deep link analysis and pattern matching to detect fraud across various industries, including banking, insurance, and ecommerce. By processing large-scale graph data in real time, it helps organizations stay ahead of emerging fraud threats.

Cybersecurity Incident Response

In the event of a cybersecurity incident, time is of the essence. Graphs can significantly enhance the speed and effectiveness of incident response by providing a clear and comprehensive view of the attack surface and the relationships between compromised assets. By visualizing the attack path as a graph, security teams can quickly understand the scope of the breach, identify affected systems, and prioritize their response efforts.

Moreover, graph-based systems can automate parts of the incident response process by using predefined rules and patterns to trigger alerts or remediate actions. For instance, if a graph-based analysis detects a known attack pattern, it can automatically isolate compromised systems, block malicious traffic, or deploy countermeasures to contain the threat. Related enterprise products include:

Splunk Enterprise Security (ES)

Splunk ES uses graph analytics to map out attack vectors and understand the relationships between different events in a cybersecurity incident. This enables security teams to respond more effectively by focusing on the most critical threats.

Cortex XSOAR (by Palo Alto Networks)

Cortex XSOAR integrates graph-based analysis into its automation and orchestration platform for incident response. By leveraging graph data, it can correlate incidents across various sources and automate response workflows, reducing the time to resolution.

Risk Management and Compliance

Risk management in an enterprise context involves understanding the interplay between various risk factors and their potential impact on the organization. Graphs are particularly well-suited for this task as they can model the dependencies and relationships between different risk factors, such as third-party vendors, regulatory requirements, and internal processes. This allows enterprises to perform more comprehensive risk assessments and scenario analyses, identifying potential vulnerabilities that could be exploited by cyber threats.

Graphs also play a vital role in compliance management by enabling organizations to track and document complex regulatory requirements and their implementation across the enterprise. By representing compliance data as a graph, organizations can more easily identify gaps, overlaps, and conflicts in their compliance efforts, ensuring that they remain aligned with legal and regulatory standards. Related enterprise products include:

RiskIQ

RiskIQ uses graph technology to provide organizations with a comprehensive view of their external attack surface. By mapping out the relationships between internet-facing assets, third-party services, and potential vulnerabilities, RiskIQ helps enterprises manage cyber risk more effectively.

RSA Archer

RSA Archer's risk management platform integrates graph analytics to help organizations visualize and analyze risk relationships. This enables more dynamic risk assessments and supports better decision making in response to emerging threats and compliance challenges.

The integration of graph technology into enterprise security and risk management marks a major advancement in how organizations defend against threats. By harnessing the power of graphs to model complex relationships, detect anomalies, and automate responses, enterprises can significantly enhance their security posture. As cyber threats become more sophisticated, adopting graph-based solutions will be critical for organizations aiming to stay ahead of adversaries and protect their most valuable assets.

The different techniques and applications of graph learning methods in the wider security and risk management domain that we have discussed provide valuable analytical and predictive services. These services can enhance the quality of the different products and offerings in the risk and security space. Furthermore, graph learning approaches can be extended to other domains that utilize interconnected information and concepts. In the following section, we will focus on the applications of graph learning methods in the healthcare and life science domain, where we show how these methods can be translated to various healthcare and life sciences problems.

Healthcare and Life Sciences

Graph technology has found a fertile ground in the healthcare and life sciences sector, where the complexity and interconnectedness of data naturally lend themselves to graph-based solutions. In this industry, the relationships between entities of patients, diseases, treatments, or biological pathways are often as critical as the entities themselves. By leveraging graphs, organizations can unlock new insights, streamline operations, and enhance the quality of care.

Patient Journey Mapping and Personalization

In healthcare, understanding a patient's journey through the system is crucial for improving outcomes and patient satisfaction. Traditional data models often struggle to capture the nuanced paths that patients take, which can include a wide range of interactions with various healthcare providers, treatments, and outcomes over time. Graph databases excel in modeling these complex journeys, where advanced patient relationship management systems, powered by graph databases, enable real-time tracking and analysis of the patient journey. By mapping each interaction—such as appointments, medications, diagnoses, and lab results—healthcare providers can tailor personalized care plans. For instance, a graph-powered system can detect patients at risk of readmission by analyzing patterns from prior cases, allowing for proactive interventions. This approach not only enhances patient outcomes but also helps reduce costs within healthcare systems, making care more efficient and responsive.

Drug Discovery and Development

The process of drug discovery is inherently complex and data-intensive, involving vast amounts of biological data, chemical compounds, and clinical trial information. Graphs are particularly well-suited to model the sophisticated relationships between these entities, facilitating more efficient and effective drug discovery processes.

Pharmaceutical companies use knowledge graphs to connect disparate data sources, such as genomic data, chemical compounds data, etc., into a unified, searchable framework. This allows researchers to identify potential drug candidates, predict their interactions, and assess their effectiveness more rapidly than traditional methods. Graph algorithms can also be applied to predict side effects or uncover previously unknown relationships between compounds and biological targets.

In the enterprise context, these graph learning techniques offer several powerful applications, especially within pharmaceutical companies, biotechnology firms, and healthcare providers. Here's how they can be integrated into enterprise operations.

Accelerating drug discovery and repurposing

Graphs can help speed up the process of identifying new drugs or repurposing existing drugs for new applications:

Pharmaceutical R&D
Enterprises can leverage graph learning to rapidly identify new therapeutic uses for existing drugs, significantly shortening the drug development cycle and reducing costs. By analyzing relationships in drug–protein or drug–disease

networks, companies can prioritize compounds for clinical trials that show high potential for treating multiple conditions.

Collaboration platforms
Enterprises can use these techniques to build collaborative platforms where different research teams and partners share graph-based insights. This could drive open innovation across the industry, leading to breakthroughs in drug repurposing and reducing duplicative research efforts.

Optimizing drug safety monitoring

Graphs can improve the effectiveness of drug safety monitoring and allow healthcare organizations to comply with critical safety regulations:

Pharmacovigilance
Graph learning can enhance post-market surveillance by predicting potential adverse drug reactions (ADRs) before they are widely reported.[2,3] By continuously integrating new data into the graph (e.g., patient reports, clinical data, and real-world evidence), enterprises can proactively manage drug safety, alerting stakeholders to emerging risks.

Regulatory compliance
Companies can use these predictions to ensure compliance with regulatory bodies by identifying potential side effects earlier, reducing the risk of costly recalls or legal challenges.

Clinical Trial Optimization

Clinical trials are critical to the development of new therapies, but they are often costly and time-consuming. The design and execution of these trials involve managing a vast amount of data, from patient recruitment to monitoring outcomes. Graph technology can be employed to optimize this process by providing a more detailed and dynamic view of the trial landscape.

One of the most challenging aspects of clinical trials is patient recruitment, particularly when trying to match specific patient profiles to the trial's inclusion criteria. Graph databases can analyze patient data to identify suitable candidates based on a wide range of factors, including genetic markers, medical history, and demographic information. Additionally, they can model patient cohorts to predict outcomes or potential issues during the trial.

---

2 Zitnik, M., Agrawal, M., and Leskovec, J. (2018). "Modeling Polypharmacy Side Effects with Graph Convolutional Networks" (*https://oreil.ly/Euera*). *Bioinformatics* 34(13), i457-i466.

3 Nováček, V., and Mohamed, S.K. (2020). "Predicting Polypharmacy Side Effects Using Knowledge Graph Embeddings" (*https://oreil.ly/7X9fP*). *AMIA Summits on Translational Science Proceedings*, 449.

Genomics and Personalized Medicine

Personalized medicine—which customizes medical treatments based on the unique characteristics of each patient—is a rapidly advancing field in healthcare. The ability to analyze a patient's genetic data alongside other medical information is critical for delivering precise and effective treatments. Graph technology is integral to managing and analyzing these complex datasets, enabling healthcare providers to uncover complex relationships and make data-driven decisions that enhance the precision of patient care.

Graph-based systems allow for the integration and analysis of genomic data alongside other clinical data, making it possible to uncover hidden patterns and correlations. This is crucial for personalized medicine, where understanding the relationship between a patient's genetic profile and potential treatments can lead to more effective and targeted therapies.

Figure 8-5 illustrates a sophisticated knowledge representation that is instrumental in the enterprise application of graph learning for precision medicine and genomics. This model not only builds upon the foundational central dogma, where DNA is transcribed into RNA and subsequently translated into proteins, but also integrates additional dimensions such as genetic variants, biological pathways, pharmaceutical interventions, and disease mechanisms.

For enterprises focused on precision medicine, this knowledge graph is a powerful tool. It maps the relationships between various biological entities, from tissues and cells to genomic elements like DNA, RNA, and proteins. By capturing these relationships, enterprises can apply graph learning techniques to analyze complex biological data, identify patterns, and predict how genetic variants may influence disease states or treatment responses. This is crucial for the development of targeted therapies and personalized treatment plans.

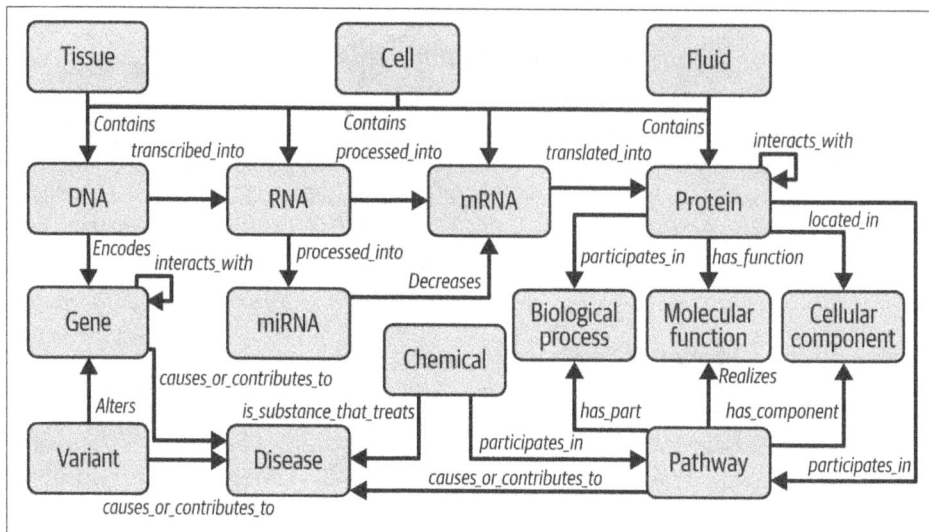

Figure 8-5. A knowledge graph representation of the levels of biological organization underlying human disease (adapted from Callahan et al. (2024) (https://oreil.ly/y-awQ))

The graph also includes information on how proteins—which are synthesized based on genetic instructions—interact within biological pathways and contribute to cellular processes. This level of detail enables companies to model the effects of different interventions, such as pharmaceutical treatments, on these pathways. By simulating these interactions within a graph-based framework, enterprises can optimize drug development processes, predict adverse effects, and refine therapeutic strategies.

Moreover, the integration of genetic variants into this knowledge graph is particularly valuable for genomics-driven enterprises. Variants can alter gene function, leading to disease; understanding these connections is key to developing precision treatments. Graph learning models can analyze these variants in the context of the broader biological network, uncovering novel insights that drive innovation in personalized medicine.

Popular Life Science Products

In the rapidly evolving field of life sciences, graph-based technologies have emerged as a transformative force, particularly in drug repurposing, genomic analysis, and clinical trials. This section delves into how popular enterprise products leverage graphs and learning on graphs to drive innovation and efficiency in these critical areas.

BenevolentAI drug repurposing

Drug repurposing, or repositioning, involves discovering new applications for existing medications, which can substantially decrease the time and cost of drug development. Graph-based methods have become crucial in this process, as they facilitate the identification of new indications for approved drugs by analyzing complex relationships and patterns within biomedical data.

BenevolentAI is a prominent example of a company harnessing graph technology for drug repurposing. The BenevolentAI Platform integrates various forms of biological and chemical data into a unified graph database. This graph connects genes, proteins, diseases, and drugs, enabling sophisticated analysis and hypothesis generation.

The platform uses machine learning algorithms on these graphs to predict new drug–disease associations. For instance, BenevolentAI's system successfully identified a potential new use for a well-known anti-inflammatory drug in treating a rare neurological condition, demonstrating the power of graph-based analysis in accelerating drug repurposing.

Tempus genomic analysis

Genomic analysis involves studying genomes to understand genetic variations and their implications for health and disease. Graph-based approaches in genomic analysis help in visualizing and interpreting complex relationships between genetic elements.

Tempus employs a graph-based approach in their platform to enhance genomic analysis. Their solution integrates various data types—genomic sequences, clinical data, and patient outcomes—into a comprehensive graph structure. This allows for an enriched understanding of how genetic mutations impact disease progression and treatment responses.

Tempus's graph-based analytics support precision medicine by identifying correlations between genetic variants and therapeutic responses. This capability is crucial for developing personalized treatment plans and advancing research into genetic disorders.

Scientists at BenevolentAI have also utilized learning on graph methods to explore graphs for mechanisms associated with viral infections and inflammatory responses similar to the graph illustrated in Figure 8-6. They identified baricitinib, which is a drug developed by Eli Lilly and Company and approved for rheumatoid arthritis—as the top candidate. This finding was based on new insights extracted from existing literature, suggesting that baricitinib might have an additional off-target antiviral effect beyond its established anti-inflammatory properties.

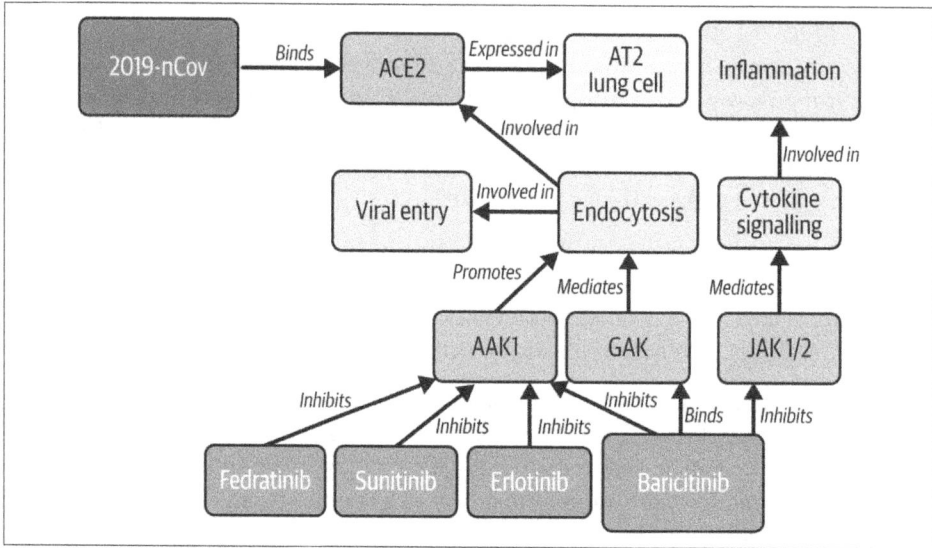

Figure 8-6. Illustration of a graph analysis of Covid-19 interaction with human body proteins, and relevant drugs to these proteins (adapted from Benevolent (https://oreil.ly/9X1I2))

Medidata Rave for clinical trials

Clinical trials are vital for assessing the efficacy and safety of new treatments. Graph-based technologies can enhance these trials by optimizing trial design, streamlining patient recruitment, and improving data analysis.

Medidata Solutions offers a platform called Medidata Rave (*https://oreil.ly/KIRYW*), which incorporates graph-based analytics to enhance clinical trials. Medidata Rave's graph technology helps in mapping out patient data, trial protocols, and outcomes. This mapping supports better patient stratification and trial design.

For instance, Medidata's platform uses graphs to visualize patient recruitment patterns and treatment pathways, which improves the efficiency of identifying suitable candidates for trials. Additionally, by analyzing trial data through graph-based methods, researchers can gain insights into treatment efficacy and adverse effects more effectively.

Summary

As we conclude this chapter on the enterprise applications of graphs and graph learning methods, it's evident that the transformative potential of these technologies extends far beyond theoretical discourse. Graphs and graph-based techniques have emerged as pivotal tools across various domains, driving innovation and efficiency in ways that were previously unattainable.

In the domain of customer and market insights, we have explored how graph analytics discover patterns and relationships within customer data, facilitating personalized experiences and strategic market decisions. Through the lens of operations and supply chain management, graph methods have proven indispensable in optimizing complex networks, enhancing logistics, and mitigating risks associated with supply chain disruptions. These applications highlight the strength of graphs in managing interdependencies and facilitating real-time insights that are crucial for operational excellence.

The domains of security and risk management and life sciences both experience substantial benefits from graph-based approaches. In security and risk management, graphs enhance anomaly detection and fraud prevention by uncovering hidden threats and vulnerabilities through sophisticated analysis of complex relationships between entities. This capability enables enterprises to proactively address security challenges and protect their assets. In life sciences, graph technology accelerates drug discovery, patient care, and genomics research, showcasing its profound impact on advancing medical science and improving patient outcomes.

The case studies and methodologies explored in this chapter highlight the versatility and effectiveness of graph technologies. The transition from traditional data analysis methods to graph-based approaches represents a significant advancement in how businesses derive value from their data. By harnessing the power of graphs, enterprises gain deeper insights into their operations, make more informed decisions, and foster innovation across various industries.

Looking ahead, the integration of graph learning with emerging technologies such as AI and machine learning promises to further amplify the capabilities of graph-based solutions. As organizations increasingly adopt these advanced techniques, they will unlock new opportunities for growth and efficiency, paving the way for a future where data-driven insights are not just a competitive advantage but a fundamental element of business success.

## CHAPTER 9

Privacy-Preserving Graph Learning

Privacy-preserving graph learning has become increasingly important as organizations seek to analyze graph-structured data without compromising sensitive information. Graphs are powerful tools for modeling complex relationships between entities and are widely used in domains such as social networks, biological systems, communication networks, and financial transactions. However, as the amount of data represented as graphs grows, so does the risk of exposing private or confidential information.

This chapter explores various techniques and applications for privacy-preserving graph learning, focusing on techniques that enable effective analysis and learning from graph data while ensuring the privacy of individuals and businesses. We will explore approaches ranging from data anonymization to advanced computation methods like federated learning—highlighting how these techniques address privacy concerns in various domains.

The Importance of Privacy in Graph Learning

Graphs encode rich relational information that reveals sensitive details about individuals and organizations. Nodes in a graph represent users, patients, or customers; the nodes contain attributes such as personal identifiers, health records, or financial data. Edges denote relationships or interactions, such as friendships, transactions, or communications, which can be confidential or sensitive. Even the structural patterns and topology of a graph expose community structures or relationships that allow eavesdroppers to reidentify anonymized data.

Privacy breaches in graph data have critical consequences—including identity theft, discrimination, and financial loss. For example, de-anonymization attacks on social networks have demonstrated that individuals can be reidentified by matching structural patterns with external information. Moreover, regulatory frameworks impose strict requirements on data privacy, and being noncompliant can lead to legal penalties and business reputational damage.

Ensuring privacy in graph learning is essential for protecting individuals by safeguarding personal information and respecting user consent. It also involves meeting legal obligations under data protection laws, maintaining user trust and organizational integrity, and enabling collaboration by allowing multiple entities to collectively analyze data without exposing their confidential information.

Enterprise Examples and Applications

Privacy-preserving graph learning has significant implications across various industries. In social networks, platforms like Meta's Facebook and LinkedIn analyze user interactions to recommend connections or content. Privacy-preserving graph learning ensures that sensitive user data is not exposed during analysis. For instance, a social media company may want to improve its friend recommendation system without accessing users' private messages or personal details.

In healthcare, hospitals and research institutions benefit from shared analysis of patient data to improve diagnoses and treatments. Privacy-preserving methods allow for collaborative learning without violating patient confidentiality. For example, multiple hospitals might collaboratively train a model to predict disease outbreaks using patient admission data, without sharing individual health records.

In the finance sector, banks and financial institutions detect fraud by analyzing transaction networks. Sharing transaction data poses privacy risks and legal challenges, necessitating secure analysis methods. An example would be banks using federated learning to detect fraudulent transactions by analyzing interconnected financial networks while keeping customer data private.

In transportation, ride-sharing companies optimize routes and reduce congestion by analyzing vehicle and traffic networks. Privacy-preserving techniques protect user location data. Competing ride-sharing services might collaborate to improve traffic predictions without revealing individual trip details.

Overview of Privacy-Preserving Techniques

Privacy-preserving graph learning includes a number of methodologies carefully designed to protect sensitive information during data analysis and model training. At a high level these methodologies can be classified into broad classes:

- Privacy-preserving graph data generation
- Privacy-preserving graph computation

Privacy-preserving graph data generation involves methods such as graph anonymization, where graph data is modified to prevent the reidentification of nodes or relationships. Techniques include k-anonymity, where nodes are made indistinguishable within a group, and perturbation methods that add or remove edges. Differential privacy introduces randomness to graph data or query outputs to mask the contribution of any single node or edge, providing mathematical guarantees against certain types of privacy attacks. Synthetic graph data generation creates artificial graphs that preserve statistical nature and properties of the original data without exposing actual sensitive information, using generative models like graph GANs.

Privacy-preserving graph computation leverages advanced cryptographic and distributed learning methodologies to enable secure analysis of graph-structured data while preserving privacy. One such technique is *secure multiparty computation* (SMPC), which allows multiple parties to jointly compute a function over their respective inputs without revealing the underlying data—we'll dig more into details surrounding this later in the chapter. This approach facilitates collaborative graph analysis by enabling computations on private data without requiring data sharing between participants. *Homomorphic encryption* enhances this capability by allowing direct computations on encrypted data, supporting operations like addition and multiplication on ciphertexts, thus enabling secure graph processing without the need for decryption. *Federated learning* further advances this paradigm by allowing machine learning models to be trained across decentralized data sources. In the specific case of federated graph learning, clients compute updates on their local graph data and share only model parameters, not raw data, ensuring that sensitive information remains protected. Additional privacy guarantees are provided through techniques such as differential privacy and secure aggregation, which add noise to the data and obscure individual contributions, further safeguarding privacy during the model training process.

These techniques address different aspects of privacy concerns in graph learning, including:

- Data-level privacy by protecting raw graph data from unauthorized access or inference attacks
- Model-level privacy by ensuring that learning algorithms do not leak sensitive information through model parameters or outputs
- Communication privacy by securing the transmission of data and model updates between parties

Throughout this chapter, we will explore these techniques in detail, discussing how they work at a high level, practical implementations, and applicability to real-world problems. We will also explore a number of trade-offs related to privacy, utility, and computational efficiency, providing insights into how these methods can be integrated into existing graph learning pipelines.

Privacy Threats in Graph Learning

As graph learning techniques become more sophisticated and widespread, the methods attackers use to compromise the privacy of graph data have also evolved. Graphs inherently contain rich structural and relational information, making them particularly vulnerable to privacy breaches. Understanding the types of privacy attacks, the adversarial models, and the role of background knowledge is important for designing and developing effective privacy-preserving techniques.

Types of privacy attacks

Privacy attacks on graph data are methods used by adversaries to compromise the anonymity and confidentiality of individuals or relationships represented within a network. These attacks can be broadly classified into two primary categories: node identity disclosure attacks and link reidentification attacks.

Node identity disclosure attacks aim to reidentify anonymized nodes within a graph by exploiting structural and attribute information. Even when explicit identifiers are removed, attackers can leverage unique patterns in the graph's structure to link anonymized nodes back to real-world entities. For example, in an anonymized social network graph where user identities are replaced with random identifiers, an attacker who knows that a particular user, Alice, is connected to three specific individuals, each with a unique number of connections, can analyze the degrees of nodes and their connectivity patterns to identify the node representing Alice.

Mechanisms of node reidentification include *degree-based attacks*, where attackers exploit the degree of nodes as unique identifiers; *neighborhood attacks*, where attackers use the subgraph of a node's immediate neighbors to search for matching patterns within the anonymized graph; and *structural queries*, where attackers employ complex queries about the graph's structure to find unique patterns that lead to reidentification.

Link reidentification attacks focus on inferring the existence or nature of relationships between nodes, which may be sensitive or confidential. Even when node identities are protected, the presence or absence of edges can reveal critical information about interactions between entities. For instance, in a company's communication network where nodes represent employees and edges represent email communications, an attacker might aim to determine if two high-profile employees are communicating, which could signal confidential activities such as mergers or acquisitions.

Mechanisms of link inference include link prediction algorithms, where attackers use algorithms that predict the likelihood of a link between two nodes based on observed patterns and similarities within the graph, and statistical attacks, where attackers leverage statistical properties of the graph, such as edge densities and clustering coefficients, to infer missing links or the nature of existing ones. Risks associated with link reidentification include exposure of sensitive relationships, violation of confidentiality, and indirect disclosure that can allow malicious actors to deduce other sensitive information.

Adversarial models and background knowledge

The effectiveness of privacy attacks often depends on the attacker's capabilities and the amount of background knowledge they possess. Adversarial models help in understanding and anticipating potential threats by categorizing attackers based on their methods and resources.

Passive attackers observe and analyze released data without altering it. They utilize available data and background knowledge in order to perform statistical analysis and pattern matching. Their capabilities include using publicly available information and prior knowledge, as well as analyzing data patterns to identify unique structures. Strategies employed by passive attackers include background knowledge exploitation and structural analysis. Passive attacks are difficult to detect because the attacker does not interact with or modify the data directly.

Active attackers can influence the data before it is anonymized and released. They may add, remove, or alter nodes and edges within the graph. Their capabilities include direct manipulation of the graph's structure and insertion of artificial patterns or nodes. Strategies involve the insertion of signature structures, embedding unique patterns or subgraphs that can later be used to identify specific nodes or relationships, and Sybil attacks, where attackers create fake identities to manipulate the graph's structure. Active attacks often require more resources and access but can be more potent in breaching privacy.

Attackers frequently enhance their capabilities by incorporating external knowledge, significantly increasing the risk of privacy breaches. Sources of external knowledge include publicly available data from public records, social media profiles, or online publications; previously leaked data from prior breaches or releases; and domain expertise or insider information about a particular industry or organization. Attack strategies using external knowledge involve attribute matching, network alignment, and temporal analysis.

For example, an attacker may match publicly available information about individuals' ages and occupations with attributes in the anonymized graph to reidentify nodes. They might align an anonymous friendship network with a public professional network like LinkedIn, using shared connections to identify individuals. Temporal analysis could involve matching login times in one dataset with transaction times in another to infer user behaviors and identify nodes.

Case Studies of Privacy Breaches

Analyzing real-world incidents where privacy was compromised helps illustrate the practical implications of the discussed attacks.

The Netflix Prize data leak

In 2006, Netflix launched a competition to improve its recommendation algorithm, releasing an anonymized dataset containing movie ratings from nearly 500K subscribers. Academic researchers from the University of Texas demonstrated that this anonymized data could be de-anonymized (*https://oreil.ly/NDyUd*). By cross-referencing the Netflix dataset with publicly available reviews on IMDb, they matched rating timestamps and movie titles to reidentify several users. This breach unveiled sensitive information about users' viewing habits and led to a lawsuit against Netflix, ultimately causing the company to cancel a subsequent competition. The incident highlighted the risks of releasing anonymized datasets without accounting for the potential of reidentification through external information.

Social network de-anonymization

In 2007, researchers showed that anonymized social network graphs could be de-anonymized (*https://oreil.ly/05f6s*). They collected data from a social networking site like Flickr using a web crawler and aligned this collected network with an anonymized network released by another platform. By matching structural patterns within the networks, they identified users despite the anonymization efforts. This case demonstrated that traditional anonymization techniques were insufficient for protecting user identities in social network data, emphasizing the need for stronger privacy-preserving methods.

Privacy-Preserving Techniques for Graph Data

Protecting privacy in graph data involves preprocessing and transforming the graph data in such a way that sensitive information is concealed while preserving the utility of the graph data for learning and analysis tasks. This section explores various techniques developed to achieve privacy preservation in graphs, including traditional anonymization methods adapted for graph structures, differential privacy applications, and synthetic data generation.

Graph Data Anonymization

Graph data anonymization involves modifying the graph to prevent reidentification of nodes and relationships while retaining as much useful information as possible. Traditional data anonymization methodologies like k-anonymity and t-closeness, among others, have been adapted for graphs, along with specialized graph modification methods.

k-Anonymity and t-Closeness in Graphs

Originally developed for tabular data, k-anonymity (*https://oreil.ly/Etkrl*) aims to make each record indistinguishable from at least $k - 1$ other records based on certain identifying attributes (quasi-identifiers). In the context of graph data, k-anonymity is extended to ensure that each node is structurally indistinct from at least $k - 1$ other nodes.

Definition: A graph G' is said to be k-anonymous if, for every node v in G', there exist at least $k - 1$ other nodes in G' such that their anonymity sets are identical. An anonymity set can be defined based on node degrees, labels, or more complex structural features.

t-closeness (*https://oreil.ly/uN5bf*) goes further by requiring that the distribution of a sensitive attribute within an anonymity set is close to the overall distribution in the graph, with a threshold t.

Graph Modification Techniques

In order to have graph learning systems that meet the usefulness threshold of businesses, it's critical to anonymize the graph data to protect users' identities without significantly compromising the utility of the information that will eventually used to train the graph ML model. Several techniques have been developed to modify graphs in ways that preserve privacy while maintaining the structural properties necessary for meaningful analysis. Modifying the structure of a graph is a common approach to anonymization. The primary methods include *edge perturbation*, *node aggregation*, and *subgraph generalization*.

Edge perturbation

Edge perturbation involves altering the connections between nodes to mitigate the risk of reidentification of individuals within the graph. This method can be executed through:

Edge addition
> Randomly adding edges between nodes that were not previously connected. This introduces uncertainty about actual relationships and obscures the original network structure.

Edge deletion

Removing certain edges from the graph to eliminate identifiable connections. This reduces the risk of linking nodes to specific individuals based on their relationships.

Edge switching

Swapping connections between pairs of edges. For example, if edges exist between nodes (A, B) and (C, D), switching would result in edges (A, C) and (B, D). This maintains the overall degree distribution while altering specific connections.

Node aggregation

Node aggregation combines multiple nodes into a single entity, known as a super-node, to obscure individual identities. This method includes:

Clustering

Grouping nodes based on similarities, such as attributes or connectivity patterns, and representing each group as a single node.

Aggregation

Edges between nodes in different clusters are represented as edges between the corresponding super-nodes. This process effectively decreases the granularity of the graph, making it harder to trace connections back to individual nodes.

Utility considerations

When modifying graphs for privacy, striking an optimal balance between privacy preservation and data utility is critical, requiring carefully designed techniques that safeguard sensitive information while retaining the analytical value necessary for meaningful insights:

Preservation of key properties

The anonymized graph should maintain essential properties of the original graph, such as connectivity, clustering coefficients, and shortest path lengths. Preserving these properties ensures that analyses performed on the anonymized graph yield meaningful and accurate results.

Balance between privacy and utility

Over-modification can strip the graph of valuable information, rendering it useless for analysis. Conversely, under-modification may fail to provide adequate privacy protection. Finding the optimal level of modification is key to achieving both privacy and utility.

Edge Differential Privacy

Edge differential privacy aims to protect sensitive information about relationships between entities represented in a graph. It guarantees that the addition or removal of a single edge within the graph has a negligible impact on the results of any analytical processes. This means that an attacker cannot confidently determine whether a specific relationship exists between two entities based solely on the analysis results. To achieve edge differential privacy, the following techniques are commonly used:

Noise addition to query results
> Random noise is added to the outputs of graph queries, such as counting the number of triangles (three nodes all connected to each other) or computing the degrees of nodes (the number of connections each node has). The noise added is calibrated according to the query's sensitivity, which quantifies the potential variation in results because of the inclusion or exclusion of a single edge. For example, the Laplace mechanism introduces noise sampled from a Laplace distribution to the query result, with the noise scale determined by the query's sensitivity and inversely related to the privacy parameter, balancing privacy and utility.

Edge randomization
> This involves directly modifying the graph by randomly adding or removing edges. Edges are altered based on certain probabilities that are designed to satisfy differential privacy constraints. This technique obscures the true presence or absence of specific edges in the graph.

Node Differential Privacy

Node differential privacy offers enhanced protection for graph data by ensuring that the inclusion or exclusion of entire nodes, along with all their associated edges, remains confidential. This approach is crucial when safeguarding the privacy of individual participants represented as nodes within a graph.

Implementing node differential privacy presents unique challenges due to high sensitivity. When a node is added or removed, it can significantly impact the results of graph queries because each node is interconnected with others through its edges. As a result, nodes and their edges are treated as a group, and mechanisms must account for this group sensitivity rather than considering each node independently.

To address these challenges, several techniques are employed:

Subgraph sanitization
> This technique involves removing or altering subgraphs associated with individual nodes before performing any analysis. By modifying these subgraphs, the influence of any single node's presence or absence on the overall graph is

reduced. This reduction in impact lowers the sensitivity of the data, making it easier to apply differential privacy mechanisms without excessively distorting the results.

Smooth sensitivity

Instead of relying on *global sensitivity*—which measures the maximum potential change across the entire graph—*smooth sensitivity* prioritizes local sensitivity, evaluating the impact of adding or removing a node within a specific region of the graph. This localized assessment often yields lower sensitivity values compared to global sensitivity, allowing for the addition of less noise while upholding the required differential privacy guarantees. Consequently, this approach enhances data utility by minimizing the extent to which noise distorts the underlying information.

Synthetic Graph Data Generation

Generative models are advanced ML tools for synthesizing data that replicates the characteristics of real datasets. Applied to graph data, these models produce synthetic graphs that retain the structural and statistical properties of the original graphs while safeguarding sensitive information. Two widely used generative models for graphs are *generative adversarial networks* (GANs) and *variational autoencoders* (VAEs).

Graph GANs

Graph generative adversarial networks (also known as *graph GANs*) are specialized adaptations of the traditional GAN architecture, designed to handle graph-structured data. A graph GAN consists of two neural networks, generator (G) and discriminator (D): they are trained concurrently through adversarial optimization:

Generator (G)

Generates synthetic graph structures from random noise, aiming to closely mimic the statistical properties of real graph data, making them indistinguishable from actual graphs.

Discriminator (D)

Evaluates whether a given graph is real or synthetic, outputting a probability that reflects its classification confidence.

During training, the generator progressively refines its ability to create more realistic graphs to fool the discriminator, while the discriminator concurrently improves its ability to distinguish real graphs from generated ones. This adversarial training continues until the generator produces graphs that the discriminator can no longer consistently differentiate from real graphs.

Variational autoencoders (VAEs)

VAEs are a class of generative models that transform data into a latent space (*https://oreil.ly/Jzdpg*) and then reconstruct it, effectively capturing its essential characteristics. In graph applications:

Encoder
Transforms the graph data into a latent representation, compressing its key features into a lower-dimensional space

Decoder
Reconstructs the graph from the latent representation, aiming to generate a structure that closely resembles the original graph

The training process minimizes the reconstruction error between the original and reconstructed graphs while enforcing a predefined distribution, typically a normal distribution, on the latent space. This regularization promotes meaningful latent representations, enabling the generation of new graphs by sampling from the latent space.

Privacy-Preserving Graph Computation

With the growing collaboration among organizations in graph analytics and machine learning, there is a critical demand for performing computations on distributed graph data while maintaining privacy. Privacy-preserving graph computation enables multiple parties to collaboratively compute functions over their private graph data without disclosing sensitive information. Core techniques in this field include SMPC, homomorphic encryption, and differentially private learning algorithms.

SMPC for Graphs

SMPC (*https://oreil.ly/2tPKS*) is a cryptographic protocol that facilitates collaborative computation of a function among multiple parties while preserving the confidentiality of their inputs. For graph data, SMPC allows parties to perform computations on combined graphs without revealing the structure, nodes, or edge attributes of their individual graphs.

Concept of SMPC

The core principle of SMPC is to enable parties to collaboratively perform computations as though a trusted third party were aggregating their inputs, executing the computation, and delivering the result without requiring any actual data sharing. Each participant gains no additional information beyond what can be deduced from their own input and the computation's output. This ensures both privacy and accuracy, maintaining the integrity of the process while safeguarding private data.

SMPC Protocols for Graph Computation

Several cryptographic protocols have been adapted for use in SMPC to facilitate graph computations:

Secret sharing schemes

Additive secret sharing distributes a secret into multiple shares, with each party holding a share such that the sum of all shares reconstructs the original secret. Shamir's secret sharing divides a secret into parts, requiring a predefined threshold of shares to reconstruct it. These methods enable computations on shared data without disclosing the actual secret values.

Oblivious transfer

This cryptographic protocol enables a sender to transmit one of several potential pieces of information to a receiver without knowing which specific piece was chosen. It is especially valuable for performing computations on data from another party without disclosing the exact data points being utilized.

Garbled circuits

In this method, one party creates an encrypted version of a computation (the "garbled circuit") and another party evaluates it using their input without learning anything about the other party's input. This technique is particularly useful for securely computing Boolean functions over private inputs.

Example: Computing Shortest Paths Without Revealing Graphs

Consider two organizations, A and B, each possessing their own private transportation network graphs. They wish to compute the shortest path between two locations that may span both networks without revealing their individual network details.

Protocol steps:

1. *Graph representation*: Each organization represents its graph in a suitable data structure, such as an adjacency matrix or list.

2. *Secret sharing of edge weights*: The edge weights (which might represent distances or costs) are shared using an additive secret sharing scheme. Each organization splits its edge weights into shares and distributes them accordingly.

3. *Distributed computation*: Utilizing a secure protocol like Yao's garbled circuits, the organizations collaboratively compute Dijkstra's algorithm over the combined secret-shared graph. This allows them to find the shortest path without exposing their individual graph structures.

4. *Result reconstruction*: After the computation, the parties collaboratively reconstruct the shortest path length and the path itself, gaining the desired information without having revealed any sensitive graph details.

Homomorphic Encryption in Graph Learning

Homomorphic encryption enables computations to be carried out directly on encrypted data, negating the need for decryption. The decrypted result matches the outcome of operations as if they were performed on the plaintext data. This feature is especially beneficial for privacy-preserving graph learning, as it allows for secure computations on sensitive graph data while maintaining the confidentiality of the underlying information.

Concept of homomorphic encryption

Homomorphic encryption schemes come in three different forms:

Partial homomorphic encryption (PHE)
Allows operations limited to either addition or multiplication on encrypted data, but not both. For example, RSA supports multiplicative operations, while Paillier encryption facilitates additive operations.

Somewhat homomorphic encryption (SHE)
Allows a limited number of additions and multiplications on encrypted data, but the ciphertext becomes too noisy for accurate decryption after exceeding this limit.

Fully homomorphic encryption (FHE)
Allows for unrestricted computations on encrypted data, supporting both addition and multiplication without restriction. Although highly flexible, FHE schemes are computationally intensive and demand substantial computational resources.

Applying homomorphic encryption to graph learning

In graph learning tasks, homomorphic encryption can be applied in two ways:

Encrypted node features
Node-associated features are encrypted—enabling computations, such as those in neural network models, to be performed directly on the encrypted data. This ensures the confidentiality of sensitive node attributes throughout the learning process.

Encrypted adjacency matrices
The graph's structure is encoded in an encrypted adjacency matrix—allowing operations involving graph connectivity, such as message passing in GNNs, to be executed securely on the encrypted representation.

Differentially Private Learning Algorithms

Differential privacy (*https://oreil.ly/Xp-A_*) offers formal assurances that the inclusion or exclusion of a single data point has an insignificant effect on the outcome of a computation. Incorporating differential privacy into machine learning algorithms safeguards individual privacy throughout the training process (see Figure 9-1). In Step 1 of Figure 9-1, fingerprint images are transformed into graph representations. In Step 2, these graphs are input into a graph neural network (GNN) and trained using *differentially private stochastic gradient descent* (DP-SGD). Gradients are clipped individually, averaged, and perturbed with Gaussian noise in order to ensure differential privacy.

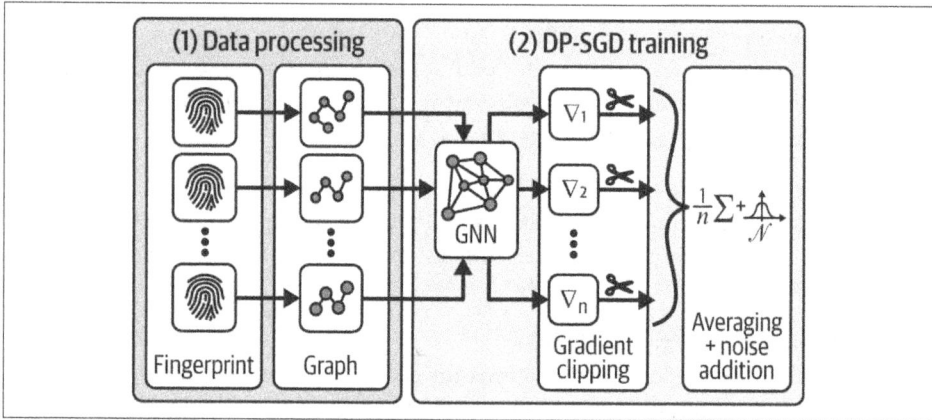

Figure 9-1. Overview of a differentially private training method for graph classification using a fingerprint dataset (adapted from Mueller et al. (2023) (https://oreil.ly/cteXK))

Concept of differential privacy in learning

In the context of graph models, differential privacy ensures that sensitive information about individual nodes or edges does not leak through the trained model. This is important in graphs where data points are interconnected, and changes to one node or edge can influence many others.

Techniques for differentially private learning

Several methods have been developed to incorporate differential privacy into machine learning:

Differentially private stochastic gradient descent (DP-SGD)
  An adaptation of standard stochastic gradient descent, this method incorporates gradient clipping to restrict the impact of individual data points by capping gradient norms. Random noise is added to the clipped gradients before updating model parameters, ensuring differential privacy.

Private aggregation of teacher ensembles (PATE)
> This technique trains multiple teacher models on separate, non-overlapping data subsets. The predictions of these teacher models are then aggregated using a differentially private mechanism to train a student model, enabling it to generalize effectively without direct access to raw data.

Applying differential privacy to graph models

Applying differential privacy to graph models introduces unique challenges originating from the inherently interconnected structure of graph data:

Interconnectedness
> Nodes and edges in a graph are not independent. A single node or edge can influence many parts of the graph, making it difficult to isolate the impact of individual data points.

High sensitivity
> Small changes in the graph can lead to significant variations in the model parameters, requiring careful calibration of the noise added to maintain privacy without excessively degrading utility.

Here are two strategies to mitigate these challenges:

Node-level privacy
> Targets the protection of information pertaining to individual nodes by employing DP-SGD with meticulously calibrated noise scales and clipping parameters. This ensures that the inclusion or exclusion of a node minimally impacts the model's behavior.

Edge-level privacy
> Aims to protect the existence of individual edges. This requires adjusting sensitivity calculations to account for the impact of adding or removing edges and ensuring that the model does not reveal sensitive relationships.

Example: Training a GNN with differential privacy

A social network platform wants to train a GNN to provide friend recommendations while preserving user privacy. By integrating differential privacy into the training process, the platform can prevent sensitive user information from being leaked through the model.

Protocol steps:

1. Gradient clipping
> During training, gradients are constrained to a specified maximum norm for each batch, limiting the impact of any single data point on the model updates.

2. Noise addition

Random noise, usually drawn from a Gaussian distribution, is introduced to the clipped gradients. The level of noise is carefully calibrated to meet the desired privacy thresholds.

3. Parameter update

Model parameters are updated based on the noisy gradients, effectively obfuscating the influence of individual data points.

4. Privacy accounting

Methods such as the *moments accountant* are used to track cumulative privacy loss during training, ensuring that the overall privacy budget is adhered to throughout the process.

Training with differential privacy considerations

Implementing differentially private learning algorithms requires careful consideration:

Choice of parameters

The clipping norm and noise scale must be selected to balance privacy and utility. Smaller clipping norms and larger noise scales increase privacy but can degrade model performance.

Privacy budget

The total privacy budget determines how much information leakage is acceptable. Deciding how to allocate this budget over training epochs is crucial for maintaining privacy throughout the training process.

Advanced techniques

Methods such as adaptive clipping, which adjusts the clipping norms dynamically based on the distribution of gradient norms, can improve the balance between privacy and utility. Learning private graph embeddings with differential privacy guarantees can also facilitate downstream tasks without compromising privacy.

Federated Graph Learning

With the rising ubiquity of graph-structured data in domains such as social networks, biological networks, and financial transaction networks, the demand for privacy-preserving graph learning has become increasingly critical. *Federated learning* (FL) (*https://oreil.ly/WAkun*) provides an effective framework for decentralized model training, eliminating the need to share raw data among participants (Figure 9-2). This methodology facilitates collaborative training of a global model while ensuring the privacy of individual datasets.

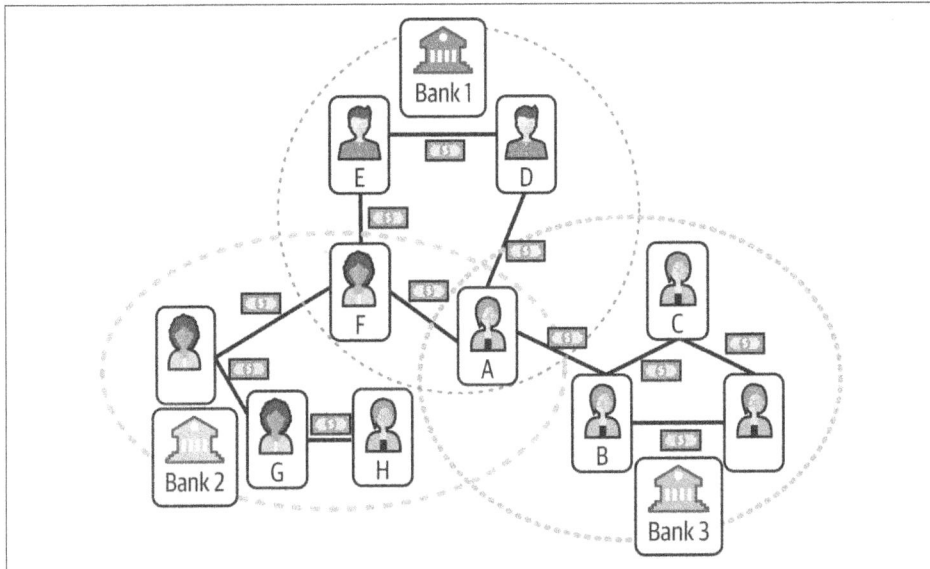

Figure 9-2. Example of privacy-preserving personalized federated graph learning (adapted from Zhang et al. (2022) (https://oreil.ly/mbpKh))

Principles and Architecture

Federated learning is a decentralized ML framework that enables multiple clients or servers, such as user devices or organizations, to collaboratively train a shared global model under the coordination of a central server, all while maintaining strict data privacy. In this paradigm, two main principles guide the use of federated learning:

Data decentralization
> Data remains securely stored on local devices or servers (clients), and only model updates are exchanged with the central server. This approach significantly mitigates the risk of data breaches and ensures compliance with privacy regulations.

Client contributions
> Clients compute model updates using their local datasets and transmit these updates to the central server. The server aggregates these updates to enhance the global model—maintaining privacy by avoiding the transfer of raw data.

To overcome the inherent challenges of distributed learning, federated learning algorithms are designed to optimize communication efficiency, minimizing the overhead between clients and the server. This ensures scalability and practicality for large-scale implementations.

Federated learning architecture

The architecture of a federated learning system comprises several key components. Clients are the individual entities, such as mobile devices or organizations, that hold local data and execute model training on this data locally. A central server plays a pivotal role in supervising the overall training process, aggregating the model updates received from the clients, and maintaining the globally shared model. Finally, a well-defined communication protocol is essential for managing the secure and efficient exchange of model updates between the numerous clients and the central server.

Training process

The federated learning training process begins with an *Initialization* phase. During this stage, the central server generates the initial global model, which serves as the starting point for collaborative learning. This initial model is then distributed to all participating clients, ensuring a synchronized starting point for the subsequent local training.

Following the distribution of the initial model, the process enters the *Local Training* phase. In this crucial step, each client or server leverages its unique local dataset to train the received global model independently. This training occurs over a specified number of epochs, allowing the model to learn patterns and relationships specific to each client's data. As a result of this local training, each client calculates a set of parameter updates that reflect the learning achieved on their local data.

Once the local training is complete, the *Transmission of Updates* phase commences. Here, each client securely transmits the computed model updates back to the central server. This exchange of information is paramount for the collaborative learning process, as it allows the server to gather insights learned across the distributed client base without requiring access to the raw, privacy-sensitive data.

Upon receiving the updates from all participating clients, the central server initiates the *Aggregation* phase. In this stage, the server employs various aggregation techniques, often involving weighted averaging, to synthesize the individual model updates into a refined global model. The weighting applied during aggregation can take into account factors such as the size or quality of each client's local dataset, ensuring that contributions are appropriately valued.

Finally, the process enters the Iteration phase. The newly updated global model, resulting from the aggregation of client updates, is then sent back to the participating clients. This iterative exchange of model parameters continues, with clients performing local training on the updated global model and subsequently transmitting their new updates to the server for aggregation. This cycle repeats until the global model converges to a satisfactory level of performance or a predefined stopping criterion, such as a maximum number of iterations, is reached. This iterative process ensures that federated learning maintains data privacy while enabling effective collaborative model training across decentralized datasets.

Relevance to graph data

Applying federated learning to graph data introduces unique challenges due to the inherent properties of graph structures:

Non-IID data distribution

One of the main challenges arises from the inherently non-independent and identically distributed (non-IID (*https://oreil.ly/M127D*)) nature of graph data across different clients. In simpler terms, this means that the graph datasets held by individual clients often exhibit significant variations in their structure (e.g., number of nodes and edges, density), overall size, and the underlying distributions of node features and edge attributes. For instance, one client might possess a large, densely connected social network graph, while another holds a smaller, sparser graph representing a biological interaction network. These substantial disparities in the local graph data can introduce complexities to the federated learning process, potentially hindering the convergence speed and the overall generalizability of the collaboratively trained model.

Graph heterogeneity

Further compounding the non-IID challenge is the issue of *graph heterogeneity*. This refers to the fact that clients' graphs can differ considerably not only in their size and density but also in the types of node features present, the categories of edges connecting nodes, and their overall topological arrangements. Training a single, unified model that can effectively learn from such diverse graph structures requires careful consideration and the development of specialized aggregation techniques capable of handling these inherent differences.

Cross-client dependencies

In certain real-world scenarios, the graph data held by different clients might not be entirely independent. There could be instances of overlapping nodes, representing the same entities across different local graphs, or shared edges, indicating relationships that span across client boundaries. Managing these cross-client dependencies during the aggregation of model updates becomes a significant challenge, as it is crucial to avoid inadvertently revealing sensitive information related to these shared elements.

Privacy concerns

Finally, the inherent sensitivity of graph data necessitates careful attention to privacy considerations. Even seemingly anonymized graph structures can potentially leak private details about individuals, their relationships, or organizational structures. Therefore, ensuring that the federated learning process for graph data preserves the privacy of the underlying information, beyond just the node features, is a critical requirement.

Motivation for federated graph learning

Despite these considerable challenges, the motivation for pursuing federated graph learning remains strong due to its potential for significant benefits:

Collaborative knowledge sharing
> Federated learning offers a powerful paradigm for entities to collaboratively leverage the information contained within their respective graph datasets to enhance the performance of machine learning models. This collaboration can occur without the need to centralize the sensitive graph data, thereby enabling knowledge sharing in a privacy-preserving manner.

Compliance with privacy regulations
> By keeping the graph data localized on the clients' premises and only sharing model updates, federated learning aligns well with increasingly stringent legal requirements and industry standards for data protection and privacy. This decentralized approach can facilitate compliance with regulations that restrict the transfer and central storage of sensitive information.

Resource utilization
> The distributed nature of federated learning allows participating clients to utilize their own computational resources for local model training. This distributed computation can potentially reduce the burden on centralized infrastructure, making large-scale graph learning tasks more feasible and efficient.

Federated Graph Neural Networks

GNNs have become highly effective for extracting insights from graph-structured data. Adapting GNNs to federated settings facilitates collaborative learning across distributed datasets while maintaining the privacy and security of local data.

Model architectures

Adapting GNNs for federated learning requires significant modifications to traditional architectures to account for the distributed and private nature of the data. Unlike centralized GNNs, which assume access to the entire graph, federated GNNs are designed to operate on local graphs while aggregating knowledge without sharing raw data.

In federated GNN architectures, local GNNs are trained independently on each client's graph data, and the clients share model parameters or updates to a central server, which aggregates them to construct a global model. Hierarchical GNNs extend this concept by using client-level GNNs to learn local graph structures, while the server combines higher-level representations from clients to construct a global understanding. To further protect privacy, edge-privacy-preserving GNNs limit computations to node features and local operations, eliminating the need to share sensitive edge information.

Fintech example

Imagine a scenario where multiple banks, each representing a client, have their own transaction networks modeled as graphs and wish to collaboratively develop a fraud detection model without exposing sensitive transaction data.

Each bank conducts local training with a GNN to detect fraudulent transactions within its own dataset. The banks then transmit model updates, including parameters such as weights or gradients, to a central server. The server aggregates these updates to build a global fraud detection model, which is subsequently redistributed to the banks. This federated approach allows the banks to collectively improve the model while maintaining the privacy of their individual transaction networks.

Training and Communication Protocols

Training federated models across distributed nodes involves careful coordination to ensure efficiency and privacy.

Federated training protocol for GNNs

The process of adapting GNNs for federated learning involves the following iterative steps:

1. *Initialization*

    The central server initializes the global GNN model parameters and distributes them to all the participating clients.

2. *Local training*

    Each client trains the model on its local graph data by performing forward and backward passes to compute gradients and update the parameters based on its dataset.

3. *Communication*

    Clients transmit their model updates or the updated parameters to the central server, ensuring only learned insights, not raw data, are shared.

4. *Aggregation*

    The server combines the received updates to produce the new global model. Aggregation methods can include simple averaging or weighted combinations that consider factors such as the size of each client's dataset.

5. Iteration

The updated global model is sent back to the clients, and the process continues iteratively until the model converges to the desired accuracy or satisfies a predefined stopping criterion.

Communication protocols

Effective communication protocols are fundamental to federated learning, governing how clients and the central server exchange model updates. Two main strategies exist: synchronous and asynchronous updates.

Synchronous updates require all clients to send their updates in each communication round before the server aggregates them. This ensures model consistency but can be slowed by slower or unavailable clients.

Asynchronous updates allow clients to send updates independently, with the server updating the global model upon each receipt. This improves efficiency but complicates maintaining model consistency.

To minimize communication overhead, compression techniques are often employed. Quantization reduces the precision of model updates, while sparsification transmits only the most significant changes. These methods are crucial for the scalability of federated learning.

Privacy Enhancements in Federated Graph Learning

While federated learning enhances privacy by retaining data on local devices, supplementary measures are essential to mitigate potential privacy leaks that may arise from shared model updates.

Secure aggregation protocols

Secure aggregation protocols are designed to ensure that neither the central server nor any adversary can infer individual client updates, addressing potential privacy risks even when data remains on local devices. These protocols mitigate threats such as inference attacks, where adversaries attempt to reconstruct original data from model updates.

Secure aggregation protocols are crucial in federated learning, ensuring that neither the central server nor malicious actors can deduce individual client updates, thereby mitigating privacy risks even with decentralized data. These protocols effectively counter inference attacks, where adversaries attempt to reconstruct original data from shared model updates.

Two primary categories of secure aggregation methods exist. *Encryption-based methods* involve clients encrypting their model updates before transmission. The central server can then aggregate these encrypted updates without needing to decrypt them.

Techniques such as homomorphic encryption are particularly valuable here, as they allow specific computations to be performed directly on the encrypted data, guaranteeing privacy throughout the aggregation process.

Alternatively, *secret sharing protocols* involve each client dividing its model update into multiple random shares. These shares are then distributed among other participating clients and the central server. The server can only reconstruct the final aggregated update by combining these shares, ensuring that no single entity, including the server itself, can access any individual client's original update.

Example of a secure aggregation protocol

An illustrative example of a secure aggregation protocol involves the following steps. First, during setup, clients establish shared cryptographic parameters and, if required, generate encryption keys. Next, in the sharing phase, each client processes its local model update to create encrypted or shared versions that effectively conceal the original data. The aggregation step then sees the central server collecting these processed updates from all participating clients and performing the aggregation operation in a manner that respects the underlying encryption or secret sharing scheme. Finally, in the reconstruction phase, the server obtains the final, aggregated model update without ever gaining access to the individual contributions of each client, thus upholding data privacy.

The adoption of secure aggregation protocols results in significant benefits. Foremost is privacy preservation, as the confidentiality of individual client updates is maintained, substantially reducing the potential for data leakage. Furthermore, well-designed secure aggregation protocols offer robustness; they are capable of tolerating a certain number of malicious or unresponsive clients without jeopardizing the overall aggregation process and the integrity of the final global model.

Differential privacy in federated settings

Differential privacy offers a rigorous mathematical framework to limit the information that can be inferred about any individual data point from the output of an algorithm, making it a critical component in privacy-preserving federated learning. Even with secure aggregation protocols, model updates can inadvertently reveal sensitive information about individual data points. Integrating differential privacy mechanisms addresses this vulnerability by introducing controlled randomness to the learning process.

Differential privacy mechanisms offer a rigorous mathematical framework for quantifying and limiting the disclosure of private information during data analysis or machine learning processes. In the context of federated learning, these mechanisms are employed to further bolster privacy guarantees beyond the inherent decentralization of the data. Two primary approaches to applying differential privacy exist within this framework: local differential privacy and global differential privacy.

Local differential privacy (LDP) operates at the client level. Here, each client adds a carefully calibrated amount of random noise directly to its model updates before transmitting them to the central server. This ensures that the server cannot definitively infer sensitive details from any single client's contribution, providing strong, per-user privacy protection. The level of noise added is controlled by a privacy parameter, ϵ, which dictates the trade-off between privacy and data utility.

Global differential privacy (GDP), in contrast, involves the central server adding noise after aggregating the model updates received from all clients. This approach is generally more computationally efficient than LDP, as noise is introduced only once at the server level. However, it relies on the assumption that the central server is trustworthy and will correctly implement the privacy mechanism, as the privacy guarantee is applied to the aggregate result rather than individual contributions.

To effectively integrate differential privacy into federated learning workflows, several key techniques are employed:

Noise addition
    As described earlier, random noise, calibrated according to the desired level of privacy (often defined by the privacy parameter ϵ and a failure probability δ), is added to the model updates. This noise can be introduced either locally by the clients (in LDP) or globally by the server (in GDP) to obfuscate the influence of individual data points.

Gradient clipping
    Clients can also employ *gradient clipping*, a technique that limits the norm (magnitude) of their model updates before transmission. This helps to ensure that no single data point or outlier in a client's local dataset can exert a disproportionately large influence on the global model update, thereby indirectly enhancing privacy by limiting the potential for inferring sensitive information from extreme gradient values.

Privacy accounting
    To manage the cumulative privacy loss across multiple rounds of federated learning, privacy accounting tools, such as the moments accountant, are utilized. These tools track how the repeated application of noise addition affects the overall privacy budget. By carefully accounting for the accumulated privacy loss, practitioners can ensure that the total privacy leakage remains within acceptable and predefined limits throughout the training process.

Applying differential privacy in federated learning involves key trade-offs:

Privacy versus utility
>   Introducing noise to protect privacy inevitably reduces model performance. Finding the right balance is crucial to ensure sufficient privacy without significantly sacrificing accuracy.

Communication overhead
>   Some privacy techniques increase computational demands and communication costs, which can be challenging in resource-limited settings.

By carefully managing these trade-offs, differential privacy mechanisms enable federated learning systems to maintain robust privacy protections while delivering practical utility.

Applications of Privacy-Preserving Graph Learning

Privacy-preserving graph learning techniques have broad applicability across various domains where graph-structured data is prevalent and sensitive information must be protected. This section explores some key applications, illustrating how these techniques enable valuable insights while maintaining privacy.

Privacy-Preserving Techniques in Social Network Analysis

Social networks offer an extensive dataset for exploring human behavior, relationships, and the dissemination of information. Through the analysis of these networks, researchers can identify communication patterns, pinpoint influential individuals, and study the dynamics of community formation and evolution. However, the sensitive nature of personal information embedded in social network data necessitates stringent privacy-preserving measures to protect user confidentiality. To balance the insights gained from social network analysis with the need to protect individual privacy, several techniques have been developed.

Anonymization of social graphs

One fundamental approach is the anonymization of social graphs, which involves modifying the graph data to prevent the identification of individuals or relationships.

Node anonymization focuses on removing or masking personal identifiers associated with the nodes in the graph. This might include stripping names, user IDs, or other unique attributes that could directly reveal a person's identity. By replacing these identifiers with pseudonyms or random labels, the risk of direct reidentification is reduced.

Edge anonymization aims to obscure the existence of relationships between individuals, particularly when those connections are sensitive. This can involve removing certain edges from the graph or aggregating connections in a way that prevents outsiders from determining whether a specific relationship exists.

Structural anonymization goes a step further by applying techniques like *k-anonymity* to the graph's structure. This ensures that individuals cannot be uniquely identified based on their connections and network positions. Graph modification methods, such as adding, deleting, or swapping edges, are used to alter the network's topology sufficiently to prevent reidentification while preserving the overall structural properties needed for analysis.

Differential privacy in social networks

Differential privacy establishes a mathematical foundation to guarantee that the inclusion or exclusion of a single individual's data minimally impacts the results of an analysis, effectively safeguarding individual privacy.

Edge differential privacy extends this concept to graph data by ensuring that the presence or absence of a single edge, representing a relationship between two individuals, does not significantly alter the analysis outcomes. This approach is particularly valuable for calculating aggregate statistics such as average degree or clustering coefficients. By injecting precisely calibrated noise into the computations, it becomes statistically improbable for an adversary to deduce the existence of any specific edge.

Node differential privacy extends this protection to entire nodes (individual users) in the network. It ensures that analyses do not reveal whether a specific user is part of the network at all. This higher level of privacy is more challenging to achieve because adding or removing a node can significantly alter the network's structure. Techniques for node differential privacy often involve more sophisticated methods of noise addition and sensitivity analysis.

Federated social network analysis

Federated learning techniques can be applied to social network analysis to enhance privacy preservation further.

Distributed learning empowers user devices, or clients, to perform localized model training on their individual social interaction datasets. Instead of transmitting raw data to a central server, each device computes model updates based on its own data.

Model aggregation is managed by a central server that collects these locally computed updates and integrates them to refine the global model. By sharing only model parameters or gradients rather than raw data, this approach significantly enhances the protection of individual users' privacy.

Privacy preservation is further enhanced through techniques such as *secure aggregation*, which prevents the server from inferring individual updates, and *differential privacy*, which introduces noise into the updates to mitigate the risk of sensitive information leakage regarding users' behavior.

Use Cases

Privacy-preserving techniques in social network analysis enable several important applications while maintaining user confidentiality.

Community detection involves identifying groups of users who interact more frequently with each other than with those outside the group. By applying anonymization and differential privacy, analysts can study community structures without exposing the identities of the individuals involved. By effectively applying techniques such as graph anonymization and differential privacy, analysts can effectively study the formation and characteristics of these community structures without the risk of exposing the individual identities of the users involved.

Influence maximization seeks to find the most influential users within a network for purposes like marketing campaigns or information dissemination. Privacy-preserving methods empower organizations to accurately identify these key influencers and understand their network positions without needing to reveal their personal connections or otherwise compromise their privacy.

Sentiment analysis examines the attitudes or emotions expressed by users across the network. By protecting individual opinions through anonymization and differential privacy, it's possible to analyze overall trends and patterns in sentiment without exposing personal viewpoints.

Case Study: Applying FedGraphNN to a Recommender System Using Epinions Data

Recommender systems are a cornerstone of online platforms, delivering personalized suggestions to users based on their preferences and behaviors. However, training these systems effectively often necessitates access to sensitive user data, which raises significant privacy concerns. Federated learning provides a solution by enabling decentralized model training while keeping raw data local. This case study examines the application of FedGraphNN, a federated learning framework for GNNs, to develop a recommender system using the Epinions social network dataset.

Dataset

The Epinions dataset represents a who-trusts-whom social network from the consumer review site Epinions.com. Users can decide whether to "trust" each other, forming a Web of Trust that influences which reviews are displayed to them. The dataset contains 75,879 nodes (users) and 508,837 edges (trust relationships), making it a rich source of information for analyzing social interactions and building recommendation models.

The goal is to develop a recommender system that can predict user preferences and suggest items (e.g., products, reviews) they might be interested in, based on the trust relationships in the network. However, directly using user data raises privacy issues, as personal preferences and connections are sensitive information. Therefore, we employ federated learning to train the model in a decentralized manner, ensuring user data remains on their devices.

Importance of Applying Federated Learning

Federated learning facilitates collaborative model training among multiple clients, such as individual user devices or organizations, while ensuring that local data remains securely stored and private. This paradigm is particularly crucial for recommender systems due to several significant considerations:

Privacy preservation
   Users' trust relationships and behavioral interactions are confined to their local devices, mitigating the risk of data breaches and ensuring adherence to privacy regulations.

Data ownership
   Individuals retain autonomy over their personal data, fostering greater trust and transparency within the platform.

Regulatory compliance
   Federated learning is in compliance with rigorous data protection regulations such as GDPR and HIPAA, which impose rigorous requirements for safeguarding sensitive information.

By integrating federated learning with graph neural networks using the FedGraphNN framework, it becomes feasible to harness the relational insights from the Epinions dataset while upholding robust privacy protections for users.

Data Processing

The data processing stage involves loading the Epinions dataset, partitioning it into subgraphs for each client, and preparing it for training:

```
def split_graph(graph, train_ratio=0.8, val_ratio=0.1, test_ratio=0.1):
    """
    Split the graph edges into training, validation, and test sets.
    """
    edge_size = graph.edge_label.size(0)
    indices = torch.randperm(edge_size)
    train_end = int(edge_size * train_ratio)
```

```
        val_end = train_end + int(edge_size * val_ratio)

        train_indices = indices[:train_end]
        val_indices = indices[train_end:val_end]
        test_indices = indices[val_end:]

        graph.edge_train = graph.edge_index[:, train_indices]
        graph.label_train = graph.edge_label[train_indices]
        graph.edge_val = graph.edge_index[:, val_indices]
        graph.label_val = graph.edge_label[val_indices]
        graph.edge_test = graph.edge_index[:, test_indices]
        graph.label_test = graph.edge_label[test_indices]

        return graph

    def load_data(args, path, client_number):
        """
        Load and partition the Epinions dataset among clients.
        """
        # Load the preprocessed subgraphs for each client
        with open(os.path.join(path, args.dataset, 'subgraphs.pkl'), 'rb') as f:
            graphs = pickle.load(f)

        data_local_num_dict = {}
        train_data_local_dict = {}
        val_data_local_dict = {}
        test_data_local_dict = {}

        for client_id in range(client_number):
            graph = graphs[client_id]
            graph = split_graph(graph)

            # Create DataLoader for each client's data
            train_loader = DataLoader([graph], batch_size=1, shuffle=True)
            val_loader = DataLoader([graph], batch_size=1, shuffle=False)
            test_loader = DataLoader([graph], batch_size=1, shuffle=False)

            train_data_local_dict[client_id] = train_loader
            val_data_local_dict[client_id] = val_loader
            test_data_local_dict[client_id] = test_loader
            data_local_num_dict[client_id] = 1  # Number of samples per client

        return train_data_local_dict, val_data_local_dict, test_data_local_dict,
            data_local_num_dict
```

The two methods that are part of the preceding preprocessing module handle the following:

split_graph

Splits the edges of a graph into training, validation, and test sets based on the specified ratios. It shuffles the edges and partitions them accordingly.

```
load_data
```
Loads the preprocessed subgraphs (assumed to be saved in a pickle file) and splits each graph for a client. It creates `DataLoader` objects for training, validation, and testing for each client.

Federated Training Logic

The *federated training logic* defines the model, the trainer, and the methods required for training and testing the model in a federated environment.

Model definition: GCN for link prediction

Let's first start by defining the graph convolutional network (GCN) model for the link prediction task that would run on each client:

```python
import torch
from torch_geometric.nn import GCNConv

class GCNLinkPred(torch.nn.Module):
    """
    Graph convolutional network model for link prediction tasks.
    """
    def __init__(self, in_channels, hidden_dim, out_channels):
        super(GCNLinkPred, self).__init__()
        self.conv1 = GCNConv(in_channels, hidden_dim)
        self.conv2 = GCNConv(hidden_dim, out_channels)

    def encode(self, x, edge_index):
        """
        Encode node features into embeddings using GCN layers.
        """
        x = self.conv1(x, edge_index)
        x = x.relu()
        x = self.conv2(x, edge_index)
        return x

    def decode(self, z, edge_index):
        """
        Decode node embeddings to reconstruct edges.
        """
        # Compute dot product between pairs of node embeddings
        return (z[edge_index[0]] * z[edge_index[1]]).sum(dim=-1)

    def decode_all(self, z):
        """
        Decode all possible node pairs in the graph.
        """
        prob_adj = z @ z.t()
        return (prob_adj > 0).nonzero(as_tuple=False).t()
```

The GCN model definition mainly consists of the following methods:

init
:   Initializes two GCN layers (conv1 and conv2) with specified input, hidden, and output dimensions

encode
:   Applies GCN layers to node features x and edge indices edge_index, producing node embeddings z

decode
:   Computes the likelihood of edges existing between pairs of nodes by calculating the dot product of their embeddings

decode_all
:   Optionally decodes all possible node pairs, useful for evaluating the model on the entire graph

Trainer definition: Federated training logic

Now that we have the plain GCN model defined, we can run the model within the following federated training environment:

```
class FedSubgraphLPTrainer(ModelTrainer):
    def train(self, train_data, device, args):
        """
        Train the model on local client data.
        """
        self.model.to(device)
        self.model.train()

        # Choose optimizer
        if args.client_optimizer == 'sgd':
            optimizer = torch.optim.SGD(self.model.parameters(), lr=args.lr,
                                        weight_decay=args.wd)
        else:
            optimizer = torch.optim.Adam(self.model.parameters(), lr=args.lr,
                                         weight_decay=args.wd)

        # Training loop
        for epoch in range(args.epochs):
            for batch in train_data:
                batch.to(device)
                optimizer.zero_grad()

                # Encode and decode
                z = self.model.encode(batch.x, batch.edge_train)
                link_logits = self.model.decode(z, batch.edge_train)
                link_labels = batch.label_train
```

```
                # Compute loss
                loss = F.mse_loss(link_logits, link_labels)
                loss.backward()
                optimizer.step()

    def test(self, test_data, device, args):
        """
        Evaluate the model on test data.
        """
        self.model.to(device)
        self.model.eval()
        scores = []

        with torch.no_grad():
            for batch in test_data:
                batch.to(device)
                z = self.model.encode(batch.x, batch.edge_train)
                link_logits = self.model.decode(z, batch.edge_test)
                link_labels = batch.label_test

                # Compute mean absolute error
                score = mean_absolute_error(link_labels.cpu(), link_logits.cpu())
                scores.append(score)

        average_score = np.mean(scores)
        return average_score

    def test_on_the_server(self, train_data_local_dict, test_data_local_dict,
                           device, args=None):
        """
        Aggregate results from all clients for evaluation.
        """
        total_score = 0
        num_clients = len(test_data_local_dict)
        for client_id in test_data_local_dict.keys():
            test_data = test_data_local_dict[client_id]
            score = self.test(test_data, device, args)
            total_score += score
            logging.info(f"Client {client_id}, Test MAE: {score}")
        average_score = total_score / num_clients
        logging.info(f"Average Test MAE: {average_score}")
        return True
```

The main components of this trainer are the `train` and `test` methods where:

train

Performs local training on the client's data:

- Moves the model to the specified device
- Chooses an optimizer (SGD or Adam) based on arguments

- Iterates over epochs and batches, encoding node features, decoding edge probabilities, computing loss, and updating model parameters

test
  Evaluates the model on test data, computing the mean absolute error

test_on_the_server
  Collects and logs test results from all clients, calculating the average performance

Running the Federated Pipeline

The final script orchestrates the entire federated learning process, initializing the environment, loading data, creating the model and trainer, and simulating the federated training rounds:

```
def average_weights(w):
    """
    Average model weights from multiple clients.
    """
    w_avg = copy.deepcopy(w[0])
    for key in w_avg.keys():
        for i in range(1, len(w)):
            w_avg[key] += w[i][key]
        w_avg[key] = torch.div(w_avg[key], len(w))
    return w_avg

def create_model(args, feature_dim):
    """
    Create the GCN model and trainer.
    """
    model = GCNLinkPred(feature_dim, args.hidden_size, args.node_embedding_dim)
    trainer = FedSubgraphLPTrainer(model)
    return model, trainer

if __name__ == '__main__':
    # Parse command-line arguments
    parser = argparse.ArgumentParser()
    args = add_args(parser)

    # Initialize logging
    logging.basicConfig(level=logging.INFO)

    # Set random seed for reproducibility
    setup_seed(42)

    # Load data and partition among clients
    train_data_local_dict, val_data_local_dict, test_data_local_dict, \
    data_local_num_dict = load_data(
        args, args.data_dir, args.client_num_in_total)

    # Assume feature dimension is known (e.g., from data)
```

```
feature_dim = 10  # Example value
device = torch.device('cuda' if torch.cuda.is_available() else 'cpu')

# Create model and trainer
global_model, trainer = create_model(args, feature_dim)

# Start federated training simulation
for round_idx in range(args.epochs):
    logging.info(f"Round {round_idx}")
    local_weights = []
    client_ids = range(args.client_num_in_total)

    # Training on each client
    for client_id in client_ids:
        # Set model parameters to the global model
        trainer.set_model_params(global_model.state_dict())

        # Train on local client data
        train_data = train_data_local_dict[client_id]
        trainer.train(train_data, device, args)

        # Collect model updates
        local_weights.append(trainer.get_model_params())

    # Aggregate updates from clients
    global_weights = average_weights(local_weights)
    global_model.load_state_dict(global_weights)

    # Evaluate the global model
    trainer.test_on_the_server(None, test_data_local_dict, device, args)

    # Save the final global model
    torch.save(global_model.state_dict(), 'fedgcn_epinions.pth')
```

The module outlined here orchestrates the complete end-to-end training and testing process for the link prediction task within this federated learning environment. Several core components work in concert to manage this distributed pipeline. The average_weights function plays a crucial role in consolidating the knowledge learned by individual clients; it takes the model parameters submitted by each client and computes their average, which is then used to update the central global model. Complementing this, the create_model function handles the initial setup of the learning model itself, specifically a GCN, and integrates it with the *federated trainer*, which is essential for coordinating the distributed training process.

The main execution of this pipeline follows a structured sequence of steps. Initially, the load_data function is invoked to retrieve the graph data and distribute it across the simulated clients—mimicking a real-world federated setting where data resides locally. Subsequently, the global model and its associated trainer are instantiated, representing the central entity in the federated system. The core of the learning process then unfolds through a series of simulated federated training rounds.

Within each training round, the system iterates through all participating clients. For every client, a synchronization step occurs where the parameters of the client's local model are set to match the current parameters of the global model, ensuring a consistent starting point for local learning. The client then engages in local training, updating the model's parameters based on the patterns and relationships present in its private data. Once the local training is complete, the updated model parameters from that client are collected. After all clients have completed their local training and submitted their updates, the `average_weights` function is employed to aggregate these individual model parameters, effectively synthesizing the knowledge gained across the federation into an improved global model. Finally, upon the completion of the designated training rounds, the performance of the resulting global model is assessed using the `test_on_the_server` method, providing a measure of its effectiveness on unseen data. The culmination of this process is the saving of the final, trained global model to a persistent file for future use.

This case study illustrates how FedGraphNN can be applied to build a privacy-preserving recommender system using the Epinions dataset. By leveraging federated learning and GNNs, we can train effective models without compromising user privacy and with an acceptable approximation for the system utility. The full E2E example is available as part of the book's GitHub repo as well as more examples that can help demonstrate the other key techniques explained as part of this chapter.

Summary

In this chapter, we explored the importance of privacy in graph learning and the various techniques developed to protect sensitive information within graph data. We began by examining the privacy threats in graph learning, such as node identity disclosure and link reidentification attacks. These threats highlight how attackers can exploit structural properties and background knowledge to reidentify anonymized nodes or infer sensitive relationships between them.

We explored privacy-preserving techniques for graph data, emphasizing adaptations of traditional data anonymization techniques such as k-anonymity and t-closeness, tailored specifically for graph structures. Various graph modification techniques were examined, including edge perturbation, node aggregation, and subgraph generalization, designed to prevent reidentification while retaining the utility of the data. The application of differential privacy to graphs was also discussed, focusing on edge differential privacy and node differential privacy, along with the challenges posed by the intricate dependencies inherent in graph structures.

The chapter also addressed privacy-preserving graph computation methods. We detailed how SMPC enables collaborative computations over private graphs without exposing the underlying data. The use of homomorphic encryption in graph learning was highlighted, demonstrating its ability to support computations directly on encrypted graph data, ensuring both privacy and functionality. Additionally, we covered the integration of differentially private learning algorithms into the training of graph models, providing formal privacy guarantees.

Finally, we explored federated graph learning, outlining the principles and architecture of federated learning and its specific relevance to graph data. We presented federated GNNs, discussing architectures suited for federated settings and how models are trained and communicated across distributed nodes. Techniques for handling data heterogeneity and non-identically distributed data across clients were introduced to mitigate the challenges posed by diverse graph structures. Through an application in social network analysis, we demonstrated how privacy-preserving graph learning enables valuable insights while ensuring data confidentiality.

## CHAPTER 10

Graph Inference and Deployment Strategies

Graph inference refers to the process of utilizing trained graph models to make predictions or derive actionable insights from graph-structured data. It is one of the most critical stages in the graph learning pipeline, where models transition from development to practical application. In enterprise environments, graph inference serves as the engine that powers a wide array of use cases, including product recommendations, relationship predictions, fraud detection, and knowledge discovery. By leveraging the sophisticated connections and dependencies within graph data, enterprises can unlock insights that traditional data models often overlook.

Unlike inference in traditional machine learning systems, graph inference must contend with the complexities inherent to graph-structured data. In graphs, data is not isolated into independent rows or instances but exists as interconnected nodes and edges, each carrying both individual attributes and relational context. This interconnected nature requires inference models to consider not just the features of each node but also the structural relationships and dependencies across the entire graph. As a result, graph inference often demands significant computational power, particularly in large-scale settings where the graph may contain millions or billions of nodes and edges.

The role of inference within the graph learning pipeline is pivotal. After a graph model is trained and validated, inference is the step where the model is applied to new or unseen data to generate predictions. These predictions must be accurate, timely, and actionable in order to deliver real-world value. For example, in a recommendation system, graph inference identifies the most relevant products or services for a user based on their preferences and connections. In a fraud detection system, it evaluates relationships between transactions to flag suspicious patterns. In each case, the effectiveness of the inference phase determines the success of the entire graph learning system.

Deploying graph inference at scale, however, is far from straightforward and involves navigating a series of challenges that we have previously discussed in Chapter 7 in the context of scaling the graph learning process. First, latency is a significant concern—especially for real-time applications such as recommendation engines, where even slight delays can lead to a poor user experience. Achieving rapid inference is essential for maintaining the responsiveness of these systems. Next, scalability poses another critical obstacle. Enterprise graphs—particularly in industries such as social media, finance, and ecommerce—are often vast in size, consisting of billions of entities and relationships. Managing inference workloads across such large datasets requires sophisticated strategies to distribute computations efficiently.

Resource constraints further complicate the process, as inference systems often operate in environments with limited computational capacity. Enterprises must carefully balance the trade-offs between performance and cost, particularly when deciding between CPU-based and GPU-based inference solutions or exploring emerging hardware accelerators like TPUs. Finally, accuracy remains a non-negotiable requirement. While optimizing for speed and scalability, it is crucial to ensure that the model's predictions remain reliable. Errors in inference—such as misclassified nodes or incorrect predictions—can lead to adverse outcomes, including financial losses, reputational damage, or regulatory violations.

This chapter explores the techniques and methodologies of graph inference, focusing on strategies to overcome these challenges while ensuring efficient and robust deployment in enterprise applications. It explores various deployment methodologies, such as *canary* and *blue–green* deployments, which allow for safe and controlled model rollouts. Additionally, the chapter examines hardware considerations, runtime optimizations, and scalability techniques, providing a comprehensive framework for implementing graph inference at scale. By addressing these key areas, enterprises can realize the full potential of graph learning, transforming complex data into meaningful insights and driving impactful business decisions.

Deployment Strategies

Transitioning graph learning models from the development environment to production for inference is a critical phase demanding meticulous planning and execution. Unlike models trained on simpler data structures, graph models must contend with the inherent complexities of graph data—which often includes vast scale, intricate interdependencies between nodes, varying sparsity, and potentially dynamic structures. These unique characteristics mean that generic, one-size-fits-all deployment tactics frequently prove inadequate.

Selecting an appropriate deployment strategy is therefore not merely a procedural step but a crucial decision that significantly impacts system stability, inference performance, resource utilization, and the ability to update models without disrupting service. A well-aligned strategy facilitates seamless rollouts, mitigates risks associated with new model versions, and ensures robust, continuous operation. Conversely, a mismatched approach can lead to performance bottlenecks, operational challenges, poor user experience, or even significant system downtime.

In this section, we will navigate the landscape of deployment strategies pertinent to graph inference systems. We will examine established patterns such as canary, blue–green, and shadow deployments, alongside specialized approaches including edge deployments and A/B testing frameworks. For each strategy, we will explore its operational principles, advantages, disadvantages, and specific considerations when applied to the unique demands of graph-based models in enterprise settings.

> While this section focuses on considerations specific to graph learning models, numerous excellent online resources including the following provide comprehensive discussions of general software deployment strategies in broader contexts:
>
> - "8 Deployment Strategies Explained and Compared" (*https://oreil.ly/mRkzn*) by David Berclaz (Apwide)
> - "Deployment Strategies" (*https://oreil.ly/LD1Fv*) by Attila Uhrin (Baeldung)
> - "6 Deployment Strategies (and How to Choose the Best for You)" (*https://oreil.ly/Ak1Ic*) (LaunchDarkly)

Canary Deployments: Testing the Waters

Canary deployments offer a cautious approach to introducing a new graph inference model version. The core idea is analogous to the historical use of canaries in coal mines to detect toxic gases before they affected the miners. Here, a small subset of traffic acts as the "canary" to detect potential problems with the new model before a full rollout, as illustrated in Figure 10-1. This strategy involves directing a limited, controlled portion of production traffic (e.g., requests from a specific user segment, geographic region, or a percentage of overall requests) to the new model version while the majority continues to be served by the stable, existing version.

The performance and behavior of the new model are closely monitored within this limited scope. If the model performs as expected according to predefined metrics (such as latency, error rates, prediction quality, and resource consumption), the traffic percentage directed to it is gradually increased. This incremental process continues until the new model serves all traffic—at which point the old version can be decommissioned. If issues arise during this phased rollout, traffic can be quickly redirected back to the stable version, minimizing the impact on the overall user base.

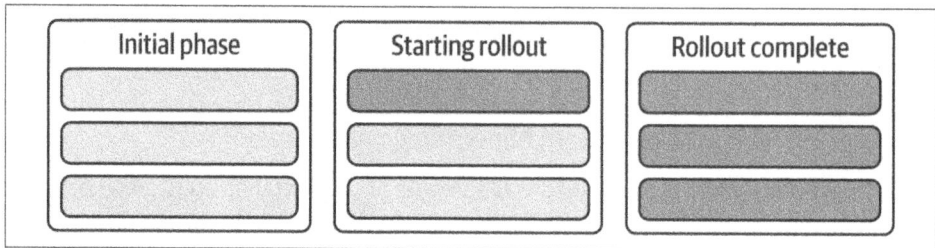

Figure 10-1. Canary deployment

Why is this particularly relevant for graph inference? Graph structures can exhibit complex and sometimes unpredictable behaviors. Changes in model logic or updates based on new graph data might have nonlocal effects due to the interconnected nature of nodes. A seemingly minor modification could inadvertently affect predictions for distant parts of the graph. Canary deployments provide a safety net, allowing teams to observe these real-world effects in a contained environment. For instance, when deploying an updated fraud detection model, one might initially route transactions from a small, low-risk customer segment to the new model. This allows evaluation of its accuracy and performance without exposing the entire system to potential errors.

There are several key considerations for graph canary deployments:

Selecting the canary group
> The subset of traffic or data chosen for the canary phase should be representative enough to yield meaningful insights. For graph models, this might involve selecting a subgraph or a user cohort that covers diverse node types, degrees, and edge patterns. Simply choosing random users might not adequately test scenarios involving highly connected "hub" nodes or specific community structures within the graph.

Monitoring critical metrics
> Beyond standard operational metrics like latency and CPU/memory usage, specific graph-related metrics are crucial. This could include monitoring the distribution of prediction scores, the model's behavior on specific node types, or its performance on queries involving multihop neighborhoods. Anomalies in these metrics can signal problems specific to the graph model's logic or its interaction with the data.

Robust rollback mechanism

A critical component of a successful canary strategy is the ability to rapidly and reliably revert traffic away from the new model if problems are detected. Automating the rollback process based on predefined alert thresholds is highly recommended to minimize reaction time and potential negative impact.

Why is this good for graph reasoning? Graphs often have unpredictable quirks: a small change in one part of the graph can ripple through the rest in unexpected ways. Canary deployments let you observe these behaviors in a controlled setting. For example, in a recommendation system, you could test a new model on users with diverse browsing histories to see how well it handles different patterns. Here's how to nail canary deployments for graphs:

Pick the right canary group

Use a subset of the graph that represents the diversity of your system. You want a mix of high-activity nodes (e.g., power users) and low-activity ones.

Monitor the right metrics

Keep an eye on latency, prediction accuracy, and system resource usage. Are you seeing weird spikes or drops? Time to hit pause and investigate.

Have a rollback plan

If things go wrong, you need a quick, seamless way to revert to the old model. Automating this step can save you many headaches.

Blue–Green Deployments: Smooth Transitions

Blue–green deployments prioritize seamless transitions and rapid rollback capabilities by maintaining two distinct, identical production environments: *blue* (the current live environment) and *green* (the idle environment hosting the new model version). Before deployment, the green environment is thoroughly tested. Once confidence in the new version is established, the load balancer or routing mechanism is updated to direct all incoming traffic from the blue environment to the green environment. The blue environment is kept on standby, ready to receive traffic again if any critical issues emerge in the green environment post-deployment. This allows for near-instantaneous rollback by simply switching the traffic back.

This strategy is particularly valuable for mission-critical graph inference systems— such as real-time financial fraud detection or supply chain optimization—where downtime or performance degradation is unacceptable. It provides a high degree of safety and predictability during updates.

Next, we'll cover a few things about fine-tuning blue–green for graphs:

Environment parity and testing
> Ensuring that the green environment truly mirrors blue is crucial. This includes replicating infrastructure, configurations, data access patterns, and ideally, simulating realistic production load, including complex graph query patterns. Stress testing the graph model in the green environment under these conditions helps uncover potential bottlenecks or integration issues before going live.

Gradual traffic shift (canary on blue–green)
> While the classic blue–green approach involves a swift, complete traffic switch, it can be combined with canary principles for added safety. Instead of redirecting 100% of traffic at once, you can initially route a small percentage (e.g., 5%, 10%) to the green environment. Monitor its performance closely, just like a canary deployment. If stable, gradually increase the traffic percentage routed to green until it handles the full load. This hybrid approach provides the safety net of a full standby environment (blue) while still allowing for gradual exposure and monitoring before committing all traffic.

State and data synchronization
> Graph models often rely on shared resources such as databases, precomputed embeddings, feature stores, or cached graph structures. Ensuring consistency and synchronization of these resources between the blue and green environments during the transition is vital. Stale data or caches in the green environment could lead to incorrect inferences. Strategies for managing this might include read-only replicas, dual-writing during the transition phase, or ensuring cache invalidation mechanisms work across both environments.

Shadow Deployments: Flying Under the Radar

Shadow deployments (also known as *dark launches*) offer a way to test a new model version with real production traffic without impacting users. In this setup, incoming requests are duplicated. One copy goes to the stable, live model (which generates the actual response sent back to the user), and the other copy goes to the new "shadow" model running in parallel as shown in Figure 10-2. The shadow model processes the request and generates predictions, but its results are not returned to the user; instead, they are logged and compared against the live model's outputs.

This strategy is excellent for validating the performance, stability, and prediction consistency of complex graph models, such as GNNs, under real-world conditions before exposing them to users. Since graph model behavior can be sensitive to specific data patterns and graph structures, shadow deployments allow for risk-free evaluation. For example, a new recommendation GNN can run in shadow mode, comparing its suggested items against the current system's recommendations for the same users, helping identify divergences or improvements.

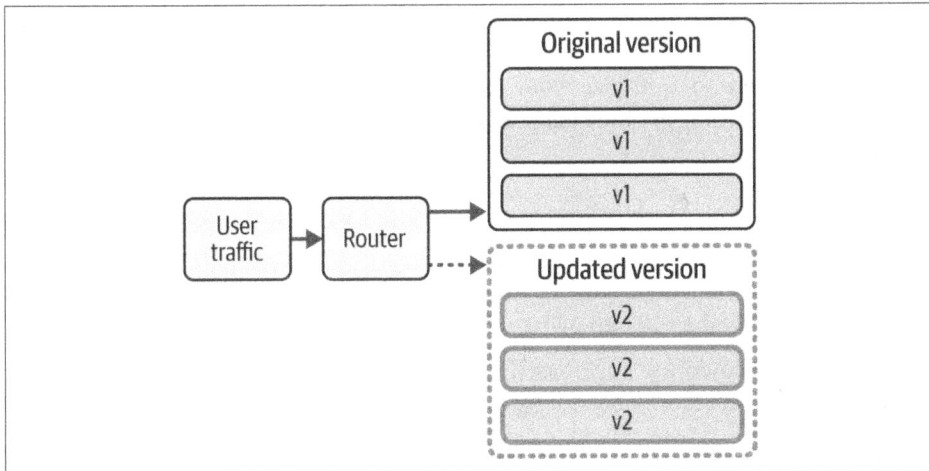

Figure 10-2. Shadow deployment

Here are some best practices for graph shadow deployments:

Detailed result comparison
> Log and meticulously compare the outputs (e.g., prediction scores, classifications, generated embeddings) of the shadow model against the live model. Analyze discrepancies to understand *why* they occur—is it improved accuracy, a bug, or sensitivity to different graph features? Automated analysis and alerting for significant divergence are beneficial.

Performance and scale testing
> Shadow deployments provide a realistic environment to verify that the new graph model can handle production-level traffic volume and query complexity without performance degradation (latency, resource usage). Ensure that the shadow infrastructure can sustain the load.

Sufficient evaluation duration
> Allow the shadow model to run long enough to encounter a diverse range of inputs and graph interaction scenarios. Short evaluation periods might miss edge cases or behaviors that only manifest under specific conditions or over time.

Edge Deployments: Taking It to the Edge

Edge deployments bring graph inference closer to where the action happens: on edge devices like sensors, smartphones, or local servers. This approach reduces latency (since you're not waiting for a round trip to the cloud) and can enhance privacy by keeping sensitive data on the device.

While this sounds great, deploying graph inference at the edge comes with its own set of challenges, like limited computational power and memory. To overcome these, you'll need to optimize your graph models, often using techniques like pruning, quantization, or knowledge distillation. Here are some examples of edge deployments:

- In IoT networks, graph inference might predict when a machine is likely to fail, enabling proactive maintenance.
- Retail stores might use edge devices to run localized recommendation models that suggest products based on in-store behavior.
- Mobile apps could use edge-based graph inference for personalized features like real-time social recommendations.

A/B Testing Deployments: Controlled Experiments

A/B testing, a familiar concept from optimizing user interfaces and marketing campaigns, is also a highly effective strategy for rigorously evaluating the real-world impact of a new graph inference model. The core principle involves splitting production traffic (users, requests, or data points) into distinct groups, typically two. Group A (the control group) continues to interact with the existing, stable model, while Group B (the treatment group) receives predictions or results generated by the new model candidate as shown in Figure 10-3.

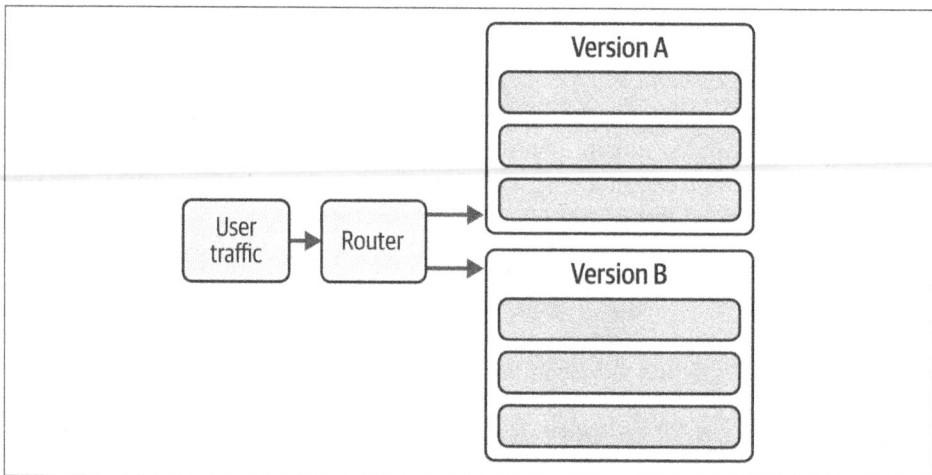

Figure 10-3. A/B testing deployment process

The key advantage of A/B testing lies in its ability to provide statistically significant comparisons of user behavior or business outcomes directly attributable to the model change. By tracking relevant key performance indicators (KPIs) for both groups over a defined period, you can objectively measure whether the new model leads to improvements, degradations, or no significant change.

You can also apply A/B testing to graph models. Imagine deploying a new graph-based recommendation engine. In an A/B test:

Group A (Control)
Users in this group receive recommendations generated by the current, established algorithm.

Group B (Treatment)
Users in this group receive recommendations from the new graph model.

Over the course of the experiment, you would compare metrics such as:

- Click-through rates (CTR) on recommended items
- Conversion rates (e.g., purchases made after clicking a recommendation)
- User engagement metrics (e.g., time spent on site, session duration)
- Diversity or novelty of recommendations

If Group B consistently shows statistically significant improvements in the target KPIs compared to Group A, it provides strong evidence that the new graph model is superior in practice. Conversely, if Group B performs worse or shows no difference, it might indicate that the new model isn't delivering the expected value or requires further tuning. Careful selection of metrics and rigorous statistical analysis are crucial for drawing valid conclusions from A/B tests involving complex graph models.

Progressive Rollouts: Scaling Up Gradually

Progressive rollouts are about taking baby steps. You start small, deploying your graph inference model to a small and trusted fraction of users or nodes, and then gradually increase the scope as you gain confidence. This strategy combines elements of canary deployments and full rollouts, giving you a way to scale up while keeping risks low.

Containerized Deployments

Leveraging containerization technologies like Docker (*https://docker.com*) and container orchestration platforms such as Kubernetes (*https://kubernetes.io*) can significantly streamline the deployment and management of graph inference models. Containers encapsulate the model, its dependencies (libraries, frameworks, specific runtime versions), and necessary configurations into a standardized, portable unit. This "package" can then be run consistently across different environments—from a developer's laptop to staging servers and large-scale cloud clusters.

Kubernetes builds upon containerization by providing powerful tools for automating the deployment, scaling (adjusting the number of running instances based on load), monitoring, and lifecycle management of containerized applications. For graph inference services, this means easier handling of updates, automatic recovery from failures, and efficient resource utilization. Deploying a graph model as a containerized service within Kubernetes simplifies integration into larger microservice architectures and CI/CD pipelines.

By mixing and matching these deployment strategies, potentially facilitated by containerization, you can tailor your approach to fit the unique needs and constraints of your graph inference system. Whether deploying to a centralized cloud environment, a distributed edge network, or a hybrid setup, selecting and implementing the right strategy ensures your models are not just computationally powerful but also operationally reliable, scalable, and ready to deliver value in the real world.

Hardware Considerations

Hardware selection is pivotal for the performance, scalability, and cost-effectiveness of graph inference systems. Graph tasks often blend computational intensity with significant memory demands, making the choice between CPUs, GPUs, or emerging specialized hardware a critical optimization decision.

CPU inference

CPUs offer versatility and cost-efficiency, suitable for general-purpose computation. They excel in batch inference scenarios where real-time latency is not paramount (e.g., overnight processing, periodic updates). While potentially struggling with low-latency demands or the highly parallel nature of some graph algorithms on massive graphs, CPUs remain viable, especially with optimized software libraries and multithreading. They are often the default for budget-conscious environments.

GPU inference

GPUs, designed for massive parallelism, are well-suited for graph inference tasks involving simultaneous operations like feature aggregation or matrix manipulations. They shine in real-time, large-scale applications (e.g., social media recommendations, ecommerce personalization) requiring high throughput and low latency. High memory bandwidth is another advantage for memory-intensive graph data structures. However, GPUs involve higher costs and might offer diminishing returns for smaller graphs or less parallelizable workloads due to data transfer overhead.

Emerging hardware technologies

The hardware landscape is evolving with specialized processors targeting AI and graph workloads:

Tensor processing units (TPUs)
Optimized for matrix computations common in deep learning, TPUs excel with GNNs and other neural network-based graph models, particularly in cloud environments.

Graph processing units (Graph PUs / GPUs)
A newer category specifically designed for graph computations, focusing on optimizing the sparse data structures and irregular memory access patterns typical in graph algorithms, promising performance gains for large-scale tasks.

Balancing hardware choices

Selecting hardware involves aligning capabilities with specific application needs (latency requirements, scale, batch versus real time) and budget. Consider the ecosystem: compatibility with existing infrastructure, library support, and scalability needs. Hybrid approaches, using CPUs for orchestration and GPUs/TPUs for core inference, can offer balanced solutions. Understanding the trade-offs between CPUs, GPUs, and specialized hardware enables informed decisions to maximize the efficiency of graph inference systems.

Inference Runtimes

The choice of inference runtime is a critical factor in determining the performance, scalability, and efficiency of graph inference systems. Inference runtimes act as the bridge between graph models and the underlying hardware, translating the abstract logic of machine learning models into executable operations. Given the unique demands of graph-based tasks—such as their irregular data structures, memory-intensive computations, and real-time requirements—it is essential to select the right runtime environment and optimize its usage. In this section, we will dive into inference frameworks and libraries, precomputation and caching strategies, and the key distinctions between online and offline inference.

Inference Frameworks and Libraries

Inference for graph models has seen rapid advancements in tooling, with several frameworks emerging to streamline the process. These frameworks aim to optimize performance, simplify deployment, and provide flexibility across different hardware environments. Let's explore some of the most popular inference frameworks and their capabilities:

TensorRT

Developed by NVIDIA, TensorRT is a high-performance deep learning inference library optimized for NVIDIA GPUs. It is particularly well-suited for large-scale and real-time inference tasks, including GNNs. TensorRT provides features like precision calibration (e.g., FP16 and INT8), layer fusion, and hardware-specific optimizations that can significantly accelerate graph model inference. For graph tasks that involve neural networks, such as node classification or link prediction, TensorRT can deliver notable performance improvements, especially on edge or embedded devices equipped with NVIDIA GPUs.

ONNX Runtime

The ONNX Runtime is an open source inference engine that supports the Open Neural Network Exchange (ONNX) format. It is hardware-agnostic and integrates with a wide range of accelerators, including CPUs, GPUs, and TPUs. One of the key advantages of ONNX Runtime is its flexibility—it allows you to export graph models from popular training frameworks such as PyTorch or TensorFlow and deploy them efficiently across different platforms. For graph models built with frameworks such as Deep Graph Library (DGL) or PyTorch Geometric (PyG), ONNX Runtime ensures smooth and optimized inference, especially when deploying across heterogeneous environments.

Deep Graph Library (DGL)

DGL is a Python-based library designed specifically for graph learning. It provides end-to-end support for graph neural network training and inference. While DGL excels in the training phase, it also offers inference functionalities optimized for large-scale graphs. It provides utilities for sampling, batching, and managing dynamic graph structures during inference, making it ideal for applications like social network analysis and recommender systems. DGL's integration with backend frameworks like PyTorch and TensorFlow further enhances its flexibility.

PyTorch Geometric (PyG)

PyG is another powerful library for graph-based deep learning. Focusing on simplicity and speed, PyG is optimized for implementing and deploying GNNs. Its modular design makes it easy to extend for custom graph models. PyG supports GPU acceleration, enabling high-throughput inference for tasks such as graph embeddings, clustering, and link prediction. For enterprises focused on scalability, PyG's integration with distributed computing frameworks offers significant advantages. Each of these frameworks has strengths and trade-offs as shown in Table 10-1.

Table 10-1. Strengths and trade-offs of inference frameworks

Feature	TensorRT	ONNX Runtime	Deep Graph Library (DGL)	PyTorch Geometric (PyG)
Primary focus	High-performance deep-learning inference on NVIDIA GPUs	Hardware-agnostic inference via ONNX format	End-to-end GNNs (training and inference)	GNN implementation and deployment (focus on simplicity)
Hardware support	NVIDIA GPUs	CPUs, GPUs (NVIDIA, AMD), TPUs, other accelerators	CPUs, GPUs (via PyTorch/TensorFlow backend)	CPUs, GPUs (via PyTorch backend)
Key strengths	Speed, optimization (FP16/INT8, fusion)	Flexibility, portability, broad hardware support	Graph-specific optimizations (sampling, batching)	Simplicity, speed, modularity, distributed support
Considerations	NVIDIA hardware lock-in, optimization expertise needed	May require fine-tuning for graph specifics	May lack some hardware-specific accelerations	Primarily tied to PyTorch ecosystem
Best suited for	Latency-critical GNNs on NVIDIA hardware	Deploying models across diverse hardware platforms	Large-scale graph applications, dynamic graphs	Rapid GNN development and deployment, scalable systems

Choosing the right framework depends on your application's requirements, including hardware constraints, performance goals, and the complexity of the graph model.

Precomputations and Caching

Graphs are inherently resource-intensive due to their irregular structures and large-scale data requirements. To mitigate these challenges, precomputations and caching are invaluable techniques for optimizing inference.

Precomputed embeddings

One common strategy involves precomputing node or edge embeddings. In this approach, the graph model generates embeddings during an initial computation phase (e.g., after training), and these embeddings are stored for subsequent use. During inference, instead of recalculating embeddings for every query, the system retrieves precomputed embeddings, drastically reducing latency.

This technique is especially effective for static or semi-static graphs, where the structure and node attributes change infrequently. For example, in a recommendation system, user and item embeddings can be precomputed and periodically updated based on new interactions. By reusing these embeddings, the system can deliver real-time recommendations without the computational overhead of full graph inference.

Caching inference results

Caching is another powerful optimization for graph inference. Frequently accessed nodes, edges, or subgraphs can have their inference results cached, reducing redundant computations. For example:

- In a graph-based fraud detection system, common transaction patterns can be pre-inferred and cached.
- In social networks, popular content recommendations can be cached for quick retrieval.

To implement effective caching, it's essential to balance storage and computational costs. Techniques like least recently used (LRU) caching or weighted caching strategies can help manage cache size and prioritize high-value inferences.

Trade-offs in precomputation and caching

While these techniques reduce latency and resource utilization during inference, they come with trade-offs. Precomputations are less effective for highly dynamic graphs where nodes and edges change frequently. Similarly, maintaining large caches can strain memory resources—requiring careful management and invalidation strategies to ensure accuracy.

Online Versus Offline Inference

The choice between online (real-time) and offline (batch) inference depends on the application's requirements for responsiveness and computational efficiency.

Online inference: Real-time predictions

Online inference is performed in real time, generating predictions as input data arrives. This mode is essential for latency-sensitive applications where immediate decisions are required. Examples include:

- Fraud detection systems that need to flag suspicious transactions instantly
- Ecommerce recommendation engines that update suggestions as users browse

Real-time inference prioritizes low latency, often at the expense of throughput. Achieving functional real-time inference requires careful hardware optimization (e.g., GPUs for parallelism), efficient data pipelines, and lightweight models that minimize computational demands.

Offline inference: Batch processing

In contrast, offline inference processes large batches of data at scheduled intervals. This mode is suited for applications where real-time predictions are unnecessary, such as:

- Periodic updates to user embeddings in a recommendation system
- Large-scale graph analytics for trend forecasting

Offline inference offers the advantage of high throughput, as the system can process data in bulk. It also enables more complex models without strict latency constraints. However, the lack of real-time responsiveness may limit its applicability for dynamic, user-facing systems.

Balancing online and offline inference

Many enterprise applications combine online and offline inference in order to balance responsiveness and efficiency. For instance, a recommendation engine might use offline inference to generate a base set of recommendations and then refine these suggestions in real time as users interact with the system. Similarly, a fraud detection system might precompute risk scores offline and use online inference to fine-tune predictions based on new transactions.

Inference runtimes are a cornerstone of graph model deployment, influencing everything from latency and scalability to hardware utilization and cost. Whether leveraging frameworks like TensorRT for high-performance GPU inference, employing precomputations and caching to optimize resource use, or balancing online and offline strategies for dynamic applications, the choice of runtime and techniques must align with the specific needs of the task at hand. By understanding the capabilities and trade-offs of different approaches, enterprises can build graph inference systems that are not only powerful but also efficient and adaptable to evolving demands.

Model Optimization Techniques

Optimizing graph models is crucial for achieving efficient inference in real-world applications, where latency, computational resources, and scalability are often constrained. Model optimization techniques such as quantization, pruning, and knowledge distillation allow organizations to deploy graph models that perform efficiently without compromising significantly on accuracy. These methods not only improve inference speed and reduce resource requirements but also enable the deployment of graph models in environments with limited hardware capabilities, such as edge devices or cost-sensitive data centers.

Quantization

Quantization is a technique used to optimize machine learning models by reducing the precision of the numerical values representing model parameters. In the context of graph models, this technique is particularly valuable because it helps reduce memory usage, increases inference speed, and makes models more efficient, especially when deployed on hardware with limited resources like edge devices or GPUs. By converting high-precision floating-point values to lower bit-width formats, quantization significantly speeds up computations and reduces the model's storage footprint without sacrificing too much accuracy.

> Check the following courses for a detailed explanation of quantization and how it works:
>
> - "Quantization in Depth" (*https://oreil.ly/lEkEO*) (DeepLearning.AI)
> - "Quantization Fundamentals with Hugging Face" (*https://oreil.ly/08ytQ*) (DeepLearning.AI)

How quantization works

At the core of quantization lies the idea of mapping the continuous values of model parameters (e.g., weights, activations) to a discrete set of values represented by fewer bits. In traditional deep learning models, parameters are typically stored in 32-bit floating-point (FP32) format. Quantization reduces the bit width of these parameters, often to 16-bit floating-point (FP16), 8-bit integer (INT8), or 4-bit integer (INT4) formats as shown in Figure 10-4. This reduction drastically cuts down on memory requirements and computation—as operations involving smaller data types are faster.

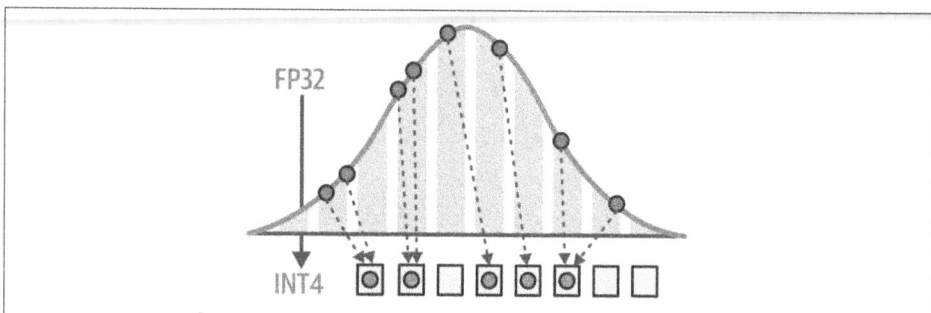

Figure 10-4. The range of quantization from FP32 to INT4 (adapted from Maarten Grootendorst (2024) (https://oreil.ly/lRDbe))

The process of quantization involves three key steps:

1. *Normalization*

   The first step is to rescale the original floating-point values to fit within the target range of the lower precision. For instance, if quantizing to 8 bits, the values are scaled to fit within the range of 0 to 255 (for unsigned integers), or –128 to 127 (for signed integers).

2. *Rounding*

   Once the model's parameters are normalized, they are rounded to the nearest value that can be represented within the target bit width. This rounding process essentially introduces a small error due to the reduced precision.

3. *Rescaling*

   After rounding, the final step is to adjust the scale of the quantized values so that the loss of precision is minimized, and the model still behaves similarly to the original model during inference.

These steps allow a model to be represented and executed with fewer bits while maintaining much of its original accuracy and functionality.

Types of quantization

There are several methods of quantization, each with advantages and trade-offs depending on the specific requirements of the application:

Post-training quantization

Post-training quantization is the simplest and most widely used approach. It is applied after a model has been fully trained in its original, high-precision format. During this phase, the model's weights and activations are converted into lower precision (e.g., from FP32 to INT8).

The main advantage of post-training quantization is that it can be done quickly and easily, without requiring changes to the training process. However, since the model has not been specifically trained with quantization in mind, this approach can sometimes cause a loss of accuracy, particularly for certain types of models and tasks. For this reason, some level of fine-tuning is often required after quantization to recover accuracy.

Quantization-aware training (QAT)

QAT takes a more sophisticated approach by integrating quantization into the training process itself. During QAT, the model is trained with simulated lower-precision operations, which allows the model to learn how to best handle quantized weights and activations. This results in a model that is more robust to the effects of quantization and retains higher accuracy after the process.

QAT is especially useful for models that are sensitive to quantization, such as deep neural networks or complex graph models. Although QAT can lead to better results in terms of accuracy retention, it requires additional computational resources and longer training times.

Weight quantization versus activation quantization

Weight quantization

In this approach, only the model weights are quantized, while activations (i.e., the intermediate outputs of neurons) remain in higher precision. This is the most common form of quantization, as it focuses on the most memory-intensive components of a model.

Activation quantization

This method involves quantizing both weights and activations. While it offers further memory reduction, it is more challenging to implement and may cause greater accuracy degradation due to the increased loss of precision in intermediate values.

Use weight quantization primarily to reduce model size/memory with minimal accuracy loss, leveraging hardware efficiently with floating-point activations. It's a simpler starting point. Opt for activation quantization (often part of "full quantization") to maximize speed and minimize computation on integer-optimized hardware (like edge devices), accepting higher complexity and potential accuracy impact, often requiring mitigation like QAT.

Symmetric versus asymmetric quantization

Symmetric quantization

In symmetric quantization, the range of values is centered around zero, and the same scaling factor is applied to both positive and negative values. This approach simplifies the implementation and is commonly used for weight quantization.

Asymmetric quantization

Here, the scaling factor is applied separately to positive and negative values. This can lead to more efficient storage when the distribution of values is skewed, but it is slightly more complex to implement.

The key difference lies in the handling of the zero point: symmetric quantization maps floating-point zero to or near integer zero, simplifying calculations, especially for hardware optimized for signed arithmetic often used with weights. Asymmetric quantization uses an explicit integer "zero-point" offset, offering potentially better precision for skewed data distributions (like activations after ReLU) at the cost of slightly more complex arithmetic.

Technical considerations

For graph models, particularly those using GNNs, the typical use of matrix multi-plications and aggregations of node and edge features can be highly sensitive to precision loss. In this context, quantization can be both beneficial and challenging:

Precision and accuracy trade-offs
One of the main challenges of quantization is the trade-off between performance gains and accuracy degradation. Lowering the precision of model parameters can lead to a loss of information, which can manifest as reduced accuracy. For graph models, which rely heavily on the relationships between nodes and edges, maintaining sufficient precision to capture these connections while still achieving efficiency is crucial. Models with dense feature spaces or complex relationships might require careful fine-tuning post-quantization to minimize the impact on performance.

Handling dynamic and irregular graph structures
Graphs are inherently irregular in structure, with variable numbers of neighbors for each node. This irregularity can complicate quantization, as uniform quanti-zation methods might not adequately capture the relationships between nodes. To address this, graph models often use techniques such as *dynamic quantization*, which allows different parts of the model to be quantized at different levels of precision, based on their importance.

Hardware considerations
The hardware used for deploying quantized graph models also plays a crucial role in the effectiveness of quantization. GPUs, for example, are often optimized for low-precision arithmetic, which can cause significant speed-ups when running quantized models. Moreover, specialized accelerators like TPUs and graph pro-cessing units can further enhance the performance of quantized models. For edge deployments, where energy efficiency and memory are critical, quantization is an especially valuable tool for enabling graph inference on devices with limited computational resources.

Quantization is a powerful optimization technique that significantly enhances the efficiency of graph models, particularly for large-scale inference tasks. By reducing the bit width of model parameters, quantization helps lower memory usage, increase computational speed, and reduce resource consumption. This makes it ideal for deploying graph models on edge devices, mobile platforms, and cloud systems with limited resources. While quantization can lead to some loss of precision, techniques such as quantization-aware training and post-training quantization provide ways to minimize these effects. By carefully applying quantization to graph models, organiza-tions can achieve both high performance and cost-effective deployment in real-world, production environments.

Pruning

Pruning is a widely used model optimization technique that helps reduce the size and complexity of machine learning models, including graph models, by eliminating unnecessary components without significantly affecting their performance. For graph models, pruning typically focuses on removing weights, neurons, layers, or even entire nodes and edges that do not contribute meaningfully to the final predictions or classifications. The goal is to maintain the model's performance while reducing its computational requirements, making it more efficient for inference tasks—especially in environments where computational resources and memory are limited.

How pruning works

The basic idea behind pruning is to identify and remove parts of the model that have little impact on its performance. This is generally achieved by evaluating the importance of individual model components—whether that's the weights in a fully connected layer, certain nodes or edges in a graph-based model, or entire subgraphs in GNNs. Once less important components are identified, they are either set to zero or removed from the model entirely, thus reducing the model size.

There are a few key steps involved in the pruning process:

1. *Weight evaluation*: In traditional neural networks, pruning often starts with evaluating the magnitude of individual weights. Weights that are close to zero (i.e., have little effect on the model's output) are considered less important and can be pruned.

2. *Criteria for pruning*: The importance of graph model components is usually determined by:

   Magnitude of weights
   > In simple pruning approaches, weights with smaller magnitudes are deemed less important and are pruned.

   Gradient magnitude
   > In some methods, components that have a smaller gradient during backpropagation are considered less important, as they contribute less to model updates during training.

   Performance sensitivity
   > Advanced pruning techniques evaluate the sensitivity of the model's accuracy to the removal of specific weights, nodes, or edges. Components with a minimal impact on the overall prediction are pruned first.

3. *Pruning execution*: Once the importance of various components is determined, pruning can be performed. There are two main approaches:

Unstructured pruning

Individual weights or neurons are removed based on their importance, resulting in sparse models. Although unstructured pruning can yield large reductions in model size, it often results in sparse matrices that require specialized hardware or software to fully exploit the speed-up.

Structured pruning

Entire neurons, layers, or graph edges are removed. Structured pruning typically leads to more efficient models since the remaining components are usually organized in a way that allows for more straightforward computation on standard hardware.

4. *Fine-tuning*: After pruning, the model typically undergoes a process called fine-tuning. Fine-tuning involves retraining the pruned model, often with a smaller learning rate, to ensure it can recover any lost accuracy and adjust to the new, reduced network structure.

Advantages of pruning for graph models

Pruning offers several key benefits for improving the efficiency and scalability of graph-based machine learning models:

Improved inference speed

By removing redundant or unimportant components, pruning reduces the number of operations required during inference. This results in faster predictions, making graph models more suitable for real-time applications, such as fraud detection, recommendation systems, and social network analysis.

Lower memory usage

Pruned models have fewer parameters to store, which directly translates to reduced memory usage. This is particularly important when deploying graph models on edge devices or mobile platforms, where memory is often limited.

Resource efficiency

Pruned models typically require fewer computational resources, enabling more efficient use of processing power—especially on CPUs, GPUs, and specialized hardware like TPUs. This can help reduce the operational costs of running graph models in production environments.

Enhanced scalability

Smaller, pruned models can handle larger datasets or scale to process more graph data without requiring proportional increases in hardware or memory. This is particularly useful for applications that deal with massive graphs, such as social network analysis or large-scale recommendation engines.

Maintainability

Pruned models are often easier to maintain and update. The reduced complexity of the model makes it simpler to interpret, debug, and make incremental improvements.

Limitations and challenges of pruning

While pruning can significantly enhance the efficiency of graph models, it is not without its challenges and limitations:

Risk of accuracy degradation

One of the main risks of pruning is that removing certain weights, nodes, or edges might lead to a loss of accuracy. Since pruning reduces the model's capacity to capture certain relationships within the graph, it can degrade performance if important features or connections are removed. This risk can be mitigated through techniques like fine-tuning, but it is still a concern, especially for models that are highly sensitive to structural changes.

Sparse representations

Unstructured pruning often results in sparse models, where most of the parameters are zero. While this can reduce memory usage, sparse matrices can be inefficient to store and process, as they may not fully exploit the hardware's capabilities. Specialized libraries and hardware are often required to efficiently handle sparse models, which can complicate deployment.

Computation overhead during pruning

The pruning process itself can require significant computational resources, especially in large-scale graph models. Evaluating which weights, nodes, or edges to prune may involve running multiple training iterations or performing a deep analysis of the model's performance, which can be time-consuming.

Challenges in graph structure pruning

Unlike traditional neural networks, graph models involve complex relationships between nodes and edges. Removing or pruning parts of a graph (e.g., certain nodes or edges) can be more difficult and error-prone, as it can disrupt the graph's underlying structure and impact the way that information is propagated through the network. For example, pruning key nodes or edges in a graph neural network could negatively affect message passing, leading to degraded performance.

Effectiveness depends on model type

The effectiveness of pruning varies depending on the model and its structure. For deep and highly complex models—such as those used in large-scale recommendation systems or dynamic graph analysis—pruning may be less effective because of the complex dependencies between components. Additionally, pruning might not work well for tasks where a high level of model complexity and detail is necessary to achieve competitive performance, such as in some natural language processing (NLP) or image recognition tasks.

Pruning is a powerful optimization technique that enhances the efficiency and scalability of graph models by reducing their size and complexity. By eliminating unnecessary weights, nodes, or edges, pruning can lead to faster inference times, lower memory usage, and more resource-efficient graph models. While pruning offers numerous advantages, including improved scalability and reduced operational costs, it also comes with limitations such as the risk of accuracy degradation and the challenges of handling sparse representations. Careful application of pruning, coupled with fine-tuning and other optimization techniques, can help overcome these challenges and make pruning an effective tool for deploying high-performance graph models in enterprise applications.

Knowledge Distillation

Knowledge distillation is a powerful technique for compressing large, complex models into smaller, more efficient ones without significant loss of performance. In this approach, a high-capacity model, often referred to as the *teacher*, transfers its learned knowledge to a more compact *student* model (Figure 10-5).[1] This process is particularly valuable for graph models, enabling the deployment of resource-efficient models capable of maintaining strong predictive accuracy while reducing computational demands.

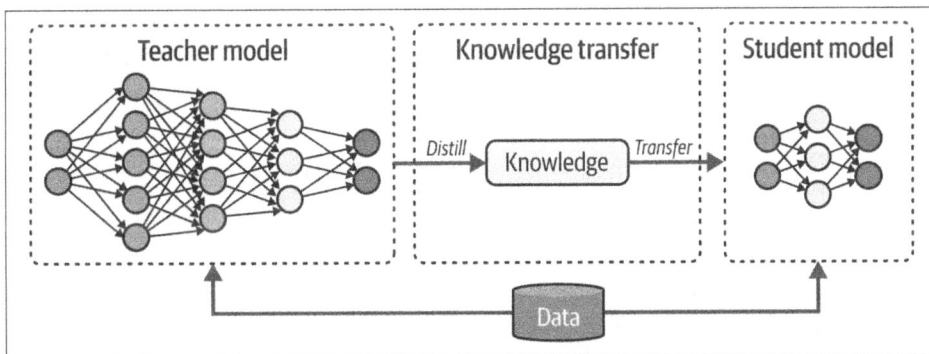

Figure 10-5. An illustration of teacher–student knowledge transfer to distill knowledge from a large model to a smaller model (Yan et al. (2024))[2]

---

1 Gou, J. et al. (2021). "Knowledge Distillation: A Survey" (*https://oreil.ly/OpsWH*). *International Journal of Computer Vision* 129(6), 1789-1819.

2 Yan, X., Liu, B., and Qu, G. (2024). "Efficient Monocular Human Pose Estimation Based on Deep Learning Methods: A Survey" (*http://dx.doi.org/10.1109/ACCESS.2024.3399222*). *IEEE Access*.

How knowledge distillation works

The process of knowledge distillation involves training the smaller student model to mimic the behavior of the larger teacher model as illustrated in Figure 10-5. Unlike traditional training that uses ground-truth labels, knowledge distillation leverages the teacher model's "soft labels" or probabilistic outputs. These soft labels contain rich information about the teacher's learned patterns, such as inter-class relationships and fine-grained decision boundaries.

For graph models, the process works as follows:

1. A large, pre-trained graph model—such as a deep GNN—acts as the teacher, generating soft predictions for nodes, edges, or entire graph-level tasks.

2. The student model is trained to replicate these soft predictions, learning to emulate the teacher's decision-making process.

3. By optimizing a loss function that compares the student's outputs to the teacher's soft labels, the student gradually acquires the essential patterns and relationships captured by the teacher.

This transfer of knowledge enables the student model to deliver comparable accuracy while being far smaller and faster during inference.

Advantages of knowledge distillation for graph model inference

There are several advantages of knowledge distillation for graph model inference:

Reduced model complexity
Distilled models are significantly smaller, with fewer layers or reduced parameter counts, making them ideal for inference tasks requiring quick response times. For instance, a deep GNN with many message-passing layers can be distilled into a shallower GNN that still captures the core graph features and relationships.

Enhanced deployability
The compact size of distilled models makes them easier to deploy in resource-constrained environments, such as edge devices, mobile platforms, or systems with limited memory and computational power. This is particularly relevant for graph-based tasks in IoT networks or real-time recommendation systems.

Retained predictive power
Despite their reduced size, distilled models retain much of the accuracy and expressive power of the teacher model. This makes them suitable for critical applications where precision and reliability are essential—such as fraud detection or personalized recommendations.

Teacher–student architectures for graph models

Designing effective teacher–student architectures is crucial for the success of knowledge distillation. For graph models, this involves simplifying the structure of the teacher model while ensuring the student can still capture the critical patterns and relationships inherent in the graph data:

Simplifying GNN layers
A deep teacher GNN with many message-passing layers can be distilled into a shallow student GNN with fewer layers. This reduction maintains core capabilities, such as capturing local graph structure, while lowering computational requirements.

Embedding dimensionality reduction
In some cases, the teacher's high-dimensional node or graph embeddings can be distilled into lower-dimensional embeddings for the student. This not only reduces model size but also improves inference speed and memory efficiency, especially in large-scale graphs.

Distilling global and local knowledge
For graph-level tasks, the teacher may capture both local (node-level) and global (graph-level) patterns. The student model can be trained to replicate these patterns using carefully designed loss functions that balance local and global knowledge transfer.

Knowledge distillation offers a pragmatic solution to the challenges of deploying graph models in enterprise systems. By simplifying complex architectures while preserving their predictive capabilities, it enables faster and more scalable graph inference—paving the way for broader adoption of graph learning across diverse applications.

Quantization, pruning, and knowledge distillation are powerful techniques for optimizing graph models to meet the demands of real-world inference tasks. Quantization streamlines computations and reduces resource consumption, making it ideal for latency-sensitive applications. Pruning trims unnecessary components from the model, boosting inference speed and scalability. Knowledge distillation simplifies large models, enabling faster and more efficient inference while maintaining accuracy for one or more tasks. By incorporating these techniques, enterprises can deploy graph models that are not only performant but also cost-effective and adaptable to diverse operational contexts.

Scaling Inference for Large Graphs

As the size and complexity of graphs grow in enterprise applications, scaling inference becomes a critical challenge. Large graphs—with millions or billions of nodes and edges—require innovative strategies to deliver timely and accurate predictions.

Scaling inference is particularly vital in applications such as social network analysis, recommendation systems, and fraud detection, where real-time insights from massive datasets drive decision making. In this section, we'll explore key strategies for scaling graph inference, including distributed inference systems, graph partitioning, and incremental inference.

> We have already started the discussion on scaling inference for large graphs in Chapter 7 in a general context. However, in this section we focus on scalability in the context of inference.

Distributed Inference Systems

Distributed inference systems leverage multiple computational nodes to parallelize inference tasks, making them an effective solution for scaling graph-based models. The primary goal of such systems is to distribute the computational workload across a cluster of machines or devices (e.g. multiple GPUs), ensuring that large-scale graphs can be processed efficiently.

There are several architectural considerations for distributed graph systems:

Horizontal scalability
Distributed systems achieve scalability by adding more computational nodes, each responsible for a subset of the graph. These nodes work in parallel, aggregating results to produce final predictions. Proper orchestration of these nodes is essential to ensure seamless communication and synchronization, which minimizes bottlenecks.

Communication overhead
Distributed systems for graph inference often face challenges related to communication overhead. Graph models, especially GNNs, require information propagation between nodes. When the graph is partitioned across multiple machines, this leads to frequent inter-node communication, which can degrade performance if not optimized. Techniques like hierarchical aggregation and asynchronous updates can mitigate this issue.

Hardware utilization
Distributed inference systems must effectively utilize a mix of hardware resources as we have previously discussed, such as CPUs, GPUs, and specialized accelerators like TPUs. GPUs, in particular, are ideal for processing dense computational tasks, while CPUs handle pre- and post-processing tasks. Balancing the workload across different hardware types can maximize efficiency.

Graph Partitioning for Scalable Inference

In Chapter 7, we showed that graph partitioning is a critical strategy for scaling graph learning in general, especially when computational resources are distributed across multiple nodes or machines. In this part, we focus on its effectiveness in the inference time frame. The essence of this technique lies in dividing a large graph into smaller, manageable subgraphs, allowing each partition to be processed independently.[3] By distributing the workload, partitioning not only enhances efficiency but also enables inference on graphs too large to fit into the memory of a single machine. However, partitioning must be performed thoughtfully to avoid trade-offs that can affect performance and accuracy.

How graph partitioning works

Partitioning a graph involves splitting its nodes, edges, or both into subsets that minimize the dependency between partitions. The objective is to reduce communication overhead between computational nodes while ensuring that each partition contains enough local information for accurate inference. Depending on the graph structure and the type of inference being performed, different partitioning methods are employed to achieve these goals.

Techniques for graph partitioning

Next, let's cover some techniques for graph partitioning:

Edge-cut partitioning
Edge-cut partitioning is a widely used technique where the graph is divided by minimizing the number of edges that cross between partitions. Each partition is designed to contain a dense set of nodes, with minimal connections to nodes in other partitions. This approach is particularly effective for graphs where dense local clusters dominate the structure, as it keeps related nodes together.

For instance, algorithms like Metis (*https://oreil.ly/5OphI*) and ParMETIS (*https://oreil.ly/7grqi*) are commonly employed for edge-cut partitioning. These tools use heuristics to find partitions that minimize the *cut size* (the number of edges that are split across partitions). The fewer the cut edges, the less communication is required between computational nodes during inference, resulting in faster execution times.

One challenge with edge-cut partitioning is that the graph's connectivity may be disrupted, potentially impacting applications like GNNs, which rely on message passing across edges. To address this, replicated *ghost nodes* (nodes mirrored in

---

3 Buluç, A. et al. (2016). *Recent Advances in Graph Partitioning*. Springer International Publishing.

multiple partitions) can be used to maintain critical connections—though at the cost of increased memory usage.

Node-cut partitioning

Node-cut partitioning takes a different approach by minimizing the number of shared nodes across partitions rather than focusing on edges. In this method, some nodes are duplicated across partitions, ensuring that their neighbors have access to their information when needed.

This technique is particularly useful for GNNs, as it accommodates the message-passing mechanism inherent to these models. By replicating critical nodes across multiple partitions, this technique reduces the latency associated with cross-partition communication. However, the trade-off lies in higher memory consumption, as duplicated nodes increase storage requirements.

This approach is often favored when maintaining high model accuracy is a priority. The graph contains dense clusters that would otherwise require extensive communication between partitions.

Community-based partitioning

Graphs often exhibit a community structure, where nodes within a community are more interconnected than nodes between communities. Community-based partitioning exploits this natural property by dividing the graph along community boundaries.

For example, in a social network, users who frequently interact with each other might form a tightly connected community. By partitioning along these boundaries, most interactions remain within a single partition, reducing the need for inter-partition communication. This makes community-based partitioning a highly efficient choice for inference tasks like recommendation systems or fraud detection.

Techniques like the *Louvain* or *Label Propagation* (*https://oreil.ly/PFKgf*) algorithms are often used to detect community structures before partitioning the graph. While effective, this method assumes that the graph's community structure is well-defined, which may not always be the case in highly interconnected or random graphs.

Random partitioning

Random partitioning is a simple and fast method that divides the graph into equal-sized chunks without considering its structure. While it lacks the sophistication of edge-cut or community-based methods, random partitioning has its advantages in specific scenarios, such as when speed is critical or when the graph structure is unknown or unpredictable.

However, the simplicity of random partitioning has a cost. Without considering the graph's topology, this method often results in frequent inter-partition communication, significantly increasing latency and resource utilization during inference. As a result, random partitioning is typically used as a baseline or fallback method rather than the primary approach.

Challenges and trade-offs in graph partitioning

Partitioning a graph for inference is not without its difficulties. Striking the right balance between computational efficiency and model accuracy requires careful consideration of several factors:

Balancing workload and communication
Effective partitioning must balance the computational workload across partitions while minimizing communication between them. If partitions are unevenly distributed, some computational nodes may become bottlenecks, leading to inefficiencies. Conversely, excessive inter-partition communication can negate the benefits of distributed processing.

Partitioning algorithms often include heuristics to equalize the workload, but achieving perfect balance is challenging, particularly for irregular or highly skewed graphs.

Maintaining accuracy across partitions
Partitioning can disrupt the graph's connectivity, which is particularly problematic for models like GNNs that rely on information propagation across edges. If neighboring nodes are split into different partitions, the quality of inference can degrade, as message-passing mechanisms become less effective.

To mitigate this, techniques like ghost nodes are often employed. These replicated nodes ensure that information can flow seamlessly between partitions, preserving model accuracy. However, this approach increases memory usage and computational overhead, creating a trade-off between accuracy and resource efficiency.

Handling dynamic graphs
Partitioning static graphs is relatively straightforward, but dynamic graphs, which evolve over time, introduce additional challenges. As new nodes and edges are added, or existing ones are removed, partitions must be updated to reflect the changes. This can disrupt ongoing inference tasks, requiring frequent repartitioning or adaptive algorithms that can adjust partitions in real time.

In general, dynamic partitioning algorithms are an active field of research, with techniques like incremental partitioning or online clustering showing promise. These methods aim to update partitions efficiently without disrupting inference or incurring excessive computational costs.

Out-of-vocabulary inference

Out-of-vocabulary (OOV) inference in graph learning is the challenge of predicting for nodes absent during training, common in dynamic graphs with newly appearing entities. Traditional graph models struggle with these novel nodes due to a lack of learned representations and relationships.

Addressing OOV inference necessitates methods leveraging the new node's context, such as attributes and connections to known nodes. Inductive learning enables generalization to unseen graph parts. By learning underlying patterns, models can infer OOV node representations through interactions with existing nodes, often using node features or graph attention to understand local context and make informed predictions.

Incremental Inference

Real-world graphs are dynamic, constantly evolving as new nodes, edges, and data are introduced. Social networks grow with every new connection or post, recommendation systems adjust as user preferences shift, and transaction networks evolve as financial activities unfold. In such contexts, recomputing predictions across the entire graph for every update is computationally prohibitive. Incremental inference offers a smarter approach by updating only the portions of the graph affected by changes. This localized strategy not only reduces computational overhead but also ensures that predictions remain timely and responsive in dynamic environments.

The fundamentals of incremental inference

At its core, incremental inference operates on the principle of locality. When changes occur, they often impact only a subset of the graph. For example, adding an edge between two nodes primarily affects their immediate neighborhoods, and updating a node's feature may only influence predictions involving that node. Instead of treating every change as a global problem, incremental inference narrows its focus to the areas of the graph directly impacted, enabling faster updates with minimal disruption.

The process begins by identifying affected regions of the graph. This requires tracking dependencies—knowing which nodes and edges influence each other. Once the impacted areas are identified, inference calculations are localized, avoiding the need to reprocess the entire graph. This targeted approach ensures computational efficiency while maintaining high accuracy in most cases.

Techniques in incremental inference

One key method used in incremental inference is *localized updates*. This involves recalculating embeddings or predictions only for the directly affected nodes, edges, or subgraphs. For instance, if a new edge is added between two nodes, the embeddings of those nodes—and possibly their immediate neighbors—might need updates. The rest of the graph remains untouched, saving significant processing time.

Another common strategy involves caching and precomputing results. Many graph systems store precomputed embeddings or intermediate results, which can be incrementally updated rather than recomputed from scratch. For example, embeddings for frequently queried nodes can be stored in a cache and updated only when changes occur. This approach reduces latency and improves system responsiveness.

Dynamic neighborhood sampling is particularly relevant in GNNs, where node embeddings depend on their neighbors. Incremental inference selectively updates only the relevant neighborhoods, propagating changes efficiently without unnecessary computations. This approach also minimizes redundant updates, ensuring resources are allocated effectively.

Temporal graph techniques are often employed to manage updates in a chronological sequence. By timestamping nodes, edges, and features, systems can track the order of changes and process them incrementally. This not only improves efficiency but also ensures that updates are handled in a logical and consistent manner.

Challenges in incremental inference

Despite its advantages, incremental inference is not without challenges. One significant issue is the complexity of tracking dependencies in a graph. In highly connected or dense graphs, identifying all the elements influenced by a single change can be computationally expensive. The broader the ripple effect of a change, the harder it becomes to efficiently localize updates.

Error propagation is another concern. Incremental updates often rely on propagating changes through the graph, which can amplify small inaccuracies over time. For instance, if an embedding update is slightly off, the error may cascade through subsequent computations, degrading overall model accuracy. Periodic full recomputations may be necessary to reset the system and maintain consistency.

Balancing latency and accuracy is also a critical challenge. Incremental inference is designed for speed, but prioritizing speed can sometimes compromise precision. Approximate algorithms or heuristics, while faster, may introduce trade-offs in accuracy, which must be carefully managed, especially in high-stakes applications like fraud detection or critical decision-making systems.

Dynamic resource allocation poses an additional hurdle. As graph updates occur, the computational demands of incremental inference can vary. Managing these fluctuations requires adaptive systems that can scale resources in response to workload changes, ensuring steady performance without overprovisioning.

Addressing challenges in incremental inference

To tackle these issues, hybrid approaches are often employed. Systems can use incremental inference for most updates while scheduling periodic full recomputations to reset errors and validate model accuracy. This hybrid model strikes a balance between efficiency and reliability, ensuring that the benefits of incremental updates are realized without compromising long-term system integrity. Approximate methods can also help mitigate resource demands. Techniques like stochastic updates or sampling-based inference simplify computations without significantly affecting accuracy. While these methods may not be suitable for all applications, they work well in contexts where minor deviations are acceptable.

Scalable frameworks are another avenue for improvement. Modern tools like DGL and PyG now include support for distributed and incremental inference, enabling large-scale systems to process updates efficiently across clusters of machines. These frameworks are designed to handle the complexities of dynamic graphs, offering built-in optimizations for communication and memory management.

Adaptive systems that dynamically adjust resource allocation in response to graph changes can further enhance incremental inference. For instance, a spike in updates might trigger the provisioning of additional computational resources, while periods of low activity could scale down usage to conserve costs. In general, incremental inference is a powerful strategy for maintaining efficiency and responsiveness in dynamic graph systems. By focusing computational effort on localized updates, it minimizes unnecessary work and ensures real-time performance in evolving environments. While challenges like dependency tracking, error propagation, and resource management remain, innovations in hybrid approaches, approximate methods, and scalable frameworks continue to advance the field. As dynamic graphs become increasingly central to enterprise applications, mastering incremental inference will be essential for creating systems that are both efficient and adaptable.

Summary

Graph inference is a cornerstone of deploying graph learning models in enterprise applications, bridging the gap between model training and real-world impact. This chapter explored the diverse strategies, tools, and challenges associated with scaling graph inference, providing a roadmap for implementing effective and efficient inference pipelines.

The chapter began by defining graph inference and its critical role in enterprise workflows, highlighting challenges such as maintaining low latency, achieving scalability, and balancing accuracy with resource constraints. These considerations set the stage for discussing practical deployment strategies tailored to enterprise needs.

Deployment strategies examined include canary deployments for incremental risk mitigation, blue–green deployments for seamless model transitions, shadow deployments to validate model behavior without affecting live traffic, and edge deployments to enable localized inference on devices such as IoT systems. Each approach was dissected to show its benefits, limitations, and applicability to graph-based systems.

A detailed discussion on hardware considerations illuminated the trade-offs between CPU- and GPU-based inference. CPUs were shown to excel in batch processing and cost-sensitive environments, while GPUs are indispensable for real-time, high-throughput tasks. The chapter also touched on emerging hardware solutions like TPUs and graph-specific processors—hinting at future possibilities for improving graph inference performance.

The exploration of inference runtimes provided a practical guide to popular frameworks such as TensorRT, ONNX Runtime, DGL, and PyG. Strategies like precomputations and caching were highlighted for their ability to reduce latency and resource demands. A comparison between online (real-time) and offline (batch) inference emphasized the importance of choosing the right approach based on application-specific trade-offs between responsiveness and computational cost.

To further optimize inference pipelines, the chapter explored model optimization techniques such as quantization, pruning, and knowledge distillation. These methods were shown to accelerate inference by reducing model size and complexity while preserving essential accuracy. Each technique was elaborated with examples relevant to graph neural networks and embedding models.

Scaling inference for massive graphs was addressed through strategies such as distributed inference systems, which distribute workloads across multiple nodes, and graph partitioning, which divides large graphs into smaller subgraphs for parallel processing. Techniques such as edge-cut, node-cut, and community-based partitioning were analyzed for their ability to balance computational efficiency and accuracy. Incremental inference was also discussed as a real-time strategy to handle dynamically evolving graphs without sacrificing performance.

By synthesizing deployment strategies, optimization techniques, and scaling considerations, this chapter provided a comprehensive guide to mastering graph inference in enterprise settings. Looking forward, advancements in federated inference, specialized hardware, and dynamic graph handling promise to further transform this space, presenting new opportunities and challenges for scalable graph learning in enterprises.

## CHAPTER 11

Monitoring and Feedback Loops

In the rapidly evolving landscape of machine learning and graph-based systems, ensuring consistent performance and adaptability is a paramount concern. Monitoring and feedback loops play a central role in addressing these challenges by providing the mechanisms to observe, evaluate, and refine graph models over time. As graphs are inherently dynamic, with new nodes, edges, and patterns emerging, a robust monitoring framework ensures that the models remain relevant, accurate, and scalable in the face of change.

The monitoring and tracking of deployed machine learning is a critical part of the cycle of developing AI-powered solutions, as shown in Figure 11-1, as it assesses how good the deployed models are in tackling real-world data. It also detects when the deployed models face difficulties in terms of both predictive accuracy and runtime performance. Monitoring involves tracking system performance, detecting anomalies, and assessing the stability of the graph structures and embeddings. It enables practitioners to identify when models start to drift—whether due to shifts in underlying data distributions, changing graph topologies, or evolving user behavior. Complementing monitoring, feedback loops introduce a mechanism for continuous improvement by leveraging insights from monitored metrics, user interactions, or system behavior in order to refine the models and processes. Together, these two components form the backbone of a self-sustaining and adaptive graph learning pipeline.

This chapter explores the necessity of monitoring and feedback loops, particularly in large-scale and real-world graph systems—where model degradation can lead to significant downstream failures. We will discuss common challenges, effective strategies for designing monitoring frameworks, and the role of feedback in maintaining and improving model performance. Additionally, we will explore the tools, technologies, and best practices that can aid in the seamless implementation of these systems.

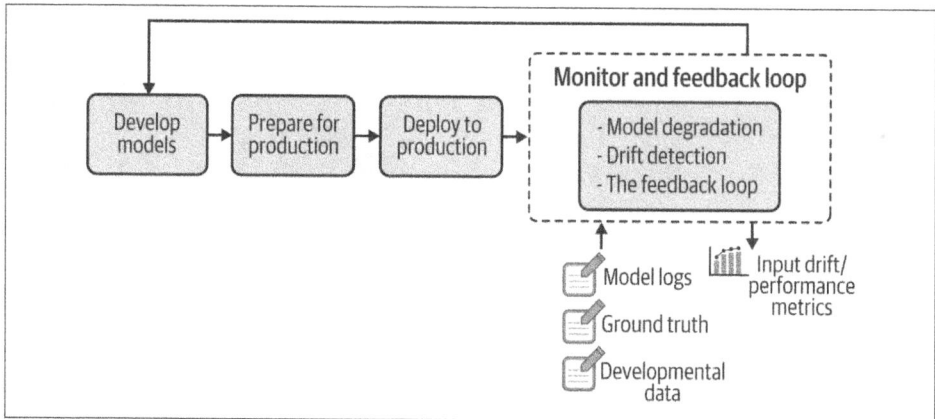

Figure 11-1. The overall development cycle of building machine learning models from training to deployment and monitoring[1]

Ultimately, monitoring and feedback loops are not just about maintaining the status quo—they are about enabling evolution of the deployed system with fixes, updates, and added features. By establishing a feedback-driven culture, organizations can create graph systems that adapt to new challenges, scale effortlessly, and consistently deliver value in dynamic environments.

Challenges in Monitoring Graph Models

Monitoring graph models is tricky. You're not just looking at individual data points; you're monitoring the *relationships* between them and the *overall structure* of the graph itself. This structure can be massive and may change rapidly in real-world scenarios. On top of that, practical issues like getting data in real time, handling sheer scale, and dealing with the limitations of your actual hardware and software setup make building good monitoring systems a real head-scratcher.

So, let's break down the four main hurdles you'll likely encounter:

Figuring out the right metrics

What does "good performance" even mean for a graph? Simple accuracy scores often don't cut it. You need metrics that tell you if the *relationships* are being captured correctly and if the graph's overall *shape* and *health* are sound. Pinpointing these relevant metrics is challenge number one.

---

1 Image from *Introducing MLOps* by Mark Traveil et al. (O'Reilly).

Keeping up with dynamic graphs

Real-world graphs are rarely static; they evolve. New users join, connections are made or broken, information gets updated. Your monitoring can't just rely on occasional snapshots; it needs to handle this constant change, which is much harder than monitoring static datasets.

Taming scale and complexity

Many production graphs are enormous, with millions or even billions of nodes and edges. Just processing this data for monitoring, let alone analyzing it deeply, can overwhelm systems and requires careful planning and efficient tools. The intricate web of connections adds another layer of complexity.

Dealing with system and deployment realities

There are many practical, on-the-ground limitations you face when actually running your graph model and trying to monitor it. Think of these assets and limitations as the environment your system lives in.

That last point—"system and deployment realities"—often boils down to what we call system constraints. These aren't theoretical problems; they're the real-world limits of your infrastructure and setup that directly impact your monitoring efforts. Getting a handle on these is key:

Compute power limits (CPU, GPU, memory)

Graph operations, especially analysis for monitoring, can be hungry for resources. If you don't have enough processing power or memory, you might have to monitor less often, sample data instead of using it all, or give up on real-time insights.

Storage bottlenecks (capacity and speed)

Good monitoring often means storing historical data—logs, metrics, maybe even graph snapshots over time—in order to spot trends or debug issues. Limited or slow disk space makes it tough to keep this valuable history around.

Network speed bumps (bandwidth and latency)

If your graph data, model, and monitoring tools are spread across different servers or locations (common in cloud setups), slow network connections can really hamper efforts to collect monitoring data quickly. This makes near real-time feedback a major hurdle.

Integration headaches

Sometimes, just getting your chosen monitoring tool to talk nicely with your specific graph database, processing engine (like Spark or Flink), or deployment system (like Kubernetes) can be a technical challenge in itself. Compatibility isn't always plug-and-play.

Your specific environment's rules

> Where you run your system matters. Cloud platforms have costs you need to manage, your company's data center might have older hardware, security policies might restrict access needed for monitoring, and edge devices can have very tight power and compute limits.

Scalability walls

> Can your monitoring system grow alongside your graph? If your graph doubles in size or usage spikes, but your monitoring tools can't keep up without breaking the bank or falling over, that's a critical constraint.

Real-time processing capacity

> Does your system *actually* have the horsepower to crunch monitoring data almost instantly? For graphs tracking things like live fraud attempts, a delay in processing monitoring alerts could be costly.

So, while graph models offer incredible insights, effectively monitoring them requires tackling these challenges head-on. Understanding the need for graph-specific metrics, planning for dynamic changes, respecting the scale, and crucially, working within your real-world system constraints are all part of building a monitoring framework that truly tells you what's going on with your graph. It's a complex task, but getting it right is vital for ensuring these powerful systems are reliable and delivering the value they promise.

Graph-Specific Metrics

A fundamental difficulty arises from selecting appropriate metrics. While standard metrics such as accuracy or F1 score are useful for evaluating specific prediction tasks (e.g., classifying node types), they don't adequately capture the overall structural integrity or relational dynamics of the graph itself. To gain a holistic view, we need metrics designed for graphs:

Modularity

> This measures how well a network is partitioned into distinct communities or groups.

> *Example:* Consider a university's internal social network. High modularity might indicate that students primarily interact within their own departments (e.g., engineering students mostly connect with other engineers). A sudden drop in modularity could mean increased inter-departmental collaboration (a positive evolution) or perhaps the breakdown of distinct academic communities (potentially negative). Monitoring modularity helps understand the stability and nature of these group structures.

Clustering coefficients

This quantifies how interconnected the neighbors of a node are. Essentially, it measures the "cliquishness" around nodes.

Example: On a platform like LinkedIn, if many of your connections are also connected to each other, your local network has a high clustering coefficient, suggesting a tightly knit professional circle. In contrast, if your connections are largely unacquainted, the coefficient is low. Tracking this metric across the network could reveal trends in collaboration or fragmentation within professional fields.

Centrality measures

These identify the most important or influential nodes in a network based on different criteria.

Example (degree centrality): On Twitter, an account followed by millions has high degree centrality—it's a major hub for information dissemination.

Example (betweenness centrality): In Ireland's road network graph, a town situated on the primary route between Galway and Dublin might have high betweenness centrality, as much traffic passes through it. Monitoring this can identify critical infrastructure points or bottlenecks.

Example (closeness centrality): In a small company, the office manager might have high closeness centrality—they can quickly reach anyone in the company through a short chain of connections. This indicates efficiency in information flow around that node.

Interpreting changes in these metrics requires context. A shift doesn't automatically signal an error; it could be normal network evolution. For instance, is the emergence of a new high-centrality node in a communication network a sign of a new team lead (normal) or a potential spam source (anomaly)? Differentiating requires deeper analysis beyond the metric value itself.

Furthermore, many models rely on *graph embeddings*, which are essentially numerical representations (like coordinates on a map) learned for each node or edge, placing similar items closer together in a mathematical space. Monitoring involves checking if these representations remain stable and meaningful as the graph changes. Are nodes representing similar concepts still close together in the embedding space, or have updates caused them to drift apart nonsensically? This adds another layer of monitoring complexity, often requiring significant computational effort.

Dynamic Graphs

Real-world graphs are rarely static; they are dynamic entities constantly changing over time. This dynamism presents significant monitoring hurdles:

Real-time change tracking

Networks evolve continuously—users join, connections form, transactions occur. Effective monitoring often requires near-real-time observation to detect critical events promptly.

Example: In a financial transaction network, a sudden, rapid series of connections originating from a newly active account to many disparate merchants might signify fraudulent activity (e.g., using stolen credit card details). A delay in detecting this pattern could result in significant financial loss. Systems must be able to process updates and recalculate relevant metrics quickly.

Model adaptation to evolving data (staleness/drift)

Models trained on past graph data can become outdated as the network structure and patterns shift over time (concept drift). This will reduce the predictive power of the model.

Example: An ecommerce recommendation engine learns user preferences based on past purchase patterns and connections. If a new trend emerges (e.g., a shift from Product A to Product B), a model trained on older data might keep recommending the now unpopular Product A, leading to poor user experience. Monitoring must detect this performance degradation and signal the need for model retraining or adaptation.

Handling temporal dependencies

In many graphs, the timing of connections is crucial. Edges might have time-stamps or be valid only during specific intervals.

Example: Consider a graph representing road networks for a navigation app. A particular road segment (an edge) might be closed during specific hours (e.g., 7-9 a.m. for a school zone). A routing algorithm (graph model) must respect these time constraints to provide accurate directions. Monitoring needs to ensure this temporal information is accurate and correctly utilized by the model.

Monitoring dynamic graphs inevitably involves a trade-off between the detail and frequency of monitoring (granularity) and the computational resources required. Continuously recalculating complex metrics for every small change might be infeasible, while infrequent checks might miss important transient events. Striking the right balance is essential for effective and efficient monitoring.

Scale and Complexity

When we use graphs to model real-world systems like social networks, recommendation engines, or biological pathways, these graphs can become incredibly large and intricate. Monitoring them effectively—checking their health, performance, or how they change over time—presents some significant hurdles:

The sheer scale

Think big! We're often dealing with graphs that have millions, or even billions, of points (nodes) and connections (edges). Imagine trying to keep an eye on every single interaction happening on a massive social media platform simultaneously.

Why it's a challenge: Just storing this much data is hard, let alone processing it repeatedly for monitoring. Standard calculations that might be quick on small graphs can take too long or require immense computing power (computation) and memory (storage). Making sure our monitoring methods can even handle this scale (scalability) is a primary concern.

Lots of detail (high dimensionality)

To understand nodes and their roles (like grouping similar users or classifying content), we often describe them using many characteristics or features. Think of giving each node a very detailed profile. This creates a "high-dimensional" representation.

Why it's a challenge: Checking if these detailed profiles remain consistent and meaningful across the entire graph takes a lot of computational effort. Also, if we want to monitor specific groups or communities within the graph (like "active users in Ireland"), calculating summary statistics for these groups can be difficult without efficient ways to split up the graph and process it in parallel.

Working across many computers (distributed architectures)

Because these graphs are so huge, they often don't fit on a single computer. Instead, they are spread across a network of computers (a distributed system) that work together.

Why it's a challenge: Our monitoring tools need to work seamlessly across all these computers. Getting a consistent, up-to-date picture can be tricky because of delays in sending information between computers (network overhead) and ensuring everything is synchronized. This is especially tough if we need real-time monitoring.

Intricate structures (topological complexity)

Real-world graphs aren't usually neat and simple grids. They have complex, often messy patterns. Think of groups of friends that overlap (overlapping communities), company structures with departments inside divisions (hierarchical structures), or maps showing roads, railways, and flight paths all at once (multi-layered relationships).

Why it's a challenge: A monitoring system needs to understand this complexity in order to give accurate insights. For example, imagine monitoring how connected a node is (its centrality). If a node in a sparsely connected part of the graph loses a few connections, it might not be a big deal. But if a node in the middle of a dense, tightly knit cluster loses the same number of connections, it could signal a critical failure. The monitoring needs to interpret changes within the context of the graph's structure.

To handle these challenges, engineers use clever techniques. These include looking at representative smaller parts of the graph instead of the whole thing (graph sampling), using faster algorithms that give good-enough approximate answers (approximation algorithms), and designing systems that can effectively spread the monitoring workload across many computers (distributed computation). The trade-off is that sometimes these methods might sacrifice a little bit of accuracy or fine-grained detail to gain speed and manageability.

System and Deployment Issues

In Chapter 10, we discussed model inference and deployment, where we showed how critical the deployment strategy for efficient model performance is. After deployment, monitoring the status of the deployment is critical to ensure smooth model operation; hence implementing monitoring frameworks in real-world systems is critical. However, this involves practical challenges related to system performance, resource utilization, and deployment constraints:

Latency
> In applications like fraud detection or recommendation systems, monitoring must happen in real time. Latency in detecting and responding to anomalies can lead to missed opportunities or adverse outcomes. Monitoring frameworks must optimize data pipelines to minimize delays while maintaining accuracy.

Data freshness
> Graph data often arrives in streams, requiring systems to maintain up-to-date models and metrics. Stale data can lead to inaccurate monitoring and incorrect conclusions about model performance.

Resource utilization
> Monitoring large-scale graphs demands substantial computational and memory resources. Continuous computation of metrics such as modularity or centrality may strain system capacity, especially when scaling to billions of edges. Balancing the trade-off between resource allocation for core operations and monitoring tasks is a critical consideration in system design.

Deploying monitoring systems within enterprise environments often involves integrating with existing infrastructure, such as databases, logging systems, or cloud platforms. Compatibility issues, lack of standardization, and varying data formats can hinder the seamless deployment of monitoring frameworks.

Monitoring graph models is a multifaceted challenge that spans technical, computational, and practical domains. From defining meaningful metrics to managing dynamic updates and handling large-scale deployments, each aspect requires tailored solutions in order to ensure effective and efficient monitoring. As graph applications continue to grow in scope and complexity, addressing these challenges will be essential for building reliable, scalable, and adaptive graph systems. By leveraging advancements in algorithms, distributed systems, and automation, practitioners can overcome these obstacles and establish robust monitoring frameworks that support the long-term success of graph-based models.

Designing a Monitoring Framework

Think of creating a monitoring framework for your graph models as building the central nervous system for your entire graph-based application. Just like your brain constantly receives signals from your body, processes them, and triggers appropriate responses (like pulling your hand away from a hot stove), this framework is where all the critical information about your graph model flows. Monitoring frameworks are the hub that collects data, spots patterns or problems, and alerts you when things aren't quite right.

However, monitoring graph models isn't the same as watching over simpler, more static systems. Graphs have unique characteristics that make monitoring a bit more complex.

Dealing with Ever-Changing Connections (Graph Topology)

Imagine monitoring a city's road network versus monitoring a dynamic social network like Twitter or Facebook. In the city, roads are mostly static. But in a social network, new friendships form, old ones break, and people join or leave constantly. Graph models often represent real-world systems where relationships (edges) and entities (nodes) change frequently. Your monitoring system needs to track not just the *state* of the graph but also how its *structure* is evolving. Is a critical connection suddenly missing? Is a new cluster of nodes forming unexpectedly? If a popular product node suddenly loses most of its "also bought" connections (edges), the monitoring system should flag this structural change, as it might indicate a data issue or a shift in user behavior.

Checking the "Meaning" (Evaluating Embeddings)

Many graph models turn nodes and edges into numerical "fingerprints" called embeddings. These fingerprints capture the essence or meaning of a node/edge within the graph's context. Monitoring needs to check if these fingerprints are still accurate representations. Think of it like ensuring a person's description (their fingerprint) still matches their actual appearance and characteristics over time. The quality of these embeddings is crucial for tasks like recommendations or fraud detection. The monitoring framework must have ways to evaluate if these embeddings are still meaningful and haven't "drifted" or become outdated as the graph changes or new data comes in.

In a fraud detection graph, embeddings might represent users. If the embedding for a known "good" user starts looking numerically similar to embeddings of known "fraudulent" users, the monitoring system should raise an alarm. This indicates the model might be starting to misinterpret that user's behavior.

The Balancing Act (System Performance Versus Graph Tasks)

Imagine trying to track every single conversation happening in a massive, bustling town square (complex graph tasks) without causing huge traffic jams or slowing everyone down (system performance). Graph operations can be computationally intensive. Running detailed monitoring checks constantly might slow down the very system you're trying to monitor. The framework needs to be smart about *what* to monitor, *how often* to check, and *how efficiently* to do it, balancing the need for detailed insights with the need for a responsive system. Instead of recalculating complex graph-wide statistics every second, the monitoring system might calculate them every hour but monitor simpler metrics (like the rate of new edge creation) in real time to get an early warning of potential issues without overwhelming the system.

In essence, designing a monitoring framework for graph models requires thinking beyond simple metrics like CPU usage or error rates. It demands tools and techniques that can handle dynamic structures, evaluate abstract representations like embeddings, and intelligently manage the trade-offs between insight depth and system performance. We'll explore how to tackle these challenges, covering everything from data collection strategies to effective visualization techniques. Now, let's look at how we actually gather the necessary information.

Data Collection Mechanisms

First things first—how do you get your data? A monitoring system is only as good as the data it receives. It needs a constant or periodic feed of information to track performance, detect anomalies, and alert you to potential issues. There are two primary approaches to collecting this vital data: real time and batch.

Real-time monitoring: Catching things as they happen

Think of real-time monitoring as having a live security camera feed where you see events unfold the moment they occur. Data streams continuously from your graph model, application logs, or data pipelines directly into the monitoring system. This approach is essential for applications where immediate action is critical, such as instant fraud detection (flagging a suspicious transaction the second it appears in the graph), identifying rapidly trending topics on social media by watching connection patterns, or adjusting recommendations on the fly based on a user's current browsing path. To manage these continuous data streams, systems like Apache Kafka (*https:// kafka.apache.org*), AWS Kinesis (*https://aws.amazon.com/kinesis*), or Google Cloud Pub/Sub (*https://cloud.google.com/pubsub*) are often used, feeding data into processing engines like Apache Flink (*https://flink.apache.org*) or Spark Streaming (*https:// spark.apache.org/streaming*). However, this immediacy comes at a cost: it requires more robust infrastructure to handle the constant flow and potentially complex stream processing logic, much like needing more guards and faster communication lines for that live security feed.

Batch monitoring: Scheduled check-ups

Batch monitoring is more like reviewing the security footage from the past day or week; you get a comprehensive overview but not instant alerts. Here, data is collected in chunks (batches) and processed at regular intervals—such as every hour, daily, or weekly. This method is suitable for analyzing trends over time or for metrics that don't change dramatically minute by minute. It's ideal for tasks like generating daily reports on overall graph health (e.g., average node degree changes), tracking slow-moving trends in user communities, calculating model performance metrics over a specific period, or triggering model retraining cycles based on detected data drift over the past week. Frameworks such as Apache Hadoop (*https://hadoop.apache.org*) (MapReduce), Apache Spark (*https://spark.apache.org*) (in batch mode), or scheduled database queries are common for processing these batches. The main trade-off is that you won't catch sudden spikes or issues immediately between processing intervals. On the plus side, it's generally less resource-intensive and simpler to implement than real-time monitoring, similar to needing fewer resources to review recorded footage compared to maintaining a live monitoring station.

Often, the most effective monitoring frameworks use a hybrid approach, employing real-time collection for critical, fast-changing metrics and batch collection for deeper, less time-sensitive analysis. We'll explore how to tackle these challenges further, covering everything from specific metrics to collect to effective visualization techniques.

Monitoring Deployed Graph Models

When a graph learning model moves from development to a live production environment, the journey isn't over. Continuous monitoring becomes essential to ensure the model performs reliably over time, adapts to changing data, and continues to deliver value. Monitoring helps detect performance degradation or unexpected shifts (drift) in data or concepts, providing crucial signals to trigger feedback loops like model retraining, updates, or investigations.

Effective monitoring involves observing different facets of the system. Let's explore the key areas: performance (of downstream tasks), structure (of the graph itself), and embeddings (learned representations)—along with the specific metrics used to track them, complete with intuitive examples and runnable Python code.

Performance monitoring: Is the model achieving its goal?

This area focuses on how well the model performs its intended *downstream task*. These tasks often rely heavily on the quality of the underlying graph structure and learned embeddings. Evaluating task performance requires using appropriate metrics in order to understand different aspects of the model's success and failures. A drop in these performance metrics is a clear signal that something needs attention.

Before diving into specific graph tasks, let's understand the common metrics used to evaluate them—particularly for classification and prediction scenarios:

Accuracy
> Gives the overall percentage of correct predictions. It's simple, but it can be misleading if data is imbalanced (e.g., predicting a very rare event).

Precision
> Measures how accurate the positive predictions are. High precision is crucial when the cost of a *false positive* is high (e.g., flagging a legitimate transaction as fraud).

Recall (sensitivity)
> Measures how well the model finds all actual positive instances. High recall is vital when the cost of a *false negative* is high (e.g., failing to detect a critical disease or a security threat).

F1 score

The harmonic mean of precision and recall, providing a single score that balances both, especially useful for imbalanced datasets.

ROC-AUC score

Evaluates the model's ability to distinguish between positive and negative classes across all decision thresholds, useful when the model outputs probabilities or scores. A higher AUC indicates better separability.

Confusion matrix

A table showing the detailed breakdown of correct and incorrect predictions (true positives, false positives, true negatives, false negatives) per class, essential for understanding *what kind* of errors the model is making.

The choice of which metric(s) to prioritize depends heavily on the specific graph task and the real-world implications of different types of errors.

Let's see how these metrics apply to common graph learning tasks:

Node classification and embedding tasks

Task goal: Assigning labels to individual nodes within a graph (e.g., classifying users, identifying protein functions). This often relies heavily on the quality of learned node embeddings.

Relevant metrics: Accuracy provides an overall view. Precision, recall, F1 score, and the confusion matrix are crucial, especially for imbalanced classes (e.g., detecting rare "bot" accounts) or when misclassifying specific node types has different costs.

Real-life scenario: Consider the task of classifying user accounts in a social network as "human" or bot." Missing a bot (false negative) might be acceptable if precision (avoiding flagging humans as bots—false positive) is paramount, or vice versa depending on the platform's goals. F1 score helps balance this:

```
import numpy as np
from sklearn.metrics import accuracy_score, f1_score, confusion_matrix,
                            classification_report

# Example: True vs. predicted labels for user nodes (0: Human, 1: Bot)
# Assume bots are rarer (imbalanced)
# 3 bots out of 15
true_node_labels = np.array([0, 0, 0, 1, 0, 0, 0, 0, 1, 0, 0, 0, 0, 1, 0])
# Model found 2/3 bots, but flagged 2 humans as bots
pred_node_labels = np.array([0, 0, 1, 1, 0, 0, 0, 1, 1, 0, 0, 0, 0, 0, 0])

# Calculate metrics
accuracy = accuracy_score(true_node_labels, pred_node_labels)
# Calculate F1 score specifically for the 'Bot' class (positive label = 1)
f1_bot = f1_score(true_node_labels, pred_node_labels, pos_label=1)
```

```
# Calculate the confusion matrix
cm = confusion_matrix(true_node_labels, pred_node_labels)

print(f"Node Classification Accuracy: {accuracy:.2f}")
print(f"F1 Score (Bot Detection): {f1_bot:.2f}")
print("Confusion Matrix (Rows: True, Cols: Pred):")
# [[TN, FP], [FN, TP]]
# [[10  2]  <- True Human: 10 correct (TN), 2 predicted Bot (FP)
#  [ 1  2]] <- True Bot:    1 predicted Human (FN), 2 correct (TP)
print(cm)
# Generate a full classification report (includes precision, recall,
# f1 per class)
print("\nClassification Report:\n", classification_report(true_node_labels,
    pred_node_labels, target_names=['Human', 'Bot']))
```

Link prediction

Task goal: Predicting whether an edge (connection) exists or is likely to form between two nodes (e.g., recommending friends, predicting protein interactions).

Relevant metrics: Precision, recall, F1 score, and ROC-AUC are key. The trade-off between precision (accuracy of predicted links) and recall (finding all true links) is often critical. ROC-AUC gives a threshold-independent view of ranking quality.

Real-life scenario: Recommending research papers to users based on citation networks. High precision means recommendations are relevant (low false positives), while high recall means users don't miss many relevant papers (low false negatives). ROC-AUC helps evaluate the underlying ranking quality:

```
import numpy as np
from sklearn.metrics import precision_score, recall_score, roc_auc_score,
                            f1_score
```

```
# Example: True link existence vs. predicted probability scores for
# potential paper recommendations
# 1: Relevant link (should recommend), 0: Irrelevant
true_links = np.array([1, 0, 1, 1, 0, 0, 1, 0, 1, 0]) # 5 relevant links
# Model's predicted relevance scores
pred_scores = np.array([0.9, 0.4, 0.8, 0.6, 0.3, 0.2, 0.7, 0.1, 0.45, 0.55])

# Apply a threshold to get binary predictions (e.g., recommend if
# score >= 0.5)
threshold = 0.5
# [1, 0, 1, 1, 0, 0, 1, 0, 0, 1]
pred_links = (pred_scores >= threshold).astype(int)

# Calculate metrics based on the threshold
precision = precision_score(true_links, pred_links) # TP=4, FP=1 -> 4/5 = 0.8
recall = recall_score(true_links, pred_links)       # TP=4, FN=1 -> 4/5 = 0.8
f1 = f1_score(true_links, pred_links)                # F1 based on threshold
```

```
# Calculate ROC-AUC score (uses scores directly, threshold-independent)
roc_auc = roc_auc_score(true_links, pred_scores)

print(f"Link Prediction Precision (Threshold={threshold}): {precision:.2f}")
print(f"Link Prediction Recall (Threshold={threshold}): {recall:.2f}")
print(f"Link Prediction F1 Score (Threshold={threshold}): {f1:.2f}")
print(f"Link Prediction ROC-AUC Score: {roc_auc:.2f}")
```

Graph classification

Task goal: Assigning a label to an entire graph (e.g., classifying molecules by property, identifying types of communities).

Relevant metrics: Accuracy gives an overall picture. F1 score is important for imbalanced graph classes. The confusion matrix helps understand misclassifications between different graph types.

Real-life scenario: Consider the task of classifying molecular graphs based on whether they are toxic or nontoxic. Accuracy might be high if most molecules are nontoxic, but F1 score is crucial to ensure the model effectively identifies the rare but important toxic ones:

```
import numpy as np
from sklearn.metrics import accuracy_score, f1_score, confusion_matrix,
                            classification_report

# Example: True vs. predicted labels for molecular graphs
# (0: Non-Toxic, 1: Toxic)

# Assume toxic molecules are less common
# 3 toxic out of 12
true_graph_labels = np.array([0, 0, 1, 0, 0, 0, 1, 0, 0, 1, 0, 0])
# Model missed 1 toxic, flagged 1 non-toxic as toxic
pred_graph_labels = np.array([0, 0, 0, 0, 1, 0, 1, 0, 0, 1, 0, 0])

# Calculate metrics
accuracy = accuracy_score(true_graph_labels, pred_graph_labels)
# Calculate F1 score specifically for the 'Toxic' class (positive label = 1)
f1_toxic = f1_score(true_graph_labels, pred_graph_labels, pos_label=1)
# Calculate the confusion matrix
cm = confusion_matrix(true_graph_labels, pred_graph_labels)

print(f"Graph Classification Accuracy: {accuracy:.2f}")
print(f"F1 Score (Toxic Detection): {f1_toxic:.2f}")
print("Confusion Matrix (Rows: True, Cols: Pred):")
# [[TN, FP], [FN, TP]]
# [[8  1]  <- True Non-Toxic: 8 correct (TN), 1 predicted Toxic (FP)
#  [1  2]] <- True Toxic:    1 predicted Non-Toxic (FN), 2 correct (TP)
print(cm)
# Generate a full classification report
print("\nClassification Report:\n", classification_report(true_graph_labels,
    pred_graph_labels, target_names=['Non-Toxic', 'Toxic']))
```

Structural monitoring: Is the graph itself changing?

Graphs representing real-world systems (social networks, financial transactions, citation networks) are dynamic. Monitoring the graph's structure (topology) is crucial because unexpected shifts can affect model performance or signal data pipeline issues, even if performance metrics seem stable initially. Let's take a look at some key structural monitoring metrics (note: the code requires the NetworkX library, which can be installed with the pip install networkx command):

Average node degree

Concept: The average number of connections (edges) per node in the graph.

Intuitive example: In a social network graph, a significantly decreasing average degree might indicate users are becoming less active or connected over time. A sudden spike could signal mass friending activity or potentially bot behavior:

```python
import networkx as nx

# Create a simple example graph
G = nx.Graph()
G.add_edges_from([(1, 2), (1, 3), (2, 3), (3, 4), (4, 5)])
# Nodes: 1, 2, 3, 4, 5
# Degrees: 1:2, 2:2, 3:3, 4:2, 5:1 -> Sum = 10
# Number of nodes = 5

num_nodes = G.number_of_nodes()
if num_nodes > 0:
    # Calculate the sum of all node degrees
    total_degree = sum(dict(G.degree()).values())
    # Calculate average degree
    avg_degree = total_degree / num_nodes
    print(f"Average Node Degree: {avg_degree:.2f}") # Output: 2.00
else:
    print("Graph has no nodes.")
```

Clustering coefficient (average)

Concept: Measures the degree to which nodes in a graph tend to cluster together (i.e., are neighbors of a node also connected?). A high value indicates tightly knit groups.

Intuitive example: In a scientific collaboration network, a high average clustering coefficient suggests researchers tend to form closed groups where collaborators also collaborate with each other. A sharp increase might indicate the formation of isolated research silos:

```python
import networkx as nx

# Using the same graph G
G = nx.Graph()
G.add_edges_from([(1, 2), (1, 3), (2, 3), (3, 4), (4, 5)])
```

```
# Calculate the average clustering coefficient using networkx function
avg_clustering = nx.average_clustering(G)

print(f"Average Clustering Coefficient: {avg_clustering:.2f}")
# Example calculation for node 3: neighbors are 1, 2, 4. Possible links
# between neighbors = 3 ((1,2), (1,4), (2,4)). Actual links = 1 ((1,2)).
# Local C = 1/3.
# NetworkX averages these local coefficients.
```

Number of connected components

Concept: Counts the number of distinct, separate subgraphs within the overall graph. In an undirected graph, nodes in the same component can reach each other via some path.

Intuitive example: Monitoring a supply chain network graph. A sudden increase in the number of connected components might indicate disruptions or failures in data feeds, causing parts of the supply chain to appear disconnected in the graph when they shouldn't be:

```
import networkx as nx

# Create a graph with two separate components + isolated node
G = nx.Graph()
G.add_edges_from([(1, 2), (2, 3)]) # Component 1
G.add_edges_from([(4, 5)])         # Component 2
G.add_node(6)                      # Component 3 (isolated node)

# Calculate the number of connected components using networkx function
num_components = nx.number_connected_components(G)

print(f"Number of Connected Components: {num_components}") # Output: 3
```

Graph density

Concept: The ratio of the actual number of edges present in the graph to the maximum possible number of edges the graph could have (given its number of nodes). It ranges from 0 (sparse) to 1 (dense/complete). In a "follows" graph on a platform like Twitter, density is typically very low (sparse). A sudden, significant increase in density might indicate anomalous behavior like bot activity creating many connections rapidly:

```
import networkx as nx

# Using the first example graph G
G = nx.Graph()
G.add_edges_from([(1, 2), (1, 3), (2, 3), (3, 4), (4, 5)])
# 5 nodes, 5 edges. Max possible edges in
# undirected graph = n*(n-1)/2 = 5*4/2 = 10

# Calculate graph density using networkx function
density = nx.density(G)
```

```
# Output: 0.50 (5 edges / 10 max possible)
print(f"Graph Density: {density:.2f}")
```

Embedding monitoring: Are learned representations still meaningful?

Graph learning models often produce embeddings (numerical vectors) representing nodes, edges, or entire graphs. These embeddings power the downstream tasks evaluated in performance monitoring. Therefore, monitoring their quality is crucial, as degradation here can silently undermine task performance:

Stability

> *Concept*: Measures how much an entity's embedding changes over time or between model retraining cycles. While embeddings should adapt to real changes, excessive fluctuation without cause indicates instability, potentially affecting downstream task consistency.

> *Intuitive example*: Consider embeddings for products on an e-commerce site. The embedding for a specific "blue running shoe" shouldn't change dramatically day-to-day unless its relationship to other products (e.g., user viewing patterns, copurchases) genuinely shifts significantly. High instability suggests training problems. Stability is often tracked using distance metrics (Euclidean distance):

```
import numpy as np

# Embedding for 'blue running shoe' yesterday and today
embedding_yesterday = np.array([0.5, -0.1, 0.9, 0.2])
embedding_today = np.array([0.51, -0.12, 0.88, 0.21]) # Small change

# Calculate Euclidean distance between the two vectors
# np.linalg.norm calculates the magnitude (L2 norm) of the difference vector
distance = np.linalg.norm(embedding_yesterday - embedding_today)

print(f"Embedding Distance (Stability): {distance:.4f}")
# Monitor this distance over time; large spikes indicate instability
```

Representation quality

> *Concept*: Assesses if the embeddings continue to capture the intended relationships, which directly impacts how well downstream tasks can use them. Cosine similarity measures the directional similarity between embedding vectors (ranging from –1 to 1). Similar entities should have high cosine similarity (close to 1).

> *Example*: In a knowledge graph, embeddings for concepts like "London" and "England" should have a higher cosine similarity than embeddings for "London" and "Tokyo." If monitoring reveals that related concepts start drifting apart (lower cosine similarity), the model's representation quality might be degrading, likely leading to poorer performance on tasks relying on these embeddings (e.g., link prediction between related entities):

```
import numpy as np
from sklearn.metrics.pairwise import cosine_similarity

# Example embeddings (ensure they are 2D arrays for sklearn)
embedding_london = np.array([[0.6, 0.1, -0.2]])
# Vector pointing in a similar direction
embedding_england = np.array([[0.55, 0.15, -0.18]])
# Vector pointing in a different direction
embedding_tokyo = np.array([[-0.4, 0.8, 0.1]])

# Calculate cosine similarities
sim_london_england = cosine_similarity(embedding_london, embedding_england)
sim_london_tokyo = cosine_similarity(embedding_london, embedding_tokyo)

# Extract the scalar similarity value from the resulting 1x1 matrix
# Expect high value
print(f"Similarity(London, England): {sim_london_england[0][0]:.2f}")
# Expect low/negative value
print(f"Similarity(London, Tokyo): {sim_london_tokyo[0][0]:.2f}")
```

Effective monitoring of deployed graph models requires a multifaceted approach. Tracking performance metrics ensures the model achieves its downstream task goals (like classification or link prediction). Monitoring graph structure reveals changes in the underlying data that could impact performance or signal data issues. Observing embedding quality verifies that the core representations learned by the model remain stable and meaningful, as these directly influence task performance. By combining insights from these different areas using appropriate metrics and setting intelligent alert thresholds, you create a robust feedback loop, enabling timely interventions—like retraining, debugging, or feature updates to maintain the health and reliability of your graph models in production.

Thresholds for Alerts

What's the point of monitoring if you don't know when something's genuinely off? Collecting data is only half the battle; you need rules to decide when that data indicates a potential issue that requires attention. That's where thresholds come in— they define the specific conditions under which your monitoring system should raise a red flag or trigger an alert. There are two main philosophies for setting these trigger points:

Manual thresholds: The fixed rules
> These are predefined limits set based on existing knowledge, experience, or specific requirements of your system. Think of them as fixed rules you establish up front. For instance, you might decide that if your graph model's prediction accuracy drops below 85%, or if the number of disconnected components in your graph suddenly jumps above 10, you want an alert. Manual thresholds are straightforward to understand and implement but can be quite rigid. They don't

automatically adjust if the normal behavior of your system changes over time (e.g., due to seasonality or organic growth), potentially leading to false alarms or missed issues.

Adaptive thresholds: Learning from history

Adaptive thresholds offer a more dynamic approach by adjusting based on the data's observed patterns and natural variability over time. Instead of fixed rules, they often employ machine learning techniques, particularly anomaly detection algorithms. These algorithms learn the typical range and behavior of your metrics (like embedding distances, node centrality scores, or edge creation rates) and automatically flag significant deviations from this learned norm. For example, an adaptive threshold could detect that the density of connections in a specific community within your graph is unusually low for a Tuesday afternoon, even if the absolute value isn't below a fixed manual limit. They are more sophisticated and can adapt to evolving systems and seasonal trends, but they require more data, careful setup, and ongoing computation to maintain their learning.

Choosing between manual and adaptive thresholds (or often, a combination of both) depends on the specific metric being monitored, the predictability of its behavior, and the resources available for implementing and managing the alerting system.

Most systems benefit from a mix: use manual thresholds for critical metrics where you know the acceptable range and adaptive thresholds for metrics prone to gradual shifts. With data collection methods and alerting thresholds in mind, let's dive into the specific *types* of things we need to monitor within our graph model framework.

Visualization Tools

The ability to effectively monitor and analyze graph learning models hinges on more than just collecting metrics; it also depends on how well you can interpret and act on that data. Visualization tools are indispensable for transforming raw performance metrics into meaningful insights. These tools enable researchers and engineers to quickly identify issues, assess trends, and optimize model performance over time. Here we explore their key functionalities in the context of graph learning models.

Real-time dashboards

Graph learning models are often employed in dynamic environments, such as social network analysis, recommendation systems, or fraud detection, where real-time feedback is essential. Visualization tools like Grafana, Kibana, or TensorBoard can present up-to-the-minute metrics, helping users detect and address anomalies as they occur. Real-time dashboards display information such as node embeddings, edge predictions, or classification outputs, providing a clear snapshot of the model's current performance.

Historical trends

Understanding how your graph learning model evolves over time is crucial for identifying gradual performance degradation or concept drift in the data. Visualization tools can track and plot historical metrics like accuracy, loss, or computational efficiency across training epochs or production timelines. These visualizations help uncover trends, such as deteriorating edge prediction accuracy in certain subgraphs, enabling proactive adjustments to the model or data pipeline.

Custom alerts

To ensure timely intervention, many visualization tools support custom alerts that notify users when predefined thresholds are breached. For graph learning models, this could include alerts for rising training loss, memory usage spikes, or declining node classification accuracy. Integrating these alerts with messaging platforms like Slack or PagerDuty ensures that critical issues are addressed promptly, reducing downtime or degraded performance in production systems. By leveraging these visualization capabilities, teams working on graph learning models can maintain better oversight, quickly diagnose problems, and continuously refine their models for optimal performance.

In the end, designing a monitoring framework for graph models isn't a one-size-fits-all process, but by focusing on the right components, metrics, and tools, you can create a system that keeps your models running smoothly. Whether you're dealing with real-time fraud detection or periodic graph analysis, a well-designed monitoring framework ensures you're always a step ahead of potential problems. Keep it modular, start with the essentials, and expand as your needs grow.

Feedback Loops in Graph Systems

Feedback loops, as shown in Figure 11-2, are a crucial part of maintaining and improving graph-based systems. Unlike traditional machine learning systems, graph systems are often deeply integrated into dynamic, interactive environments. Whether it's a social network adapting to user interactions, a recommendation engine learning from clicks, or a fraud detection system responding to new types of malicious behavior, feedback loops ensure that models stay relevant and responsive to changes.

Feedback in graph systems generally comes from three main sources: user actions, system performance, and changes in the data itself. Each type of feedback has its nuances, challenges, and opportunities for optimization. In this section, we'll explore how these feedback loops work, why they matter, and how to make the most of them.

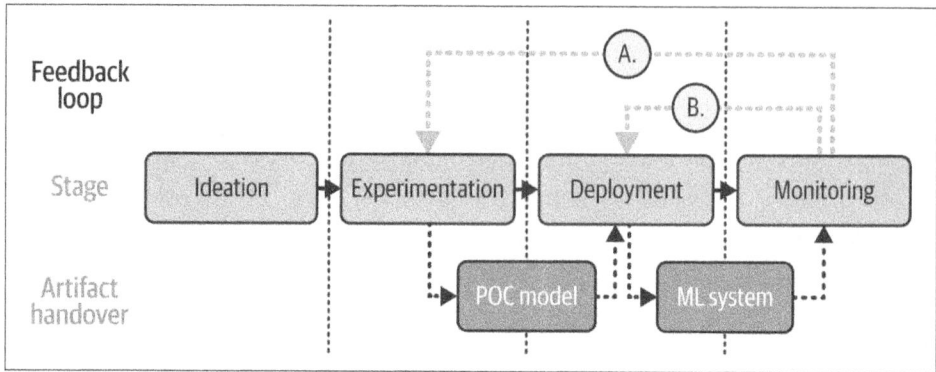

Figure 11-2. Feedback loop in machine learning systems (adapted from Aurimas Griciūnas (2023) (https://oreil.ly/xVi9A))

User Feedback: Learning from Interaction

User actions are the ultimate measure of success in many graph systems. Interactions like clicking recommendations, flagging content, or general platform engagement provide direct feedback on the system's effectiveness.

Take graph-based recommendation systems. They often map user-item relationships. When you click a suggested item (e.g., a movie or product), this positive feedback reinforces the connection the model found. If you ignore or explicitly dislike a suggestion, it signals that the model needs adjustment.

However, using this feedback effectively requires care. User signals can be noisy (like accidental clicks) or inconsistent. Therefore, systems often employ strategies like:

Weighting
Giving more importance to stronger signals (e.g., a purchase over a simple view)

Filtering
Identifying and removing anomalous data (like bot activity)

Iterative Updates
Gradually refining the graph model with new feedback, avoiding drastic shifts based only on recent trends.

This process creates a vital user feedback loop. As users interact, the system continuously learns and adapts to their potentially evolving preferences. This dynamic adjustment is key to keeping the system relevant, personalized, and engaging over time, enabling it to improve alongside its users. Figure 11-3 illustrates the feedback loop in machine learning systems. It highlights how feedback from various sources, such as user interactions, system performance, and changes in data, is crucial for maintaining and improving graph-based systems.

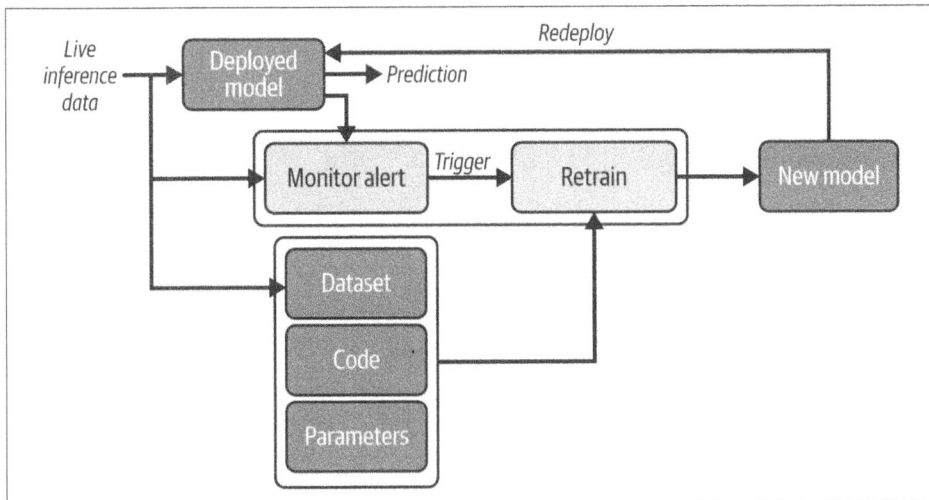

Figure 11-3. Auto retraining based on alert: this can be based on user or system feedback (adapted from DKube blog (https://oreil.ly/52IXe))

System Feedback: Optimizing Model Performance

Beyond user interactions, system-level feedback provides a wealth of information about how well a graph model is functioning. This type of feedback focuses on the internal metrics of the system—how accurate predictions are, whether resource usage is efficient, and how well the model scales as the graph grows. By closing the loop between performance monitoring and model retraining, system feedback ensures that graph systems remain robust and scalable.

For example, consider a link prediction model used in a knowledge graph. During deployment, system feedback might reveal that the model is struggling with certain types of relationships. Perhaps its predictions for rare or newly introduced node types are less reliable. By analyzing these performance gaps, developers can identify where the model needs improvement—whether it's better feature engineering, additional data, or fine-tuning hyperparameters.

System feedback also includes operational metrics like latency, throughput, and error rates. A spike in query latency might indicate that the graph has grown too large for the current infrastructure or that specific computations are becoming a bottleneck. Similarly, an increase in resource consumption might point to inefficiencies in the model pipeline.

To make the most of system feedback, graph systems often employ automated retraining pipelines. These pipelines continuously evaluate performance metrics, detect when the model's accuracy or efficiency drops below acceptable levels, and trigger updates. For instance, a recommendation system might automatically retrain its graph embeddings when it notices a decline in click-through rates. This automation minimizes downtime and ensures that the system stays responsive to real-world demands.

Data Feedback: Adapting to a Changing World

Perhaps the most challenging type of feedback comes from the data itself. Graphs are inherently dynamic structures. Nodes and edges are added, deleted, or modified as new information becomes available. In social networks, new users join, connections form and dissolve, and trends emerge. In transaction graphs, purchases, transfers, and new entities reshape the graph daily. Keeping a model up-to-date with these changes requires a robust data feedback loop.

One key challenge is determining how often to update the graph and retrain the model. In fast-changing domains, like real-time fraud detection, updates might need to happen continuously. In others, like scientific research graphs, periodic updates might be sufficient. The balance depends on the speed of data changes and the sensitivity of the application to those changes.

Another challenge lies in handling graph drift. Over time, the structure of a graph can shift in ways that affect model performance. For example:

- Community structures in a social network might evolve, making previous embeddings less relevant.
- New types of nodes or relationships might emerge, requiring the model to generalize beyond its training data.
- Patterns of interaction, such as seasonal or cyclical trends, might introduce variability that models need to account for.

Data feedback loops help address these issues by continuously monitoring changes in the graph and updating models accordingly. For instance, if a recommendation model notices that a user's connections are shifting toward a new cluster, it can adjust its predictions to better reflect the user's changing preferences. Similarly, in a transaction graph, detecting new fraud patterns can trigger updates to the fraud detection model, ensuring it remains effective against evolving threats.

Incorporating data feedback also involves preprocessing and feature engineering. New data often needs to be cleaned, integrated, and transformed into formats the model can use. Automating these steps reduces delays and ensures that the feedback loop operates smoothly.

Synergy Between Feedback Loops

While user, system, and data feedback loops each serve distinct purposes, their true power lies in how they work together. Consider an ecommerce recommendation system. User feedback provides direct signals about preferences, system feedback highlights performance bottlenecks, and data feedback captures the ever-changing relationships between users and products. Together, these feedback loops form a cohesive ecosystem, enabling the system to adapt holistically.

For example, suppose a new product category is introduced on the platform. Data feedback identifies the new nodes and edges, updating the graph to reflect the change. User feedback reveals how shoppers interact with the new category, helping refine recommendations. System feedback ensures that the model updates don't introduce latency or degrade overall performance. By integrating insights from all three feedback loops, the system can respond effectively to the new category, ensuring a seamless experience for users.

Closed-Loop Systems: Automating Adaptation

In the world of graph systems, a closed-loop system represents the gold standard of adaptability. These systems take feedback—whether from users, performance metrics, or data changes—and automatically incorporate it into the model without requiring extensive manual intervention. By closing the loop between feedback and action, these systems can operate more efficiently, scale better, and respond faster to changes.

What is a closed-loop system?

A closed-loop system automates the entire feedback process, from data collection and analysis to decision making and model updates. It eliminates the need for human oversight at every stage, allowing the system to function autonomously while maintaining high levels of accuracy and relevance. In graph systems, closed loops are especially valuable due to the complexity and dynamic nature of the data.

For example, consider a social network graph where new users and interactions are added every second. A closed-loop recommendation system can:

1. Detect changes in graph structure (e.g., new nodes, edges, or clusters).
2. Update embeddings or predictions in real time based on these changes.
3. Monitor how users respond to the new recommendations and further refine the model.

Key components of closed-loop graph systems

There are several key components of closed-loop graph systems:

Automated feedback processing
> At the heart of any closed-loop system is its ability to process feedback efficiently. This involves:

> *Real-time ingestion*
>> Systems like Apache Kafka or Flink handle continuous streams of data, ensuring that updates are captured as they happen.

> *Analysis pipelines*
>> Machine learning models or rule-based systems analyze feedback to identify actionable insights, such as performance bottlenecks or emerging trends in graph topology.

Dynamic model updates
> Once feedback is processed, the system needs to adapt. Closed-loop systems use mechanisms such as:

> *Incremental learning*
>> Instead of retraining the entire model from scratch, they update only the affected parts, saving time and computational resources.

> *Automated hyperparameter tuning*
>> Tools like Bayesian optimization or reinforcement learning algorithms adjust model settings dynamically to maintain optimal performance.

Self-monitoring
> Closed-loop systems continuously monitor themselves to ensure the changes they implement don't introduce new issues. For example, they compare new predictions against historical benchmarks to detect anomalies. In addition, they use adaptive thresholds in order to fine-tune alerts and avoid unnecessary disruptions.

Closed-loop systems are particularly effective in scenarios where quick adaptation is critical:

Fraud detection
> In transaction graphs, fraudsters constantly change tactics. A closed-loop system can identify new fraud patterns, retrain its detection model, and deploy updates within minutes.

Recommendation engines

> User preferences evolve rapidly in domains like ecommerce or entertainment. Closed-loop systems continuously learn from clicks, purchases, and other interactions, ensuring recommendations stay relevant.

Dynamic networks

> In transportation or communication networks, topology changes (e.g., road closures or new routers) need to be incorporated into graph models quickly to maintain accurate predictions.

In summary, feedback loops are the lifeblood of graph systems, enabling them to learn, adapt, and evolve in response to real-world interactions, performance metrics, and data changes. Whether it's capturing user preferences, addressing system inefficiencies, or staying in sync with dynamic graphs, feedback loops keep graph models robust and relevant. The key to designing effective feedback loops lies in understanding the unique requirements of each type and integrating them into a cohesive framework. By doing so, organizations can create graph systems that not only meet today's needs but also anticipate and adapt to the challenges of tomorrow.

Adaptive Retraining Pipelines

Graph learning models, like all machine learning systems, face the challenge of *concept drift*—where the relationship between input features and target variables changes over time. Implementing adaptive retraining pipelines helps maintain model performance in the face of evolving data distributions.

Monitoring model health

To keep our graph models effective in a changing world where concept drift (the natural evolution of data patterns) occurs, we need continuous monitoring. This acts as the eyes and ears of our feedback loop, constantly checking the model's "health" and the data it uses. We track key performance indicators like accuracy, precision, and recall on recent data to catch any degradation early. For example, if a fraud detection model's precision drops significantly, it might start incorrectly flagging many legitimate transactions, causing customer frustration. We also monitor operational aspects: is it responding quickly enough (latency)? A sudden slowdown in an ecommerce site's "related products" feature could hurt sales. Or is it suddenly demanding excessive computing power (resource utilization)? These are clear signals that something is amiss.

Beyond the model's direct performance, we monitor the data itself. Has the nature of the incoming data changed significantly (covariate shift)? Imagine a ride-sharing app expanding into a new city; the traffic patterns and user demographics might differ greatly from its initial training data, requiring the model to adapt. Has the relationship between user actions and the outcomes we want to predict evolved (concept drift)? For instance, during the initial COVID-19 lockdowns, online shopping behaviors shifted dramatically, making models trained on pre-pandemic data less effective at predicting purchase intent. Assessing these aspects, including data quality metrics like missing values, is crucial to understand if the model's current understanding aligns with the latest reality.

Auto retraining triggering

This continuous monitoring isn't just for passive observation; it actively feeds into automated retraining triggers. These are predefined conditions based on the monitored metrics that automatically kickstart the model's "refresher course"—the retraining process. When model performance dips below an acceptable threshold (e.g., if the fraud model's recall falls below 90%, meaning it's missing too many actual fraudulent cases), when latency spikes beyond acceptable limits for user experience, or when significant shifts are detected in the data's characteristics (like the ride-sharing app detecting a sustained change in average trip duration compared to its training baseline), the system knows it's time to learn from the latest data. This ensures the model adapts proactively. We might even identify completely new patterns emerging in the data—perhaps a novel type of user interaction—that warrant retraining the model to understand and leverage them, keeping it effective and relevant.

Anomaly detection

For systems dealing specifically with graph data, such as social networks, financial transaction systems, or fraud detection systems, real-time anomaly detection within the graph structure itself adds another vital layer of vigilance. This involves monitoring specific graph properties in real time, such as how connected nodes are on average (node degree distribution) or how tightly knit communities are (cluster density). A sudden, unexpected change acts as an early warning. For example, in a financial transaction graph, the sudden appearance of many new accounts making small, rapid transfers to a single central account could be an anomaly indicating potential money laundering. On a social media platform, a coordinated network of new accounts suddenly liking or sharing the exact same content might signal a disinformation campaign. Detecting such anomalies instantly allows the system to react swiftly. This might trigger an immediate alert via the notification system (which we'll explore next) for investigation, and can also serve as a trigger for retraining, ensuring the model adapts to maintain system integrity and performance against new or unusual activities.

Notification Systems

Detecting anomalies or performance degradation is crucial, but even the most sophisticated automated systems require human oversight. When monitoring flags an issue—whether it's a performance dip triggering retraining or a real-time anomaly—well-designed notification systems ensure that the right people are alerted promptly.

Alert design principles

Effective notifications are built on actionability. Each alert shouldn't just state a problem; it must be tied to specific, documented response procedures. Imagine receiving an alert: instead of just saying "High Latency Detected," a good alert might say "P1 Critical: API Latency > 500ms for 5 mins. Responders: See runbook [link]. Escalate if unresolved in 15 mins." It should contain enough context (like affected service, specific metric, duration) for responders to begin investigation immediately. Clear escalation paths must be defined—if the primary on-call person doesn't acknowledge, who gets notified next? Integrating alerts with incident management systems like Jira or ServiceNow allows for seamless tracking, assignment, and resolution workflows—the alert might automatically create a ticket.

Precision and clarity in the message itself are vital. Alerts should clearly state the issue and its severity (e.g., Critical, Warning, Info). Supporting data, perhaps a link to a real-time dashboard showing the problematic metric, should be easily accessible. Knowing if an alert is a recurring issue (historical context) also helps responders diagnose faster.

Timeliness and relevance ensure alerts aren't just noise. The delivery mechanism should match the urgency. A critical system outage might trigger an immediate PagerDuty alert involving phone calls and push notifications to the on-call engineer's phone. A warning about rising disk space might generate a message in a specific team's Slack channel. Non-urgent updates or daily performance summaries could be sent via email. Smart aggregation policies are needed to prevent an "alert storm"—receiving hundreds of similar alerts during a major incident is counterproductive. Configurable delays can also help filter out brief, transient spikes that resolve themselves.

Integration strategies

Modern alert systems integrate into existing workflows. Direct messaging via Slack allows teams to quickly discuss less critical alerts. PagerDuty or Opsgenie handle critical issues requiring immediate wake-up calls. Email serves well for reports and non-urgent notifications.

Visualization is key. Real-time dashboards (e.g., using Grafana or Datadog) showing system health enable proactive monitoring *before* alerts trigger. Trend analysis tools can identify patterns, perhaps showing that latency spikes every Tuesday morning, prompting investigation. Historical alert logs are invaluable for post-incident reviews.

As systems evolve, so must monitoring and alerting. Future directions include using machine learning for smarter alert prioritization or even automated root cause analysis. Predictive capabilities might anticipate issues based on subtle patterns. Developing distributed monitoring architectures and efficient data handling becomes crucial for large-scale systems. Ultimately, enhanced automation might lead to self-healing capabilities where the system attempts automated fixes for common issues, further reducing the burden on human operators while ensuring the reliability and performance of complex graph learning systems.

Summary

In this chapter, we dove deep into the challenges and nuances of monitoring graph models at scale. We began by laying out the unique hurdles enterprises face when dealing with graph-specific metrics, dynamic graphs, and the sheer scale and complexity of modern systems. These aren't your run-of-the-mill monitoring concerns; they require tailored strategies to capture the sophisticated web of relationships and constantly evolving structures that define graph-based learning.

We explored the nitty-gritty of designing an effective monitoring framework. From data collection mechanisms to metrics tailored specifically for graph tasks, we stressed the importance of precision in defining thresholds for alerts. After all, a good monitoring system should be proactive, not reactive, in addressing performance issues.

The chapter also covered different mechanisms of performance, structural, and embedding monitoring, each critical for keeping your graph models running smoothly. Whether you're tracking latency, throughput, or resource usage, it's clear that understanding system metrics isn't just nice-to-have; it's a necessity. And of course, what's the point of metrics without visualization? We highlighted the value of real-time dashboards, historical trend analysis, and custom alerts for turning raw data into actionable insights.

Feedback loops took center stage as we looked at the symbiotic relationship between user feedback, system feedback, and data feedback. Each of these loops offers opportunities to optimize model performance, adapt to changing data landscapes, and incorporate real-world insights. When these loops work in harmony, they create closed-loop systems that enable automated adaptation—turning monitoring from a passive watchdog into an active participant in system improvement.

Finally, we talked about how automation, real-time anomaly detection, adaptive retraining pipelines, and notification systems are no longer futuristic luxuries but practical tools for ensuring scalability and reliability in graph learning systems. Alert design principles and integration strategies rounded out the discussion, reminding us that well-designed notifications can make or break a monitoring setup.

In essence, this chapter laid out the blueprint for building robust, scalable monitoring systems that not only keep your graph models in check but also help them thrive in dynamic, real-world environments. Monitoring isn't just a safety net, it's a competitive edge. And as your graph systems grow and evolve, having these tools and strategies in place will ensure you're always one step ahead.

## CHAPTER 12

Future Trends: Graph Learning and LLMs

Introduction to Graph-Enhanced LLMs

This chapter explores the significant intersection of *large language models* (LLMs) and graph learning. LLMs—such as ChatGPT, Gemini, and Claude—represent a paradigm shift in information processing. Trained on vast textual corpora, they exhibit remarkable proficiency in natural language understanding, text generation, document summarization, and code development. Their capabilities stem from identifying and replicating complex linguistic patterns learned during their extensive training phases.

Despite their power, LLMs possess inherent limitations. Their knowledge base is typically static, reflecting the data available up to their last training date, rendering them unaware of subsequent developments. Furthermore, they are susceptible to generating inaccurate or "hallucinated" responses, particularly when addressing queries that demand highly specific, current, or domain-expert knowledge. A core challenge lies in their processing of linear text sequences, which often hinders their ability to fully comprehend and reason over the complex, interconnected relationships embedded within data.

To mitigate these limitations, the *retrieval-augmented generation* (RAG) framework was developed. This approach equips the LLM with access to an external, dynamic information repository. When presented with a query, the RAG system first *retrieves* pertinent data segments from this external source. Subsequently, the LLM utilizes this retrieved information to *generate* responses that are demonstrably more accurate, timely, and contextually relevant compared to those generated solely on its internal knowledge base. The basic RAG architecture substantially enhances the factuality and applicability of LLM outputs.

However, the effectiveness of standard RAG can be constrained by the nature of the retrieved information, which often consists of isolated text fragments identified through keyword matching. Such fragments may lack the explicit relational context required for sophisticated reasoning. Consider, for instance, retrieving separate documents detailing a company's CEO and a recent product introduction; standard RAG might not inherently establish the causal or strategic links between the CEO's decisions and the product's market performance.

This is the juncture where graph structures offer a distinct advantage. *Graph-enhanced RAG*, commonly termed *GraphRAG* (*https://oreil.ly/-oDNN*), refines the RAG process by employing knowledge graphs as the external memory source. Knowledge graphs provide an explicit representation of entities (e.g., individuals, organizations, locations, concepts) and the diverse relationships connecting them (e.g., "founded by," "affiliated with," "located in," "component of"). Instead of retrieving disconnected text passages, GraphRAG leverages this inherent structure. It enables the system to navigate relational pathways, identify interconnected entities, and grasp the broader context surrounding information far more effectively than conventional RAG. The integration of graph structures yields considerable advantages—including improved reasoning over complex interdependencies, enhanced factual consistency, a reduction in model hallucination, and the capacity to synthesize insights from multiple, linked data sources.

This chapter provides an in-depth examination of graph-enhanced LLM workflows, concentrating on the GraphRAG methodology. Our exploration will encompass:

The core concepts
Analyzing the limitations inherent in standard LLMs and RAG frameworks that motivate the integration of graph structures

GraphRAG pipeline
Elucidating the essential stages, from indexing source data into a structured knowledge graph (involving entity extraction, relationship identification, and embedding generation) to sophisticated graph querying techniques (utilizing global and local search strategies) for augmenting LLAMA's contextual understanding

Enhanced capabilities
Demonstrating how GraphRAG facilitates advanced reasoning across comprehensive datasets

Practical considerations
Addressing implementation specifics and providing a comparative analysis of GraphRAG versus baseline RAG methodologies

Illustrating the practical utility of GraphRAG through a relevant case study, such as enhancing question-answering systems in customer service domains

We invite you to delve into how the structured representation of knowledge via graphs unlocks superior levels of intelligence and reliability in LLMs, thereby contributing to the development of more robust and trustworthy AI systems.

LLMs and Their Transformative Impact

LLMs represent a new chapter in the field of natural language processing—so much so that their ability to generate coherent yet contextually rich text has opened opportunities for several applications. From Figure 12-1, organizations in sectors as diverse as finance, high-tech, media, and healthcare have begun using LLMs to automate rote processes, distill best practices from immense amounts of unstructured content, and in some cases, power creative workflows in areas like marketing and product development. Because of the size of these models and the corpura of text that they are trained on, they are able to generalize across topics and domains and thus become integral components in our modern digital ecosystems.

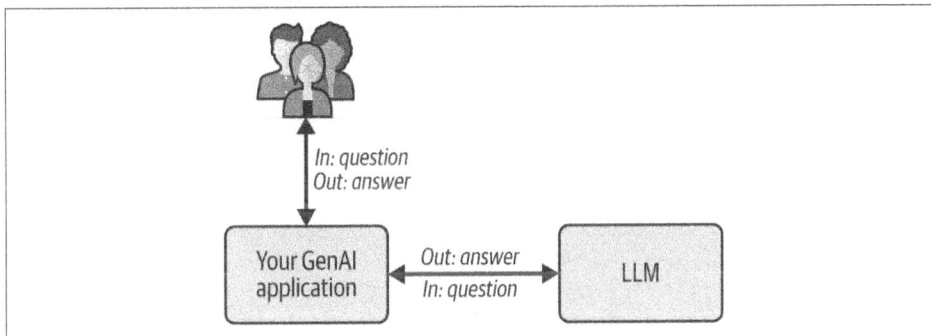

Figure 12-1. Using "out of the box" pre-trained LLMs for generative AI solutions

Even though LLMs are transformative, they also have their limitations. These models, when deployed "out of the box," may struggle in enterprise settings where precision, reliability and transparency are critical. Another major hurdle is the issue of *hallucination*, wherein models produce information that may sound credible but is not factual or completely made up. This is particularly problematic in high-stakes environments like legal, financial, or healthcare applications, where inaccuracy means the stakes could be high. Additionally, LLMs often face difficulties with attribution. Because they generate content based on patterns learned from extensive training data, they may fail to cite the sources of their information, making it hard for users to verify the output. Another challenge is *stalling*, where models sometimes produce repetitive or uninformative responses, particularly when confronted with complex, multistep queries. These limitations underscore the need for a more structured approach in order to enhance the reliability of LLM outputs.

The Need for External Memory: The RAG Setup

To overcome these challenges, researchers and practitioners have turned to external memory systems that provide additional context beyond what is stored in the model's parameters. This approach, known as RAG, involves integrating an external database or memory component with the language mode, as shown in Figure 12-2. In a typical RAG setup, when a query is received, the system first retrieves relevant documents or data fragments from a curated knowledge base. This retrieved information is then used to augment the model's internal context, enabling it to generate more accurate and contextually grounded responses.

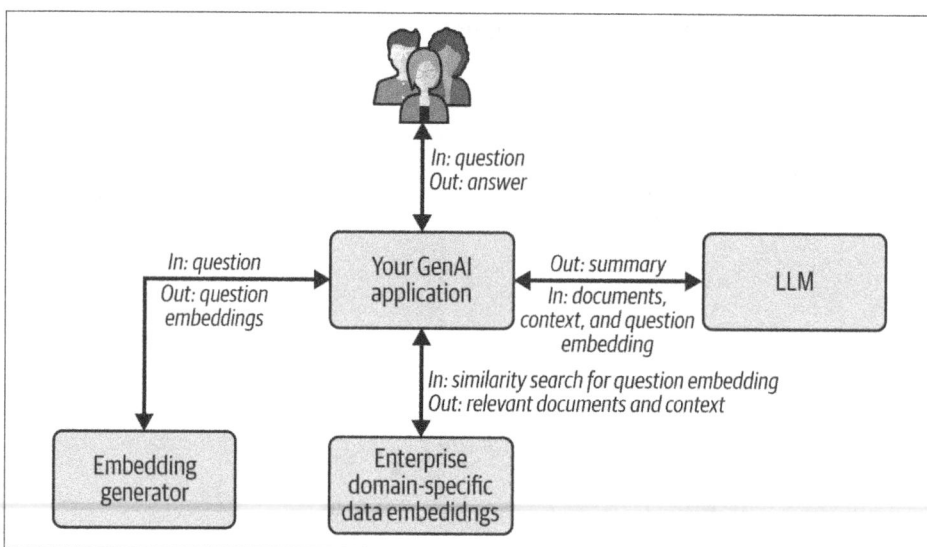

Figure 12-2. Diagram of a RAG pipeline: user questions are embedded, relevant documents are retrieved from domain-specific data embeddings, and both are fed into an LLM via the GenAI application to generate a contextualized answer

The generation process is anchored in verifiable data in the RAG setup, mitigating the hallucination issue. Rather than relying only on the model's built-in knowledge (which may be stale or incorrect), it can look up external sources that are updated and curated constantly. This both bolsters the factual reliability of the responses and improves attribution, as the model can reference particular documents or sources that underlay its output. Moreover, the addition of external memory also can reduce stalling as it provides a larger context in which to answer complex multihop questions, enabling the model to answer questions that require connecting several pieces of information.

Benefits of Graph-Enhanced RAG Setup

RAG significantly boosts LLMs by letting them consult external information before answering, much like giving an AI access to a digital library to look up facts. While this standard RAG setup improves accuracy, it often treats information sources in isolation. It's good at finding relevant text snippets but can struggle when the real answer lies in understanding the complex web of connections *between* different pieces of information—similar to trying to grasp a major historical event by only reading disconnected articles, potentially missing the crucial cause-and-effect links or alliances.

This is where graph-enhanced RAG introduces a powerful evolution. It organizes information not just as separate documents, but as a knowledge graph. This structure allows the AI to navigate these relationships directly, going beyond simple keyword or semantic searches in isolated texts.

The advantages of this approach become clear when we see how it improves responses. Graph-enhanced RAG enables a much deeper contextual understanding. While standard RAG might find documents mentioning *Company A* and *Product B*, the graph-enhanced version can trace the connections to reveal *how* they are linked. For instance, answering "Why did *Company A* launch *Product B*?" might involve following a path in the graph like *Company A* acquired *Startup X*, whose key technology was *Technology Y*, which formed the basis for *Product B*. The graph uncovers the narrative behind the launch.

Furthermore, this structure facilitates multihop reasoning—the capacity to link several pieces of information across multiple steps or "hops" in the graph to address complex queries. Consider a medical question about potential negative interactions between treatments for *Disease Z* and *Drug X*. A graph could connect *Disease Z* to a treatment—*Drug Y*—which targets *Protein P*, which is also affected by *Drug X*, thereby highlighting a potential interaction that might be missed by just searching documents.

Graph exploration also leads to more comprehensive information gathering, assembling a fuller picture around the query's core entities and their web of connections, much like putting together all related pieces of a puzzle. In legal analysis, for example, a graph can link a primary case to related precedents, involved parties, and relevant statutes, offering a holistic view. Finally, because the retrieval process follows explicit, traceable paths within the graph, graph-enhanced RAG improves transparency and trust. In a financial audit, if an AI flags a transaction, the graph can clearly display the chain of related transactions and entities leading to that conclusion, making the reasoning verifiable and auditable.

In essence, while standard RAG equips LLMs with external knowledge, graph-enhanced RAG adds relational intelligence. By leveraging knowledge graphs, it empowers AI systems to reason more effectively, grasp context more profoundly, and deliver more accurate, comprehensive, and trustworthy answers—especially in fields where understanding the connections is paramount.

Retrieval Augmentation with Graph Integration

In the evolving landscape of AI, the fusion of graph-based methodologies with RAG systems has emerged as a pivotal advancement. This integration addresses the limitations inherent in traditional RAG setups, particularly in handling complex, multihop queries that require nuanced reasoning across interconnected data points (see Figure 12-3). This section delves into the intricacies of advanced retrieval augmentation through graph integration, elucidating its methodologies, benefits, and transformative impact on information retrieval and generation.

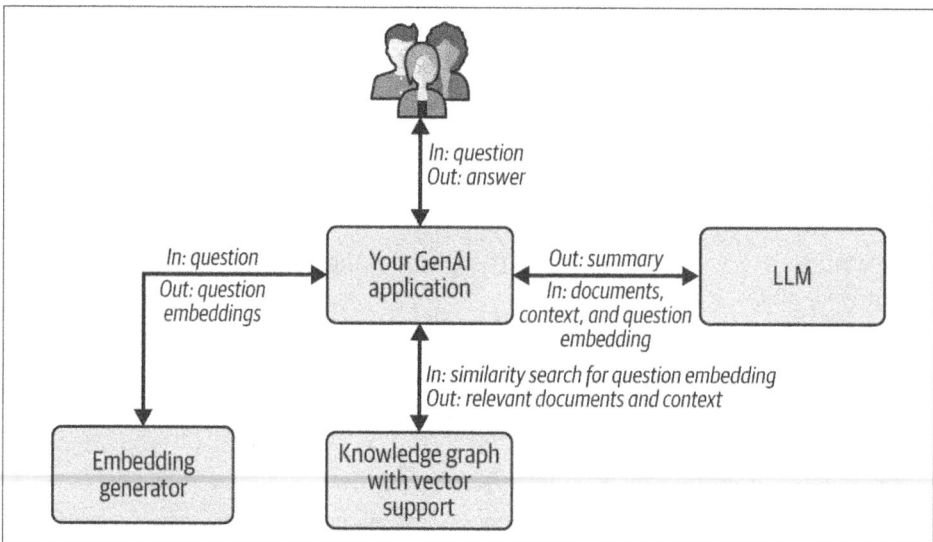

Figure 12-3. Enriched RAG setup with knowledge graph to enhance system transparency and accuracy

Challenges in Traditional Retrieval-Augmented Generation

Traditional RAG systems give LLMs a boost by fetching relevant text snippets from external knowledge bases, helping to ground their answers in facts. While this is useful, these systems often hit limitations when faced with complex questions. Imagine asking, "Which actors starred in movies directed by the person who directed *Inception*?" This requires connecting multiple pieces of information: first identifying Christopher Nolan as the director of *Inception* and then finding actors who worked with him on *other* films.

This is called *multihop reasoning*, and standard RAG struggles here because it usually retrieves documents focused on *either Inception or* Christopher Nolan's filmography but might not easily bridge the gap between them in a single retrieval step.

Furthermore, conventional retrieval methods, whether they rely on keyword matching (sparse) or meaning similarity (dense), often fail to grasp the complex *relationships* between different entities described across various texts. For example, understanding the intricate relationship between a parent company, its subsidiary, a specific product line developed by that subsidiary, and the market competitors requires seeing how these entities are connected—not just finding documents that mention them individually. Standard RAG might pull up separate documents about each entity but miss the crucial links like "subsidiary of," "developed by," or "competes against," leading to incomplete or less insightful answers when deep contextual understanding is needed.

Graph Integration

Integrating graph structures into RAG systems enhances their ability to understand and reason about interconnected information. Let's explore the key ways this integration happens, using a running example involving a fictional tech ecosystem. Imagine our knowledge base contains information about founders, companies, and products:

1. *Graph-based indexing*
   Instead of just storing text, we first build a knowledge graph:

   Concept: We represent key entities (such as people, companies, and products) as *nodes* and the relationships between them (such as "founded," "developed," and "acquired") as *edges*

   Example: Our graph might have nodes for Alice (Person), Bob (Person), Inno vate Inc (Company), DataWidget (Product), and AcquireCorp (Company). Edges could represent relationships like: (Alice) -[FOUNDED]-> (Innovate Inc), (Bob) -[FOUNDED]-> (Innovate Inc), (Innovate Inc) -[DEVELOPED]-> (DataWidget), (AcquireCorp) -[ACQUIRED]-> (Innovate Inc). This structured index maps the connections inherent in the data.

2. *Graph-guided retrieval*
   When a query comes in, the system uses the graph to find relevant information clusters, not just isolated facts:

   Concept: The system navigates the graph's nodes and edges to find paths or subgraphs connecting entities mentioned or implied in the query. This allows it to follow connections across multiple steps (multihop reasoning).

Example: For the query, "Who founded the company acquired by AcquireCorp?", the system doesn't just look for documents mentioning AcquireCorp. It navigates the graph: `AcquireCorp` -> finds incoming `ACQUIRED` edge from -> `Innovate Inc` -> finds incoming `FOUNDED` edges from -> `Alice` and `Bob`. The retrieval process follows the relationships to pinpoint the relevant founders.

3. *Graph-enhanced generation*

The information retrieved from the graph (the subgraph including Alice, Bob, Innovate Inc., AcquireCorp, and their connections) is then fed to the LLM to help generate the final answer:

Concept: By providing this structured, relational context, the LLM can generate responses that are more accurate, comprehensive, and explain the *connections* between facts.

Example: Instead of just saying "Alice and Bob founded Innovate Inc. AcquireCorp acquired Innovate Inc.," the LLM, using the graph context, can generate a more integrated response like: "Innovate Inc., which was acquired by AcquireCorp, was founded by Alice and Bob." This directly answers the query by leveraging the relationships discovered during graph retrieval.

By integrating these graph methodologies, RAG systems move beyond simple document lookup to perform more sophisticated reasoning based on the inherent structure and relationships within the knowledge base.

Integrating graph-based methods into RAG systems offers several notable benefits:

Enhanced multihop reasoning

Graphs inherently represent relationships between entities. This structure enables the system to perform multihop reasoning naturally by traversing the graph edges to connect related pieces of information, which is crucial for answering complex queries that require synthesizing information from multiple sources or steps.

Improved retrieval accuracy

Graph structures allow for more precise information retrieval. By considering the relationships between entities, the system can identify the most relevant information paths specifically related to the query, reducing the retrieval of irrelevant data often found in broader text searches.

Mitigation of hallucinations

Grounding the generation process in structured graph data makes the system less likely to produce fabricated information (hallucinations) that might appear plausible but lacks factual basis. The graph provides a verifiable factual backbone that guides the generation process, enhancing the reliability and trustworthiness of the outputs.

Transparency and explainability

The explicit representation of entities and relationships in graphs allows users to trace the path of reasoning followed by the system. Seeing how the system navigated from one node to another via specific relationships leads to greater understanding and trust in the system's conclusions.

GraphRAG Methodology and Pipeline

These benefits become particularly crucial when extending the power of LLMs to vast amounts of enterprise or private data—information like proprietary research, internal communications, or specialized news feeds that the model wasn't originally trained on. In such scenarios, the LLM's built-in knowledge is insufficient, making external context essential. While standard RAG techniques provide some external information, their typical reliance on vector similarity searches often falls short when faced with complex, multistep questions or when answers require weaving together insights from disparate sources.

This is where specific methodologies like GraphRAG (developed by Microsoft Research) offer a significant advancement. GraphRAG leverages LLMs themselves to construct knowledge graphs from private datasets. This process creates a structured map of the information, capturing not just the content but also the underlying semantic and relational concepts. This structured representation serves as a robust foundation for the AI to retrieve relevant context and generate answers. Essentially, GraphRAG empowers LLMs to effectively "learn" and reason over new, private information, producing responses that are not only contextually rich but also traceable back to their source data, providing clear evidence provenance.

The GraphRAG approach generally unfolds in two main phases. First comes the *indexing process*, where the system analyzes the raw, unstructured data and transforms it into that hierarchical, structured knowledge graph. Following this, the *querying process* takes over. When a user asks a question, the system utilizes the generated graph to find the most relevant interconnected information and then uses this structured context to augment the LLM's ability to provide precise, well-grounded answers. Together, these phases bridge the gap between raw data and insightful, reliable AI-driven responses.

Indexing Process

The indexing process is the backbone of GraphRAG. It transforms a vast and diverse corpus into an organized, searchable knowledge graph. This process involves several key steps.

Text segmentation

The first step is to take the raw corpus—be it thousands of news articles, technical support tickets, or enterprise documents as shown in Figure 12-4—and segment it into manageable pieces, commonly referred to as "text units." Segmentation is not arbitrary; it is designed to preserve the inherent structure of the documents. For example, a long report might be divided into paragraphs, sections, or even sentences—with some overlap to ensure that the context is not lost. This careful segmentation is critical because it allows subsequent processing to be both detailed and context-aware.

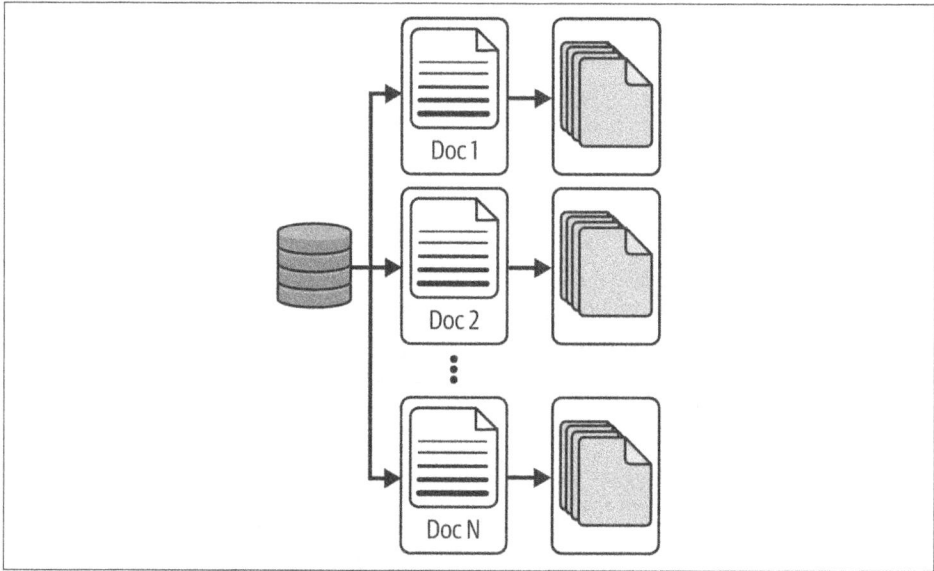

Figure 12-4. Document chunking

Entity, relationship, and claim extraction

Once the text is segmented, the next step involves running each text unit through an LLM or a combination of rule-based systems and LLM prompts to extract meaningful entities and the relationships between them. Entities might include people, places, organizations, or abstract concepts. Relationships capture how these entities are connected, for example, "caused by," "located in," "related to," or "implicated in." Besides simple entity recognition, GraphRAG also extracts claims or key statements that will later serve as evidence for the generated responses.

Knowledge graph construction

With the extracted entities and relationships in hand, GraphRAG then constructs a knowledge graph. In this graph, each entity is represented as a node, and each relationship is represented as an edge connecting two nodes. The resulting graph is a structured representation of the underlying corpus, capturing both the intra-document (or intra-issue) structure and the inter-document relationships. This dual-level representation is crucial for understanding complex queries that require linking information from multiple parts of the dataset.

Hierarchical clustering and community formation

Knowledge graphs can be huge and complex. To make them more manageable and useful, GraphRAG applies hierarchical clustering techniques, such as the Leiden algorithm, to group related nodes into "communities." Each community represents a cluster of entities that are densely connected, often corresponding to semantic themes or topics within the data. Once communities are identified, the system generates summaries for each cluster using a bottom-up approach. These summaries encapsulate the main ideas or claims within the community and provide a high-level overview that can be used during query time (Figure 12-5).

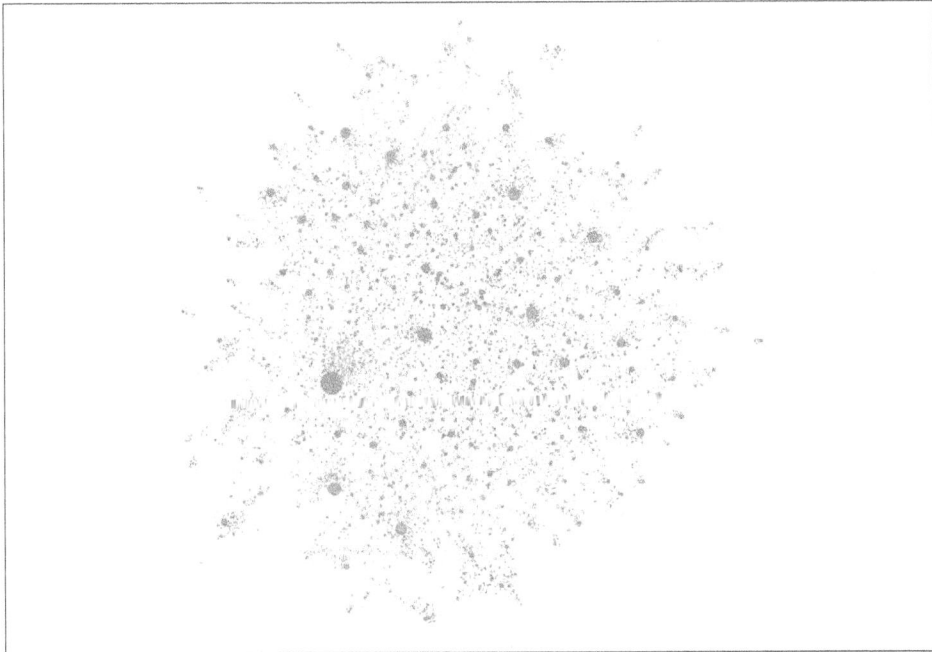

Figure 12-5. LLM-generated knowledge graph built from a private dataset using a GPT model (color version available online at Microsoft GraphRAG (https://oreil.ly/S5Lph))

Embedding generation for graph nodes

For each node and relationship in the graph, embeddings are generated using state-of-the-art text-embedding models. These embeddings provide a numerical representation of the textual content, which is critical for later semantic search and matching operations. By storing these embeddings in a vector database, GraphRAG ensures that each node in the graph can be quickly retrieved based on semantic similarity during the querying process.

Finalizing the index

The culmination of the indexing process is a fully constructed, multilayered knowledge graph that represents the entire corpus. This graph includes detailed nodes, inter-node relationships, community summaries, and vector embeddings. The graph is stored in a manner that supports fast querying and efficient traversal, providing the necessary groundwork for the next phase.

Querying Process

Once the knowledge graph is built, the querying process allows the system to answer user queries by tapping into the structured knowledge stored within the graph. This phase is responsible for bridging the gap between the user's question and the vast repository of structured data.

Query parsing and understanding

When a user submits a query, especially one that involves complex or multihop reasoning, the system first analyzes the query to identify key entities, intents, and underlying themes. The query is parsed using the LLM, which extracts relevant keywords and determines the type of information required. For instance, a query like "What has Novorossiya done?" would prompt the system to identify "Novorossiya" as the primary entity and recognize that the user is asking about actions or events related to it.

Global search via community summaries

For queries that require a holistic understanding of the dataset, GraphRAG leverages the community summaries generated during the indexing process. In what can be called a "global search" workflow, the system retrieves relevant community reports from the knowledge graph. These reports provide aggregated, high-level context for the query, which is particularly useful for queries that require understanding themes or summarizing complex relationships across multiple documents.

Localized entity search and graph traversal

For more focused queries that require precise information about specific entities, GraphRAG initiates a "local search" workflow. In this mode, the system uses the vector embeddings stored in the graph to perform a similarity search. It identifies the most relevant nodes corresponding to the query's entities and then traverses the graph to collect adjacent nodes and relationships. This traversal is not merely a flat search; it leverages the structure of the graph to follow multihop paths, connecting the dots between disparate pieces of information that are related through shared attributes or relationships

Contextual augmentation for the LLM

The information gathered from both the global and local searches is then used to augment the context provided to the LLM. By integrating the structured data from the knowledge graph, the LLM's response is grounded in verifiable evidence. For example, if the query is about the actions of Novorossiya, the system might retrieve specific subgraphs that detail relationships between Novorossiya and other entities (such as news reports or documented events). This augmented context not only improves the factual accuracy of the response but also provides provenance data, allowing users to trace back the answer to its original source documents.

Answer generation with evidence provenance

With the enriched context in place, the LLM generates a comprehensive answer. The response is not a mere synthesis of unrelated text chunks; it is a carefully crafted answer that integrates multiple layers of structured information. Importantly, the output includes citations or provenance markers that reference the specific nodes or community summaries from the knowledge graph. This feature is particularly valuable in enterprise and research applications, where the ability to verify and audit the response is critical.

Enhanced Capabilities and Whole-Dataset Reasoning

One of the most compelling advantages of GraphRAG is its ability to perform *whole-dataset reasoning*, a capability that baseline RAG approaches struggle to achieve. Whereas traditional RAG relies on retrieving semantically similar text segments, GraphRAG uses its structured knowledge graph to understand and synthesize high-level themes across an entire dataset.

For example, as shown in Table 12-1, when asked "What are the top 5 themes in the data?" baseline RAG might return unrelated or superficial text segments based solely on keyword matching. In contrast, GraphRAG leverages its hierarchical clustering and community summaries to identify coherent themes, such as conflict and military activity, political dynamics, infrastructure concerns, community threat assessments, and humanitarian issues. The system not only lists these themes but also provides detailed context and supporting evidence for each, all of which is traceable to the original source documents.

Table 12-1. Whole-dataset reasoning with GraphRAG (source: GraphRAG (https://oreil.ly/S5Lph))

Baseline RAG	GraphRAG
1. Improving the quality of life in cities and urban development.	The data presents a wide range of themes, but the top five most prevalent themes can be identified as follows:
2. The meeting between Vladimir Putin and the President of the United Arab Emirates, Mohammed bin Zayed Al Nahyan.	1. **Conflict and military activity**: A significant portion of the data revolves around the ongoing conflict in Ukraine, with numerous reports detailing military activities, occupations, and attacks by various entities. This theme includes the actions of the Ukrainian military, Russian forces, and various other military units and entities [Data: Reports (513, 241, 151, 493, 343, +more)].
3. The National Rating of the Investment Climate in the Regions of Russia.	2. **Political and governmental entities**: Many reports focus on political figures and governmental entities, highlighting their roles, relationships, and actions in the context of the current situation. This includes entities like the Kremlin, the President of Ukraine, the US State Department, and various regional administrations [Data: Reports (98, 493, 265, 129, 196, +more)].
4. The state of the Russian economy and the growth of domestic brands.	3. **Infrastructure and environmental concerns**: Several reports highlight potential environmental impacts and infrastructure threats. These include potential environmental damage due to industrial activities, flooding crises, and threats to infrastructure due to military conflicts [Data: Reports (308, 154, 201, 348, 216, +more)].
5. The discussion on the meaning of life and the role of science in understanding it.	4. **Community analysis and threat assessment**: Several reports provide detailed analyses of specific communities, often centered around a particular location or entity. These analyses typically discuss the key entities within the community, their relationships, and any associated threats. Many reports also include assessments of potential threats associated with the entities or situations they discuss [Data: Reports (323, 596, 518, 583, 179, +more)].
	5. **Health, humanitarian concerns, and emergency situations**: Some reports focus on health and humanitarian issues, such as the Shereshevsky-Turner Syndrome community and the potential risk of intestinal diseases in the Odessa region. The data also covers emergency situations, including natural disasters, accidents, and attacks [Data: Reports (204, 149, 372, 154, 532, +more)]. These themes provide a comprehensive overview of the current situation, highlighting the complexity and interconnectedness of the issues at hand.

Implementation Considerations

Successfully implementing a system like GraphRAG in a real-world production environment involves careful planning across several key areas. Moving from concept to practice requires attention to the details of data handling, model selection, infrastructure, and how we interact with the AI:

Data preparation: The foundation

Before any graph can be built, the raw input data (the *corpus*) needs meticulous preparation. Think of this as preparing ingredients before cooking:

Segmentation

Large documents often need to be broken down into smaller, manageable chunks (e.g., paragraphs or sections). This helps the LLM focus on extracting information from localized contexts without becoming overwhelmed.

Cleaning

Raw text can be messy, containing irrelevant formatting, boilerplate text (such as headers/footers), or errors. Cleaning involves removing this noise to ensure the LLM processes meaningful content, leading to more accurate entity and relationship extraction. The cleaner the input, the higher the quality of the resulting knowledge graph.

LLM selection: Choosing the right brains

The performance of GraphRAG heavily depends on the capabilities of the LLMs used. Different LLMs might be optimal for different tasks within the pipeline:

Extraction LLM

The model responsible for reading text chunks and extracting entities and relationships needs strong analytical and structured data generation capabilities. It must accurately identify key pieces of information and their connections.

Generation LLM

The model that synthesizes the final answer based on the retrieved graph context needs strong reasoning and natural language generation skills. It must effectively use the structured graph data to provide coherent and accurate responses to user queries. Using state-of-the-art models for both roles is crucial for maximizing the system's effectiveness.

Graph database technology: the right storage

Once built, the knowledge graph needs to be stored efficiently. Choosing graph database technology is critical for performance and scalability; a few important considerations are:

Traversal speed

The database must allow for rapid navigation (traversal) between connected nodes and edges. This is essential for quickly executing multihop reasoning during the retrieval phase.

Scalability

Enterprise datasets can be enormous. The database must be able to handle potentially billions of nodes and edges without significant performance degradation.

Embedding support
> Modern graph approaches often store vector embeddings alongside nodes and edges to capture semantic meaning. The database should ideally support efficient storage and retrieval based on these embeddings, combining structured graph traversal with semantic similarity searches.

Prompt engineering: Guiding the AI
> As discussed previously, crafting precise instructions (prompts) for the LLMs is vital. This applies throughout the pipeline:

Indexing prompts
> These guide the LLM to extract specific types of entities and relationships, often requiring output in a structured format like JSON. Clear examples and constraints in the prompt are key to building an accurate and consistent graph.

Querying prompts
> These instruct the LLM on how to use the retrieved graph context (nodes, edges, summaries) to answer the user's specific question, ensuring that the answer is grounded in the provided data and directly addresses the query.

Community summarization prompts
> GraphRAG often involves summarizing clusters or communities within the graph. Specific prompts are needed to guide the LLM in generating concise yet informative summaries of these graph sections.

Addressing these considerations thoughtfully is essential for building a robust, scalable, and effective GraphRAG system. As the field progresses, ongoing work aims to streamline these processes, particularly through increased automation in graph construction and further optimization for real-time performance.

Baseline RAG Versus GraphRAG

RAG enhances LLMs by integrating external data sources into the generation process. The traditional or baseline RAG approach retrieves relevant information from a dataset using vector similarity searches, which are then used to augment the LLM context window. While effective for straightforward queries, this method can struggle with complex questions that require synthesizing information across multiple documents or understanding intricate relationships between entities.

In practical applications, such as analyzing the Violent Incident Information from News Articles (VIINA) dataset, GraphRAG has demonstrated superior performance over baseline RAG, for instance, when queried "What is Novorossiya?" as shown in Table 12-2.

Table 12-2. Enhanced accuracy with GraphRAG over baseline RAG
(source: GraphRAG (https://oreil.ly/S5Lph))

Baseline RAG	GraphRAG
The term "Novorossiya" is not mentioned in the provided context. However, to provide some information, Novorossiya, or New Russia, is a historical term referring to a region in the south of Ukraine that was conquered by the Russian Empire in the 18th century. In recent years, the term has been revived by Russian-backed separatists in Eastern Ukraine to refer to the territories they claim, but it is not officially recognized as a separate entity by international bodies.	Novorossiya, also known as New Russia, is a term with historical and contemporary significance. Historically, it referred to a region in the southern part of the Russian Empire that is now part of Ukraine. In the contemporary context, it has been used by pro-Russian separatists to refer to certain areas of Ukraine [Data: Entities (6494, 912, 6493)]. The term Novorossiya has been used in the context of a political movement in Ukraine, particularly by Russian nationalists. This movement has been associated with efforts to destabilize Ukraine and create a so-called "Novorossiya" [Data: Entities (912); Relationships (15211, 15206)]. The term has also been used to denote a separatist state in Ukraine, known as the Federal Republic of Novorossiya (FRN) [Data: Entities (7690)].

As shown in Figure 12-6, the baseline RAG system failed to provide specific information due to the absence of direct mentions in the retrieved context.

Relevant chunks of source documents:

	text	source
0	The substance did not go beyond the enterprise." The activities of Meta (social networ	ria
1	The problems that the West is causing her. The sanctions list, published on the depar	ria
2	They ignore Kiev's constant refusals to negotiate in the West. Earlier, the official repre	ria
3	They plan to export grain to Russia. Russian military are robbing Ukrainians - what is	unian
4	Countries have begun to fight not only against Soviet history, but also against everytł	ria
5	Energy, defense industry, military administration, and communications in Ukraine. A:	ria
6	About anti-Ukrainian content on the air of the Russian channel "Soloviev.live" and fu	unian
7	and dentistry, resuscitation departments and operating rooms. The hospital grounds	ria
8	"of the kind that has been going on for over a year," Medvedev stated. It should be no	unian
9	They are deploying their weapons directly in the cities of people on the edge of the se	unian

Figure 12-6. Limited context of baseline RAG (source: GraphRAG (https://oreil.ly/ S5Lph))

In contrast, GraphRAG utilized the knowledge graph to identify relevant entities and relationships—enabling it to generate a detailed and informative response.

This included insights into the historical and contemporary significance of Novorossiya, its association with political movements in Ukraine, and its involvement in various activities, all supported by provenance links to the original source documents, as demonstrated in Table 12-3.

Table 12-3. Enhanced accuracy with GraphRAG over baseline RAG (source: GraphRAG (https://oreil.ly/S5Lph))

Baseline RAG	GraphRAG
The text does not provide specific information on what Novorossiya has done.	Novorossiya, a political movement in Ukraine, has been involved in a series of destructive activities, particularly targeting various entities in Ukraine [Entities (6494, 912)]. The movement has been linked to plans to destroy properties of several Ukrainian entities, including Rosen, the Odessa Canning Factory, the Odessa Regional Radio Television Transmission Center, and the National Television Company of Ukraine [Relationships (15207, 15208, 15209, 15210)]. In addition to these, Novorossiya has also been associated with plans to destroy properties of Roshen, the Odessa Conservatory Factory, the Odessa Regional Radio Television Transmission Center, and the National Telecommunications Company of Ukraine [Relationships (8329, 8330, 8331, 8332)]. Furthermore, Novorossiya has been implicated in plans to blow up ATMs of PrivatBank, the largest state bank in Ukraine [Relationships (8335, 8335)]. The Office of the General Prosecutor in Ukraine has reported on the creation of Novorossiya, indicating the government's awareness and potential concern over the activities of this movement [Relationships (8264, 8264)]. The destructive activities of Novorossiya have had significant impacts on the targeted entities and have likely contributed to the ongoing tensions and conflicts in the region. In summary, Novorossiya has been involved in a series of destructive activities targeting various entities in Ukraine. These activities have had significant impacts on the targeted entities and have likely contributed to the ongoing tensions and conflicts in the region. The Ukrainian government, through the Office of the General Prosecutor, has acknowledged the existence and activities of Novorossiya, indicating a level of concern over the movement's actions.

By enhancing the retrieval process with a structured knowledge graph, GraphRAG not only improves the relevance and accuracy of the information provided to the LLM but also offers clear provenance for each piece of information. This ensures that users can trust and verify the generated responses, making GraphRAG a powerful tool for complex information retrieval and reasoning tasks.

RAG with Knowledge Graphs
for Customer Service Question Answering

Integrating knowledge graphs into RAG systems has shown significant promise in enhancing customer service question-answering capabilities. Traditional RAG approaches often treat historical customer service data as unstructured text, which can overlook the inherent structure and relationships within the data. By constructing knowledge graphs from past issue tickets, it's possible to retain both the intra-issue structure and inter-issue relations, leading to more accurate retrieval and generation of responses.

In this integrated approach, the system first builds a comprehensive knowledge graph from historical customer service tickets, capturing the hierarchical structure of each issue and linking related issues based on contextual relationships. During the question-answering phase, the system parses incoming customer queries and retrieves relevant subgraphs from the knowledge graphs. These subgraphs provide structured context that aids the LLM in generating precise and contextually relevant answers.

Empirical evaluations have demonstrated the effectiveness of this method. For instance, a study reported improvements of 77.6% in mean reciprocal rank (MRR) and a 0.32 increase in bilingual evaluation understudy (BLEU) scores compared to baseline models. Furthermore, deploying this knowledge graph (KG)–enhanced RAG system within a customer service team resulted in a 28.6% reduction in median issue resolution time over a six-month period.

The integration of KGs into RAG systems not only enhances retrieval accuracy by preserving the structured information of customer service data but also improves the quality of generated responses by mitigating issues related to text segmentation. This approach represents a significant advancement in the application of AI for customer service, leading to more efficient and effective resolution of customer inquiries.

Let's dig deeper into the approach:

- Knowledge graph construction

Data structuring
> Historical customer service issue tickets are transformed into a tree-structured format, capturing the hierarchical nature of each issue.

Interlinking issues
> Issues are interconnected based on their relational context, forming a comprehensive knowledge graph that reflects both intra-issue structures and inter-issue relationships.

Node embeddings
> Each node within the knowledge graph is assigned an embedding to facilitate efficient semantic searching during the retrieval process.

- Question-answering process

Query parsing
> Incoming customer queries are analyzed to identify named entities and discern user intent.

Subgraph retrieval
> Relevant subgraphs from the knowledge graph are retrieved based on the parsed query, ensuring that the response is contextually relevant and informed by past issues.

Answer generation
> Leveraging the information from the retrieved subgraphs, the system generates accurate and context-rich answers to address customer inquiries effectively.

Figure 12-7 illustrates the dual-phase framework of the proposed system:

Left side
> Depicts the knowledge graph construction phase, showing how historical issue tickets are structured into a tree format, interlinked, and embedded to form the comprehensive knowledge graphs

Right side
> Illustrates the question-answering phase, demonstrating the process of parsing a customer query, retrieving the pertinent subgraph from the knowledge graph, and generating a well-informed answer

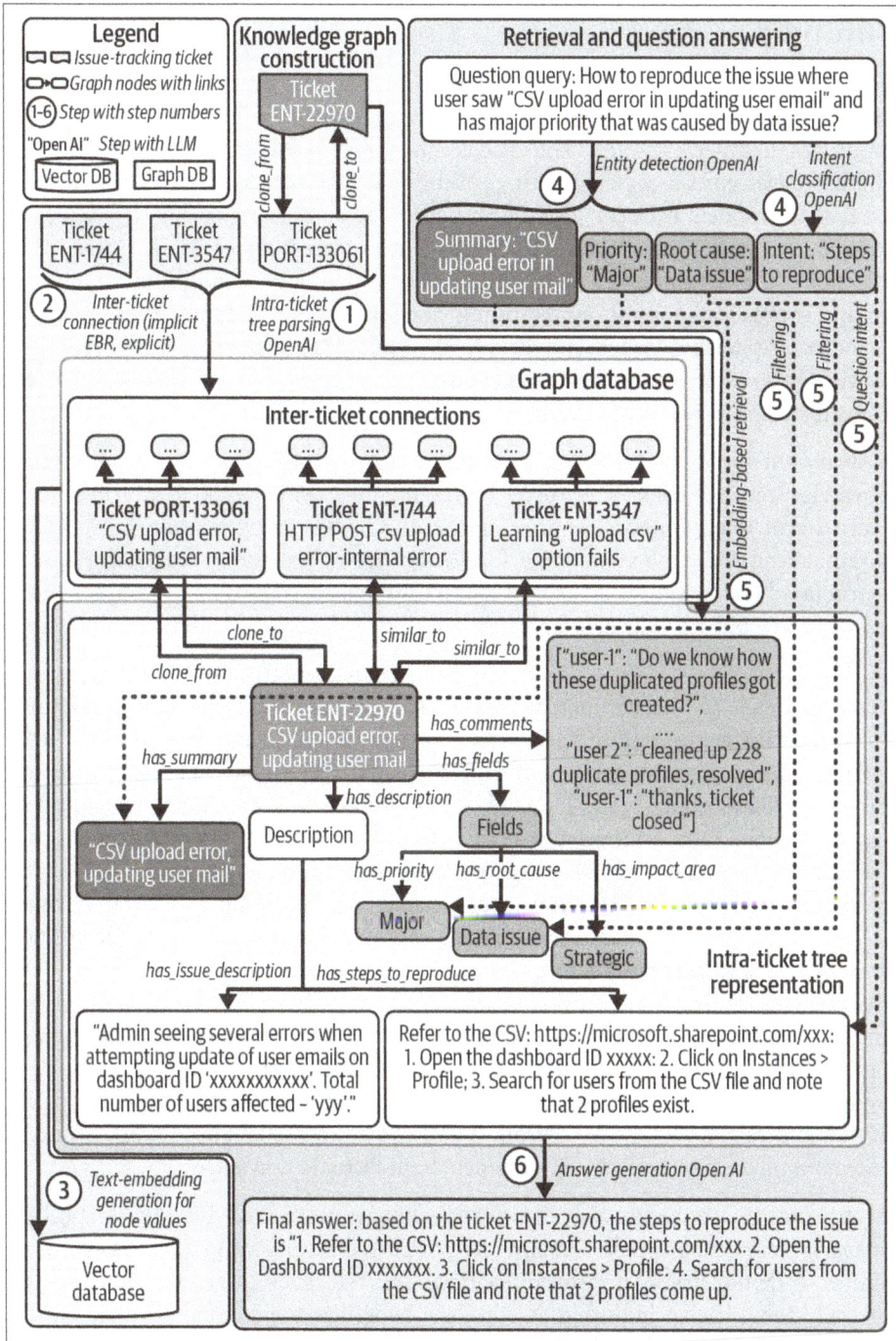

Figure 12-7. Enhanced accuracy with GraphRAG over baseline RAG (architecture from this paper by Xu et al. (2024) (https://oreil.ly/f0_3r) about the proposed solution)

Summary

This chapter provided an in-depth exploration into the integration of knowledge graphs within RAG systems, elucidating how graph-centric methodologies significantly enhance performance. The discussion commenced with an analysis of the inherent constraints associated with conventional RAG approaches. While foundational RAG models excel at leveraging dense vector representations for semantic retrieval, they often encounter difficulties when processing complex queries that necessitate the synthesis of information distributed across multiple sources or demand sophisticated multistep reasoning. Such limitations frequently stem from the absence of explicit relational structures in the underlying data, potentially leading to fragmented context retrieval and an increased risk of generating factually inconsistent or unsubstantiated responses, commonly referred to as hallucinations.

To surmount these obstacles, the chapter introduced the strategic incorporation of knowledge graphs. These structured representations, which model information as a network of interconnected entities and their corresponding relationships, offer a more nuanced and contextually rich foundation for information access compared to unstructured text or simple document chunks. By explicitly encoding the connections between concepts, knowledge graphs facilitate a deeper level of understanding within the retrieval process.

A central focus was placed upon the GraphRAG framework, an advanced architecture specifically engineered to harness the power of graph structures within the RAG pipeline. The exposition detailed the fundamental techniques that constitute this framework. First, graph-based indexing was examined as a method to transform or map source data onto a knowledge graph, thereby creating an interconnected index that mirrors the relational fabric of the knowledge domain. Second, the chapter investigated graph-guided retrieval mechanisms. These techniques actively navigate the graph's structure, identifying not merely relevant documents but specific entities, relationships, and pertinent subgraphs that directly address the nuances of a query. This capacity for graph traversal is instrumental in enabling complex multihop reasoning, allowing the system to logically bridge information gaps across different parts of the knowledge base. Third, graph-enhanced generation was discussed, highlighting how the structured information retrieved from the graph—such as specific paths, entities, and relations—serves to ground and constrain the language model's output generation phase, ensuring closer alignment with factual knowledge.

Throughout this analysis, the distinct advantages conferred by the GraphRAG approach were emphasized. Notably, the structured nature of graph retrieval contributes to demonstrably improved accuracy and relevance in generated responses, especially for intricate inquiries. A corollary benefit is the significant reduction in model hallucination, as the generation process remains tethered to the verified facts and relationships resident within the knowledge graph. Furthermore, GraphRAG inherently promotes enhanced explainability and transparency. The explicit pathways and connections utilized within the graph to formulate an answer can often be surfaced, providing users with valuable insights into the system's reasoning trajectory.

In summation, this chapter established that the integration of knowledge graphs represents a significant maturation for RAG systems. By adopting graph-based methodologies for indexing, retrieval, and generation, frameworks such as GraphRAG furnish a more robust, precise, interpretable, and context-aware paradigm for addressing complex information requirements. This evolution signals a promising direction for developing AI systems capable of more profound reasoning and understanding over richly interconnected knowledge landscapes.

Index

A

A/B testing deployments, 252-253
activation quantization, 262
active attackers, 213
active monitoring, 24
adaptive retraining pipelines, 305-306
    anomaly detection, 306
    auto retraining triggering, 306
    monitoring model health, 305
adjacency list, 50
adjacency matrix, 50
advanced techniques in graph learning,
    131-157
    CiteSeer use case example, 150-156
        data preprocessing/visualization,
            150-153
        embeddings visualization, 155
        model testing, 155
        model training using PyG, 153-155
    graph attention networks, 145-149
        attention mechanism, 146
        example: citation network, 147-149
        feature vectors, 145
        multihead attention, 147
    graph embedding models, 134-145
        embedding interaction methods,
            136-138
        example: learning on freebase dataset,
            140-145
        knowledge graph embeddings basics,
            134
        strengths of graph embedding models,
            139-140

        training knowledge graph embedding
            models, 135-136
        training objectives, 139
    graph types, 131-134
        heterogeneous graphs, 132
        homogeneous graphs, 132
        temporal graphs, 133
Airbnb, 185
alerts
    custom alerts, 299
    design principles, 307
    thresholds for, 297
Amazon
    copurchasing dataset and node embeddings,
        69-73
        feature extraction, 61-62
        generating node embeddings, 70-73
        navigating graph tasks, 53-56
        node embeddings use case for Amazon
            copurchasing dataset, 69
        representing copurchasing networks as
            graphs, 50-53
        use case for, 69
    copurchasing dataset graph-learning work-
        flow using PyGraf, 93-97
        development and monitoring, 96
        evaluation and model selection, 96
        model training, 95-96
        preprocessing and transformation, 94
    recommendation engine, 191
    supply chain and logistics optimization, 196
anomaly detection, 306
approximation techniques, for scaling GNNs,
    180

asymmetric quantization, 262
attention mechanism, 146
attention on graphs (see graph attention networks)

B

batch monitoring, 289
batch processing, 259
Benevolent AI (drug repurposing), 205
betweenness centrality, 58
bipartite graphs, 163, 195
blue–green deployments, 249-250

C

caching, of inference results, 258
canary deployments, 247-249
centrality measures, 283
citation network use case, 147-149
    feature combination, 147
    normalization with softmax function, 148
    score calculation, 148
    update paper i information, 149
    weighted sum, 148
CiteSeer use case, 150-156
    data preprocessing/visualization, 150-153
    embeddings visualization, 155
    model testing, 155
    model training using PyG, 153-155
clinical trial optimization, 202
closed-loop systems, 303-305
clustering coefficient, 61, 283
community detection, 235
community-based partitioning, 272
complex systems, defined, 3
computationally intensive workloads, 23
connectors (PyGraf), 84-87
containerized deployments, 253
copurchasing networks (see under Amazon)
Cora dataset node classification, 120-125
    data preparation, 120-121
    embedding the Cora network, 122
    GCN model architecture, 122
    model testing, 124
    model training/evaluation, 123
CPU inference, 254
customer relationship management (CRM) systems, 183
customer segmentation, 185-186
customer service, 329

cybersecurity incident response, 199

D

dark launches (shadow deployments), 250-251
dashboards, 298
data feedback, 302
data harmonization
    challenges for enterprise-ready systems, 22
    in graph data preparation, 38-40
Deep Graph Library (DGL), 256
degree centrality, 58
demand forecasting, 195
deployment strategies, 246-255
    A/B testing deployments, 252-253
    blue–green deployments, 249-250
    canary deployments, 247-249
    containerized deployments, 253
    edge deployments, 251
    hardware considerations, 254-255
    progressive rollouts, 253
    shadow deployments, 250-251
DGL (Deep Graph Library), 256
differential privacy
    edge differential privacy, 217, 234
    global differential privacy, 232
    in federated settings, 231-233
    local differential privacy, 232
    node differential privacy, 217, 234
differentially private learning algorithms, 222-224
    applying differential privacy to graph models, 223
    concept of differential privacy in learning, 222
    example: training a GNN with differential privacy, 223
    techniques for differentially private learning, 222
    training with differential privacy considerations, 224
differentially private stochastic gradient descent (DP-SGD), 222
directed graphs, defined, 8
DistMult model, 138
distributed graph learning tools, 173-176
    Paddle Graph Learning, 174-176
    PyTorch Geometric (PyG), 174
distributed inference systems, 270
distributed learning, 234

teacher–student architectures for graph models, 269

temporal graphs, 133

Tempus genomic analysis, 205

tensor processing units (TPUs), 255

TensorRT, 256

third-party data, integrating with enterprise data, 37

threat detection/analysis, 197

time-series graphs, 195

timestamps, 60

TPUs (tensor processing units), 255

traditional machine learning for graphs, 47-73
  basics, 48
  feature learning with node embeddings, 67-73
    Amazon copurchasing dataset and node embeddings, 69-73
    random walk algorithm, 68
  graph feature engineering, 56-62
    extracting features for the Amazon copurchasing graph, 61-62
    importance and challenges, 57
    types of graph features, 58-61
  graph features in ML modeling, 62-64
    graph clustering, 64
    link prediction, 63
    node classification, 63
    task and techniques overview, 63
  nontraditional graph-based machine learning versus, 48
  predicting high-rated products with a prediction model, 64-67
  representing graphs for traditional ML, 49-56
    graph representation basics, 49-50
    navigating graph tasks in the Amazon copurchasing dataset, 53-56

representing Amazon copurchasing networks as graphs, 50-53

TransE (translating embedding) model, 137-138

travel-time predictions on Google Maps, 16

traveling salesman problem (TSP), 195

TriNetX, 203

Triton Inference Server, 91

U

Uber Eats recommendation engine, 192

undirected graphs, defined, 8

uniform (homogeneous) graphs, 132

unstructured data, 33

UPS, transportation and logistics optimization, 196

user feedback, 300

V

variational autoencoders (VAEs), 219

vector representations, 68

vehicle routing problem (VRP), 195

vertices (defined), 7

visual graph data, 35

visualization tools (monitoring), 298-299
  custom alerts, 299
  historical trends, 299
  real-time dashboards, 298

VRP (vehicle routing problem), 195

W

Walmart, inventory and supplier relationship management, 196

weight quantization, 262

weighted graphs, 195

About the Authors

Ahmed Menshawy is the vice president of AI engineering at Mastercard. In this role, he leads the AI engineering team, driving the development and operationalization of AI products and addressing the broad range of challenges and technical debts surrounding ML pipelines. Ahmed also leads a team dedicated to creating a number of AI accelerators and capabilities, including serving engines and feature stores, aimed at enhancing various aspects of AI engineering.

Ahmed is the coauthor of *Deep Learning with TensorFlow* and the author of *Deep Learning by Example*, focusing on advanced topics in deep learning.

Sameh Mohamed is a senior applied scientist at Microsoft and an expert in machine learning and health informatics. He has more than a decade of both academic and industrial experience in machine learning and AI solutions. He obtained his PhD from the University of Galway, where he did research on machine learning on graphs and its applications in biomedical applications, and a master's degree in cardiovascular intervention medicine.

He later worked for Mastercard, Carelon, and Microsoft in technical leadership roles where he built machine learning powered solutions in the domains of finance, healthcare insurance, and content generation. His contributions are mainly focused on the topics of representation learning, natural language processing, and health informatics.

Maraim Rizk Masoud is a leading machine learning engineer at Mastercard's Cyber and Intelligence division, concurrently serving as an AI researcher. With a diverse background spanning both industry and academia, Maraim has delved into various AI domains, including natural language processing and AI governance. She holds an MSc in machine learning from Imperial College London and an MEng from the University of Southampton.

Colophon

The animal on the cover of *Scaling Graph Learning for the Enterprise* is a long-tailed pangolin (*Phataginus tetradactyla*). Also known as the African tree pangolin, it is a rare and distinctive species of pangolin found primarily in the dense tropical rainforests of Central and West Africa, including countries such as Cameroon, Equatorial Guinea, and the Democratic Republic of the Congo.

Unlike its ground-dwelling relatives, the long-tailed pangolin is almost entirely arboreal, using its exceptionally long, prehensile tail—often longer than its body—to grip branches and navigate the tree canopy with agility. Its body is covered in overlapping keratinous scales that provide protection from predators, and it has powerful curved claws for climbing and stripping bark in search of food. Small compared to other pangolins, it typically weighs less than 5.5 pounds.

The long-tailed pangolin's diet consists mostly of ants and termites, which it extracts using a long, sticky tongue. It is a solitary and nocturnal creature, although it may exhibit some diurnal activity, especially in undisturbed habitats. Females give birth to a single young after a gestation period of about 140 days. The typical lifespan in the wild is not well documented due to the species' secretive nature and limited observation, but pangolins in general can live up to 20 years in captivity. The long-tailed pangolin is currently classified as Vulnerable by the IUCN Red List, largely due to deforestation and illegal hunting for the bushmeat and traditional medicine trades. Conservation efforts are underway, but the species remains elusive and understudied—making focused protection all the more critical.

Many of the animals on O'Reilly covers are endangered; all of them are important to the world.

The cover illustration is by Karen Montgomery, based on a black-and-white engraving from *Natural History of Animals*. The series design is by Edie Freedman, Ellie Volckhausen, and Karen Montgomery. The cover fonts are Gilroy Semibold and Guardian Sans. The text font is Adobe Minion Pro; the heading font is Adobe Myriad Condensed; and the code font is Dalton Maag's Ubuntu Mono.

O'REILLY®

Learn from experts.
Become one yourself.

60,000+ titles | Live events with experts | Role-based courses
Interactive learning | Certification preparation

**Try the O'Reilly learning platform
free for 10 days.**

www.ingramcontent.com/pod-product-compliance
Lightning Source LLC
Chambersburg PA
CBHW080716220326
41598CB00033B/5437